POINT AND
FIGURE CHARTING

POINT AND FIGURE CHARTING

Founded in 1807, John Wiley & Sons is the oldest independent publishing company in the United States. With offices in North America, Europe, Australia, and Asia, Wiley is globally committed to developing and marketing print and electronic products and services for our customers' professional and personal knowledge and understanding.

The Wiley Trading series features books by traders who have survived the market's ever changing temperament and have prospered—some by reinventing systems, others by getting back to basics. Whether a novice trader, professional, or somewhere in-between, these books will provide the advice and strategies needed to prosper today and well into the future.

For a list of available titles, please visit our web site at www.WileyFinance.com.

POINT AND FIGURE CHARTING

The Essential Application for Forecasting and Tracking Market Prices

Third Edition

Thomas J. Dorsey

John Wiley & Sons, Inc.

Designations used by companies to distinguish their products are often claimed as trademarks. In all instances where John Wiley & Sons, Inc. is aware of a claim, the product names appear in initial capital or all capital letters. Readers, however, should contact the appropriate companies for more complete information regarding trademarks and registration.

Published by John Wiley & Sons, Inc., Hoboken, New Jersey.
Published simultaneously in Canada.

Wiley Bicentennial Logo: Richard J. Pacifico

No part of this publication may be reproduced, stored in a retrieval system, or transmitted in any form or by any means, electronic, mechanical, photocopying, recording, scanning, or otherwise, except as permitted under Section 107 or 108 of the 1976 United States Copyright Act, without either the prior written permission of the Publisher, or authorization through payment of the appropriate per-copy fee to the Copyright Clearance Center, Inc., 222 Rosewood Drive, Danvers, MA 01923, (978) 750-8400, fax (978) 646-8600, or on the web at www.copyright.com. Requests to the Publisher for permission should be addressed to the Permissions Department, John Wiley & Sons, Inc., 111 River Street, Hoboken, NJ 07030, (201) 748-6011, fax (201) 748-6008, or online at http://www.wiley.com/go/permissions.

Limit of Liability/Disclaimer of Warranty: While the publisher and author have used their best efforts in preparing this book, they make no representations or warranties with respect to the accuracy or completeness of the contents of this book and specifically disclaim any implied warranties of merchantability or fitness for a particular purpose. No warranty may be created or extended by sales representatives or written sales materials. The advice and strategies contained herein may not be suitable for your situation. You should consult with a professional where appropriate. Neither the publisher nor author shall be liable for any loss of profit or any other commercial damages, including but not limited to special, incidental, consequential, or other damages.

For general information on our other products and services or for technical support, please contact our Customer Care Department within the United States at (800) 762-2974, outside the United States at (317) 572-3993 or fax (317) 572-4002.

Wiley also publishes its books in a variety of electronic formats. Some content that appears in print may not be available in electronic books. For more information about Wiley products, visit our web site at www.wiley.com.

Library of Congress Cataloging-in-Publication Data:

Dorsey, Thomas J.
    Point & figure charting : the essential application for forecasting and tracking market prices / Thomas J. Dorsey. -- 3rd ed.
    p. cm. — (Wiley trading series)
    Includes index.
    ISBN-13: 978-0-470-04351-6 (cloth/cd-rom)
    ISBN-10: 0-470-04351-2 (cloth/cd-rom)
    1. Stocks—Prices—Charts, diagrams, etc. 2. Speculation. 3. Stock price forecasting. I. Title. II. Title : Point and figure charting.
HG4638.D67 2007
332.63'222—dc22

                                              2006031242

Printed in the United States of America.

10 9 8 7 6 5 4

CONTENTS

Acknowledgments   vii

Part One
Learn the Point and Figure Methodology

Chapter 1   Introduction   3

Chapter 2   Point and Figure Chart Fundamentals   21

Chapter 3   Chart Patterns   55

Chapter 4   Foundations of Relative Strength   103

Chapter 5   Advanced Relative Strength Concepts   141

Chapter 6   Primary Market Indicators for Gauging Risk   177

Chapter 7   Secondary Market Indicators   223

Chapter 8   Sector Rotation Tools   249

Part Two
The Point and Figure Methodology
—A Complete Analysis Tool

Chapter 9   Fixed Income Indicators   279

Chapter 10 Utilizing the Exchanged Traded Fund Market   295

**Chapter 11 Evaluating the Commodity Market
                      for Opportunities   323**

Part Three
Apply the Point and Figure Methodology
to Your Investment Process

Chapter 12 Portfolio Construction and Management   361

About the CD-ROM   371

Index   375

ACKNOWLEDGMENTS

It's been 11 years since the first edition of *Point and Figure Charting* was printed and 20 years since Watson Wright and I walked down Main Street in Richmond, Virginia, to our new quarters, Dorsey, Wright & Associates (DWA). Watson and I have been together for the better part of 26 years, almost as along as I have been married to my wife Cindy. Watson and I have found a way to make $1 + 1 = 3$. Our partnership has worked well for 20 years and I look forward to another 20 years.

The first edition of *Point and Figure Charting* was a labor of love. I knew it had to be written if for no other reason than to express my gratitude for having being shown my manifest destiny and giving me a vision to develop DWA with Watson. As soon as I learned this method of investment management, I knew I had to pass the word to any and all investors who were searching for a more secure financial future. The success of the first edition and the consistency of sales told me this was the right method for the majority of investors. When John Wiley asked me to write the second edition I knew it would be an all-hands evolution. We had developed many new concepts for Point and Figure analysis over the years similar to the spokes extending from the hub of a bicycle wheel. My two top analysts, Tammy and Susan, joined in with me in writing the second edition. Tammy and Susan have been with DWA since the beginning and are like family to me. They have accumulated 20 years each in experience in this method of investment analysis. In my opinion, they are the best on the planet when it comes to our little slice of Wall Street.

Well, here we are five years after the debut of the second edition and John Wiley & Sons asked me to write the third edition of the book. It was quite fortuitous, because we at DWA had just been discussing the need for a third edition for many reasons. There has been a whirlwind of changes on Wall Street these past five years. We experienced the end of a 20-year bull market, the beginning and the end of a major bear market, and the beginning but not the end of what I called a "structural fair market." Here's why the book is necessary at this time. The structural fair market is simply my way of saying that the market is likely to move sideways for many years; however, it will experience many up and down moves of 20 percent or more. Skill at Sector Rotation will be the key to success during this period. Sectors will move in and out of favor as produce does in the supermarket. Since 2002, this has been the case. Since 1998, the market as dictated by the S&P 500 has gone nowhere. A quick look at the Point and Figure chart in July 1998 shows a high of 1175 and here we are eight years later and the S&P 500 is at 1220. Investors are about to experience a lost decade. Wall Street has had to come to grips with the fact that the buy-and-hold theory is simply not working for their investors. It is because of these changes that we too have changed, focusing much more on sector rotation and relative strength. Also the debut of the Exchange Traded Fund, the most important new product I have seen in my 32 years on Wall Street, is discussed in detail in this book, expanding extensively the discussion we began in the second edition. This third edition of *Point and Figure Charting* deals with what is happening *today* in the markets, examines the forces of supply and demand that will continue to drive the markets, and provides a framework that will be instrumental in helping investors both professional and individual in growing their assets so a comfortable retirement can become a reality.

To accomplish writing this book in a timely manner required that I rope in all the analysts who live with these concepts and methods day in and day out. Jay Ball who is first an analyst and second in charge of our whole database was instrumental in creating the study guide CD that accompanies this book. Jay has made some incredible advances in our web-based Productivity System with the help of Justin Knight who makes sure the nuts and bolts of our system are greased and operating at top efficiency. I am continually amazed each and every day I use this Productivity

System. It truly takes you to the edge of what some call the future. Paul Keeton didn't escape the net of this monumental project either. Paul has been with DWA for six years now and has risen to become one of our top analysts. He writes for our research reports daily and is instrumental in much of the creative thought process at DWA. Paul's fingerprints are on just about everything we do. We consulted frequently with Steve Raymond when it came to mutual funds—also a new addition to this book. Steve heads up our mutual fund department and is one of the best managers on Wall Street in this area. When you read the book and see all those fantastic charts and graphs, think of Sarah Lepley. She is a sophomore at Pennsylvania State University and is now in her second year of internship at DWA. She has done such a great job here we entrusted her with the visual portions of the book. It's amazing that we were able to martial such brainpower to accomplish one task. We have had zero turnover of key personnel in DWA's 20 years. Each person here simply becomes better and better at what he does. We have 10 full-time employees in the home office at DWA. We also hire five or more of the best minds the local universities can provide us each year as interns. We try to make our intern force as international as possible and have had interns from Bolivia, Ghana, Spain, Estonia, and Germany to name just a few of the countries represented.

Watson Wright is my partner, but Tammy DeRosier is my right hand. She headed up the whole operation for this third edition. Without her help, it might have taken another year to finish this book. Heading up this operation was a massive undertaking for her mainly because it was in addition to her other management duties at DWA. We write over 5,000 pages of original research each year at DWA but the logistics of choreographing and constructing a book suitable for publishing at a major publishing house is a different task all together. Tammy is like the foreman on the DWA Ranch. She has been working at DWA since she was 16 and worked her way through the University of Virginia, working vacations and weekends at the company.

Susan is the head of all stock research at DWA. She was the first person outside Watson and me to work at DWA. Sue was a municipal bond trader at Signet Bank in Richmond, and heard me speak at a bank function one night. That was all it took; she embraced a method of investing that would become her business life from that night forward. She is world class without a doubt and she is one of the integral parts of this family. Susan also worked her way through Virginia Commonwealth University while working at DWA.

As with everything we do at Dorsey, Wright, this book is a family affair. I hope you enjoy the book; our heart is in it.

Part One

LEARN THE
POINT AND FIGURE
METHODOLOGY

Chapter 1

INTRODUCTION

Point and Figure Charting: A Lost Art

I would never have thought we would be embarking on the third edition of this book when I wrote the first edition. I know now that this will not be the last edition either. Technology and the Internet have significantly changed the way we approach technical analysis. Over the years, we have been able to develop new and interesting indicators that the founders of the Point and Figure method over a hundred years ago could not have fathomed. Dorsey, Wright & Associates (DWA) has been in business for 20 years now and the changes we have seen are amazing. When we first started DWA, we used a Tandy 3000 computer that was considered to be state of the art. We did not have enough money to buy it outright, so we leased it. When all of those rent payments were totaled up, that computer cost $3,000 and only did a small fraction of what computers today can do that cost one-tenth the price. Twenty years ago, there was no such thing as an online charting system. We updated 2,500 stock charts by hand for close to a decade. Our Relative Strength charts were updated by hand once a week. It was a right of passage for each intern to maintain the Relative Strength charts each week. Distribution of our research each day was done by fax machine. The machine we used to fax out our 20-page report each day cost $1,800. This fax machine was state of the art technology, and we borrowed it from

3

friends. Since we had no money, only debt, in the beginning we had to go downstairs each day and fax out our report by hand, page by page. This machine could only fax to one phone number at a time. This was in 1987. I think we paid seven cents a page to use this fax. When you start a business with nothing, you do what you have to do to make it work. By 1994, we were on the Internet; however, our clients were not up on that technology curve yet and still wanted our reports by fax. Those who wanted to take down stock charts did so through the, by then, outdated DOS system. Most of us will hold on to the old way of doing things when new technology and new ways of doing things come into existence. This is called the technology gap. I remember one of the largest brokerage firms on Wall Street saying the Internet was a flash in the pan, and they were not putting any significant resources into it. We knew from the start how important this new technology would be and put all our resources into it. With this new technology, we were able to begin creating new and important indicators that stemmed from the Point and Figure method of analysis. We continue to push the envelope with technology, and every few years we have new and innovative things we have created to help investors and professionals become more successful at the investment process. This is why I am sure that at some point in the future there will be a need for *Point and Figure Charting*, Fourth Edition. For now we have more than enough new things to discuss in the Third Edition.

Let's start with the basics. The Point and Figure method is not new by any stretch of the imagination. It is, however, a lost art simply because most investment professionals and individual investors have lost sight of the basics that cause fluctuations in the prices of securities. Even though we have been championing this method of analysis for 20 years, we have barely made a dent in the 50 million investors in America. We've scratched the surface; that's about all, and our business has grown every year for 20 years. We have a lifetime of work ahead of us. In today's rapidly evolving technologies, the irrefutable law of supply and demand has been all but forgotten and that is one thing that doesn't change in any market. In the end, the only thing that will outlive technological change that is truly sustainable is the transcendent competence of an individual's workmanship. New methods of security analysis continue to crop up capturing the ever-expanding curiosity of the investing public. It seems everyone is searching for the Holy Grail, yet few are willing to become craftsmen at the investment process. Many are looking for a computer program that will define the winning trades each day without any effort from the investor or professional who has ultimate responsibility for the portfolio of stocks. A long time ago when I was a stockbroker at a major firm on Wall Street, I learned there is no Holy Grail. The key to success in this business, and any business for that matter, is confidence. According to my dictionary, confidence means "firm belief or trust; self-reliance; boldness; assurance." In the securities business, the key term in that definition is *self-reliance*, and it is the one trait most investors and stockbrokers lack. Investors today are increasingly averse to making their own decisions, which is why the mutual fund business has grown to record levels. Not only that, investors look to the television to provide them ideas on where to invest their hard-earned money. There are also investors who have taken control of their own investments and of their training and education in the investment process. The irony is that 75 percent or more of professional money managers never outperform the broad stock market averages, so looking for professional help has proved ill fated in many cases. Nevertheless, most investors look at the stock market as an enigma. It confounds them that the market reacts in what seems to be an illogical pattern. Increased earnings expectations should result in price appreciation of the underlying stock, right? Not necessarily. In many cases, the opposite happens. In the year 2000, we saw exactly that. Stocks with great fundamentals collapsed under their astronomical valuations. Companies like Lucent Technologies declined from 80 to the single digits. Major firms on Wall Street were in love with the stock's fundamentals at 80. Lucent's only problem was not in the company itself, but in its customers' ability to pay for the products they had purchased from Lucent. This information did not show up in the fundamental research until the stock collapsed. It did, however, show up in the Point and Figure chart. Those who were well versed in evaluating the supply demand relationship of the stock saw trouble early on. The game of golf is like the market, often counterintuitive. It took me a long time to realize that the harder I hit at the ball the less distance it would go. I found that if I hit down on the ball it made the ball go up. Like I mentioned earlier, the market, like golf, can often seem counterintuitive.

Over the past 11 years, since the first edition of this book was published, my confidence in this methodology has increased tremendously. While nothing in the method has changed, how we use it has expanded and grown. We have developed a number of new indicators, many based on the Bullish Percent and Relative Strength concepts covered in the first edition, and have found new ways to use many of the old indicators. One of the most interesting and useful products that was just coming into existence when the last edition was published was the Exchange Traded Fund. This class of investment vehicle is growing by leaps and bounds and I think it is the most important new product to hit the market in my 30 plus years in the business so we discuss this investment vehicle extensively throughout the entire book.

In the past five years, we have gone through some of the most volatile markets anyone has seen. Negotiating the markets in this volatile and changing economy points out the need for an operating system to guide investors. This book provides that operating system. The old paradigm of buying quality stocks with real products and visible earnings has gone right out the window. At least the media and most investors think so. In the late 1990s, the mantra on Wall Street was: "Forget earnings they aren't important, only revenues are important." We heard 22-year-old CEOs suggesting that the old-line companies, the backbone of the United States, "just don't get it." Well, the crash of the dot-com companies that thought they "got it" has awakened Americans to a market that both gives and takes away. The 22-year-old CEOs "didn't get it." Investors have come to realize that real wealth is made in the stock market. They have also come to realize that the market can take it away just as fast. Attention to the bottom line is now back in vogue as investors recognize that net earnings are in fact important. In the latter part of the 1990s, firms attempted to create brand names by simply throwing millions of dollars into advertising. Companies were trying to create solid brand names in one month that took companies like Procter & Gamble 40 years to create. Some companies even sell products below cost, with the expectation of making up the difference in advertisement revenues.

This all came to roost in the second quarter of 2000 when the Nasdaq stocks literally melted down in a matter of a few weeks. All of a sudden, the market that once valued The Street Dot Com (TSCM) at 71 now valued it at 3. MicroStrategy (MSTR) once traded as high as 330, fell to $14, and is now back to $108. The high-flier Priceline.com was as high as 165, declined to $5, and is now at $22. How quickly the market corrects over exuberance, as Alan Greenspan warned. The high-fliers were not the only ones that were hit in 2000; some stocks, many New York Stock Exchange names, hit their peaks in 1998 and are just beginning to show signs of life again. Quality companies like Eastman Kodak, Cisco Systems, AT&T, Worldcom, and virtually countless others have seen their stocks become burned out stars as their stock prices have been cut in half or worse. There was basically nowhere investors could hide. It was an interesting market from April 1998 to March 2000 in which the indexes did fairly well while the stocks underlying them were killers. Since 2000, the Dow Jones, only considering price change, no commissions to buy it and no dividends, is down 2.5 percent at this writing in 2006. So a buy-and-hold investor, who wanted the safety of the largest capitalization stocks available today, would have basically been spinning his wheels for the past five and a half years. If, however, an investor had a way to know that the play was in small capitalization (small cap) stocks, not large capitalization (large cap) stocks, and bought the Standard & Poors Small Capitalization Universe stocks, he or she is up 90 percent at this writing in 2006.

You know what concept never wavered once during this treacherous period? It was the irrefutable law of supply and demand. In almost all the cases cited, the charts foretold trouble down the road and they also foretold demand taking control in instances like the small cap stocks. In later chapters, I point out how these supply-and-demand indicators "saw" the 2000/2002 crash coming and told us the risk was high. We were then able to get our clients out of harm's way. We have once again gone through a market condition never seen before. The Internet has injected change into the whole game on Wall Street. Barriers to entry in almost any business are nonexistent and the freedom of the Internet brings tremendous competition. The playing field is being leveled every day. The one constant that has not changed in over 100 years is supply and demand and the Point and Figure method of analyzing markets. It's interesting that the Internet stocks that became so inflated and eventually collapsed are the very stocks that have the most potential in the weeks and months ahead. The Internet is here to stay and, in my opinion, is only in the first foot of a 26-mile marathon. Knowing "when to hold 'em and when to fold 'em," is the key to success.

What Do Investors Have in Common with an 18-Year-Old Bungee Jumper?

The answer is no fear. During the 1990s, investors came to believe that buying the dips is the key to success: Stocks always come back, don't panic; just buy more. Some people leveraged their homes to put money in the stock market. This kind of situation never ends well, and in the year 2000 it didn't. The crash in Nasdaq stocks caught just about everyone off guard, and massive losses were generated buying the dips, averaging good money after bad. I don't believe investors have broken this habit yet, because not a week goes by that I don't talk to someone who still owns a Cisco Systems or SunMicrosystems or Microsoft in their account. Many investors have recently turned to the real estate markets but now that the housing markets are losing strength, investors are wondering if there is a safe haven anywhere on the investing landscape. The only safe harbor an investor has is his own education and training in the investment process.

The "buy every dip" mentality is what I call false courage. False courage is confidence you may feel when under the influence of alcohol or drugs. It dulls the senses and gives you the confidence to do things you otherwise would not consider. A friend of mine, the late Cornelius Patrick Shea, used to say, "My pappy use to tell me the 'sauce' makes ya say things ya don't mean and believe things that ain't true." The "sauce" for investors consisted of the seemingly never-ending rise in high-flying tech stocks and of late in real estate. It was so intoxicating that investors were "saying things they didn't mean (buy 1,000 more) and believing things that weren't true (revenues are increasing with no end in sight)." During the latter part of the 1990s and first quarter of 2000, investors were enamored with the seemingly never-ending ascent of the stock market and in particular the Nasdaq. The media aided this belief with the ceaseless chant of zero inflation and endless increases in worker productivity due to technological advances. Because of their intoxication, investors kept taking more risks through leverage in high volatility stocks beyond any rational measure. I even had a broker call me with a story of how her aunt was not allowed to use margin at her firm because of her advanced age (she was 80). Do you know what she did? She took a second mortgage out on her house, put the money in her stock account, and continued trading. In essence, she skirted the brokerage firm's margin requirement and margined the account anyway with the money the bank loaned her when she margined her house. I wonder how she fared after the crash of March 2000, May 2000, and November 2000. She may have lost her house.

The decline in stocks from 2000 to 2002 certainly woke many an investor up to the fact that markets go both ways—up and down. But I also fear that markets of 2003 through 2006 have lulled investors back to sleep. From July 1998 to present, someone who bought and held the S&P 500 is finding him- or herself with an annualized rate of return of about 1 percent per year. You might first think, that's not too bad, at least I didn't lose any money. But the fact of the matter is for a great many people that means you have lost, although maybe not in actual dollars, almost a decade of investing. When you consider that so many investors were made to believe that they would get 11 percent a year rate of return on equities, dropping that just 1 percent a year can really put a dent in your retirement planning. Not only are you not making any headway, but you've now lost eight years. Many investors have forgotten that having a logical, organized, well-founded method of investing in the markets is the only way to success. Haphazard, overleveraged, method-less investing will always lead to disaster, just as it did in 2000. The Nasdaq not only corrected, it headed south like a migrating bird. Its decline was so swift that, in a matter of weeks, it had lost 37 percent from its high, and that even masked what happened to so many stocks. Many individual stocks lost 80 percent or more of their value. Investors with a whole portfolio of high-tech/high-wreck Internet and technology stocks may not see the light of day in their accounts for many years to come, and it's now 2006. The average gain in the stock market over the past 80 years is around the 10 percent level. If an investor loses 50 percent of his portfolio value, that portfolio will have to rise 100 percent to get back up to even. How long will that take at an average 10 percent per year? About seven years. We are now five and a half years after the bottom and the Dow Jones has not made any headway. If an investor bought at the top in 1973 and rode the market down, it took seven and a half years to get even. Can you wait seven and a half years to get your money back if you ride a bear market down as the media and mutual funds suggest you should do? If your answer is no, then you are ultimately interested in risk management, which is what this book is all about.

I was in a store the other day purchasing a new laptop computer. I got into a conversation about investing in the market with the head of the computer department. He was having a hard time understanding what I did. I told him that successful investing requires an operating system like the one in every computer. The computer's operating system allows it to effectively read and run all the software products. Operating systems like Windows 2000 simply provide a set of instructions that tells the computer how to run. Without an operating system, software cannot run on the computer. Investing is the same. Investors must have an operating system firmly in mind to work from *before* they can become successful at the investment process.

This operating system is the core belief in some method of analysis an investor both understands thoroughly and embraces wholeheartedly. It's like getting religion on Wall Street. At some point, all successful investors have to find some church on Wall Street that they can attend every week. This is why we entitled the motivational book we wrote; *Finding Religion Among the Rapids.* Many investors subscribe strictly to the fundamental approach of investing. This method only delves into the internal qualities of the underlying company. It does not take into consideration timing entry and exit points in that stock and, above all, supply and demand imbalances. Supply and demand imbalances are nothing more than investor sentiment. Other methods of analysis might involve astrology, Fibonacci retracement numbers, Gann angles, waves, cycles, candlestick charts, bar charts, or any other method you are willing to embrace. At DWA, we only subscribe to one irrefutable method—the law of supply and demand. If you want to go back to the basics, with a methodology that has stood the test of time, in bull and bear markets, and one that is easy enough to learn whether you are age 8 or 80, then you are reading the right book. This operating system will carry you through your investment endeavors, from stocks and mutual funds to commodities.

Why Does This Method Make Sense and Where Did It Originate?

We humans have certain limitations when coping with rapid decision making. Most investors find it difficult to think through the complex decisions they need to make when it comes to investing. The problem is not that we have too much information. The problem is managing and processing this information. It is like a fire hose of information that hits us in the face every day. The question is how to control that massive information flow and break it down into understandable bits that we can use to make effective decisions. In essence, we have decision overload.

To help you organize this information, we have some powerful tools (see our web site: www.dorseywright.com). The simplest example of how information is organized is telephone numbers. We have an ability to remember three or four numbers in succession easily but seven is difficult. This is why our phone numbers are divided up in threes and fours. The pound sign and the star sign on the phone were there for years with no apparent function. Now we routinely use them. They had no function when they first appeared on phones, but the phone companies knew that eventually there would be a use for them in managing information. Similarly, Charles Dow found a way to organize data back in the 1800s. He was the first person to record stock price movement and created a method of analysis called Figuring that eventually led to the Point and Figure method described in this book. The Point and Figure method of recording stock prices is simply another way of organizing data.

At the turn of the twentieth century, some astute investors noticed that many of Dow's chart patterns had a tendency to repeat themselves. Back then, there was no Securities and Exchange Commission; there were few rules and regulations. Stock pools dominated the action and outsiders were very late to the party. It was basically a closed shop of insiders. The Point and Figure method of charting was developed as a logical, organized way of recording the imbalance between supply and demand. These charts provide the investor with a road map that clearly depicts that battle between supply and demand. It allowed the outsider to become an insider.

Everyone is familiar with using maps to plan road trips. When we drive from Virginia to New York, we start the trip on I-95 North. If we don't pay attention to our navigating and inadvertently get on I-95 South, we are likely to end up in Key West, Florida. To prepare for a journey with your family to New York from Virginia, you need to familiarize yourself with the map, check the air in your car's tires, begin with a full tank of gas, and make sure the children have some books and toys. In other words, plan your trip. Most investors never plan their investment trip. The Point and Figure method of analyzing supply and demand can provide that plan. Nothing guarantees success, but the probability of success is much higher when all the possible odds are stacked in the investors' favor. Somewhere along the road, you may be forced to take a detour, but that's okay as long as you stick to your original plan. This book outlines the best plan for financial success when you are investing in securities.

When all is said and done, if there are more buyers in a particular security than there are sellers willing to sell, the price will rise. On the other hand, if there are more sellers in a particular security than there are buyers willing to buy, the price will decline. If buying and selling are equal, the price will remain the same. This is the irrefutable law of supply and demand. The same reasons that cause price fluctuations in produce such as potatoes, corn, and asparagus cause price fluctuations in securities.

Two methods of analysis are used in security evaluation. One method is *fundamental analysis.* This is the method of analysis familiar to most investors. It deals with the quality of the company's earnings, product acceptance, and management. Fundamental analysis answers the question: What security should I buy? *Technical analysis* is the other basic method. It answers the question: When should I buy that security? Timing the commitment is the crucial step. Fundamental information on companies can be obtained from numerous sources. There are many free Internet sites that deal strictly with fundamental analysis. The technical side of the equation is much more difficult to find because few securities professionals are doing quality technical analysis that the average investor can understand. This book is designed to teach you how to formulate your own operating system using the Point and Figure method, coupled with solid fundamental analysis.

Why You Should Use Point and Figure Charts

Although the investment industry is overloaded with different methodologies to evaluate security price movement, the Point and Figure method is the only one I have found to be straightforward and easy to understand.

The charts are made up of X's and O's. Recording the movement of a security using this method is very much like recording a tennis match. A tennis match can last 12 sets. Each player can win a certain number of sets, but the final count determines which player wins the match. In the Point and Figure method, we are only interested in the culmination of the match, not the winner of the underlying sets. The patterns this method produces are simple and easy to recognize—so simple that I have taught this method to grade schoolers in Virginia. I have always maintained that simple is best.

The concept underlying any method of analysis you choose must be valid. Supply and demand is as valid and basic as it gets. I am not criticizing the validity of other methods; it's just that most people can easily understand supply and demand because it is a part of everyday life. Why not make it a part of your everyday investing?

The greatest market indicator yet invented was developed by A. W. Cohen in 1955 called the New York Stock Exchange Bullish Percent Index. We have used it for many years with great success. In that time, we have refined it as the markets have changed, but the basic philosophy is still intact. I have devoted a whole chapter of this book to a discussion of this indicator. A part of our sector analysis, which is explained in another chapter, is a derivative of the Bullish Percent concept and we have other sector rotation models based on relative strength, just another way of measuring supply and demand. Once you learn these basic principles, your investing confidence will increase tremendously. You will soon find yourself acting rather than reacting to different market conditions. This method changed my life, and it can do the same for anyone who takes the time to read this book and then implement the investing principles contained therein.

In the Beginning

It took me years of operating in a fog in the brokerage business before I came across the Point and Figure method. I started my career at a large brokerage firm in Richmond, Virginia, in late 1974. When training new brokers, the firm focused primarily on sales. As trainees, we were drilled in the philosophy that the firm would provide the ideas and our responsibility was to sell them. We were in essence intermediaries doing the exact same work a computer does today. The first four months at the firm we devoted to study. Every potential broker must pass the Series 7 examination to become registered with the New York Stock Exchange. The course was extensive—covering everything from exchange rules and regulations to complicated option strategies. Once we had passed the exam and completed five weeks of sales training, we were ready to be unleashed on the public. I think back 32 years now and realize how unprepared I was to handle investors' hard-earned money. In fact, I came to work totally unprepared to do anything but pass on my firm's research.

As in any other profession, experience counts a lot, and we were severely lacking in that area. The market had just gone through what seemed to be a depression, losing about 70 percent of its value. Prospecting for new accounts was a difficult task at best, but those of us who survived spent the next four years building a book of business and learning by trial and error. Each morning, we had mounds of new recommendations from New York to sift through, all fundamental. We were not allowed to recommend any stocks our firm did not have a favorable opinion on; the rule was: No thinking on our own—it could cause a lawsuit. Our job was to sell the research, not question it.

Over the years, we had some tremendous successes and some spectacular failures, definitely not a confidence builder. In my spare time, I kept searching for some infallible newsletter writer. This search, however, only proved that the newsletter writers were better at selling newsletters than at picking stocks. The ship was basically rudderless, but somehow we forged ahead. Now, almost 32 years later, the landscape has changed significantly. The brokerage business now is done by computer. The broker asks some questions and gains a feeling for the investors' risk tolerances. They then key this into a computer and the computer spits out a Strategic Asset Allocation Pie. The computer makes recommendations on what funds to have in the pie and the pie is then rebalanced (good things sold and bad things bought) twice a year. That is primarily what the basic broker does today. During my tenure at that firm, I specialized in option strategies. Options were relatively new, having been first listed for trading in April 1973 on the Chicago Board Options Exchange. I spent much of my time studying this investment tool, and in 1978 I was offered the opportunity to develop and manage an options strategy department at a large regional brokerage firm based in the same town. It was an irresistible challenge, so I embarked on this new adventure.

Overnight, my clientele changed from individual investors to professional stockbrokers. I was now responsible for developing a department that would provide options strategy ideas to a salesforce of 500 brokers. At this moment, I had to be totally honest with myself. Just how much did I really know about the stock market? I knew that my success at selecting the right stocks to support our options strategies would ultimately determine the success or failure of my department. The answer to that question was startling.

After four years of working as a stockbroker, I had very little knowledge about selecting stocks on my own, much less evaluating sectors and the market itself. I was used to doing what the firm directed. The one thing I did know was that relying on any firm's research was likely to be hit or miss. I would have to be self-contained with respect to the research that came out of my department. Developing a successful options strategy department meant I would have to find someone who was adept at stock selection.

During my search for a "stock picker," one name continued to crop up: Steve Kane, a broker in our Charlotte branch. I contacted Steve and explained my new adventure to him and offered him a position in my department. He decided to join me. My grand plan was that Steve would provide the stock, sector, and market direction; and I would provide the option strategies to dovetail his work.

As any craftsman would, Steve brought along his tools, which consisted of a chart book full of X's and O's on hundreds of stocks and a Point and Figure technical analysis book written by A. W. Cohen (this book is no longer in print). The basic principles of the Point and Figure method were developed by Charles Dow, the first editor of the *Wall Street Journal*. Later, a book was first published on the subject in 1947, the year I was born, and the book was called, *Stock Market Timing*. Each week, Steve would fastidiously update these charts of X's and O's and use these charts to make his stock selections. Over the first year, Steve did very well. Stocks he selected to rise generally did. Stocks he felt would decline generally did. His calls on the market and sectors were also very good. The team was working well, and best of all, we were self-contained. We were a technical analysis and options strategy department rolled into one. We weren't always right, but we were more right than wrong and, most important, we had a plan of attack.

Just as things were looking good, a specialist firm on the New York Stock Exchange offered Steve a job with the opportunity to trade their excess capital. It was an offer Steve could not refuse, and I supported his decision to go. I found myself back in the same predicament that I had been in a year earlier. Rather than try to find someone else who understood the Point and Figure method of technical analysis that I had become accustomed to, I decided it was time to learn it myself.

Steve explained the basics to me and recommended I read his closely guarded copy of A. W. Cohen's book. That weekend I started reading it, and after reading the first three pages, my life changed. All the years of operating in a fog, searching for answers, and believing it was all too complicated to learn, came to an end. What I found in the first three pages made all the sense in the world to me. I knew in that moment what I would do for the rest of my life. This was the missing link that all brokers needed to effectively service their clients. I knew my job from that day forward was to teach this method to my brothers and sisters in this business. We now operate the only Stockbroker Institute in the United States, and it is the culmination of my dream that night. We have trained hundreds of stockbrokers in this method and watched their confidence and client profits climb. We have also held our first Individual Investor Institute in concert with Virginia Commonwealth University, and the auditorium was packed. Something right is going on here.

On Taking Risks in Life*

There are many similarities between the principles in sports and the psychology of the stock market. I am a world record holder in powerlifting, and in my endeavors to improve my lifts, I learned a lot from Judd Biasiotto's articles in *Powerlifting* magazine. I have gotten to know Judd personally, and we see so many similarities between our two businesses that we have written articles together. In fact, we published two books together in concert with my analysts at DWA. The books are entitled *Keep Peddling Zen Farmer* and *Finding Religion Among the Rapids*. These books explain how some of the psychological aspects of sports competition can be applied to investing. I think this story Judd tells about

---

* This section was written with the assistance of Judd Biasiotto, PhD.

taking risks really hits at the heart of investing—it is just an exercise is continual risk management.

When Judd was working with the Kansas City Royals baseball team, his roommate, Branch B. Rickey III, "met a guy who was willing to let us buy into a condominium project being constructed in Florida. The deal was that we could purchase up to 10 condominiums at a price of $10,000 each. At the time, $10,000 was a pretty good chunk of money, but the deal was extraordinary. If everything went as planned, there was a good chance we could double or triple our money in no time. Still, there was a risk—there always is a risk. Because it was beachfront property, the taxes were very high. Unlike Branch, I did not have the money to invest long term. I would have to borrow the money at a fairly high interest rate and then hope that I could turn the property over in a short period. Otherwise, I would lose a lot of money. In the end, I decided not to do the deal. Of course, you know the end of the story already. The property is now worth anywhere from $500,000 to $1 million.

"Yes, I could have been living in the Bahamas relaxing on the beach, but I failed to take the risk. There is one thing I'm certain of—if you don't have the guts to put yourself on the line now and then, your chances of success are limited. To reach the top, athletes—or anyone else for that matter—have to know how to live on the edge. They have to enjoy the elements of risk and a little danger. I'm not talking about taking needless, senseless, incalculable risks, like running with the bulls in Pamplona or attempting a 500-pound dead-lift when your personal best is 300; such actions prove nothing except that you have the brain of an infant. What I'm talking about is intelligent, calculated risk-taking in which the risk in question has a legitimate cost-reward relationship."

Judd's comments really speak to the business of investing. You have to be a risk taker to even survive in this business, much less flourish. Every time you buy a stock, you are risking your hard-earned money. If you are a broker, you are risking your clients' hard-earned money. If you can't operate in a high-risk environment, then the business of investing is not for you. I have met many investors and brokers who just couldn't make a buy decision for fear of losing their or their clients' money. It's good to have a healthy dose of trepidation in this business of investing money. That way you don't make stupid mistakes, but freezing only causes you to miss great opportunities. There is a big difference between having a healthy respect for risk and allowing risk to paralyze your thought processes. Many investors and brokers simply can't deal with market volatility. A fine line exists between managing risk and being controlled by risk. The stock market is not a place for the faint of heart. To reach the pinnacle in the personal or professional investment field, you have to learn to live on the edge, to enjoy the element of risk and danger—at least to a reasonable degree.

Look back through time and you'll find that people who had the courage to take a chance, who faced their fears head on, were those who shaped history. The people who played it safe, who were afraid to take a risk, well, have you ever heard of them? I love what Theodore Roosevelt said about this very issue:

> It is not the critic who counts, not the man who points out how the strong man stumbles or where the doer of deeds could have done them better. The credit belongs to the man who is actually in the arena, whose face is marred by dust and sweat and blood, who strives valiantly, who errs and comes up short again and again because there is no effort without error and shortcomings, who knows the great devotion, who spends himself in a worthy cause, who at the best knows in the end the high achievement of triumph and who at worst, if he fails while daring greatly, knows his place shall never be with those timid and cold souls who know neither victory nor defeat.

Roosevelt's words remind me of this business of investing, and how many critics are out there ready to pounce on your every misstep although they never step into the ring; they never actually put their reputation or their money on the line. In the case of a professional, these critics never lose one minute of sleep because they are worried about other peoples' well-being.

Do you see yourself in the preceding quote? Those of you who are reading this book are the people in the ring. You are here to learn this method to better help you fight the battle. You realize that nothing is perfect and at times you will err and err again; but quit, you will never do. As time goes on, you will begin to intuitively understand things in the market that used to baffle you.

Eventually, you will reach craftsman status. The critics will continue criticizing because that is what they do best. Just turn the television on to any financial station and you will come away with gibberish. I often call these TV stations, Public Enemy #1. Once you nail down these principles of analysis, you will have no need for business periodicals or financial TV.

I remember vividly my broker years. My face was marred and bloodied many times but I was in the ring trying, striving for excellence. I just didn't have a plan back then. What a difference this information and way of thinking would have made if they had been available to me when I was a broker. Mix this with my enthusiasm and dedication to excellence and the combination is unbeatable. Many of you have already done this, and it makes me feel so good to see so many of you actually making a major difference out there in your own and others financial well-being.

Theodore Roosevelt was right, the credit goes to you the investor or broker who is actually in the arena, who at times comes up short again and again but in the end experiences triumph. This is why I wholeheartedly recommend you learn these methods and manage your money yourself. Win or lose, be the one in the ring where the action is. Make the decisions; take the calculated risk; live. Don't find yourself at the mercy of others or at the end of your career having ridden the bus and looked out the window, watching others reach greatness. It's all here for the taking. You just have to want it. Sports are full of great physical specimens, but there is a real shortage of athletes who are willing to play their game with reckless abandon, and athletes who are willing to put themselves and their careers on the line. Those who do are usually the ones at the top.

The truth in that last line inspires me. If you're not willing to risk, you have no growth, no change, and no freedom. And when that happens, you are no longer involved in living; for all practical purposes, you have no life. You're dead, but you just don't know it. So risk, for goodness sake. Be a part of life. You have the power to be or do anything you want. You can produce miracles if you have a mind to. You have the magic; you just have to tap into it. Get in touch with it, make things happen, live—journey to the stars, push on to new galaxies. If you don't, you will never know your greatness!

Chapter 2

POINT AND FIGURE FUNDAMENTALS

Many investors are familiar with charts of some kind or other, whether from school or reading newspapers or magazines. Point and Figure charts were developed over 100 years ago and have stood the test of time. We've even added a new dimension to the history of their effectiveness in negotiating all markets. That new dimension is the Internet craze. The Internet has allowed us to deliver our charting system to anyone in the world who has Internet service. The major leaps in computer technology have allowed us to create some amazing indicators that only 10 years ago were not possible. When I say they have withstood the test of time, I mean right up through today in this third edition of *Point and Figure Charting*. And, I'm even more confident now about this method than I have ever been.

I have taught this method of technical analysis in many seminars and classes. I have even taught it to schoolchildren as young as 12 years old. One reason this methodology is so teachable is that it is based on supply and demand. The irrefutable law of supply and demand governs the movement of prices in stock, or anything else for that matter. If there are more buyers than sellers willing to sell, prices rise; on the other hand, when there are more sellers than buyers willing to buy, prices decline. These imbalances in supply and demand, and nothing else, cause prices of stocks to move up and down. When you cut through all the red tape and obfuscation on Wall Street, you are left with the raw facts of supply and demand. Fundamental changes in the underlying company's outlook can cause this imbalance, but it is the imbalance nonetheless that causes the stock to move. Don't get me wrong. I am not saying fundamental analysis is not important: It is the first line of defense. I want any stock I buy to be fundamentally sound. I love to start with a list of fundamentally sound stocks before I begin to evaluate the supply-and-demand relationship of the stocks. Keep that firmly in mind as we go forward. The problem with fundamentals is they change ever so slightly early on and this change is rarely picked up on the fundamental analyst's radar screen. The investors who truly understand these nuances begin to cast their vote on the stock early on and this causes the supply demand relationship to change. This change is then picked up on a Point and Figure chart, which in turn tips off the astute investor of an imminent change in the underlying stock's direction. All too often, fundamental analysts say they missed the decline in the stock because the businesses of the companies they followed were not failing. Until the underlying business begins to change, they cannot change their opinion, and rightfully so. Their expertise is evaluating the fundamentals of the underlying stock, not its supply/demand relationship.

The Point and Figure method of analyzing stock movement was designed simply as a logical, organized way of recording this battle between supply and demand. The word *organized* is the key. A basic road atlas would be difficult to use if the actual lines depicting the roads and interstates were missing. It is the same in the stock market business. Looking at an endless list of High-Low-Close quotations on any particular stock can be equally confusing. When these quotations are organized in a logical fashion, however, the battle between supply and demand becomes much more evident. The Point and Figure chart simply shows whether supply or demand is winning the battle. We use various chart patterns and trend lines to guide our buy-and-sell decisions. These patterns are covered in detail in later chapters, as is market and sector analysis.

A tennis match is a helpful analogy in describing this battle between supply and demand. Consider a match between tennis greats, Jimmy Connors and John McEnroe. Let's call demand

Jimmy Connors and supply John McEnroe. Their tennis match consists of various sets. The sets in this tennis match are similar to the Point and Figure chart moving back and forth, changing columns of alternating X's and O's. This seemingly random movement in the Point and Figure chart is similar to the seemingly random changes in sets the players win during the tennis match. Eventually, Connors or McEnroe wins enough sets to emerge victorious in the match. Likewise, only when the match between supply and demand is completed can we get a handle on which way the stock is likely to move. The Point and Figure chart considers the sets that are played as market noise and not worthy of inclusion in the decision-making process. In the short run, stock prices move about randomly but eventually demand or supply takes control and a trend begins. In this book, I refer to tennis and football in explaining many of the market indicators and stock chart patterns you are about to learn. Let's play ball!

The Basic Tenets of a Point and Figure Chart

We begin with the basics of maintaining your own chart. We use plotting a stock as our basis for explaining how to chart and then end the chapter with some of the nuisances of charting mutual funds and Exchange Traded Funds (ETFs) but the fundamentals are the same for all investment vehicles—from stocks to funds to commodities, and so on. It only takes a few minutes each day to update 20 or 30 charts by hand but why bother when we have a web site that does all the work for you on over 8,000 stocks a day? It does help in gaining a strong feeling for the process if you maintain a few by hand each day. We have a broker client who updates over 400 each day by hand and would never give up that process no matter what. At Dorsey, Wright, & Associates (DWA), positions in our managed accounts and key indicators are charted by hand each day. It gives a feel that one cannot get any other way. Most investors, however, don't have that time available after market hours, and thus the Internet is a valuable time-saver. If you should choose to maintain charts by hand, all you would need is a financial page providing the high and low prices of stocks each day. If you have a computer with Internet hookup, you will be in technical analysis heaven these days.

The Point and Figure chart uses only the price action of the stock—volume is not a consideration. Volume will have to show up in the chart patterns because there will be no movement of the stock unless there are more buyers than sellers willing to sell or more sellers than buyers willing to buy. Much of the volume in stocks today is related to option strategies and hedge fund activities that have nothing to do with a bet on the direction of the stock. You would be amazed at how much is just option related. Remember, we are only interested in the battle between supply and demand. Two letters of the alphabet are used in this method of charting, "X" and "O." The X represents demand. The O represents supply. The key to this method is how the chart moves from one column to the next. For the purposes of this book, we will use the 3-point reversal method. As you become more adept, you may want to choose other reversal points. At my company, however, we never deviate from the three-box method described in this section: We keep it simple. Figure 2.1 shows a basic chart that gives you an idea of what the Point and Figure chart looks like. Talking about the X and O reminds me of a seminar I held in Minneapolis one day. A beautiful woman in her 70s came up to me after the seminar and told me how her husband had gained new vigor and enthusiasm for life now that he charted all their stocks every day. (They had attended two other seminars I had held in Minnesota and had read my book.) She went on to tell me how she also helped him manage their considerable portfolio. She said with a

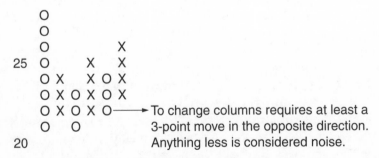

Figure 2.1　Basic Point and Figure chart.

smile, "He handles the hugs and I handle the kisses." What a wonderful story! I could, in fact, write a book devoted to stories of people who became successful investors when they embraced this operating system. It makes me feel especially good when learning this method changes a professional investment advisor's life. This simply means he or she is helping many other people become successful with their investment endeavors. Today, retirement is on many people's minds. According to the Census Bureau, over three-quarters of all the wealth in the United States is in the hands of those of us who are over 50 years old.

The chart pattern is formed by alternating columns of X's and O's. The only way a column of X's can change to a column of O's is by reversing three boxes. The same three-box reversal method applies to the column of O's. This moving back and forth from one column to the next is what causes the chart pattern to form. This is where the Point and Figure chart drastically departs from the method of the bar chart. The Point and Figure chart leaves volatility out of the equation and gives you a clear picture of the battle between supply and demand. The bar chart on the other hand includes volatility in the equation because the chart must be updated every day no matter how inconsequential the move might be. This is why bar charts are subjective and difficult to read, and are rarely effective for many people who use them.

Let's get into the mechanics of charting by looking at the values of the boxes we primarily use in constructing the chart. When I say box sizes, I mean the boxes on a simple sheet of chart paper. You know the paper; the same charting paper you use to get in Biology class in High School. The box sizes change as the stock price moves through certain levels. This is why we call this method a three-box reversal method rather than a 3-point reversal method. It is important to think in terms of boxes rather than prices. Between 20 and 100, the box size is 1 point per box. If a stock is trading below 20 or above 100, we use other box sizes. Simply stated, when a stock is between 0 and 5, the box size on the chart is ¼ of a point. Between 5 and 20, the box size moves up to ½ point per box. Between 20 and 100, the box size is 1 point per box. Above 100, the box size rises to 2 points per box. Finally, above 200, the box size is 4 points per box. Keep the following table handy while you are learning to chart:

Price ($)	Box Size
0 to 5	¼ point per box
5 to 20	½ point per box
20 to 100	1 point per box
100 to 200	2 points per box
Above 200	4 points per box

The Internet age ushered in higher priced stocks and, more importantly, more volatility. After the Internet bust, energy stocks and metals stocks became the high fliers. One of the best ways to adjust for that volatility is to increase the box size. Many stocks in the technology and Internet sectors were so volatile that we had to increase the box size enough to compress the chart and obtain a normal picture of the supply and demand relationship of the stock. In fact, stocks like Yahoo in 1998 to 2000 often required 10 points per box to compress the chart to normal. And, these Internet stocks and high-tech/high-wreck stocks absolutely wiped out many investors in 2000. Think about this for a second. If we have to increase the box size from, let's say, 1 to 5 to slow the chart down enough to get a good picture of supply and demand, this stock is too volatile for most investors. Many investors saw stocks drop 50 percent or more in a single second in 2000. Apple Computer, for example, reported less than expected earnings for the quarter. Wham! The stock was down 50 percent on the opening. This is important: As you embark on your investment endeavors, remember that stocks with 5-point box sizes are out of the realm of most investors' risk tolerance. If you find it compelling to invest in these stocks, buy 10 shares. This will help you slay that monster called volatility. On our web site, we have a system called "Smart Charts." These charts give the user the ability to raise or lower the box size on any chart. This can give the chart user some perspective when making a buy or sell decision on that stock. Often, we will gravitate to a smaller box size on a stock to help in establishing a less painful stop loss point. We have come a long way on our web site (www.dorseywright.com) since its debut in 1994 when we were one of the first to use the Internet as a delivery system.

Let's go over these different box size values once again. I want this to be set firmly in your mind. If a stock were trading below 5, then each box would have a value of ¼ point. Between 5 and 20, the box size would be ½ point. If the stock were trading between 20 and 100 (where most stocks trade), the box size would be 1 point. If the stock were trading at 100 or higher, the box size would be 2 points; and above 200, the box size would be 4 points. Again, these are the standards or the "default" box sizes. The beauty of the system is you have control of what you want the box size to be. Some stocks are high dividend payers and have very low volatility. The standard box sizes might not be right for these stocks and thus require a smaller box size. As I mentioned, you can make changes on our system. The key to making the chart relates to how the chart switches from one column to another. When a stock is rising and demand is in control, the chart will be in X's. Conversely, when a stock is declining and supply is in control, the chart will be in O's. It requires a three-box reversal or more to be significant enough to warrant changing columns. Therefore, to change columns from X's to O's when the stock was between 20 and 100 would require 3 points. We established that between 20 and 100 the box size was 1, so three boxes equals 3. The same three-box reversal would only be 1½ points if the stock were between 5 and 20. If the stock were trading below 5, the same three-box reversal would only be ¾ of a point because the box size in a stock between 0 and 5 is ¼ of a point. Think in terms of box reversals.

Figure 2.1 illustrates how much the stock must rise or fall to create a reversal on the chart. In this chart, each column has at least three X's or three O's, maybe more, but never less. Although I am being redundant, that's okay—I intend to be redundant in this chapter to help you catch on to the basics of maintaining your own chart. The rest of the book will flow easily once you understand this concept. If you don't catch on after the first reading, go back and reread this chapter again and again until you are comfortable with the concepts. Believe me; it will be worth your time. When you become a craftsman at this easy method, you will join an elite group of investors and professionals who consistently make money and manage risk with this method. I call them The SEAL Team of Wall Street.

IF THE CHART IS FALLING IN A COLUMN OF O'S

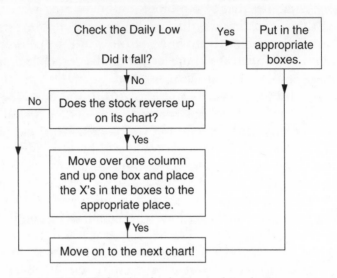

Figure 2.2   The flowchart for charting; explains charting process.

Updating a Point and Figure Chart

When I lecture on this subject, I use the flowchart shown in Figure 2.2 to demonstrate how to update a chart. The basic concept is as follows. Whichever column the chart is in, you will remain in that column as long as the stock continues in that direction by one box or more. Let's stop and think about that statement for a second: "As long as the stock continues in that direction by one box or more." So, if the chart were in a column of O's and declining, your first question of the flowchart at the close of the business day would be, "Did the stock decline one full box or more on the chart?" If the stock did decline one more box, let's say from 45 to 44, then record that move by making an O in the 44 box and stop—go no further that day. Keep in mind; all you are doing is recording what the stock does on each trading day, nothing more, nothing less. Don't think about the chart again until the close of business the following day. At the close of business the following day, you simply look at the high and low for the day (in the case we are now discussing, the low would be the most important) and ask the same question again. Since the stock is still in a column of O's, did it decline another box or more? Answer the question by looking at the low price for the day. If the stock in this case hit 43 or lower (declined one more box or lower), record the move by making an O in the box and stop. I don't care if the stock reversed later in the day and went to 100. You'll deal with that move tomorrow. You are only concerned with one direction per day. At this point, the stock is at 43 in a column of O's. Since the stock is still in a column of O's, the next day at the close of trading you ask the same question again. Did the stock decline one more box or lower? Today, the answer is no to flowchart question 1. The stock did not move lower by one box or more today.

Because the stock did not decline enough to close one more box today, you go to the second and last flowchart question. Since the stock did not decline any further, or at least enough to close another box, the second and final question of the flowchart is, did the stock reverse up three boxes? Let's think about this for a second. Did the stock reverse up three boxes? In this example, we are discussing a stock that is trading between 20 and 100 so the box size is 1 point per box. So, a three-box reversal up would be 3 points higher than the last "O." Count up three boxes from 43, which would be 44, 45, and 46. Okay, did the stock hit 46? Let's say it hit 45.75. That's not good enough. That was only a 2.75 reversal, not 3. What do you do? Nothing.

The next day, you go through the same process again. Since the stock is still in a column of O's, the first flowchart question that must be answered is, "Did the stock go down one box or more?" Get the picture? You go back to the first flowchart question and start again. At this point, there can only be two action points on the chart. The stock either does move one more box lower or it reverses up three boxes. The two action points that will cause me to make a mark on the chart are 42 or 46. Nothing else will cause a change on the chart. It either continues in its current column of "O's" or it reverses up into a column of "X's." That is about as difficult as it gets in maintaining a Point and Figure chart. Okay, back to the example, if over time, the stock does reverse up three boxes to 46 by following these two flowchart questions, you will find the chart now one column over to the right and that movement

represented by three X's. The chart is now rising. The same
process starts over again, only this time the first flowchart
question is, "Did the stock move up one box or more?" That is
really the whole ball of wax.

Once again, it takes three boxes to reverse from one direction
to the other. For example, if a stock were trading in a column of
X's with a top of 45, it would take a move to 42 to reverse this
chart to a column of O's: 45–3 = 42. Anything less than three
boxes would be considered market noise, not worthy of recording.
Conversely, if the stock in question was trading in a column of
O's with a current low at 45, it would need a rise to 48 before a reversal into a column of X's could be recorded; as before, anything
less than three boxes would be considered market noise. Figure
2.3 shows some examples of reversals.

There is one exception to the preceding pattern. If a stock
reversed from 21, for example, the required number of points
would only be 2. This is because the stock will be moving
through a level, where the box size changes. If a stock is moving
up (in a column of X's) through the upper teens and has a high of
21, a reversal would take place at 19, a move of only 2 points.
The three boxes in this case are at 20; then as the stock goes
below 20, the box size changes to ½ point per box or 19½, 19,
and so on. Once again, the box size between 20 and 5 is ½ point
per box rather than the 1 point per box above 20. Keep break
points in mind when you are charting at levels where the box
size changes. If you just price the vertical axes properly, you
need deal only with the boxes. Prices will take care of themselves. Keep it simple. Just assign the proper point value to the
box, ½, 1, and so on and then count three boxes. This brings
you to the actual charting. The daily high and low quotations
for a stock are all that you will need. In today's Internet world,

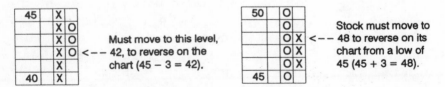

Figure 2.3   Examples of reversals.

all you need do is go to our web site and we do all the work for you. If you choose to do it by hand, most newspapers have a financial section, but quotes are limited. Sites like Yahoo Finance would serve your quote needs perfectly. Once you have the quotes, the only prices you are concerned with are those that cause changes in the chart. For example, a stock is in a column of X's and has a high of 28.875. For charting purposes, we would read this as 28 because between 20 and 100 there are no fractions in the boxes. Each box is 1 point. In this case, .875 is not enough to close the box of 29. It's .125 too low. To the Point and Figure chartist, .875 is simply market noise when the box size is 1 point. If a stock is in a column of O's, you are primarily interested in whether the stock declined on that day of trading and you would look at a stock's low first. Using the same example, a stock has a low of 28.875. You read this as a low of 29. The stock must move to 28 to add another O to the chart. When you get a reversal of three or more boxes on a chart, you plot the reversal one column over and three boxes up or down depending on the direction of the reversal. The first change in direction would always be a three-box move because that is the minimum move required to shift columns. After the shift in columns, the moves could be as low as one box. If the stock reverses down, you will plot an O one column over and three boxes down. If the stock reverses to the upside, you will plot an X one column over and three boxes higher. When reversing up or down, your count does not begin at the last number. Up means begin counting up one box. For example, to begin counting a reversal up where the last box closed at say, 28 with an O, start counting up at 29, 30, 31. The first X of the three-box reversal up would begin at 29. A reversal down suggests you begin counting down one box below the highest X.

The only record of time in the Point and Figure chart is the replacing of the X or O with the number of the month when the chartist makes the first entry of that month. Placing the month in the chart has no significance except as a reference point. As the stock moves about, it alternates back and forth from one column to the next, X to O, O to X, and so on. At no time will you have an O in a column of X's nor an X in a column of O's. As previously mentioned, the first action point on the chart in any given month is represented by the number of the month. For example, if a stock rises one box, you would add another X to its chart, but if that X, or plot, is the first one for July, you would use a 7 instead of an X in that box. Seven signifies the seventh month of the year, or July. This also holds true on down moves. For example, if a stock declined one box, and that is the first action point in August, you would put an 8 in the box instead of an O.

Let's cover it again. If the chart is rising, first check the daily high, and add an X if the stock has risen enough to close the next open box or boxes. You would add as many X's as needed to represent the stock's move. If the stock rose 4 points during the trading session, and each box equaled 1, you would put four X's on the chart. If the same stock moved up 5 points, you would add five X's. Flowchart question 1 would have been satisfied and at that point you stop charting for that day. If, on the other hand, the stock did not move high enough to add another X, you go to flowchart question 2 and check the daily low to see if it has declined enough (3 boxes) to reverse on the chart. The reversal is the key feature of the Point and Figure chart. If it did reverse, move one column over and one box down, then add the three O's representing the reversal. If the stock did not decline enough to warrant a reversal, then there is no action on the chart for the day. Remember, the three-box reversal means all three boxes must be filled before you fill any of them (2.99 points is not 3, and 3 is the requirement for a reversal if the point value of a box is 1). You cannot begin filling one box, then the next, until you get three. The chart will remain in its current column until it closes (hits) all three boxes on the reversal. I am being purposely redundant because it is incredibly important that you understand the concept of charting before we go on to the fun parts of the book.

By using a three-box reversal method, we eliminate the minor moves that often occur in the market and look for moves that are significant enough to warrant representation. If a stock is declining, use the same process in reverse. Look first to see if the stock has moved down enough to add another O. If it has, add the O or O's. If the stock did not decline enough to close another box, then look at the daily high to see if the stock has rallied enough to reverse the chart up. If it has, move one column over and one box up and add the three new X's. If it has not moved up enough to reverse, there is no action on that chart for the day. Some stocks can sit for months without any change. In volatile markets, the chart could continue in its present direction and then reverse. In other words, the stock rose enough to close another box with an X, but the last 20 minutes of trading that day, the stock declined 8 points on earnings news. You would simply stick to the flowchart, close the box with an X and forget the reversal at the end of the day. Remember, one direction per day. You will deal with that reversal tomorrow. It is a good idea to be aware of the stock's reversal at the end of the trading session, even though you don't record it on the chart that day. This can happen when earnings reports are released. The stock rises one box on the day, but late in the session the earnings are released. Let's say they are much less than Wall Street expected. This could have the effect of immediately collapsing the stock price, thus producing what might seem like a reversal back down the chart. Remember, as I mentioned earlier, a chart can only move in one direction a day. In this case, you update the chart by moving it up in the column of X's. If the stock has moved enough late in the day to reverse, you will more than likely chart that reversal the following day, but not in all cases.

If you have already gotten the hang of updating your chart, you can move along to the next section; if not, let's recap for a moment. We'll call it Study Hall. If a stock is rising in a column of X's, you will record any subsequent up-moves as long as that up-move equals or exceeds the next highest box. If the stock does not move up enough to equal the next higher box, then you look to the low to see if the stock reversed columns. To reverse into a column of O's from X's, the underlying stock must reverse three boxes to be significant enough to warrant a change in columns. Thus, the action points in a stock that is rising and has the 50 box closed with an X will be 51 for another X, or 47 to qualify for a reversal into a column of O's. The opposite is true for a stock declining. The easiest way to chart is to determine your two action points before you seek the high and low for the day. In the preceding example, your action points were 51 or 47. That's all you look for in the high and low for the day. Did the stock hit 51? If the answer is no, then did it hit 47? If one of those action points was hit, record the correct price and stop. Once you understand the concept of the reversal, you have mastered the nuts and bolts of this method. I urge you to keep studying this method. It will truly change your investment life. Sometimes we feel as if we are falling behind or failing when we try something new. Keep at it. I like to think about Thomas Edison, who failed many times before he found the right path.

Edison's life is a prime example of the American Dream. Without question, he was a giant among men. During his lifetime, he patented a record 1,093 inventions. Some of those inventions literally revolutionized the world. However, despite having one of the greatest minds in history, Edison, like all men, knew failure. In fact, he failed quite often. But like all great men, Edison accepted failure as a learning experience that would help him grow and develop. His son Charles Edison wrote about his father: "It is sometimes asked—didn't he ever fail? The answer is yes." Thomas Edison knew failure frequently. His first patent, when he was all but penniless, was for an electric vote recorder, but maneuver-minded legislators refused to buy it. Once he had his entire fortune tied up in machinery for a magnetic separation device for low-grade iron ore only to have it made obsolete and uneconomic by the opening of the rich Mesabi Range. But he never hesitated out of fear of failure. "Shucks," he told a discouraged coworker during one trying series of experiments. "We haven't failed. We now know a thousand things that won't work, so we're that much closer to finding what will." If you are reading this book, you are on your way to becoming a world-class investor by learning what works. Now it's time to take what you have learned and construct a Point and Figure chart based on a series of highs and lows. In Figure 2.4 we have provided you with a piece of graph paper to plot your practice Point and Figure chart. Using the data in Figure 2.5 and using the principles you just learned about charting and using the simple two-question flow chart as your guide, plot a Point and Figure chart. As you plot this chart, remember that you are recording the supply-and-demand relationship of the stock in a logical, organized manner.

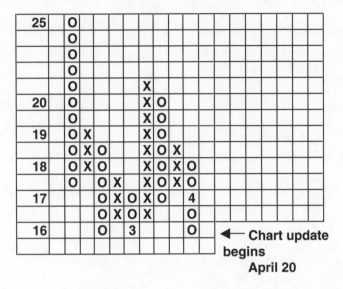

Figure 2.4   ABC Corp. starting chart.

Practice Chart: ABC Corporation

We have used the price quotations shown in Figure 2.5 to construct the chart that appears in Figure 2.6. Take a look at that chart now. Notice how the last box closed in the chart in April is at the price of 16. We begin updating the chart from that point. Remember the easiest way to maintain a Point and Figure chart is to determine where your action points are. If the chart is in a column of O's, the first action point would be one box lower than the last one recorded. If the stock does not decline low enough to record the lower box, then your second and last action point would be a three-box reversal up. In the case of ABC Corporation, the first action points from the bottom at 16 in April would be 15½ (one box lower) or 17½ (a three-box reversal up). From the 16 level, there are no other action points. Whichever action point is hit first, record it, and then determine your next action point. That basically is all there is to updating a chart. Always think of your two action points.

DATE	HIGH	LOW	LAST
20-Apr	16.625	16.000	16.000
21-Apr	16.250	16.000	16.125
22-Apr	16.875	16.375	16.625
25-Apr	16.750	16.500	16.625
26-Apr	17.375	16.500	17.375
27-Apr	17.375	17.375	17.375
28-Apr	18.125	17.500	17.750
29-Apr	18.125	17.625	17.625
2-May	18.375	17.500	18.000
3-May	18.250	17.875	18.000
4-May	18.250	17.875	18.125
5-May	18.250	17.500	17.500
6-May	17.750	17.500	17.625
9-May	17.750	17.125	17.125
10-May	17.625	17.125	17.125
11-May	17.625	17.125	17.375
12-May	17.500	17.125	17.250
13-May	17.500	17.125	17.375
16-May	17.375	17.125	17.250
17-May	17.500	17.125	17.250
18-May	17.625	17.250	17.375
19-May	17.625	17.375	17.500
20-May	17.625	17.250	17.375
23-May	18.000	17.500	17.625
24-May	18.875	17.625	18.875
25-May	19.625	18.625	18.875
26-May	19.750	18.375	18.500
27-May	19.125	18.500	18.875
31-May	19.375	18.875	19.000
1-Jun	22.250	19.625	21.750
2-Jun	20.500	19.500	19.750

DATE	HIGH	LOW	LAST
3-Jun	21.000	19.875	20.500
6-Jun	21.750	20.875	21.000
7-Jun	21.500	20.750	20.750
8-Jun	21.125	20.500	20.625
9-Jun	20.750	20.500	20.500
10-Jun	21.625	20.500	21.500
13-Jun	23.125	21.250	22.875
14-Jun	23.250	22.250	22.625
15-Jun	22.875	20.500	22.750
16-Jun	24.250	22.750	23.875
17-Jun	24.625	23.750	24.000
20-Jun	23.250	22.250	23.000
21-Jun	23.125	21.875	21.875
22-Jun	22.250	21.125	21.625
23-Jun	21.625	20.750	20.750
24-Jun	21.750	20.500	21.375
27-Jun	21.500	21.000	21.500
28-Jun	23.625	21.250	23.625
29-Jun	24.125	23.250	23.875
30-Jun	23.875	22.125	22.375
1-Jul	23.250	20.500	22.875
5-Jul	23.000	20.500	22.750
6-Jul	22.625	22.000	22.000
7-Jul	24.000	22.000	23.625
8-Jul	24.250	22.875	23.500
11-Jul	23.750	23.000	23.125
12-Jul	23.750	23.250	23.375
13-Jul	23.625	23.250	23.250
14-Jul	23.625	23.375	23.500
15-Jul	23.375	22.625	22.750

Figure 2.5 ABC Corp. price history.

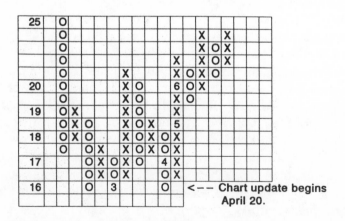

Figure 2.6 ABC Corp. chart.

36

Using Figures 2.4 and 2.5, let's update ABC Corporation stock beginning at the 16 in April. As discussed earlier, there are numbers on the chart that correspond to the months of the year and provide a convenient reference point for the following steps:

1. On April 20, determine action points with the stock currently in a column of O's at 16. They are 15½ and 17½. Let's explain how we get these numbers one more time. Since we begin with the stock in a column of O's, the 15½ action point is simply one box lower than the last one recorded at 16. The 17½ action point corresponds to a three-box reversal up. Remember that each box below 20 and above 5 equals ½ point. Three boxes represent 1½ points, thus 16 + 1½ = 17½. In this case, 17½ is hit before 15½. Notice how, on April 28, 17½ is hit as well as 18. This action causes the reversal plus one box. Now go up to 18 in a column of X's.

2. On April 28, determine your action points. They will be 18½ for a one-box rise or 16½ for a three-box reversal. Record whichever comes first. It takes until May 24 for the stock to move enough to be considered significant enough to record. The stock rose to 18.875 closing the 18½ box. This is a good example of why the Point and Figure chart is so important. The bar chartist would have been recording moves in the chart every day. The Point and Figure chartist would have done nothing from April 28 until May 24 because nothing significant happened between those dates. The Point and Figure chartist is not interested in noise.

3. On May 24, determine your action points. They are 19 on the upside and 17 for a three-box reversal. Now you wait to see which one is hit first, and then establish your next action points. Easy, huh? On May 25, the next day, ABC Corp. hit a high of 19.625. This closed the action point box of 19 as well as the next box above it at 19½.

4. On May 26, determine your action points. They are 20 and 18. If the stock increases one more box and hits 20 make an X. If—instead of rising—it falls three boxes to 18 or lower, reverse into a column of O's and represent the move. On June 1, the stock hit 22.25. You can now move up in X's to the 22 box. Notice how the box size has changed. It was ½ dollar (point)

per box below 20, now it is 1 dollar (point) per box above 20 up to 100.

5. On June 2, establish your action points. They are 23 and 19½. The 23 one is easy, the 19½ action point might confuse you a little. Remember the breakpoints in box size. Three boxes down from 22 would be 21, 20, 19½. Below 20 is ½ point per box. The very next day the stock declines to 19.50, so you will reverse into a column of O's. Supply had taken control for the time being. Your action points will now begin with one box lower to continue in the same direction, or a three-box or more reversal into a column of X's.

6. On June 3, establish your action points. The chart is now in a column of O's at the 19½ level. Your action points are 19 and 22 for a three-box reversal. Once again, we cross the equator, the point where the box size changes from ½ to 1, so a three-box reversal up from 19½ is ½ point to 20 then 1 point to 21 and 1 point to 22. Note how the box size changes when you cross the 20 mark. Let's see which one is hit first. On June 13, the stock rises to 23, so the stock reverses up into a column of X's and the 23 box is closed.

7. On June 14, establish your action points. Since you are in a column of X's, your first action point is one box higher than the last one closed. That number is 24. A three-box reversal would be 20. So we are looking for 24 and 20. On June 16, 24¼ is hit closing the 24 box.

8. On June 17, establish your action points. We are looking for 25 or 21. A one-box rise is represented by 25 and 21 the three-box reversal. On June 23, the stock declines to 20.75. This reverses it back down the chart and into a column of O's. The 21 box is now closed with an O.

9. On June 24, establish your action points. We are looking for 20 and 24. On June 29, the stock hits a high of 24.125. The stock now reverses back up into a column of X's. The reversal forms a Double Top (we cover these patterns in Chapter 3).

10. On June 30, establish your action points. They are 25 and 21 for a three-box reversal. Continue on your own for the rest.

This has been an interesting exercise because the stock crossed the equator a couple of times demonstrating three-box reversals using ½-point and 1-point box sizes.

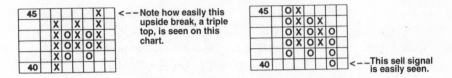

Figure 2.7 Buy and sell signals.

One of the reasons Point and Figure charts are so practical is that the chart formations stand out because we move over and down a box when making a reversal. This is easily seen by looking at a chart that has just broken out. By moving down a box when the stock reverses down, the tops, or resistance areas, stand out. By moving up a box when the stock reverses up, the lows or support areas stand out. Figure 2.7 provides examples of such movements.

Mutual Fund Charting

I've mentioned several times already in this book how technology changed the scope of analysis we do at DWA. One place this is evident is in our extensive mutual fund service. In 1997, we began to develop a database of mutual fund charts. This universe has burgeoned to over 16,000 mutual fund charts today. Many investors didn't even realize that you can plot Point and Figure charts for mutual funds but when you cut to the core of a mutual fund, it is merely a basket of stocks. The same principles for charting a stock can be applied to charting a mutual fund, with a couple of nuances. First and foremost, the flow chart for plotting a mutual fund chart is the exact same as a stock. In Figure 2.2 instead of looking at the high or the low, we look at the Net Asset Value (NAV) at the end of every trading day. The first question we ask ourselves upon looking at that NAV is if we can continue in the direction the chart is currently going. If the answer is yes, we add the appropriate X's or O's and move on to the next chart. If the answer is no, we look to see if the chart has reversed. If so, we make the appropriate marks and move on. If the chart does not reverse, there is no action on the chart for that day.

Now let's talk about the nuances of plotting a Point and Figure chart on a mutual fund. The first is the mutual fund scale.

The average fund trades at $15 a share. That is a basket of stocks, not just an individual name. Because mutual funds generally move slower than an individual issue we have to "speed up" the chart. Instead of using a scale of ½ point per box, we instead use a default scale, also called the intermediate scale, of 20 cents per box. The short-term chart is half that size at 10 cents a box. The long-term chart follows the stock scale and is at 50 cents a box for this price range. Note that this scaling does adjust as the price of the mutual fund changes but this is the scaling used for the average fund.

The box sizes differ to produce a sensitivity range that helps you in evaluating that mutual fund. Smaller box sizes make the chart more sensitive also increasing signal noise. Bigger box sizes reduce sensitivity and reduce noise. Larger box sizes are best used to establish longer-term trends because they tend to show stronger areas of support and resistance. The purpose of using several different box sizes is to uncover the short-term action within the context of the longer-term trending. If we focus only on the long-term chart, we may miss the attractive short-term benefit from the fund. If we focus only on the short term, we may lose sight of the underlying long-term trend. The art in the Point and Figure method is to correctly interpret both themes in tandem. This often leads to a better understanding of how to use a mutual fund within your asset allocation models.

Exchange Traded Funds

I have been in this business for over 30 years now and I'm almost sad to say that the rate of innovation on Wall Street has actually been pretty poor when you compare it to other industries. In 1973, the advent of the listed options market changed the financial landscape. It wasn't until the introduction of the ETF about 25 years later that I think Wall Street brought to market a new, innovative product that would forever change the way investors approached the market. I had spoken to one of the major exchanges about the need for an ETF-like product in the early 1980s but it wasn't until the introduction of the iShares ETF product in 2000 that we began to see this product expand extensively in the marketplace. Without a doubt, I think the ETF product is the most important innovation on Wall Street in my 30 years in this business. It is so important that we devoted a chapter to ETFs in the second edition of the book and we devote a chapter to ETFs in this third edition. In Chapter 10, we go into more history on ETFs but for now, I want to point out a subtle difference when charting ETFs and stocks. Much like a mutual fund is a basket of stocks, ETFs are baskets of stocks, too. Because of this we find that the charts of an ETF move, for the most part, too slowly when plotted on a typical stock scaling system. At DWA we default to 25 cents per box up to $20, 50 cents up to $50 and then we go back to the stock scaling of 1 point per box. And in some instances, an ETF of a low volatility sector might even need a scale a little lower than that. The more you work with this methodology though, the easier it will be for you to look at a chart and determine whether you need to speed it up by decreasing the box size or slow it down by increasing the box size. But again, we use the previously outlined scaling for most all of our ETFs and then tweak it from there. Our system at DWA allows us to easily change box sizes.

Trend Lines

Trend lines are one of the most important guides you have in Point and Figure charting. In fact, we have created a new sector indicator by aggregating trend lines—The Percent of Stocks Trading Above Their Trend Lines—is discussed in Chapter 8. I am always amazed how a stock will hold a trend line on the way up or down. Trend lines are very easily drawn using the Point and Figure method, whereas bar chart methods involve a lot of subjectivity. Two basic trend lines are used in Point and Figure charting: the Bullish Support Line and the Bearish Resistance Line. We discuss each of these separately as well as two other trend lines, the Bullish Resistance Line and the Bearish Support Line. For long-term investors, a stock's main trend is always bullish if it is trading above the Bullish Support Line. I call this line Interstate 95 North. On the East Coast, I-95 is the main artery moving north and south. Conversely, a stock's main trend is said to be bearish if it trades below the Bearish Resistance Line. I call this line Interstate 95 South. These trend lines are typically used for long-term investors. Traders are much more flexible and find the truth lies somewhere in between most of the time.

The Bullish Support Line

The Bullish Support Line is a major component of a stock's chart pattern. It serves as a guide to the underlying security's trend. Typically, these lines are like brick walls. It is uncanny how so many stocks will hold the trend line as they rise in price. In general, investors should not buy stocks that are not trading above their Bullish Support Lines. Drawing the line is very simple and has not changed since the inception of the Point and Figure method. Once a stock has formed a base of accumulation below the Bearish Resistance Line and gives the first buy signal off the bottom, we go to the lowest column of O's in the chart pattern and begin drawing a trend line starting with the box directly under that column of O's. You then connect each box diagonally upward in a 45-degree angle. Unlike bar charts, which connect prices, the Point and Figure chart never connects prices. The angle for a Bullish Support Line will always be a 45-degree angle. The Bearish Resistance Line will always be the reciprocal of the 45-degree angle, a 135-degree angle.

We typically give a stock the benefit of the doubt if it gives a sell signal while it is trading close to the Bullish Support Line. Once a stock rises significantly above this trend line and gives a sell signal, followed by another buy signal, a shorter-term trend line can be drawn. Simply go to a level that is one box below the bottom O in the column that gave the sell signal and connect the boxes up diagonally. This will serve to be your new trend line, although I would still leave the first trend line intact because it will give you some longer-term perspective. The first Bullish Support Line will always serve to be the long-term trend line and may very well come into play years later. These shorter-term trend lines serve as visual guides. The short-term trend lines can also be valuable in identifying the short-term direction of stocks. Traders often initiate a long trade when the stock has declined near the Bullish Support Line because the stock is then close to the stop-loss point. The most important characteristic of the Point and Figure method is its clear guidelines for whether a stock is on a buy signal or a sell signal and whether it is in an uptrend. But above all, remember this is an art not a science. H_2O does not necessarily equal water in the investment world. You are an integral part of the equation; never forget that. Many investors are looking for the black box that can make them instantly wealthy without becoming personally involved. It ain't happening. You will find that this method is equally effective in helping you avoid the big hit as it is in helping you to buy the right stock at the right time. Often in investing, it's what you did not buy that is responsible for your success.

When the stock violates the Bullish Support Line and simultaneously gives a sell signal, it is a critical event and a strong sign to sell the stock, or at a minimum, recheck the fundamentals. Something is generally wrong when this happens. Not until some days down the road will light be shed on the reason for the trend line break. A case in point is ImClone (IMCL). This stock had been trading above its Bullish Support Line for months until December 2001. In December 2001, IMCL hit $62 and violated the Bullish Support Line and changed the trend to negative. IMCL was actually on a monitored portfolio that DWA publishes and our comments at the time when IMCL hit $62 were:

12/20/2001
[IMCL] ImClone Systems Incorporated ($61.75) violated its Bullish Support Line at 62. This follows the breakdown at 66. IMCL had topped out at 75, then made a lower top at 70. We had entered this stock at 49 (when it was added to the Best Page). This move to 62, though, stops us out on the Best Page with still nice profits overall; we had previously sold a portion to lock in profits. For those long this stock we would look to lighten up or hedge positions in some way. The stock has sold off sharply in the past couple of days, so wait for a bounce over the next couple of days, and use that as a chance to sell.

A couple of days later we followed up with this comment:

12/28/2001
[IMCL] ImClone Systems Incorporated ($63.620) IMCL continues to slide and gave another sell signal on Thursday. . . . Would use this second sell signal as a stop loss for those still long.

It was a mere few days later that ImClone began to implode on negative FDA news. A month later, IMCL was trading in the mid-teens. I can't help but think that if Martha Stewart had just been using the Point and Figure methodology in her analysis, she could have avoided a lot of trouble. The Point and Figure chart spoke volumes about the supply-and-demand relationship in the stock before the fundamentals came to light.

As we mentioned in our commentary about IMCL, often when a stock gives a strong sell signal like violating a Bullish Support Line, we will begin to scale out of the position instead of selling all the stock. A stock frequently will give such a signal, then regroup, and begin moving up again giving you a better out with respect to the rest of your position but that bounce only results in a lower top. Things take time in the market. It often is not an overnight thing. I like to take my time in investing. Often the truth is not black or white; it's gray. To qualify as a violation of the trend line, the stock must move through it by one box or more, not just touch it. There is no such thing as the line being a little violated. It is or it isn't. In Figure 2.8, the stock maintained the trend line all the way up from 15 to 25. Soon after, supply took control of the stock. When the stock hit 21, it not only gave a Double Bottom sell signal but also violated the Bullish Support Line. The violated support line was the key sign

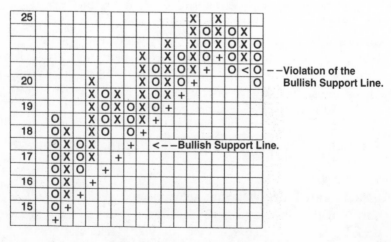

Figure 2.8   The Bullish Support Line.

there was a high probability that the trend had changed. This is what I would take to be a wake-up call. You can hit the snooze button if you wish but situations like this generally require that you take some action.

The Bullish Resistance Line

We rarely use the Bullish Resistance or Bearish Support Lines. The more lines you begin drawing, the more complicated it becomes. The next thing you see is a screen that looks like the old game of pick-up sticks. Keep it simple. That being said, the Bullish Resistance Line is drawn by moving to the left of the last buy signal (at the point the signal was given, where the X exceeds the previous column of X's) and going to the first wall of O's to the left. Remember, it is not the first column of O's but the first wall of O's. A wall of O's is usually that last down-move in the stock from which it begins to bottom out. This is the point where demand begins to take the upper hand. Figure 2.9 best demonstrates

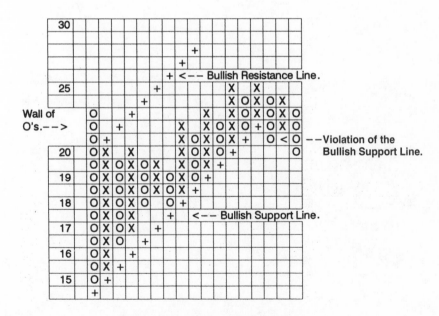

Figure 2.9   The Bullish Resistance Line.

this. Then go to the column of X's right next to the wall of O's and begin drawing your trend line, beginning with the empty box above that top X. This line will be a 45-degree angle, as is the Bullish Support Line. Typically, a stock will encounter resistance as it moves to the Bullish Resistance Line, though this line may have to be drawn a number of times. The boundaries of the Bullish Support Line and the Bullish Resistance Line form a trading channel. In Figure 2.9, the Bullish Resistance Line is drawn from the wall of O's beginning at the 21 level. In reality, we do not use these lines much at DWA and they are not drawn on our Internet site (www.dorseywright.com). We tend to be much more concerned with the Bullish Support Line when a stock is rising.

The Bearish Resistance Line

The Bearish Resistance Line, which is the exact opposite of the Bullish Support Line, is shown in Figure 2.10. When a stock forms an area of distribution above the Bullish Support Line and

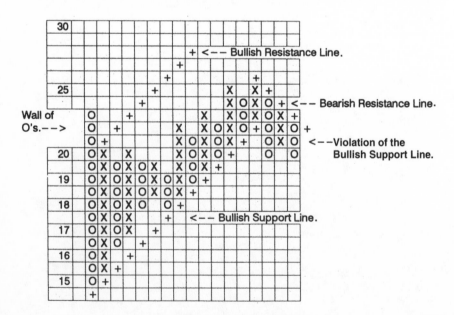

Figure 2.10   The Bearish Resistance Line.

gives the first sell signal, you can go to the top X and begin drawing the trend line in the box directly above that last column of
X's. Next connect the boxes diagonally down in a 135-degree
angle, the reciprocal of the 45-degree angle of the Bullish Support
Line. Actually, all you need to do is connect the boxes and the
angle will be 135 degrees. The same principles and trading tactics
apply in reverse to the Bearish Resistance Line. We typically prefer not to go long when below the Bearish Resistance Line. This
line, like the Bullish Support Line, can be as strong as a brick
wall. We say a stock is bearish when it is on a sell signal and
below the Bearish Resistance Line. Or, as I often say, the stock is
on I-95 South. Be wary of buy signals that come from just below
this resistance line, as they tend to be false or best suited to
traders. Stocks that are moving up to this line typically find formidable resistance there. Also, a stock must be on a buy signal to
penetrate the Bearish Resistance Line. Short sales can be initiated
in weak stocks when the underlying stock rallies up to the resistance line but is still below it. This is the optimum point to sell
short on any of the bearish chart patterns.

The Bearish Support Line

As shown in Figure 2.11, the Bearish Support Line is the reciprocal of the Bullish Resistance Line and is drawn by moving to the
left of the Bearish Resistance Line to the first wall of X's—again,
not to the next column of X's but to the first wall of X's. Then
move to the first column of O's next to it and begin drawing your
support line down from the empty box below the last O. The line,
which will automatically be a 135-degree angle by connecting the
diagonal boxes, can be used as a guide to identify where any decline might be contained. The Bearish Resistance Line and the
Bearish Support Line in combination form a channel that the
stock can be expected to trade in. Movement down to the Bearish
Support Line is likely to cause bottom fishing as investors create
demand supporting the stock at that level. As the stock rises to
the resistance level, investors who have been stuck holding the
declining stock will elect to sell on rallies.

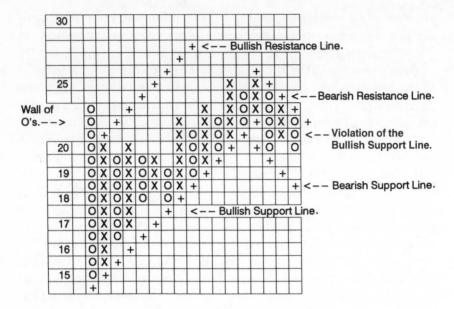

Figure 2.11   The Bearish Support Line.

Price Objectives

Price objectives in Point and Figure technical analysis are derived through two methods called the horizontal count and the vertical count. Our charts on our web site automatically calculate the vertical price objective for you. But again, while the computer saves us a lot of time in doing some of these calculations, you need to understand where they come from. The methods of determining price objectives come from the science of ballistics and have been used in Point and Figure analysis for many decades. The distance a bullet will travel can be calculated if the following factors are known—the size of the powder keg that will propel the projectile, the length of the barrel, the resistance the projectile will experience traveling through the barrel, the air temperature, and the attitude of the rifle. The best definition describing this science was written in an Encyclopedia Britannica article in the 1920s. The following passage is from the book *The Point and Figure Method: Advanced Theory and Practice* (New York: Morgan, Rogers, & Robertson, Inc., 1934):

Exterior ballistics is that part of the science of ballistics in which the motion of the projectile is considered after it has received its initial impulse. The factors involved are the pressure of the powder or gas in the chamber of the gun from which the projectile secures its initial velocity, resistance of the bore before the projectile leaves the barrel, the resistance of the air, and the influence of gravity, all must be calculated in order to determine the probable objective of the projectile.

These same principles have been applied to stock and commodity trading to arrive at a rough estimate of the price objective following a breakout of a consolidation area. The vertical count is the most reliable and should be used whenever possible. At DWA, we use the price objective as an ingredient for helping us determine our risk-reward ratio. Whenever we initiate a position, as an investor or trader, we want to have two points on the upside for every point on the downside, and the price objective is one of the tools we use in determining the risk-reward ratio. Other factors that we look at include trading bands and other resistance on the chart. We cover both of these concepts later on. But there is one statement we must make about price objectives here: Just because a stock hits its bullish price objective does not mean we will automatically sell that position. If relative strength and trend are still strong, we very well may elect to sell a partial position and hold on to the core position. In 2005, Apple Computer was on a tear. The price seemed like it would never stop. Taking profits on the first price objective would have left plenty of profits on the table. The price objective is best used for risk reward calculations.

The Vertical Count

When a stock finally bottoms out and begins to move up, it will give a simple buy signal at some point. A buy signal comes when a column of X's exceeds a previous column of X's. Once a buy signal is given, the stock will rise to a certain level where supply again takes over. It's like throwing a tennis ball up in the air. The ball will rise to a certain level before gravity takes hold and the ball begins to revert down. Stocks are the same. They will rise to a certain level where supply comes in for what ever reason. Supply overtakes demand, and the stock reverts to a column of O's. When the stock reverses into a column of O's, the first column of X's off the bottom is finished. No more X's can be placed in that column. At this point, count the number of boxes in the column of X's, and multiply times 3 (if you are using the three-box reversal method). Then multiply that figure by the value per box. Add the result to the bottom of the line of X's (where that column began). This will give you a rough estimate of the stock's price objective on that move. Remember, the price objective is a guide, not a guarantee. It is not set in concrete, because many stocks meet their first price objective and continue on up, so keep the chart formation, trend line, and relative strength in mind when deciding whether to sell the stock. Just because a stock has met its expected price move, it does not mean you must sell. It does, however, suggest you reevaluate its potential from that level.

Notice that in the example of the vertical count shown in Figure 2.12, box sizes change. You must first count the boxes below 5 as each box represents ¼ point. Then count the boxes above 5 as they represent ½ point per box. There are four boxes representing ¼ point. Multiply them times 3 and then multiply that number by ¼ $(4 \times 3 = 12 \times \frac{1}{4} = 3)$. Now count the boxes above 5 and ending at 8. There are six boxes at ½ point per box $(6 \times 3 = 18 \times \frac{1}{2} = 9)$. Now add the two counts together, and you get $(3 + 9) = 12$. Okay, here's the last step. Add the 12 to the dollar value at the first box in that column. The potential move is $4¼ + 12 = 16¼$. This example helps you understand how to use the count at breakpoints.

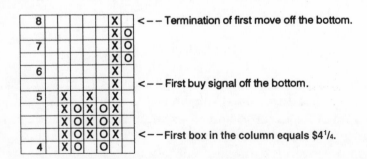

Figure 2.12   The vertical count.

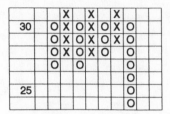

Figure 2.13   The vertical count for a short sale.

Vertical Count for Short Sale

Calculating the vertical count for a short sale is similar to that of a long position with one exception. Instead of multiplying the move by 3, you multiply by 2. In Figure 2.13, we count the number of boxes in the first down move off the top, which creates the first sell signal. There are seven boxes in that column. Multiply 7 times 2 and that comes to 14. Now multiply 14 times the box size, which is 1. That comes to 14. The last step is to subtract 14 from the level of the first O in the column, which is 30. The price objective is 30–14 = 16.

The Horizontal Count

A horizontal count is taken by counting across the base a stock has built, multiplying by three, and then multiplying again by the value per box. This is similar to the vertical count except you count horizontally across the formation as opposed to the vertical move off the bottom. We look at the horizontal count as an exercise in counting the size of the powder keg that will propel the projectile. In ballistics, the powder keg is the amount of gunpowder in the shell casing, and the projectile is the bullet that will fly when the charge is detonated. I associate the vertical count with the distance the projectile travels before gravity takes control and pulls the bullet back to earth. This analogy, as well as the tennis ball analogy earlier always helped me understand the concept of the count when I was learning this method many years ago. Try to keep this as simple as possible because the count is only a

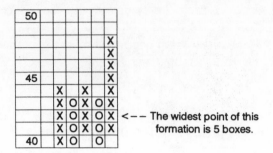

Figure 2.14   The horizontal count.

guide. It is far more important to consider the market, sector, relative strength, and chart pattern when initiating a long or short position. This book places more emphasis on these variables than on the count.

In Figure 2.14, you would simply count the number of boxes horizontally at the widest point of the formation. That number is multiplied by 3 and the product of that multiplication is again multiplied by the box size. Looking at Figure 2.14 and counting across the widest part of the formation, both X's and O's, you get 5 columns. We then multiply this by 3. Finally, in this example, the box size is 1 ($5 \times 3 = 15 \times 1 = 15$). Then add the product of this multiplication to the lowest point of the formation, which is 40. The expected move is thus $15 + 40 = 55$. Again, where the count really comes into play is in determining your risk-reward relationship. You should have at least two points of potential profit for each point of potential loss before initiating a trade. Keep in mind that there are thousands and thousands of stocks to trade. Don't get hung up on one stock for any reason. There is always another train coming down the track. All you have to do is watch for it.

Dorsey, Wright Money Management

Ten years ago we had two stockbrokers, Mike Moody and Harold Parker, both from Smith Barney's discretionary management group, who we knew very well, come to us at DWA and present their vision of developing Dorsey, Wright Money Management. We were a little surprised, and our first thought being that we were not in that business. Our second thought was that when two professionals in this business with the highest principals, integrity, and character, come to you with a vision, wanting to join your firm, you do it. So we agreed. We started the management operation at Mike Moody's house to keep costs low. As we expanded our clientele, we moved to a real office in Beverly Hills with the zip code 90210. As we expanded further, we moved to larger spaces in Pasadena, California, where we are currently located. Many people wonder how we function with the home office of DWA in Richmond, Virginia, and the money management division in Pasadena, California, and the answer is simple, computers and a shared philosophy. In today's high-tech environment it would not make a difference if they were located in Katmandu, Nepal, or down the hall here in Richmond.

Over the years, we have learned much with respect to managing money. Today we offer a number of avenues to participate in Dorsey, Wright Money Management. One way is through the systematic relative strength portfolio offerings. These portfolios are all relative strength based and rules based. We have found a way to take the knowledge we have developed over the years in money management and transform it into a disciplined management system. This has effectively taken the best of what we do at DWA and made it an emotionless, method of managing money that has served us well over the years. Our management has even expanded into managing Tax Deferred Annuities at Nationwide Insurance Company through their "MarketFlex" Program. The knowledge our money managers have about managing money and how the stock market works is astounding. Each week they produce a column we put into our daily report called "From the Managers." We decided to put some of these discussions into this book to help you become a better manager for your own account. At the end of each chapter, we reproduce an article written by the money management group. I'm sure you will find them interesting and educational. If you have an interest in learning more about Dorsey, Wright Money Management, you can visit www.dorseywright.com and there is a section devoted to Dorsey, Wright Money Management. If you are a professional and would like to talk to Dorsey, Wright Money Management, e-mail us at moneymanagement@dorseywright.com. The first article follows.

POINTS AND FIGURES BY DORSEY, WRIGHT MONEY MANAGEMENT

An *Economist* article featured a study by Glenn Jones, of Texas A&M University. Mr. Jones is a paleo-oceanographer—an archaeologist of the oceans. He investigates both the mysteries of the deep and the secrets of the past. In one of his recent projects he read old seafood menus to study the price of a catch over the years. Mr. Jones and his team read through some 40,000 menus, dating back to the 1850s (*Economist*, October 27, 2005).

Going back and looking at menus, mainly from American cities on both coasts, he was able to track the price of seafood over 150 years and gain insight into their supply. From the early 1920s to the late 1930s, for example, a San Francisco restaurant would charge only $6 to $7, in today's money, for a serving of abalone, a type of mollusk. By the 1980s, however, abalone was selling for $30 to $40 a meal. As the supply of one species of seafood would become exhausted, another would replace them. Swordfish began appearing on menus in 1909, according to Mr. Jones. From the 1920s to the 1950s, the cost of a meal of swordfish remained about $7, but by the late 1970s the cost had risen to $30 to $35 a meal. However, new suppliers from Australia and the south Atlantic then entered the market and helped to bring the price back down. I was rather surprised to read that lobsters used to be in such abundant supply that they were fed to inmates in prison and children in orphanages. Farmers even fertilized their fields with it, and servants would bargain with their employers to be given it *no more* than twice or thrice a week. A lobster meal in 1870 cost $4 (in today's money), but in 1970 cost $30 or more. Interestingly, the perceived value of seafood (and stocks) depends on the underlying supply-and-demand relationship. Lobster tasted the same in 1870 as in did in 1970, but the price was much higher due to a decrease in the supply of lobster and an increase in demand for lobster meals.

Perhaps, this is another way we can explain the concepts of supply and demand. It is hard to believe that lobster was once considered worthy for fertilizer, but now is associated with fine dining. Cisco, Sun Microsystems, and Krispy Kreme were once in high demand, but no more. Using our intuition alone, we may be tempted to avoid seemingly unknown stocks because they are not popular (even though they may be rising) or hang on to a burned out star because of how popular it used to be. All prices are a function of supply and demand and with price alone we have the tools to objectively and successfully navigate the markets.

Chapter 3

CHART PATTERNS

Recording the Battle between Supply and Demand

The backbone of the Point and Figure analysis is the chart pattern. The beauty of this method is its ability to form simple chart patterns that record the battle between supply and demand. The reason this method is so credible is that it is founded on the irrefutable law of supply and demand, which affects our life on a daily basis. Although just about everything we come in contact with has some association with supply and demand, it wasn't until my first course in college-level economics that I really thought about and came to understand this basic law. Heck, for the previous 22 years, I had simply taken price change at face value—prices changed and that was it. It was that ECON 101 class in college that taught me to appreciate the law of supply and demand. You know what? Most people never gain a full understanding of it. This is why I strongly feel that as a requirement for high school graduation every student should take an economics course using the textbook *Economics in One Lesson* by Hazlett (Random House, 1981). Since it seems unlikely I'll be elected to any office where I will be able to institute this course of instruction, it will have to remain in the pages of this book. Take it to heart and have your kids learn these basic concepts. They will be well rewarded later in life with clarity of vision others will never have. While many of the concepts I learned in ECON 101 have been improved on over the years, one remains unchanged—

supply and demand. It is the driving force behind all price changes. If there are more buyers than sellers willing to sell, then the price will rise. If there are more sellers than buyers willing to buy, then the price will decline. This is as true for the price of tomatoes as it is for the price of stocks. It is as simple as knowing why we have lemonade stands in the summer and hot chocolate stands in the winter. Although these price changes affect our lives on a daily basis, we rarely think much about the law that governs these changes. We are currently in an energy crisis. The price of oil is above $70 a barrel as I write this. The American public is up in arms looking to have someone's head on a platter. Some say it's the big oil companies that are gouging the retail customer. Others say the government is doing nothing to pass legislation to reduce the price of gasoline at the pumps. Blame is everywhere, but few understand what is truly happening. Even our elected officials have not demonstrated one shred or knowledge of economics. It truly amazes me. One idea Congress came up with was to tax the heck out of the big oil companies with a Windfall Profits Tax. If that was to be instituted, big oil would simply produce less of what is being taxed more, and the result would be shortages and higher gas prices. What it would do is gain votes for the politicians who proposed it. The votes would most likely come from those who would be most hurt by the legislation. I have not seen anyone explaining to the American investor why it takes 800 government permits to build one refinery. This is not a problem that will be fixed by legislation other than legislation allowing the oil companies to search for more oil and gas. The energy crisis is a topic for a whole book. Suffice it to say, Adam Smith's "Invisible Hand" is working well.

When I left a hotel in Phoenix, Arizona, on May 6, 2006, the highways were nearly empty. No one was driving. Those who were driving were not driving their SUVs. "The Invisible Hand" was working. High gas prices caused less driving, which caused less demand for gas, which caused the demand for SUVs to decline and demand for small cars to increase, and so it is, real life Econ. 101. The problem with television today is no one takes time to educate the public on very important things like energy costs. I have been a regular on both CNBC and FOX business shows. There is only time for sound bites. It's all about ratings, nothing else. Every time I was on one of those shows, I tried to educate the viewers in some way about how the markets worked, but the time was so short, even in a half hour show that I'm afraid I failed at my task. One day I decided to take things into my own hands. We went to a local TV station and began to tape "The James River Talks." These were hour-long talks about the markets and how we used Point and Figure analysis to help us negotiate them. We then turned the tapes into DVDs and offered them to our clients. They received rave reviews, so I decided to take myself off the national TV programs and focus on doing the right thing. All of a sudden the Podcast came into existence. This technology superseded our James River Talks, so we began doing Podcasts each week. Now you can listen to us each week for free through itunes or www.wallst.net where we are syndicated.

In the stock markets, prices change daily. Buyer and seller battle it out for control of the stock. Eventually, one side wins the battle, and the stock begins to take on a trend. Guess what? The battle between supply and demand was won by demand in oil stocks in 2002. Had investors been able to figure this out, as we did, they could have purchased oil stocks and offset any increase in gasoline along the way. Just think about how astute the American public would be if they taught basic economics in high school. I'll bet you there would be a waiting list for the class. I have taught this method of stock analysis to children in grade schools by using the analogy of a tennis match described in Chapter 1. Virtually the same pattern occurs with stocks. Over the near term, stocks seem to move back and forth randomly the same way players may win alternate sets of a tennis match. Eventually, either demand or supply will win out and establish a trend. In the Point and Figure method, a particular pattern will form signaling that either demand or supply has taken control of the stock. We are not interested in making commitments in the stock market on the evidence of the sets. We are only interested in making commitments on the evidence of a completed match.

History Repeats Itself

The usefulness of the Point and Figure chart patterns lies in their repetition. The patterns of a Point and Figure chart tend to repeat themselves, and thus provide a high degree of predictability about the future move of the underlying stock. When teaching the importance of chart patterns in the Point and Figure Institutes held in Richmond, Virginia, and we also have available the DWA Global Online University, I use this example. To begin the session, I throw a ball to someone in the audience without the participants knowing I am going to do it. (At the DWA Global Online University, we discuss the concept of throwing a ball to someone in class.) The person's reflex is to reach up and catch the ball. Then I throw another ball into the audience, and then another. Even though the participants know what is coming, the natural reflex is the same—they hold up their hands to catch the ball. This is just like a Point and Figure chart; the pattern is repeated. Every time the market throws a Triple Top, or a Bearish Signal Reversed pattern, or a Bearish Triangle pattern at me, I know the action that I must take. More often than not, the action taken was the right one. All too often investors buy stocks that are clearly being controlled by supply simply because they never venture past the fundamentals of the company. Keep in mind there are some very fundamentally sound companies whose stock price move lower. What we try to accomplish is to stack as many odds as possible in our favor before we make a stock commitment. That includes fundamentals and technicals.

While the chart pattern is very important in the decision-making process, other factors should go into any decision. This method is an art, not a science. Many investors think they can simply look at a particular chart pattern with no additional evaluation and experience instant success. It just doesn't work like that. You are an integral part of this process. Other things we evaluate along with the chart pattern are overall market, sector, trend, and relative strength. Before we get to those concepts, however, it is essential that you understand the chart patterns of individual stocks. This is of utmost importance because the markets are made up of individual stocks. The market is like the aggregate of all the fish in the sea. These fish can be broken down into schools of fish and then to individual fish. It is imperative to understand the basics of looking at a stock's Point and Figure chart before graduating to market indicators, sector indicators, and relative strength.

Increasing Your Odds of Success

A good friend of mine, the late Jim Yates, used the following analogy when explaining profits and probabilities. Consider a basketball game in which one player is dribbling the basketball down the court. Along the way, he receives a personal foul from an opposing team player. A personal foul simply means the player can go to the foul line and take two shots (free throws) at the basket, unencumbered by the opposing team. Each shot he attempts is independent of the other. Prior to his shooting, the television commentator says that this player is a 70 percent free-throw shooter. This means that he will make 7 out of 10 baskets when he attempts a free throw. Keep in mind that he has two opportunities to make a basket, each one independent of the other. What is the probability that he makes both shots? When I present this problem at seminars, most people will answer 70 percent, whereas the actual probability of making both shots is 49 percent (0.70 × .70 = .49 percent). What this suggests is this basketball player, over time, will be successful less than half the time at completing two free-throw shots.

You, as an investor, have the same problem. You must perform two tasks correctly, each one independent of the other. You must buy the stock right and you must sell the stock right. Have you ever bought a stock, had it go up, and—before you sold it— watched it go right back down again? If you haven't, I have. I have also had the distinct displeasure of buying a stock and having it go right down without the benefit of a rise first. In the latter case, I never even made the first basket. This whole book is designed to help you increase your odds of success and have the greatest probability of making both shots. We outline the whole game plan as we go along.

Right now, let's deal with chart patterns. Chart patterns are like road maps. They are really not any different from a map you might study to find the best interstate for a vacation trip to New York from Richmond, Virginia. If you were to choose I-95 South instead of I-95 North, it would take you to Key West, Florida, first. Selecting the wrong route is a common mistake most investors make. They set out on a trip to New York from Virginia and choose I-95 South to get them there. They select a fundamentally sound stock that is clearly controlled by supply and likely to go down, not up. As a broker, I did this many times simply because I didn't know any better. My approach was like starting out on a road trip and taking the first road I hit as the direction to my destination. What we did back then was simply buy the stocks that research recommended we buy without any other input. We tended to emphasize the "What" question and never considered "When."

Many stockbrokers and investors buy a stock on the fundamentals because it is usually the only form of analysis they understand, and there is plenty of this type of research around. I'll bet most of you get unsolicited stock hype research reports in your mail every day. I know I get them. This type of fundamental research is everywhere. Never forget, someone has a reason for sending it to you. That reason is not to help you become independently wealthy. It's probably to unload some stock on you. These stories catch the investors' interest because they are all hype. I'm in no way suggesting fundamental analysis isn't important. It is essential in answering the question what stock to buy; it is the first line of defense. It is our preferred method of analysis to create our inventories. Fundamentals, however, provide only half the equation. Once the stock has been selected and is determined to be fundamentally sound, the next task is to determine whether it has a high probability of going up or down. This is the point where technical analysis comes into play. When I was a stockbroker, technical analysis was never used. It was considered black magic even though it had been around in the United States for over 100 years. We sold the sizzle on the steak. That's what customers wanted to hear, and that is what we sold. Had my firm included technical analysis along with fundamental analysis and trained us to understand and use it, what a difference that would have made. It would have been like the Fourth of July for both brokers and customers. Today most broker dealers have given up on tactically managing portfolios. They have gone to Strategic Asset Allocation where a computer decides, after a risk analysis is done and an investment policy statement is drawn up, how an investor should populate his Strategic Allocation Pie. Then twice a year the computer "rebalances" the portfolio. This means the stocks that have done well in the portfolio are trimmed and this money is placed in the stocks that have done poorly. To me this is the best way to put the brakes on a portfolio. I must also add there are many firms that provide DWA research to their brokers. Over the past 20 years, we have had a major impact in the way technical analysis is used on Wall Street. Many advisors utilizing our work will use the Strategic Asset Allocation as the base from which to build and then add the Point and Figure work to tactically manage the portfolios.

The best results in investing are achieved by using fundamental and technical analysis together. At DWA, we look at several sources of fundamental recommendations to answer the "what" question. There are many excellent sources of fundamental information. Value Line and Standard & Poor's both produce fantastic rating systems that are easy to use. And for a little over a dollar a day, you can get some great earnings numbers right out of *Investors Business Daily* newspaper. These numbers coupled with Point and Figure analysis are very powerful. Most of the traditional brokerage houses also publish reports now available to all investors with their fundamental stock picks. The Internet has fundamental information everywhere you turn. It's virtually everywhere and free on the Internet. In fact, on our web site I keep several portfolios of fundamentally sound stocks that I work from. What I then do with those fundamentally sound portfolios is bring the technical side into the equation. Technical analysis is more difficult to find than fundamental but most of the time this step in the investment process truly determines whether an investment is successful. Technical analysis is different from fundamentals. Fundamentals simply deal with the same things everyone had in accounting 101 and 102, period, end of story. Chartered Financial Analysts all look at the same ratios like PEs, Cash Flow, and so on. Technicians are a diverse group. There are many methods that are used like Fibonacci numbers, waves, Gann angles, cycles, astrology, candlestick charts, line graphs, bar charts, and Point and Figure. This is the reason why many consider technical analysis black magic. I took the easy approach to it. I knew that the last part of the equation before prices change is the irrefutable law of supply and demand. No matter what method of analysis you subscribe to, there must be an imbalance between supply and demand to cause the price change. If this is the case and it is then you have arrived at the Holy Grail. As I discussed earlier, the Point and Figure method was developed by Charles Dow as a simple, logical, organized, way to view this battle between supply and demand, nothing else. So why not go directly to the source rather than learning something that is many steps removed? You are reading this book so that you can take control of the technical research yourself. There is no one who will watch over your own investments more diligently than you.

The reason technical research is so important is that it answers the question when to buy. All too often, investors and stockbrokers buy a stock because it is a great company, but great companies don't always make great stocks. In fact, I recently got a call from a broker client of ours asking what my opinion was on a stock named Integrated Devices. He related to me how the company just had an extended news release talking about how their earnings were going up 50 percent and how things were just wonderful. His question to me concerned how the stock could move down on that news by $5. I looked at the chart and 30 points higher the stock was screaming at anyone who would listen, to "get out." The supply-and-demand relationship was already suggesting supply was in control. This broker never went past the fundamental roses and was totally perplexed that he had lost his clients $5 in one day. The stock went on to lose quite a bit. If I created a balance sheet of technical indicators for that stock, it would be extremely heavy on the debit side. You need to know when a great company is also a great stock. That is where this broker went wrong. He should have listened to the fundamentals and then put the stock name in a drawer of "things to do later." Once the technicals came around to positive and the fundamentals were still positive, it would be a "go."

Here's another interesting story. General Electric has been a great company over the years. It is the only original stock left in the Dow Jones Industrial Average. The earnings had been going straight up for 10 years but in 2000 the stock topped out and began a long decline from $60 to $22. The fundamentals had not changed only investor sentiment changed. Investors decided they did not want to own GE for whatever reason. Supply overtook demand, optimism turned to pessimism, and the stock collapsed. Warren Buffett said something interesting. He in essence said there was a time to own the stock and a time to own the company. In the GE example, with the fundamentals intact but the technicals suggesting a decline in price, it was time to own GE, not GE's stock. Our problem is we are not like Warren Buffett who has the ability to buy whole companies. We are relegated to the stock market. In times when supply is clearly in control, our only play is to avoid the stock or mitigate the risk of holding it in some way.

The power of the computer has made this process much easier than it use to be. In those days before computers became a commodity, we would literally page through chart books looking up the symbols of fundamentally sound companies that had strong chart patterns. Today, we enter those fundamentally sound portfolios into our web site (www.dorseywright.com) and then use the Search/Sort function to filter out those stocks that meet our technical requirements for a stock we expect to rise in price. It is this combination of fundamental and technical analysis that is so powerful. The computer reduces to a matter of seconds the time-consuming task of looking at hundreds of stocks to come up with a small basket of actionable names. The computer can never replace the analysis of a specific issue, but it can help narrow down the list of those to evaluate to a reasonable number based on some basic technical attributes we feel are important. One of those technical attributes is the chart pattern of the stock.

Chart Patterns

If you wait for the right chart pattern to form before making a stock commitment, you dramatically increase your probabilities of success. In our day-to-day operation evaluating and trading the markets, we have found that when the market is supporting higher prices (we cover these indicators in later chapters), sticking to the bullish chart patterns when going long stock usually produces superior results. Conversely, we have found that when the market is not supporting higher prices, sticking to the bearish chart patterns when shorting a stock usually produces superior results. If the market is not supporting higher prices, the odds of success in buying a stock with a bullish chart pattern is like trying to swim against the current. You may make some headway but not nearly as much as if you just wait for the tide to change so you can swim with the current. Think for a second about the salmon. Remember the pictures you have seen where they swim upstream to spawn each year? That's what it is like trying to make headway in the market with long positions when the prevailing market is bearish. I'll bet if you could interview a salmon you would find it would prefer to swim downstream to spawn if possible.

While I cover chart patterns as one of the first concepts in this method of stock market analysis, other indicators must be added to the equation before you can decide what to buy. The tendency of those new to the Point and Figure process is to focus only on patterns when evaluating an individual equity. This is a very important step in the process, but not the whole process. That having been said, let's delve right into covering the Point and Figure chart patterns.

Had I known about this during my broker years, I would have been able to save a lot of heartache for both my clients and me. We always tried to recommend stocks that were fundamentally sound, but we never knew if we were on I-95 North or South. It is such a simple concept, yet most brokers and investors never get a handle on it. I remember a time I put on a trade for a client without paying much attention to the underlying stock. This good client of mine called to discuss some possible trades in the market. I had just learned about an option strategy called "covered writing" that involves buying a stock and simultaneously selling a call option against the position. The client and I talked at length about the stock. We discussed how Burlington Industries was a great company (the leader in the textile business at the time). He liked the covered-writing concept, so we did the trade, bought the stock, and sold the call option against the position. I sold it as a conservative strategy. I was really thrilled that I had been able to explain the concept of a covered write on the phone.

After the close of business, I went with my broker buddies to the Bull and Bear Club, as we did every evening, to have a beer and discuss the day's business. I mentioned to them that I had done a covered-write trade that day and the underlying stock was Burlington Northern. One of the fellows responded, "oh, the railroad." I broke out in a cold sweat. I said no, I had bought the textile company, not the railroad.

As it turned out, I had in fact bought the client Burlington Northern, the railroad, despite discussing the merits of Burlington Industries, the textile company. The names Burlington Northern and Burlington Industries are close, right? Well, the names might be close but their businesses are like the North and South Poles. The trade turned out fine, and I was probably better off with the railroad than I would have been with the textile company. In fact, Burlington Industries didn't even have listed options at that time. Talk about stacking the odds in your favor—I shut my eyes and took a shot in the dark. I wasn't sure what coast the stock was on, much less what interstate and what direction. This happens more often than you can imagine, but in most cases it doesn't turn out as well.

Many investors simply feel they can't grasp the nuances of the investment process to become better investors. They believe Wall Street is somehow over their heads. But, I've seen it time and again: Brokers and investors who take that first "toe dip" into learning this material are quickly hooked and eventually become true craftsmen at the investment process. It's like the first time you learned to employ a little strategy in a game of chess or backgammon. Before you know it, you are hooked. It's intoxicating!

The Chart Patterns

Double Top

In Chapter 2, you learned how to maintain your charts. The most basic chart patterns are the Double Top and Double Bottom. The Double Top requires three columns: two columns of X's and one column of O's. The key to interpreting the chart patterns is to determine where the stock exceeds a point of resistance or support. A feature of Charles Dow's charts that caught the eye of some astute turn-of-the-century investors was the charts' accurate identification of levels of distribution and accumulation. Distribution corresponds to a top (resistance) and accumulation corresponds to a bottom (support). Resistance is the point at which a stock reaches a particular price and encounters selling pressure. Back to the supply-and-demand scenario. This is the point where supply exceeds demand. For example, let's say that XYZ rises to 60 and meets selling pressure. This selling pressure exceeds the demand at that price, and the stock retreats back a few points. Remember, it requires a three-box reversal to change columns. If the selling pressure was enough to force XYZ back to 57 or lower, the chart would revert to O's from X's. In the tennis match analogy, supply would have won one set. The match continues. Let's say over the next few weeks, demand once again creeps back into the stock at 57 and causes the price to rise to 60 per share. This is another three-box reversal back up into a column of X's, and XYZ now sits at the same price level that previously found supply.

The question now is whether the sellers that forced the stock back before are still there. I have seen stocks hit resistance numerous times over many months until the selling pressure was finally exhausted. The only way to find out if the sellers are still operating at that price is to see how XYZ negotiates that level. If it is again repelled, then the sellers are still there. If it instead is able to move to 61, then we can say that demand has prevailed at this price by exceeding the level where supply was previously in control. By exceeding this level of resistance, the Point and Figure chart gives its most basic buy signal, the Double Top. Naturally, you must consider other things before purchasing the stock but in this most simple pattern, we can say demand is in control. If you could give me no other information on XYZ, my decision would be to buy the stock. By XYZ exceeding that point of resistance, we can say that demand won the match. The chart pattern would look like the one shown in Figure 3.1.

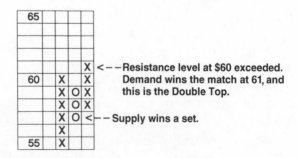

Figure 3.1   The Double Top.

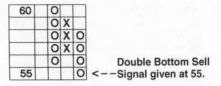

Figure 3.2   The Double Bottom.

Let's cover the Double Bottom. In this pattern, supply wins the match. Let's say instead of XYZ exceeding the previous point of resistance, it instead reversed and exceeded the previous level of support. You can see in Figure 3.2 that the stock declined to 56, at which point demand overtook supply and the stock reversed back up into a column of X's. At 59, the stock encounters selling pressure that drives XYZ back down the chart to the 56 level where demand previously took the upper hand providing support. This time, however, the buyers are not there as before, and the selling pressure persists until the stock exceeds that level of support. The match is over. Supply wins and the probability is lower prices. The reason supply overtook demand is not important. How the stock reacts to supply and demand is all that matters, for in the end, supply and demand causes stocks to move up and down and nothing else.

You can now see why we call this pattern Double Top and Double Bottom. The stock rises or declines to the same level twice. You can probably already guess what we might call the pattern if it rose or declined to the same level three times.

In Figure 3.3, you can see that when the stock rose back to 60, it was repelled for the second time. This clue suggests to us that there is formidable resistance at that level and the sell signal is that much more important. Looking at this chart, we can tell that

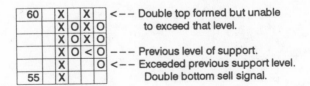

Figure 3.3   Double Bottom with resistance.

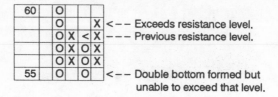

60	O			
	O			X	<– – Exceeds resistance level.
	O	X	<	X	– – – Previous resistance level.
	O	X	O	X
	O	X	O	X
55	O		O		<– – Double bottom formed but
					unable to exceed that level.

Figure 3.4   Double Top with support.

the upside potential is only 60. Naturally, things can and do change, but this is all we have to go with for the time being. Short sellers always want to know points of resistance because a penetration of these levels might signal a reversal in trend.

Figure 3.4 shows us that there is good support at 55 simply because that is the price where the stock stopped going down on two separate occasions. For some reason, there are buyers at that level. We consider this a level of accumulation or support. This Double Top buy signal is more important than the previous one because there is more information available with which to make a decision. The stock found support twice at the 55 level suggesting that the stock will hold there in the event it experiences further weakness—just a little clue the chart in Figure 3.1 did not have.

The Bullish Signal

We add one more dimension, an added clue, to the pattern this time. In Figure 3.5, notice how the last column of O's does not extend down as low as the previous column of O's. We call that a rising bottom. It signifies that supply is becoming less a factor in driving the stock. On the other side of the coin, demand is getting

| 60 | | | | X | <– – Rising top = Demand stronger.
|----|---|---|---|---|
| | | | X | X |
| | | O | X | O | X |
| | | O | X | O | X |
| | | O | X | O | | <– – Rising bottom = Selling pressure is subsiding.
| 55 | | O | | | |

Figure 3.5   Double Top with a rising bottom.

stronger as the last column of X's exceeds the previous column of X's. The rising bottom provides added guidance when evaluating the supply demand relationship of the underlying stock. Of the three Double Tops discussed thus far, this one is the strongest and would warrant the largest commitment.

The best way to understand these patterns is to take a legal pad and pencil and simply write down in 50 words or less exactly what you see (no different from the composition seven-year-olds sometimes have to write for homework, describing their room). This is what I observe in Figure 3.5:

1. I see a tennis match that only took four sets (columns) to complete.
2. I see two sets where McEnroe won (columns of O's) and two sets where Connors won (columns of X's).
3. The last column of X's exceeded the previous column, giving a Double Top buy signal at 60.
4. The second column of O's did not decline as low as the previous column of O's suggesting McEnroe is losing strength.
5. The last column of X's exceeds a previous column of X's suggesting Connors is gaining strength.

Breaking the pattern down to its lowest common denominator, simplifies analysis.

The Bearish Signal

The Bearish Signal is the opposite of the Bullish Signal. Figure 3.6 shows that demand in this case is becoming less strong as the last column of X's fails to reach the previous level. Selling pressure

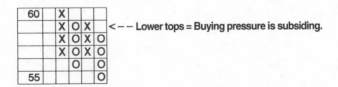

Figure 3.6 Double Bottom with a lower top.

however is increasing as evidenced by the lower column of O's. These clues simply suggest demand is losing strength and supply is gaining strength. All too often, investors buy stocks in this condition only to see them erode further.

So far, we have discussed the Double Bottom and Double Top. All other patterns that we cover are expansions of this basic form. By now, you can see how simple this method is to grasp. Let's go on to the Triple Top buy signal.

Triple Top

The Triple Top is exactly what the name suggests—a chart pattern that rises to a certain price level three times. The first two times the stock visits that level, it is repelled by sellers. The third time the stock rises to that level, it forms the Triple Top. The buy signal is given when the stock exceeds the level that previously caused the stock to reverse down. This pattern is shown in Figure 3.7.

There are many reasons a stock will encounter supply at certain levels. Think back to a time when you bought stock thinking it was the bottom, or at least an opportune price level to buy, and instead of rising the stock immediately declined. We have all had one or two experiences like that. The thought that probably crossed your mind as you saw the stock lose value was to get out if the stock got back to even. This is a perfectly normal human reaction. When you place that order to get you out at your break-even point, you are in essence creating supply at that level.

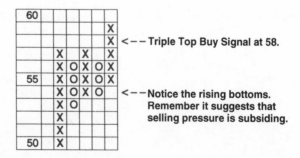

Figure 3.7   The Triple Top.

If more sellers are willing to sell their stock at that level than buyers are willing to buy, the stock will decline. The only way we know whether the selling pressure has been exhausted at a particular level is by the stock exceeding that price. If the stock is repelled again, the sellers are still there. I have seen stocks bounce off certain prices for as long as 18 months. There have been numerous examples of this over the years. Coca-Cola (KO) from 1992 to 1994 was a trading range with neither supply nor demand winning until finally, in September 1994, demand won and the stock took off. I like to use this example of KO because it was a stock I held in my children's accounts. The first time I bought KO was in August 1980. My son Thomas was born and that day I opened him a stock account. I didn't have much money then so I bought him $600 worth of KO and Alcoa (AA). Over the years, KO was a super performer, AA was not. The account was carried by KO. I held that stock for 18 years until the Relative Strength chart turned negative. We got out right at the top. KO has been a dismal performer since. That one stock however made enough money to pay for my son's college education. If you have not opened a stock account for your young children yet, do so! Another memorable example was Intuit (INTU). This is a stock from back in the wild, wild days of the Internet craze. This stock spent 11 months trading between 23 and 35. Finally, when the stock broke out, it took off like a rocket rallying to 90 in a matter of two months. When a stock trades up to an area of resistance numerous times and then finally breaks out, we refer to that as a "big base breakout" in the office. You know, it sounds a lot like a country song. Yet another big base breakout that comes to mind is Oracle (ORCL). In 1999, this stock traded up to 39 six times. Finally, the stock hit 40 breaking a spread sextuple top and there was nothing but grease between here and the trees for that stock for the next year. The ride down was just as dramatic when the dot-com stocks went bust. Centex in 2004 broke out a large base at 106 (presplit) and in the next eight months had rallied over 65 percent. Then the chart began to change and supply started to come and multiple Double Bottom sell signals were given. It is like that country song, "You gotta know when to hold them and know when to fold them." That song could have been written about the stock market.

Expansions on the Triple Top are merely patterns that take longer to complete. Patterns like the Quadruple Top or Quintuple Top are rare. The more tops a pattern has, the more bullish; and the faster the pattern develops the more bullish. The more times a stock bounces off a resistance level, the stronger the breakout will be when it comes. It was said years ago that the degree to which a stock will rise is in exact proportion to the time the stock took in preparation for that move. In other words, the wider the base from which a stock breaks out, the higher the stock will rise. In our 20 years of experience at DWA, we have found that a good strategy to use with the Triple Top or greater breakout is to buy partial positions on the breakout and then average in on a pullback. Half of the time, a stock will pull back after the Triple Top breakout.

Triple Bottom Sell Signal

The Triple Bottom sell signal, like the Triple Top, has a high degree of reliability. When I teach seminars on this subject, I use Figure 3.8 as an example of how dangerous it can be for investors to exclude technical analysis when buying a stock. Consider an investor who buys this stock at 31 per share and then leaves on vacation for one month. He checks the Internet frequently and notices that his stock is still around the price he paid for it, only down a point. Not bad for a market that had been volatile for the past month he thinks, and he continues to feel comfortable with the stock. The fundamentals are all in place. What is he missing in this puzzle? What he is missing is that a whole tennis match

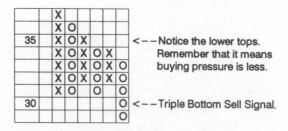

Figure 3.8 The Triple Bottom.

between supply and demand has been completed with supply winning the match. By not watching the match, he is unaware of it.

The probability of lower prices is very high. The Triple Bottom does not mean that the stock will cave in immediately; it suggests that the risk in that position has increased tremendously. Whether this investor chooses to do anything about the signal or not, he should at least be aware of it. If the investor does nothing other than increase his awareness of a potential decline, he is far ahead of the investor who holds the same position without any warning. Other considerations, such as Relative Strength, sector bullish percent, overall market condition, and trend lines, are discussed in later chapters.

In analyzing the Triple Bottom pattern, keep a close watch for declining tops. Think back to the Double Top formations. When the stock declined but was unable to decline as far as it previously did, it implied that selling pressure was drying up. Conversely, if the tops or columns of X's are making lower tops, it suggests that demand is drying up. These two clues make the chart more bullish or bearish, respectively. This will hold true with any chart pattern.

Keep in mind that other factors must be taken into consideration when evaluating a chart. We put it all together in the chapters ahead.

The Bullish and Bearish Catapult Formation

The Bullish Catapult (Figure 3.9) is simply a combination of the Triple Top and the Double Top. This pattern is a confidence builder. The Bullish Catapult comprises a Triple Top buy signal

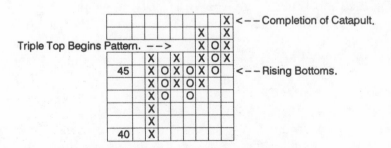

Figure 3.9   The Bullish Catapult formation.

followed by a pullback producing a rising bottom. Following the pullback, the stock resumes the trend giving a Double Top buy signal. Take a look at the pattern in Figure 3.9. Notice the Triple Top buy signal followed by the pullback into a column of O's. Notice how the column produces a higher bottom. The resumption of trend completes the Bullish Catapult by giving a Double Top buy signal.

Let's look at the Bullish Catapult in pieces to better understand what it is saying to us. The Triple Top is saying that the stock has a very high probability of rising in price, assuming the market is in a bullish mode. In fact, this type of pattern has a success probability of 87.5 percent in bull markets. The subsequent reversal producing a higher bottom suggests that supply is beginning to dry up or becoming a less significant factor. The resumption of trend and subsequent Double Top buy signal simply confirms the Triple Top. The Bullish Catapult is a confidence builder. This is one pattern that you can be more aggressive with when the overall markets are in a bullish mode, the underlying sector is in a bullish mode, and the fundamentals are superior in the stock.

The steps involved in stock selection resemble the steps involved in taking the trip from Virginia to New York City. Before you begin the trip, you need to gas the car up, check the oil, and check the water in the radiator. Then you must select the most direct route to New York (I-95 North). Gassing the car, checking the oil, and so on are similar to checking the fundamentals of the underlying stock. Selecting the proper interstate to embark on is similar to evaluating the technical (supply and demand) picture of the underlying stock. Many investors are diligent in doing the fundamental work on a stock they want to buy but ignore evaluating the probability of it rising in price. Buying a fundamentally sound stock that has just completed a chart pattern that suggests lower—not higher—prices is like making all the preparations for a trip to New York, then embarking south on Interstate 95 toward Florida. The idea is to stack as many odds in your favor before you begin the journey. There still isn't any guarantee. As much as people try to make investing a science, it remains an art.

In teaching this subject to grade school children, I have observed it takes only 30 minutes of instruction for them to make the right selection when evaluating a bearish and bullish chart together. The beauty about teaching children is that you don't have to deprogram them. Adults have preconceived ideas about how the market is supposed to work, mostly derived from watching TV programs about finance. All we are trying to ascertain with these chart patterns is whether supply or demand is in control of the underlying stock. If you go any farther than that, you've gone too far. Keep it simple. The law of supply and demand causes prices to change whether it's in the supermarket or the stock market.

Trading Tactics Using the Catapult

The Bullish Catapult is a confirmation pattern—the final Double Top that completes the Bullish Catapult simply confirms the previous Triple Top. It's a confirmation that demand is in control at this point in the stock's trend. The first part of the pattern is the basic Triple Top. In the last 15 years, buying on the pullback, or reaction from breakouts, offers a higher probability of success in the trade. Once a Triple Top exceeds the previous column of X's and then pulls back, the potential for a Bullish Catapult exists. Investors might consider buying half their position on the three-box reversal from the Triple Top. This gives them a good entry point for the first portion of the position and gets them in close to their stop point. Let's talk about the stop for a second. At what point will investors have to stop out of the position if they are wrong in their assumption that the stock will rise? In this case, with the only information being the chart pattern, the only logical stop would be the Triple Bottom. At that level, the pattern would suggest that supply was in control. If the stock is selected using strong fundamentals, has strong Relative Strength, and is trading above the Bullish Support Line, the probability of a failure in this pattern is low. Still, investors must consider what to do when things go wrong. There needs to be a plan of action if the trade begins to go sour. Remember, this is not an exact science, it's an art.

Once half the position is bought on the three-box reversal and the mental stop is in place, investors can begin to execute the plan to buy the other half of the position on completion of the Bullish Catapult. Traders can then raise their stop to the new Double Bottom sell signal that is formed when the stock reverses back up to complete the Bullish Catapult. Long-term investors will keep their stop on the violation of the Bullish Support Line, otherwise known as the trend line. In Figure 3.10, we would have to assume that supply had taken control if the stock violated the trend line and simultaneously gave a Double Bottom sell signal. The stop-loss point would come at the 42 level once the Bullish Catapult formation was complete. Just keep in mind that as long as a stock trades above the Bullish Support Line, we consider it bullish. Long-term investors will only stop out on violations of the trend line. Traders will be more apt than investors to take the sell signals above the trend line.

So far on our order entry using the Bullish Catapult, we have bought one half the intended position on the pullback to 43 and entered a mental stop-loss point at 40. Now, for the second half of our intended position, we enter an order called a "Good until Cancel" (GTC) order. The GTC order simply allows you to select a price you are willing to pay for your stock, and your order remains on the specialist's books until the stock reaches that price. In this case, you would place an order to buy the remainder of your position at 47, the level where the Bullish Catapult formation will be completed.

You can now see where you bought the second half of your intended position. Notice how the stop has risen now to the new Double Bottom sell signal that has formed at 42. This new stop allows us to protect profits should supply suddenly take control of the stock. It is important that long-term investors only use the trend line to stop out of a position. Traders are much shorter term in nature and may select a percentage of the entry price as their

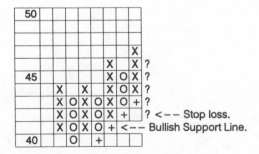

Figure 3.10   Knowing where to set the stop.

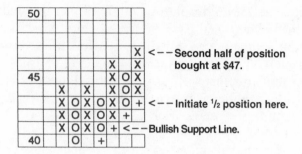

Figure 3.11 Trading with the Bullish Catapult formation.

stop. A. W. Cohen, one of the pioneers in this method of analysis, always suggested that investors risk no more than 10 percent in a stock. In today's more volatile markets, a 10 percent decline can happen fast. We find it more useful to carefully select our entry point and then give the stock some room to perform.

By looking at the Bullish Catapult formation, you can see many other combinations of entry points that you can use (see Figure 3.11). The key is you have an organized and logical guide to assist you in finding entry and exit points when investing. No other charts that I am aware of can do this. The Point and Figure charts are, without a doubt, the best and most accurate guides an investor can use.

Bearish Catapult Formation

The Bearish Catapult formation can be interpreted exactly opposite the Bullish Catapult formation and is particularly useful in timing short sales. Entry and exit points would be selected the same way we did with the Bullish Catapult. Stop points are particularly important in selling short. The risks in short selling are theoretically unlimited. In reality, that is not probable, but I have seen situations where stocks received buyout offers that significantly increased their price. The problem with being short in these unusual situations is that the stock stops trading and opens at a higher price without anyone being able to get out. These situations, however, are few and far between. It is very important to plan your entry point so you have a palatable stop price. A short seller might plan to sell half his intended position short on the first reversal back up in the chart pattern following the Triple Bottom sell signal. This will allow him to initiate the short relatively close to his stop point. Trend lines are even more important in short selling. The second half of his intended short position can be initiated when the stock reverses back down and completes the Bearish Catapult formation. Let's look at Figure 3.12.

You can see that this pattern is the exact opposite from the Bullish Catapult. Watch carefully for this pattern as it clearly suggests lower prices in the underlying stock. Whether you understood Point and Figure charting or not, if you looked at two fundamentally sound stocks, both in the same group, one with a Bearish Catapult formation and one with a Bullish Catapult formation, it wouldn't take long for you to determine which stock you wanted to buy.

These same patterns are used to assist the investor in using the options market. I have always looked at puts or calls as being surrogates for the underlying stock. We only use in-the-money calls or puts because the delta (the amount the option will move in relation to a 1-point move in the underlying stock) is much closer to 1 for 1. If an in-the-money long call is used as a substitute for buying the underlying stock, then use the same entry and exit points that you would use if you were buying the underlying stock. The same goes for put purchases as substitutes for outright short selling. Another school of thought in options buying is to let the premium be your stop. If you use this strategy, never buy more options than you would otherwise have an appetite for round lots

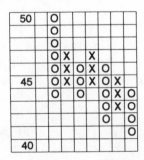

Figure 3.12   The Bearish Catapult formation.

of the underlying stock, either long or short. If you were normally a 300-share buyer, then only buy three options. If you allow the premium to be your stop, then you have the staying power to hang in the position until expiration. I have seen numerous times where a stock declines substantially early in the trade only to come back strong a few months later. We could devote a whole book to this subject, but let it suffice for now that Point and Figure chart patterns can be very useful in assisting the investor with entry and exit points for options trading as well as stock trading.

The Triangle Formation

The Triangle formation is a combination of patterns we have seen before. The key to understanding chart patterns is being able to sit down with a pencil and paper and write down exactly what you see. Don't look at the whole pattern and try to decipher it. Evaluate the parts making up the pattern, and you will then understand the pattern in total. In Figure 3.13, you can readily see the rising bottoms and lower tops in the pattern. To qualify as a Triangle, the pattern must have five vertical columns. The rising bottoms suggest that supply is drying up. You will also see the series of lower tops. The lower tops suggest that demand is becoming less of a factor in driving the stock. In our tennis analogy, the two players are getting more tired after each set, and the players have equal ability. Eventually, something will have to give. One player or the other will get a second wind or begin to take the upper hand. It is

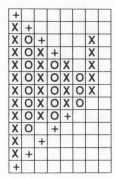 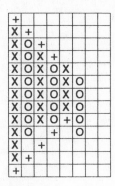

Figure 3.13 The Triangle formations.

at this point that we want to make a commitment in the underlying stock. There is nothing to do but wait and watch the match. If the pattern resolves itself on the upside, it will give a Double Top buy signal. The Double Top buy signal simply suggests that demand has won the match and the probability is higher prices in the stock. Now look at the Bearish Triangle in Figure 3.13. Notice how the match is won by supply. The Double Bottom sell signal suggests that the probability is lower prices in the stock. These patterns are simply road maps. They are not crystal balls.

There are a couple of other things that we want to point out about the Triangle pattern. First, usually a stock in an uptrend will resolve the triangle on the upside (i.e., a Bullish Triangle). Similarly, a stock in a downtrend will usually resolve the triangle on the downside (i.e., a Bearish Triangle). Second, it is usually feast or famine with the Triangle pattern. We will either see very few triangles forming, or we will see a whole host of them developing. Most of the time when we see quite a few triangles forming, it is during a choppy or sideways market and supply and demand are battling it out for control. Third, breakouts from the Triangle pattern typically result in quick, explosive moves so it behooves you to be ready to act when the signal is given. Look at the chart pattern in Figure 3.14. The stock in this graphic is forming a Triangle pattern right at the Bullish Support Line. A move to 55 would break a Double Top and complete the Bullish Trian-

60									
	X								
55	X	O			?	<-- Bullish Triangle at 55.			
	X	O	X		?				
	X	O	X	O	X				
	X	O	X	O	X	?			
	X	O	X	O	X	?	*		
50	X	O	X	O		?			
	X	O	X		*	?	<-- Bearish Triangle at 49.		
	X	O		*					
	X		*						
	X	*							
45	*								

Figure 3.14   Planning the trade with a Triangle pattern.

gle pattern and long positions could be taken. On the other hand, if the stock hits 49 it would not only complete a Bearish Triangle but also violate the Bullish Support Line. The stock could be shorted at 49. On our Internet site, we have premade reports that allow you to see the charts of all stocks breaking out of a Bullish Triangle, Bearish Triangle, and all the other different patterns.

Variations on the Triple Top

I usually call this pattern the Diagonal Triple Top, but I hesitate to use the name because it sounds too difficult. Possibly a better name would be a Bullish Signal. I have said many times if investing gets too difficult for a seventh grader to understand, the system is needlessly complex. It is important to keep it simple, especially in technical analysis. We don't usually use this pattern as a Triple Top, but older publications classify it as one. This variation is simply two Double Top buy signals, one right after the other. This is the sign of a good strong uptrend. A stock in a strong uptrend will produce rising bottoms and rising tops, and that is exactly what this pattern demonstrates. Notice in Figure 3.15 that you simply have two consecutive Double Tops with rising bottoms.

Variations on the Triple Bottom

This pattern is simply the reverse of the Diagonal Triple Top or Bullish Signal. We can simply call this the Bearish Signal. It has a series of lower tops followed by lower bottoms. Just looking at

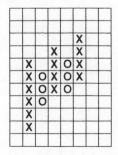

Figure 3.15   The Diagonalized Triple Top.

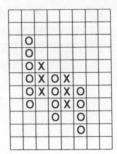

Figure 3.16   The Diagonalized Triple Bottom.

Figure 3.16 suggests that supply is in control. This is all you want your chart pattern to alert you to. Another way to look at it is two consecutive Double Bottom sell signals. We almost never evaluate this pattern as a Triple Bottom although A. W. Cohen clearly classifies it as such.

The Spread Triple Top and Bottom

This pattern is simply a Triple Top that takes a little more space on the chart to complete. Notice the gaps between the tops in Figure 3.17. This is where the spread comes in. The normal Triple Top has no gaps between the tops. The same philosophy applies

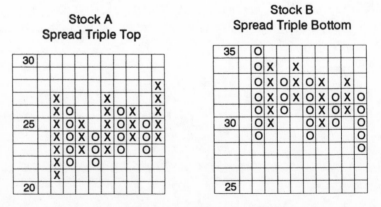

Figure 3.17   The Spread Triple Top and Bottom formation.

in this pattern as in the Triple Top. In each case, the stock rises to a certain price level and is repelled two times. The third attempt at that price is successful by the stock moving through the level shown by a column of X's exceeding the point of resistance. Since the stock was repelled twice at that same level, there are apparently sell orders there. The reason is not important. What is important is that there are sellers at that particular level. The only way to know if demand can overtake the selling pressure is to see how the stock negotiates the level again. Simply stated, if the stock is repelled again at this level of resistance, the sellers are still there. You need not know any more. If the stock exceeds that level, then demand has overcome the supply that previously caused it to reverse. This is why we always wait for a particular level to be exceeded before we make a long or short commitment in the stock. In the 1980s, we typically just bought or sold the breakouts. Starting in the 1990s, we found out that it was best to buy on the pullbacks. For most of the 1980s, stocks went up. From the 1990s forward to 2000, stocks continued their rise. Then in March 2000, something major happened. The technical balance sheet on the Nasdaq turned decidedly negative while the technical balance sheet on the NYSE turned positive—one door of opportunity closes while another one opens. For the rest of 2000 to the third quarter of 2002, tech stocks were virtually decimated. During that time though, there was money to be made in other sectors like utilities, builders, REITs, and healthcare just to name a few. For the past six years it has been a stock picker's environment and likely to remain so for the foreseeable future. Figure 3.17 shows what the pattern looks like for both the Spread Triple Top and the Spread Triple Bottom.

Notice that in these two patterns, the stocks are trading at the same price. Consider that both stocks are fundamentally sound and each is being recommended by a major firm on Wall Street. Both stocks are in the same industry group and pay about the same dividend. You have studied the fundamentals of the two stocks and are now trying to determine which stock to buy. It's the moment of truth. Which stock do you select?

Without the chart patterns shown here, you would be in a quandary. Looking at the fundamental data alone, both stocks are equal, therefore both stocks should do about as well in the future.

Not so. If you had the benefit of evaluating the Point and Figure charts in Figure 3.17, the selection process would become much easier. With the information I have just given you, which stock do you select? It doesn't take an in-depth understanding of this method to determine stock A is in an uptrend with the probability of higher prices and stock B is in a downtrend with lower prices likely.

This simple exercise shows why charts are so important and why you can achieve the best results in the market when you use both fundamental and technical analysis. The fundamental work answers the question what, and the technical side of the equation answers the question when. Both are equally important. The first question, what, is easily answered because fundamental research is everywhere on Wall Street and the Internet. Anyone doing business with a broker of a major firm on Wall Street, either through their Internet online system or direct through a broker, has access to all the fundamental ideas that the firm produces along with its related research. Technical analysis is much harder to come by, but with the information in this book, you will be perfectly capable of performing that task yourself.

The market and sector represent 75 percent of the risk in any particular stock. The problem most investors have is that they concentrate 75 percent of their effort on evaluating the fundamentals. It is extremely important to buy stocks when you are in possession of the football (the market is in a bullish mode). We cover the market indicators in later chapters. We started this book with the discussion on individual chart patterns because these patterns make up the market indicators.

Once again, stack as many odds in your favor as possible before you make a commitment in the stock market. I don't know how many times acquaintances have come up to me and asked what I think about a stock tip they just got from a friend. They usually say it's a very reliable source. My answer is always the same: If it's inside information, you won't have it. The second you have it, it's outside information and those who are really in the know have already acted on it. In almost every case, you can look back on the Point and Figure chart and see clearly where the insiders were operating. Once you get the handle on this method, which has remained true to form for over 120 years, you will see why the Point and Figure chart is as good as inside information. We have a four-step game plan that we follow, and this is the sequence of events you should follow before you make a stock commitment. Step 1 is to evaluate the overall market; Step 2 is to evaluate the sector you are investing in; Step 3 is to answer the question of "what to buy" (the fundamentals); and finally Step 4 encompasses stock selection, which answers the question of "when to buy."

Bullish Shakeout Formation

This is one of my favorite patterns. We keep a strong eye out for this pattern because it has a high degree of reliability. The Shakeout is a relatively new pattern; we've only been watching this one for the past 25 years or so, but we have found it very useful in real-life application. It is called the Shakeout because the pattern easily deceives investors when the sell signal is given.

There is a big difference between the chartist and the technician: Many chartists operate on chart patterns alone without any other input, whereas technicians use other indicators to assist them in evaluating stocks. Don't forget there are other considerations besides just the chart pattern when making a stock selection. The chart patterns should be used to determine whether supply or demand is in control of the underlying investment vehicle. Because so much risk is associated with the market and sector, it is imperative to thoroughly evaluate both factors before considering the underlying stock. If you are buying stocks in a down market, you will surely lose money. If you are selling stocks short in an up market, you will surely lose money. We want to drive home this point, because the Shakeout pattern works best in strong bull markets. We have not had much success, as you might imagine, using this pattern in a bearish market.

With that caveat, let's look at the six attributes of a Shakeout formation:

1. The stock and market should be in a strong uptrend.
2. The stock should be trading above the Bullish Support Line.

3. The stock must rise to a level where it forms two tops at the same price. Note this says "forms" two tops, not breaking the Double Top.
4. The subsequent reversal of the stock from these two tops must give a Double Bottom sell signal.
5. This sell signal should be the first in this uptrend.
6. The Relative Strength chart must be on a buy signal or at least in a column of X's.

Sounds like a lot doesn't it? It's not really. In our day-to-day operations, we fudge these parameters a little, but in general the Shakeout has these characteristics. Remember, the whole idea in using chart patterns is to determine whether supply or demand is in control. Don't forget that, and don't read too much into it because you will usually over think the position, which in turn results in losses. The best machine is the one with the fewest moving parts.

The Shakeout pattern shown in Figure 3.18 is also great for trading. Because the stock must be in a strong uptrend to qualify for the Shakeout pattern, you very well may already have an existing position in the stock. The Shakeout can provide you with an opportunity to add to that strong position or if you aren't already long, it can provide an opportunity to get in a dip.

The Shakeout begins by giving the Double Bottom sell signal. We never know what level the sell signal will carry the stock down to so our action point for entry into this stock is on the first three-box reversal back up the chart (see Figure 3.19). This is the only point where we know demand is back in con-

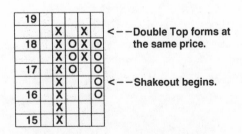

Figure 3.18   The Shakeout formation.

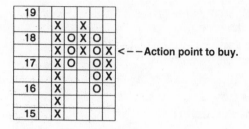

Figure 3.19 Action point on the Shakeout.

trol. Once the stock reverses back up into a column of X's, the position can be taken.

The next consideration is, what to do if things go wrong? Where is the stop-loss point? We always use the Double Bottom that is formed when the stock reverses back up as our exit point. Normally, this is 4 points' risk. Remember that the reliability of this pattern, and any other bullish pattern, diminishes when the overall market is in a bearish mode and your stop-loss point has a higher probability of being hit. Look at Figure 3.20 to see how entry and exit points are established. If the trade was established at the action point, and the stock immediately reversed, the stop point would be the first sell signal the stock gives. The stop is at 15½.

The Long Tail Down

This is one of our favorite bottom-fishing patterns. To qualify for a Long Tail Down, the stock must have declined 20 or more boxes without a reversal. After such a decline, the first reversal

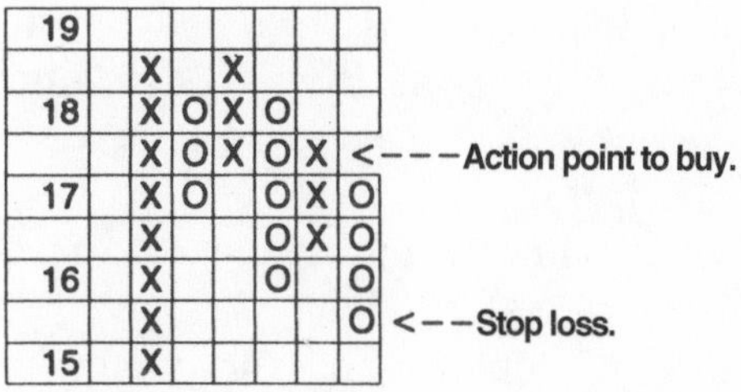

Figure 3.20 Stop loss on the Shakeout.

up usually provides a good trading opportunity. We use to see the 20-box-down movement only in stocks that were already in strong downtrends and that move was the final capitulation. However, with increased volatility in stocks, like technology in 2000, some of the Oil and Non-Ferrous Metals stocks in 2005 to 2006, we have now seen stocks in uptrends pull back 20 boxes— just above strong support areas. Of course, this begs the question, "Do you really have the risk tolerance to buy a stock that can move 20 points in one day?" Nonetheless, this pattern can be a good trading pattern.

I remember a time we thought the pattern was infallible. It had worked for a string of trades, so we decided to pound the table on the next one we came across. It seems that Murphy is always hanging around when you alert the world to a particularly lucrative situation (you know Murphy's Law: If anything can go wrong it will). One day we came across a Long Tail Down in Apple Computer. Apple is a great trading stock as the volatility is high and it seems everyone has played it at sometime or other. Apple had just gone through one of these 20-box down patterns. We knew we had a winner. This time we pounded the table with the recommendation to buy on the first three-box reversal back up the chart. I mean we pounded the table. When the reversal came, I think most of our customers took the trade and many of our customers are large institutions. You guessed it, the stock struggled up a point or so and then caved in. It was the first one in many moons that didn't work. It always seems to work out like that. The one you get everyone to buy, fakes you out. Apple did it again in 2000. The stock came with less than expected earnings and "bang" down 50 percent and over 20 boxes. The stock reversed up a few days, only to reverse down again. It did that two more times. But in 2005 Chicken Little had his revenge. Apple came out with the iPod and that stock became as hot as a firecracker. Things always seem to come full circle.

On balance, this is a good trading pattern. The idea is simple. When a stock has declined 20 boxes or more, you take the first three-box reversal back up the chart as your action point. The stop-loss point is the Double Bottom sell signal that is set up when the stock reverses up into a column of X's. The longer it takes for the stock to decline 20 boxes, the less reliable the pattern is. This is for trading purposes only and not for investors. A stock that has declined 20 boxes or more usually has something wrong with the fundamentals. One of the better ways to play the trade is through the call market. This will give you staying power to expiration, and you need not worry about your stop point being hit. If the stock rises from your entry point, you can raise your stop to each subsequent sell signal that forms. This will allow you to get the full ride if no sell signals are given. It also prevents you from taking a profit too quickly. Always allow your profits to run as much as possible and take as much subjectivity out of the equation as possible. Figure 3.21 shows the Long Tail Down pattern.

The same philosophy can be applied to a long run of X's up but with a much smaller degree of success. As a stock rises, the fundamentals are coming to fruition and there are no dissatisfied investors. For this reason, we just don't see enough selling pressure to warrant a trading commitment in a stock that rises 20 boxes without a reversal. Pullbacks in strong stocks like these appear as opportunities to buy not to sell and can easily generate

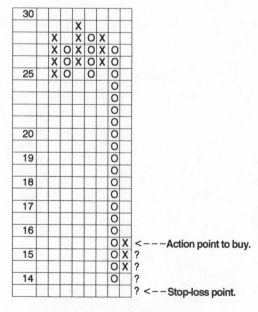

Figure 3.21   The Long Tail Down.

demand. Remember, there are no dissatisfied investors at tops. Still the very nimble can take advantage of it. I usually don't. I am much more apt to attempt a trade on a 20-box down move. However, the three-box reversal down from a run up of 20 boxes or more can be very useful in providing a stop-loss point for traders to take profits or a place for an investor to take partial positions off the table.

The High Pole Warning Formation

This pattern was pioneered by the late Earl Blumenthal. We have seldom taken action on this pattern; however, we have always used it as a warning. This pattern is most reliable in bear-configured markets. To qualify for a High Pole, the Point and Figure chart must have exceeded a previous column of X's by at least three boxes. Following the rise in X's, the stock must pull back more than 50 percent of that last up thrust on the chart. The thought behind the formation is that there must be something wrong with the supply demand relationship if the stock subsequently gave up 50 percent of the last move up. It's a warning that supply might be taking control of the stock. I will usually give the stock some room and place more emphasis on the trend line as my guide for a potential stop for stocks. The High Pole does, however, increase my awareness of a potential change in the supply demand relationship of the underlying stock especially in bear-configured markets. Figure 3.22 is an example of a

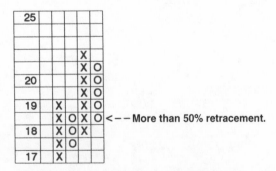

Figure 3.22   The High Pole Warning formation.

High Pole Warning formation. Over the years this pattern has become less useful to us. Often, the pullback is just that, kind of an exhale for the stock.

The Low Pole Formation

I find this pattern more useful than the High Pole simply because investors are more apt to make a commitment in a stock that appears to be a bargain than to sell a stock that has done well for them. The Low Pole simply means the selling pressure that had been driving the stock down is probably over to a great degree. This does not mean that you jump on the stock with unbridled enthusiasm. The company probably still has problems. Remember, you want to buy stocks that are fundamentally sound. That is your first line of defense. Traders, on the other hand, can attempt to make money on a bottom-fishing expedition. The trader's best play is to wait for a pullback following the Low Pole and enter the stock there (see Figure 3.23). Buying on the pullback will establish the entry point closer to the stop level. It also sets up the potential for a nice Double Top buy signal on the next reversal back up the chart. It is usually best to allow the stock to come to you if possible.

We use the High Pole and Low Pole Warnings with some of our bond indicators and the Advance-Decline indexes. Therefore, it will be important to understand the pattern when we discuss

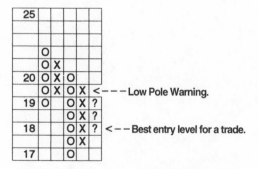

Figure 3.23 The Low Pole Warning formation.

these two indicators later in the book. In everyday practice, we rarely use the two patterns with individual stocks.

The Broadening Top Formation

The Broadening Top formation is simply a variation on the Shakeout formation. The primary difference between the two is that the Broadening Top gives a buy signal prior to the sell signal being given. Let's look back for a moment. If you don't have the Shakeout firmly in mind go back and look at the pattern (Figures 3.18 to 3.20). You will see that the underlying stock has risen up to a certain level two times but was unable to exceed that level the second time. The stock in essence formed a Double Top. Subsequently, it reversed and gave that first sell signal in the uptrend. In the case of the Broadening Top formation, the stock exceeds that previous top the stock made. In other words, it gives a Double Top buy signal. The subsequent reversal gives the sell signal. The combination of the higher top and lower bottom has the appearance of broadening the pattern. To complete the pattern, the stock then reverses back up the chart to give another Double Top buy signal (see Figure 3.24). If you look at those two consecutive Double Tops, you will see the same pattern as the Diagonal

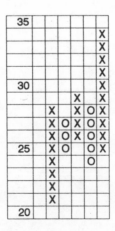

Figure 3.24   The Broadening Top formation.

Triple Top described in the section Variations on the Triple Top; the only difference is the sell signal in the pattern. I always think in terms of economics when I evaluate a Point and Figure chart. What is it telling me in economic terms? The forces that cause price changes in anything are supply and demand. Since these patterns are nothing more than a logical, organized method of recording supply and demand, the answer must lie in basic economic principles.

The Broadening Top formation usually takes place after a stock has run up nicely. What the formation is basically saying is that supply and demand had equal power at the point the pattern was broadening out. The Double Top buy signal was suggesting that demand was still in control. The Double Bottom was suggesting that supply had taken the helm and the uptrend was in question. The subsequent buy signal clearly showed that demand was still in control and that the stock had found enough sponsorship to move higher. When that Double Bottom sell signal is given, it alerts us to take a closer look at Relative Strength and the broad market and sector indicators before taking action. If all those things are positive, we will likely give the stock a little latitude.

The Bearish Signal Reversed Formation

We almost always play this pattern. It is seldom seen, but when it is, you should pay close attention. Investors can detect the pattern while it forms, which allows them to plan their trade. Often, we will show the pattern and discuss the underlying stock in our report days before the pattern is complete. In this great chess game, it helps tremendously to be able to plan your moves. To qualify for the Bearish Signal Reversed, the pattern must have seven columns in it. Each column of X's must be lower than the one before and each column of O's must carry lower than the one prior to it. In the tennis match analogy, the player symbolized by X is underperforming the player symbolized by O. You can easily see this. Remember, keep it simple. Look at the pattern in the context of a tennis match where each column in the pattern represents a set within the match. You can see that when a column of O's takes control of a set it carries lower than the previous column. Action like this demonstrates supply is getting stronger.

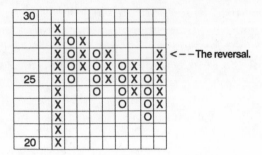

Figure 3.25   The Bearish Signal Reversed formation.

When the column of X's takes control, it is unable to carry up as high as it previously did. By evaluating a pattern in this context, you can easily see supply is stronger than demand and the probability is lower prices. This action is what we characterize as the Bearish Signal. Now let's look at the Reversed part of the pattern. The reversal up into a column of X's with the subsequent Double Top buy signal shows a change in this supply demand relationship. Something has happened to cause demand not only to win a set by reversing up but to win the match by exceeding a previous top and thus giving a buy signal. What makes this buy signal more important is that it exceeds a series of lower tops. In essence, it breaks the spell. Figure 3.25 shows this pattern.

The reversal is often caused by some sort of news that is not widely disseminated or understood by Wall Street. Insiders are usually operating at this point. Ask yourself a question. Why would such a negative pattern that is being controlled by supply change abruptly midstream? Is it possible that an upcoming earnings report is likely to be better than Wall Street expects? Usually there is some fundamental change in the stock that is not widely known. Like the Triangle pattern, the results from this pattern usually happen in a quick, explosive move.

The Bullish Signal Reversed Formation

This pattern is the reverse of the Bearish Signal Reversed. This pattern shows seven columns of rising bottoms and rising tops—the exact opposite of the Bearish cousin (see Figure 3.26). When

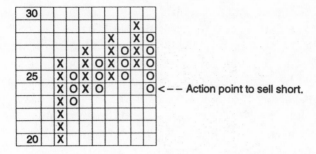

Figure 3.26 The Bullish Signal Reversed formation.

the last top is made in the seventh column, the stock reverses and without a period of distribution declines to give a Double Bottom sell signal as well as break the series of rising bottoms. We have seen this happen in drug companies where FDA approval of a particular drug was not forthcoming. Someone usually knows of this before Wall Street does. There are many other reasons for the quick reversal. It is usually brought on by insiders selling. When I say insiders, I don't necessarily mean the management of the company. What I mean is simply any investor who has information that is not widely known on Wall Street. I can truly say that I have never made money on so-called inside information. When anyone calls you with a tip or posts one on an Internet chat board, the whole street usually knows it. Whenever someone gives you a tip, ask yourself what the person had to gain from telling you. In the final analysis, you will find that frequently the reason for clueing you in was that the tipster had stock to sell. This type of action runs rampant on the Internet. So be very careful what chat room you participate in. Most investors are providing free information that serves their investment objectives, not yours. Remember, there are no disinterested parties when it comes to investing. Everyone has an ax to grind some way or another. I get e-mails all the time from professional or individual clients who point out the positive fundamentals and technicals of a particular stock. Of course, they are just giving me this information to be nice, right? Wrong! In most cases, they are hoping I will recommend it in our report in the hopes we will run the stock up for them. I've had people ask me to mention a particular stock on my next CNBC appearance. I would never do that, but it shows you there are no disinterested parties on Wall Street.

I recently saw an interview with a well-known money manager. The interviewer asked the manager for some of his best picks, and he generously named some stocks that he thought were great values at current prices. I looked in the back section of the paper for the list of stocks that the mutual funds were buying and selling and, "lo and behold," his fund was selling a stock he had just recommended for purchase. If this analyst was buying the stock, why would he publish it? So investors could compete with him in the market and possibly drive the price up? Not likely. What is likely is that he had bought the stock earlier at much better prices and was more interested in selling it. Be wary of tips, especially at cocktail parties and Internet chat rooms. Those giving the tips usually have a vested interest.

Before we leave the Bullish Signal Reversed, let's look at Figure 3.26 and discuss the pattern using the tennis match analogy. The rising tops show that demand is in control of the match. Each time the X wins a set (rises in a column), it does it more convincingly by exceeding the level it previously hit. Each time the O wins a set (declines in a column), it does so less convincingly as it is unable to decline as low as it previously did. Then, without the stock moving back and forth at the top (distribution), it declines in a straight column to give the sell signal and break the series of rising bottoms. In terms of economics, supply has taken control of the stock at 24. This is the point where you could enter a short position, especially if the stock was also violating the Bullish Support Line. It would also be a point at which if you were long, you should begin to examine that stock closer to determine what types of defensive strategies you should take. We could go through all kinds of examples of stops, but in the real world of investing it just isn't cut and dried. Many factors come into the equation, not the least of which is the investor's temperament. In most cases, long-term investors will only use the trend lines as stops. Traders have different problems that generally surround trading capital preservation. Watch for this pattern. It won't show up often but when it does, take action.

You know, one of the most asked questions I get is, "Have you got any back testing done on this method of analysis?" My answer is, yes. If you look in the first edition of this book, you will see a study done by Purdue University on the probabilities associated with the chart patterns we use. However, I have chosen not to use them in the second or third editions because it suggests this method is a science not an art. You are the most important part of the method. Yes, you! Without you—the well-educated and experienced captain of this ship—it will drift aimlessly. Like anything else in life, the more you practice and use the method, the better you will become with it. The following article explains exactly what it takes to become world class at something.

Are You Color Blind? Flash of Genius

I was cleaning up my desk to start out the new year with a clean desk and I came across an article named "Flash of Genius" from *Forbes*,* along with some of my commentary. What caught my eye was the sentence "We need to pay much more explicit attention to teaching pattern recognition." This comment was made by Professor Herbert Simon. The article went on to say, "Simon won a Nobel Prize in Economics in 1978 for theories of decision making that turn on the nature of human expertise. His central finding was that pattern recognition is critical. The more relevant patterns at your disposal, the better your decisions will be." I found it quite interesting when he discussed chess mastery. Most would think that mastering the game of chess relates to analysis but Dr. Simon suggests that isn't the case. Success in chess relates to pattern recognition. I can picture Bobby Fischer playing Kasparov of Russia in a chess match. Each is seeing patterns on the chessboard just as we would see patterns on a stock chart or a Bullish Percent chart. On Toll Brother's chart and the chart of the Building sector, it was clear to the trained eye that the stock was making higher long-term bottoms as the broad averages made lower bottoms from 2000 to 2002. The untrained eye would not have picked up on this subtlety, but this pattern spoke volumes about the probable direction of the building sector. Now we are seeing the opposite—lower tops while the indices are making new highs. It's like a color-blindness test. Have you ever taken one in a doctor's office? Most people have. The patient looks at a

* *Forbes*, November 16, 1998.

card with colored spots on it. The person who is not color-blind can, without difficulty, see the number within the dots. Those who are color-blind cannot. The craftsmen in Point and Figures can see patterns that the uninitiated will never see, and this ability shifts them up to a much higher plane compared with other professionals in the business. By understanding these patterns whether on a chessboard or the big board, the initiated have the confidence to act rather than react.

"What makes a good doctor, lawyer or stock picker?" Simon asks. It all relates to pattern recognition. It relates to experience as well. "Mozart composed for 14 years before he wrote any music you'd regard as world class, . . . you can tell juvenile Mozart from 18 year old Mozart." He suggests it's the same in all fields. "Bobby Fischer got to grand master title in chess in just under 10 years, and so did the Polgar girl. Brain power matters but so does experience." He goes on to suggest that even your doctor has probably diagnosed your problem before you finish telling him all the symptoms. We at DWA often know the answer to portfolio questions asked by our broker clients before they finish illuminating the problem.

What Does It Take to Do World-Class Work?

No matter what profession you are in, there are those who are world class and those who are other than world class. Professor Simon says: "It takes at least 10 years of hard work—say, 40 hours a week for 50 weeks a year—to begin to do world class work. We found it takes eight seconds to learn a pattern for a day, and quite a lot longer to learn it permanently. That takes you to the million pattern estimate, if you allow for certain inefficiencies in learning and also for forgetting." This is why there are relatively few professionals in the investment business who could be called world class. The term we use for it is craftsman. How long do you think it took a cobbler in the seventeenth century to learn his craft? How about a cooper? I surmise that it would have taken about 10 years. Those who have reached world-class level have seen approximately 1 million patterns. This is exactly why it takes so long to become world class in the investment business.

So many professionals jump from one thing to the next—they never take the time to do one thing well. To be world class, you must choose something to become a craftsman in. One of our analysts, Susan Morrison, calculated that during a 10 year time span when we charted by hand, in charting about 400 stocks per day for 50 weeks a year, she has seen about 1 million stock charts. This is why she has such insight into the Point and Figure Chart patterns of stocks, sectors, and the market. The rest of the analysts at DWA have similar experience. I get asked frequently, "What will happen when everyone is doing Point and Figure analysis." My response has always been that to become truly good at it one must take years of study, and most people do not have the time or the inclination to become a craftsman at this method of analysis. Only a select few will go the distance. A method becomes self-fulfilling when investors follow a "guru" (e.g., Joe Granville in years past) and simply do what he tells them to do until the inevitable happens. These investors are not interested in becoming well versed in the investment process. They simply want someone to tell them what to do.

Here is what normally happens. A broker reads our report and gravitates to the breakout reports. He looks at one symbol that says Double Top buy signal, buys that stock with no other analysis, and gets whacked. He then says this doesn't work and moves on to the next strategy. Every now and then, a broker will pick up my book *Point and Figure Charting* and read it. He will then begin to implement the strategy. Somewhere down the road, he will keep a few charts by hand himself. His feel for the subject then increases tremendously. He loves the new confidence he has. He continues to learn and apply the method; years later he looks back and can see a distinct difference between his abilities then and now. His journey has still much further to go to reach world class, but he is on the way. His client retention is now high as is his confidence. He now maintains 200 stocks a day and looks at many more through our Internet system. When he nears the tenth year, he is approaching world class and the number of chart patterns he has viewed is approaching 1 million. He no longer needs to read the financial newspapers, or watch the financial TV shows. Major statements made by Wall Street pundits have no effect on his thought process. He (or she) instinctively knows what to do in various market conditions. He is like a child who has totally memorized the multiplication tables, and now instinctively knows 9 times 9 equals 81.

How many of you have been doing this for longer than five years and are now feeling comfortable with this investment process? You're on the road to world class. There's nothing like being world class at something. To get there takes determination, patience, and hard work. There are many other methods of analyzing the market that you might choose, from astrology to Gann angles. Whatever you choose, go the distance, become a world-class investor. You only have one life to live.

Stop Loss Points

I saved this until last because it's something that everyone will decide for themselves what the best method for stopping out losing positions is. I remember reading some old manuscripts on Point and Figure and they recommended a simple 8 percent stop if a position went against you. William O'Neil one of the pioneers in technical analysis also recommends 8 percent as the stop point in a stock position. I have a problem with percents. The problem is a simple 8 percent stop may only suggest the stock has taken the "pause that refreshes." Often times a small pullback of say 2.5 points (8 percent) on a $30 stock is a market related pullback or what I call a healthy exhale. We like to use sell signals that develop on stocks we own as our "wake-up call." Traders who are quick on the trigger and need to preserve their trading capital should take every sell signal that develops. They too will be ready to go right back in on the next buy signal. This type of trading is not for most investors today. It's interesting to look at some charts of stocks and ask yourself the question: "what if I just held on to the stock until a sell signal was given"? You might be amazed how stocks trend for a very long time without giving the first sell signal. Often it's hard to stay with stocks that continue to trend up because we inherently want to nail down profits while we have them. Just take some time and look at the charts and develop your plan. In our Money Management Company we use the trend line of the stock as our "wake-up call." When a stock breaks the long-term Bullish Support Line, the stock goes on what we call Death Row. We then decide how we will execute the stock. We might sell some right then on the break and some on the next bounce up. We might consider selling all on the next bounce up. The point is we develop a plan and execute that plan. Conversely short sales would be stopped on a breakout of the Bearish Resistance Line. Another "wake-up" call we use is when the Relative Strength chart gives a sell signal. In situations like this we can easily set stop loss levels, actually put the order in on the exchange, Good Until Cancelled to sell if the stop point is hit. The stop point or escape route will be determined when the trade goes on. Remember I said we must determine what to do if things go right and what to determine if things go wrong from the onset of the trade. Always work from a plan. There are no set rules for stop points. You will intuitively begin to know what works best for you as you develop your skills in this method of analysis. Try to take a longer-term approach to investing and don't be too quick on the trigger.

POINTS AND FIGURES BY DORSEY, WRIGHT MONEY MANAGEMENT

One of the beauties of Point and Figure analysis is that the only indicator used is price. No volume, no Fibonacci retracements, no waves, no guesswork of any kind. Just pure supply and demand. Often, especially by individuals new to this form of analysis, people think that by "adding" volume or another of a host of "confirming indicators" accuracy might be improved. This, I think, is a false hope. Although using only price SEEMS overly simplistic, it is in fact much more robust than supposedly sophisticated models.

Here's an example. The normal correlation between the price of oil and 10-year bond yields has been 75 percent (Steven Wieting, Citigroup economist). That is a very high, positive correlation. Oil up, bond yields up. No doubt some sophisticated hedge fund built a predictive trading model using derivatives and leverage, making us Point and Figure practitioners look like we are back in the Stone Age.

We may still be in the Stone Age, but the hypothetical hedge fund is belly up in a negative equity position, because the correlation between November and June 2004 has become inverse and is now running at −85 percent. The new world order is oil up, bond yields down. How did that happen? Who knows? And, it doesn't matter. We'll leave that excuse to the economists.

What IS important is that a Point and Figure analyst wasn't thrown off at all. Uptrends and breakouts are clearly observable in both oil and bond futures. The Stone Age Point and Figure charts give very accurate and direct information about supply and demand in both markets, regardless of what a finance textbook says is supposed to happen. (Come to think of it, Point and Figure charts bear an uncanny resemblance to certain primitive cave etchings. To survive, Cro-Magnon man certainly had to understand relative strength from a hunting standpoint: send out the hunter who has had the most success. Perhaps the extinction of Piltdown [trend] man had something to do with selecting "value" hunters: "Let's send out Ogg. He hasn't speared a boar in months!")

Joking aside, the strength of Point and Figure is its simplicity. Supply and demand is robust. When the world changes, it changes, and can still provide accurate guidance.

Chapter 4

FOUNDATIONS OF RELATIVE STRENGTH

"Ever hear the one about the two guys camping in the woods and a bear appears? As one guy starts running, the other stops to put on his sneakers. 'What are you doing?' the first guy yells out. 'You'll never outrun the bear.' His partner replies: 'I don't have to. I just have to outrun you'" (*BusinessWeek*, May 5, 2003).

The 80/20 Rule, or Pareto's Principle (named after the Italian economist Vilfredo Pareto), is something we have all heard about. It basically means that in anything—management, wealth distribution, time spent on client relationships, and so on, a "few are vital" and "many are trivial." This same principle holds true with investment results; more specifically, that 20 percent of your trades are responsible for 80 percent of your profits. Said another way, it is not the number of winning trades versus the number of losing trades that is most attributable to your investment success, but rather it is the size of your winners versus the size of your losers. The saying is true—size does matter!

Given this proven, time-tested principle, it is imperative that you position yourself to capture the large winning trades. This is where Relative Strength comes into play. It is our contention that Relative Strength (RS) allows you to "catch the positive outliers" or big winners while helping you to avoid large losers. Others tend to agree. In *What Works on Wall Street*, Jim O'Shaughnessy found that RS was a factor in all 10 of the top performing strategies (that he tested). He also found that the worst strategy in his testing was buying stocks with the worst RS (see Figure 4.1).

At Dorsey, Wright & Associates (DWA), Relative Strength is a very important component or cornerstone of our research. Since the company's inception in 1987, RS has been part of our daily research; and yet over the past 20 years, the emphasis we place on RS has grown dramatically, as have the number of RS tools we have created to assist us in helping in the stock selection process. We have found RS to be one of the most robust and adaptable methods of security analysis. Despite it truly being a very simplistic concept, RS has been proven time and time again to be a viable methodology for outperforming the market over time. This is the essence of RS—a way to measure outperformance.

Relative Strength, as the name implies measures how one security is doing compared to another. For example, how Microsoft is performing versus the S&P 500, or how Ford is acting compared to General Motors. In essence, such a comparison allows you to determine which security is outperforming the other. The implication is that you invest in the vehicle that is outperforming the other, be it the market, or another stock. (This speaks to the transferability of the RS concept—basically you can do an RS calculation on anything! It can be applied on a stock-specific basis, with sector analysis, asset class evaluation, mutual funds, ETFs, commodities, fixed incomes, and even foreign countries.)

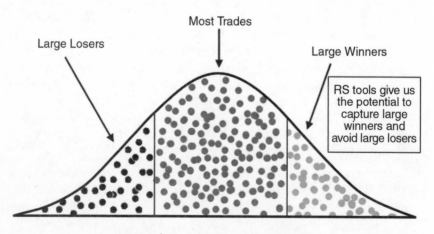

Figure 4.1   Relative Strength 80/20 Rule.

One of the visual adoptions to the RS concept is a picture of two arms, locked in an arm wrestling contest. You have all seen two people arm wrestle before. In fact, you have probably seen national arm wrestling contests on TV. It is this type of battle between investment vehicles that we pay much attention to. Let's say you brought 10 contestants to an arm-wrestling tournament. You will take the top five to the grand championships. You can't decide who to bring until the match is over. We, in essence, put stocks, indexes, bonds, and the like in an arm wrestling tournament to determine who has the strongest arm. Our tournament consists of mathematical computations to determine the winner but the computations are nothing more than a seventh grader can perform by hand. Computers simply allow us to do these computations thousands of times over in a very short time. Technology is amazing. In the end, RS steers you toward the outperformer and away from the underperformer; and helps you to invest in, and stay with, that winner for as long as the RS chart suggests outperformance. You focus your buying on those securities exemplifying the strongest RS, and sell (or sell short) those vehicles that exhibit the weakest RS.

Different Types of Relative Strength

We use two main types of RS charts when evaluating a specific stock. In both cases, the calculation is very simple, yet the results provide us with a ranking system. This is not unlike other areas of life, such as in the sports world, and in particular, college football. Each week during the college football season, we hear about the BCS rankings, which tells us what team is considered to be the best in the nation. These rankings are based on strength of schedule (opponents) and how the team has performed each week—did they win or lose, and by how much. It's interesting how this RS concept permeates our daily lives. Even when you shop at the supermarket you are employing the concept of RS. I know that the RS of summer squash is low in the winter, and the RS of winter squash is low in the summer. *Consumer Reports* is a magazine that focuses on evaluating RS of various products. We consult this magazine to determine how a certain stereo system functions versus another, or how a particular model of car ranks versus another. Although we use this concept of comparing one to another in our daily lives, few even think of it when evaluating investments. Let's now take a detailed look at each of these methods of "ranking" a particular stock.

1. *RS versus S&P 500 Equal Weighted Index.* This is the more common and most widely used of our RS calculations. It measures how a stock is performing compared with the market in general. For this comparison, we use the S&P 500 Equal Weighted Index (SPXEWI). We often refer to this as the stock's Market RS. The RS calculation is simply done by dividing the price of the stock by the price of the S&P 500 Equal Weighted Index, then multiplying by 100. (We move the decimal point merely to have an easier number to work with.) This number is then plotted on a Point and Figure chart, using the same charting principles discussed in earlier chapters. Okay, stop for a second. Let me backtrack for a moment. Just like plotting a Point and Figure chart for the trend of a stock we use a number. This number is simply the price of the underlying stock. The RS chart is plotted the exact same way but the number we use is derived by dividing something by something else. In this discussion we are dividing the price of the underlying stock by the Equal Weighted Standard & Poors 500, resulting in a NUMBER. This number is then plotted on a Point and Figure Chart just like we did when plotting the trend chart. We just get this number by dividing one thing by another instead of using the price of the underlying stock. It really is this simple. You know what? We even calculated a RS chart for Phil Mickelson versus Tiger Woods using their publicly available statistics and plotted the results on a Point and Figure Chart. We looked at Tiger as "the market" and Phil as the stock. It worked fine. It gave us some very interesting insight between the two players. We'll reserve more discussion on this for our Professional Golf Point and Figure Charts we will do in the future. Hey just kidding on the Pro Golf Charts but let your mind wander a little. What if? Okay back to the real RS charts. We use the S&P 500 Equal Weighted

Index as the divisor for a stock's Market RS, but you can choose to use another market index, such as the Nasdaq Composite or Value Line; just be consistent and always use the same index when you update your RS chart. Using the SPX-EWI makes sense to us, though, since as the name implies, it is an equal weighted index. This helps to eliminate the capitalization or price bias found in most other market indices. Previously, we used the Dow Jones Industrial Average as our benchmark to measure RS, but changed over to the SPXEWI in February 2003 after Standard & Poors announced the creation of an equal weighted version of their S&P 500 Index. Besides having the appeal of being equally weighted, the SPXEWI is a much broader based index than the Dow Jones. One point we want to make before moving on concerns the scale used for an RS chart. It differs from the basic trend chart scale in that it is not a fixed box size scale, but rather a uniform percent scaling methodology that treats all stocks equally, regardless of price. This was another change that we incorporated in February 2003 after extensive, collaborative research by the home office in Richmond and our Money Management division in Pasadena, California. The efforts to make our RS tools even more robust and adaptable is an example of our commitment of constantly striving to make Dorsey, Wright's technical analysis and research better for our clients.

2. *RS versus DWA Sector Index.* This is also known as Peer Relative Strength. It measures how a stock is performing compared with its sector peers, as measured by the Dorsey, Wright Sector Indexes. For example, the Peer RS reading would measure how Intel (INTC) is doing relative to other Semiconductor stocks. This RS chart allows you to determine the strongest stocks within a particular sector, or what we like to call "the best in class." The Peer RS calculation is equally simple, and is done by dividing the price of the stock by the appropriate DWA Sector Index chart, then multiplying by 100 to come up with a plottable number. The DWA Sector Indexes were created for each broad industry group we follow. These DWA Sector Indexes are equal weighted and include a nice

mix of stocks with varying capitalization, unlike the exchange sector indexes, which tend to be more narrow and capitalization weighted. The uniform percent scaling method is used with this type of RS chart, too, as well as all other RS charts.

How to Calculate Relative Strength

Now that you understand the two basic RS charts we use for an individual stock, let's look at an actual example of each type of RS calculation.

Relative Strength of a Stock versus the Market

$$RS\ Reading = \frac{Stock\ Price}{SPXEWI} \times 100$$

(This calculation uses closing prices and is done on a daily basis.) For example: XYZ Corp is at 81 and the SPXEWI is at 1252:

$$\frac{81}{1252} \times 100 = 6.47\ RS\ Reading$$

For example: XYZ Corp is now at 74 and the SPXEWI is at 931:

$$\frac{74}{931} \times 100 = 7.95\ RS\ Reading$$

In this case, the stock dropped in price and the S&P 500 Equal Weighted Index also fell lower, but the RS reading for XYZ went up. This tells us that the stock is performing better than the SPXEWI, and it is possible that the only reason it has fallen in price is that the overall market has dragged it down. These positive RS stocks will likely be the first ones to snap back once the overall market does. As a general rule, stocks with positive RS versus the market will typically outperform the market during a bullish market condition, and will be more likely to hold up and weather the storm in a bearish market condition over the longer term. When the market transitions from Offense to Defense, these high RS stocks that have done so well verses others will likely experience profit taking as many other stocks have no profits to be taken. Take, for example, the market beginning in early May 2006. The positive RS stocks carried the ball for most of the year. Stocks like Coca-Cola (KO) had burned out years before, and had done virtually nothing in 2006. It is natural that when optimism turns to pessimism in the market, investors rush to nail down profits but hold those stocks that have done nothing. In the two months from May 2006 to July 2006 the high RS stocks came down faster than the negative or low RS stocks because of this profit taking. Once the profits were taken they reasserted their RS and were the first to begin the run up once the offensive team came back on the field. There are a lot of little nuances in investing that make up the market.

Relative Strength of a Stock versus DWA Sector Index (Peer RS)

$$\text{Peer RS Reading} = \frac{\text{Stock Price}}{\text{DWA Sector Index}} \times 100$$

(This calculation uses closing prices and is done on a daily basis.)

For example: Intel (INTC) is at 22.50 and the DWA Semiconductor Index is at 236:

$$\frac{22.50}{236} \times 100 = 9.53 \text{ Peer RS Reading}$$

For example: Intel (INTC) rises to 22.90 and the DWA Semiconductor Index is at 244:

$$\frac{22.90}{244} \times 100 = 9.38 \text{ Peer RS Reading}$$

In this case, INTC rose in price, the DWA Semiconductor Sector Index moved higher, but the Peer RS reading for INTC went down. Now, let's substitute Advanced Micro Devices (AMD) for Intel in the previous example.

For example: AMD is at 30 and the DWA Semiconductor Index is at 236:

$$\frac{30}{236} \times 100 = 12.71 \text{ Peer RS Reading}$$

For example: AMD rises to 34.50 and the DWA Semiconductor Index is at 244:

$$\frac{34.50}{244} \times 100 = 14.14 \text{ Peer RS Reading}$$

In this case, AMD rose in price, the DWA Semiconductor Sector Index moved higher, and the Peer RS reading for AMD moved up.

This comparative example demonstrates how AMD is outperforming its Semiconductor sector peers, while INTC is underperforming its peers. AMD's Peer RS reading moved up from 12.71 to 14.14, while INTC's Peer RS reading fell from 9.53 to 9.38. This particular type of RS reading allows you to identify the stocks that are the strongest of the group—the best in class—and these are the stocks that will likely perform the best within that sector. You have all heard of "Market Neutral" Hedge Funds right? Wouldn't it make sense in the above example to buy AMD and simultaneously sell short INTC? Think about it.

How to Interpret the Relative Strength Chart

In evaluating an RS chart, buy signals are given when a column of X's exceeds a previous column of X's (also referred to as positive RS). Conversely, sell signals are given when a column of O's exceeds a previous column of O's (also referred to as negative RS). The pattern doesn't matter with the RS chart (e.g., whether it is a Double Top or Triple Top buy signal), just whether the most recent signal is a buy signal or a sell signal—a top being broken or a bottom being broken. As well, unlike other RS methods, the RS "reading" or number itself doesn't matter; the results of these RS readings really don't come to life until plotted on a PnF basis. Once the chart is plotted, the RS picture unfolds and provides guidance. Questions are easily answered, such as "Is the RS chart in X's or O's?" "Is it on a buy signal or a sell signal?" If you read my first edition book on Point and Figure Charting you will remember in the RS chapter I mentioned that I had found that the column was more important on the RS chart than the actual signal that developed, as it often indicated a change in trend was occurring. Since then we have done extensive work on the RS concept, and made improvements to these charts, as discussed earlier.

Positive Relative Strength, or an RS buy signal, suggests the stock will outperform the market (or whatever you are comparing it to), while negative Relative Strength, or an RS sell signal, suggests the stock will underperform the market. But it is important to note that just because a stock has positive RS doesn't mean that it can't fall in price; it merely means that it should not fall as much as the market averages. It's as the name suggests—it is a relative measurement, not an absolute one. It is also important to watch for RS reversals, or changes in columns, as this provides shorter term guidance. While the RS signal indicates longer term relative strength, the most recent column provides an indication as to the shorter term relative strength. If the most recent column on the RS chart is X's, it suggests the stock is outperforming in the near term; conversely, when the most recent column on the RS chart is O's, it demonstrates underperformance by the stock in the near term. As well, if you continue to see an RS chart put in another X after another X, it suggests the RS is only getting stronger, or is rising. This is a good sign for a stock, showing that it persists in outperforming the market. Conversely, if a stock is in a column of O's and continues to put in more O's, it is telling you that this stock's RS is falling, and therefore should be avoided. In sum, the best combination for the RS chart is to be on a buy signal and in a column of X's; while the worst is for it to be on an

RS sell signal and in O's. Oh, one more thing. I find it very helpful to look at the last calculation on that RS chart so you can
gauge if the RS is beginning to move in another direction. Say
the last box in the RS chart is in X's at 20. A three box reversal
will happen at 18.56. If the last reading on the calculation was
20.4 then you know the RS chart is not losing any strength.
Conversely, in this same example, if the RS chart was at 20 and
the last calculation on that RS chart was 18.72, you are close to
a reversal to O's and had better prepare for it.

The beauty of RS is that it can keep you invested in strong
stocks for a long time, allowing you to participate in the gains—
enabling you to catch the positive "outlier." Think about it for a
second. If a stock continues to have positive RS for years on end,
all while the market averages continue to record notable gains,
what does that say for the particular stock? Well, the only way a
stock can continue to have positive RS versus a market that is
moving higher, is for it to move higher in price, and at a faster
pace than the market. In essence, RS allows you to let your profits run, with the (positive) RS chart providing a clear-cut reason
to do so. This statement fits with the fact that a stock's (market)
RS signal will typically last about two years on average; and generally speaking, it tells us the overall expected trend of the
stock. Yet there are plenty of examples of how RS can stay positive or negative for years on end. For example, IBM had positive
RS from November 1996 to October 2000; its RS chart has been
on a sell signal since October 2000. More staggering is the fact
that Dell Computers (DELL) was on an RS buy signal from November 1993 to April 1999—during this time the stock was up
100 fold! If that's not impressive enough, Danaher (DHR) has
been on a RS buy signal for 16 years, since May 1993. The outperformance during this expansive time frame is incredible—
with DHR up 1545 percent compared to the SPXEWI which
posted a not-so-shabby return of 256 percent. But just as RS
works well to pinpoint outperformance, there are dramatic instances of how it warns of long term underperformance. Take
Eastman Kodak (EK)—this stock was on an RS sell signal for 12½
years, from March 1992 to September 2004; and the numbers
shouted underperformance with EK losing 22 percent in a little
over a decade while the market gained 242 percent. Another ex-

ample of this is WorldCom. On page 100 of the second edition of this book, I recommended avoiding or selling short WorldCom before any of the negative news came out. Who could have tipped me off to this? The RS chart did. I said the following: "Overall weak RS stocks that reverse back to O's are dangerous, and in most cases should be avoided, or potentially shorted. A case in point is WorldCom (WCOM)."

Another beneficial aspect of RS is it allows you (or tells you) to get off a horse not running the race and to move to one that is. This is where it's imperative to keep up with changes in Relative Strength. Each day, changes in RS will occur—some stocks will move from an RS buy signal to an RS sell signal and vice versa, and some will show changes in column on their RS chart. The point is, you must constantly monitor the RS chart for changes. Our system at www.dorseywright.com will do this for you and alert you by e-mail of any changes in stocks that warrant your attention. If you own a stock that has just given an RS sell signal, it is time to evaluate whether that stock should be sold. Also, by knowing when a stock has given a new RS buy signal, or reversed up into a column of X's, it will alert you to a potential turnaround situation or viable investment opportunity. Some graphical explanations will make this concept easier to grasp.

Examples of Relative Strength Changes for Stocks versus the Market

It never is too hard to find classic examples of relative strength, merely because the concept is so dynamic and robust. But, I must say some of the more dramatic illustrations of RS at work come from the year 2000. We all remember this time period; some fondly, while others are still licking their wounds from losses incurred following the tech meltdown. Those that used technical analysis, and in particular Relative Strength, came through the 2000–2002 time period relatively unscathed. The evidence of a major top in technology and telecom stocks was right before your eyes, if you were willing to look.

One of my favorite examples of this on a stock specific basis is AT&T (T). As we all know, the Telecom sector had recorded blistering gains in the late 1990s, with stocks like Corning (GLW), Nortel (NT), Qualcomm (QCOM) and Lucent (LU) leading the way. Even the venerable AT&T participated in the Telecom sector ascension, as it more than doubled from 1997 to its peak in 1999 to 2000. But by early 2000 the jig was up—the RS charts started shouting that it was time to get out. AT&T, and another high-profile company that you surely remember—Worldcom (WCOM) (discussed earlier), were two of the first to scream uncle. In early May 2000, T gave an RS sell signal when it broke a Double Bottom on its RS chart, as indicated in Figure 4.2. This

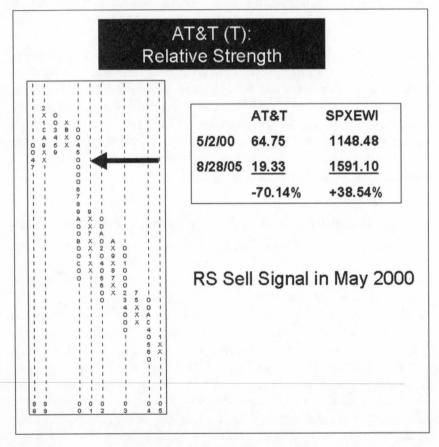

Figure 4.2   AT&T Relative Strength chart.

RS sell signal suggested the stock would underperform the market for some time to come. AT&T did exactly that! From May 2000 to August 2005, with the RS sell signal persisting, T was down 70 percent while the SPXEWI was up 38.5 percent. Similarly, WCOM gave an RS sell signal in May 2000, and we all know what happened here—RIP.

There is a saying, "as one door closes, another one opens." This couldn't have been more true in 2000. What we witnessed on an RS basis was a veritable "changing of the guard"; Technology and Telecom exited center stage while other, previously neglected sectors took the baton. This passing of the baton took the form of NYSE-type stocks giving RS buy signals. Stocks from such sectors as Building, Healthcare, Food and Beverage, and Utilities got the leading roles; and oh, what a performance they delivered. In fact, many of the RS buy signals given by these type of stocks in 2000 continue to be in place today. For example, United Healthcare (UNH) gave an RS buy signal in May 1999; its positive RS remains in force today. Throughout this time period we have seen UNH post an astronomical return of +483 percent; that is what I would call a "positive outlier" referring back to the 80/20 Rule! A similar phenomenon happened with many of the Building stocks. These stocks have proven to be a textbook example of the power of (positive) Relative Strength, and how signals can last for years on end, allowing you to capture large winners.

In all my years on Wall Street, the Building stocks were never ones that attracted much attention. The action in them, for the most part, was like watching paint dry—boring, if you will. For example, it was not unusual for Toll Brothers (TOL) to trade in a range between 16 and 22 for a couple of years on end. But that all changed in 2000 to 2001. Once again, the RS chart steered you in the right direction, unemotionally able to remove any predispositions one might have had about the "boring" Builders. The role reversal started with TOL and Lennar (LEN) in late July 2000; both gave RS buy signals, suggesting these stocks would outperform the market for some time to come. LEN stayed on an RS buy signal from July 2000 to May 2006 and during this time gained 376 percent! Not bad for a boring Building stock. But this action

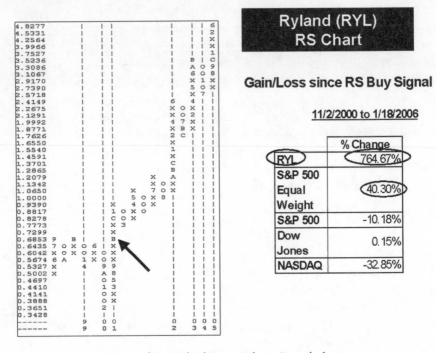

Figure 4.3 Ryland Homes Relative Strength chart.

was not relegated to just a few—others followed suit. Pulte Homes (PHM), Beazer Homes (BZH), Ryland Homes (RYL), and KB Home (KBH) all gave RS buy signals in the months to follow. Not surprisingly, the Building sector has been one of the best performing sectors since July 2000. So while the OTC/Technology arena was giving RS sell signals, other opportunities emerged in the least likely places. In Figure 4.3, we show you the Ryland Homes (RYL) RS chart. It is a great example of how RS unemotionally measures outperformance; so when doors like this open, be ready to walk through them.

Where's the Relative Strength Been, or Not Been?

We have, so far, directed our conversation about RS signals to the 2000–2001 period. But we now want to turn our attention toward more recent RS changes. Over the past couple of years, the one area that has attracted investor's attention has been the broad group of Basic Resources—Nonferrous Metals, Precious Metals, Steel and Iron, Oil and Oil Service; for good reason. Not only have the underlying commodities, such as gold and crude oil risen spectacularly, stocks in these sectors have produced unbelievable gains. Once again, RS did the job of guiding you toward these areas of outperformance. In the table that follows, we show you a sample list of some key RS buy signals that occurred in the Basic Resources group. Notice how these signals started cropping up in 2002 to 2003, and how they remain in force several years later. The returns for these stocks speak for themselves:

Where's the Beef Been Lately?

Basic Resources RS Examples

Stock	Symbol	Date of RS Buy Signal	Return Since RS Buy Signal (%)	Return of SPXEWI (%)
Nucor	(NUE)	January 2002	259	39
Halliburton	(HAL)	October 2002	382	92
Phelps Dodge	(PD)	February 2003	344	81
Valero Energy	(VLO)	February 2003	507	80
Peabody Energy	(BTU)	September 2002	701	90

While the raw materials stocks have been the "sweet spot" of the market for the past few years, it has been the large cap, and specifically Consumer Noncyclical and Cyclical stocks, that have been kicked to the curb. Old stalwarts such as Coca-Cola (KO) and Ford Motor (F), not to mention Wal-Mart (WMT), have been "taken to the wood shed." Their RS charts depict this whipping clearly—having given sell signals over the past few years. Unfortunately, many investors still own these blue-chip names, not willing to part with them. But the underperformance cannot be denied; all you have to do is look at your statement each month to see the performance lag brought about by owning weak RS names. So I ask, "Do you need to weed out some poor RS stocks from your portfolio?"

Where Have the Dogs Been Barking?
Large-Cap Consumer and Financial Examples

Stock	Symbol	Date of Return Since RS Sell Signal	Return Since RS Sell Signal (%)	SPXEWI (%)
Coca-Cola	(KO)	September 2003	0.21	38
Comcast	(CMCSA)	February 2004	8	19
Fannie Mae	(FNM)	June 2003	−29	45
Ford Motor	(F)	March 2005	−41	12
Wal-Mart	(WMT)	November 2004	−8	12

Spotting Positive Divergences

This leads us to a discussion on market divergence. It is also important to use RS to determine market divergence during times of weakness in the overall market. As discussed in later chapters, our market indicators will help dictate whether you should be playing offense or defense against the market. When defense is recommended, it becomes necessary to evaluate your portfolio positions all the more closely. This is a great time to get rid of your underperforming stocks. If those stocks haven't kept up while the market has headed higher, they are not likely to hold up well if the market moves lower. RS becomes a valuable tool to help determine which stocks get sold and which stocks are kept. Given that the market, on average, goes up two-thirds of the time, and down one-third of the time, going to 100 percent cash by selling all your positions is a huge bet. A more sensible approach is to weed out the poor RS performers and sell those stocks to raise the cash level in your portfolio. Keep the strong, positive RS stocks since they will be more resistant to decline, and will likely snap back once the market gets back on solid footing.

There is another aspect, or way to visualize market divergence and RS. During market corrections, it is important to observe whether a stock (or group of stocks in the same sector) is showing higher bottoms on its trend chart while the market averages are making lower bottoms. Often there is a change in leadership after a market correction; in many cases, subtle signs will occur even before the market as a whole has bottomed out.

We witnessed this phenomenon over the past few years, for example, with the Building stocks and Oil stocks. The market averages, for all intents and purposes, topped out in 2000. From there it was a slippery slope to drastically lower prices. This trek south persisted for a couple of years, with new lows being registered in 2001, then 2002; a test of the 2002 market lows then occurred in March 2003. Yet while all this was going on in the mainstream, underneath the surface subtle, positive changes were occurring. Certain stocks were bucking the trend, and instead were showing a series of higher tops and higher bottoms— in short, they were experiencing a positive divergence from the market. KB Homes (KBH) is one such stock. Each time the market sold off further to make a new bottom or test its old lows, KBH was showing higher bottoms. It was showing a positive divergence from the market. The trend chart itself was speaking volumes about the future prospects of KB Homes. It was displaying improvement in RS. This phenomenon was not relegated just to KBH, other Building stocks showed a similar pattern; a change in sector sponsorship was underway. KBH, as a proxy for the group, rose 139 percent from May 2000 to March 2003, and its sector brethren joined in the parade, all while the market averages were posting substantial losses (see Figure 4.4).

The KBH example displays how, as Yogi Berra used to say, "You can observe a lot just by watching." Changes in sector sponsorship often present themselves in the form of an RS change, noticeable right on the trend chart as was the case with KBH; or you may see a cluster of stocks in the same group give RS buy signals all around the same time, as we previously discussed with the Builders and Basic Materials and Natural Resources stocks. But this type of occurrence is nothing new. I remember back in October 1990, how we noticed the RS charts of Dominion Resources, Houston Industries, Scana Corporation, and Texas Utilities turned positive for the first time in four or more years. This positive RS change was an early warning system not only for the Utility sector, but boded well for the economy and market as a whole. One month later, our market indicators gave major buy signals. A similar case happened in November 1991. In one week, we saw Hercules, Briggs & Stratton, and Cummins Engine turn positive on their RS charts after being negative for years. The message was

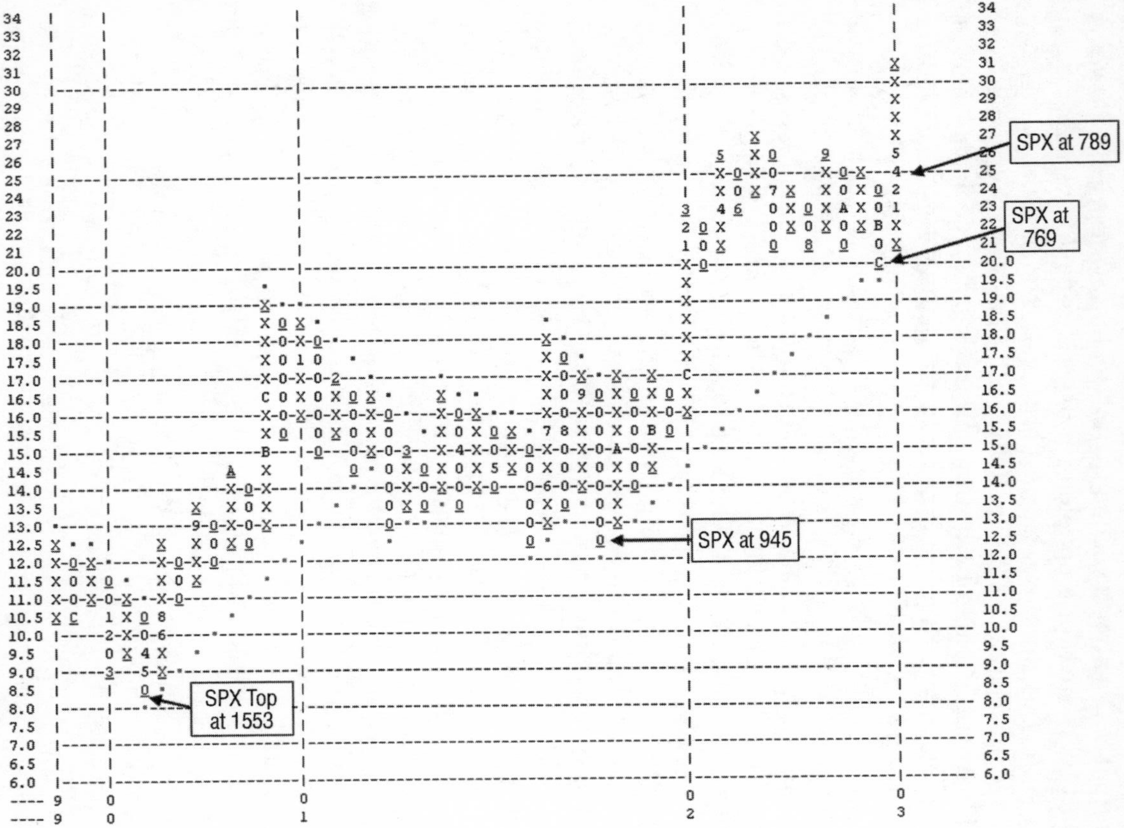

Figure 4.4 KB Homes showing Positive Divergence.

120

clear—the cyclical stocks were ready to take the lead. This work is why we have been called "Wall Street's Air Traffic Controller."

It is equally important to watch for negative divergences. Just as the trend chart of a stock can depict a positive divergence, it can also alert you to a negative divergence. This is easily seen on the chart in the form of lower tops and bottoms, all while the market averages are showing higher tops and bottoms. This situation has occurred more so over the past couple of years given that the majority of market averages have consistently made higher bottoms (since the July–October 2002 lows). When a stock shows a negative divergence from the market, it is a warning sign that something is wrong, and that the stock is losing relative strength. In most cases, it suggests you sell the stock or take some type of defensive action. A case in point is Apollo Group (APOL). The distance-learning stocks, such as APOL, had seen strong moves up, similar to the takeoff of an F4B Phantom Jet from the deck of an Aircraft Carrier. This took place for the better part of four years and in the process these stocks recorded massive gains. But that stopped in mid-2004. APOL peaked at 98 in June of that year, and has not been back to those highs since. Instead, while the S&P 500 Equal Weighted Index (SPXEWI) has made higher correction bottoms, APOL has moved to new lows on each correction and has made lower tops when the market has posted new highs during this same time period. Figure 4.5 is an example of negative divergence—APOL has fallen 48 percent since June 2004 while the SPXEWI has gained 19 percent. All told, the trend chart itself can speak to you about RS, if you are willing to listen (or should I say "look").

Changes in Relative Strength Column from Long Tails Up or Down

In a secondary fashion, it is important to pay attention to RS changes in columns. When a stock reverses back up into a column of X's on its RS chart, it is displaying positive near-term outperformance. An RS change in column (to X's) can also be helpful in identifying a turnaround situation. This can be

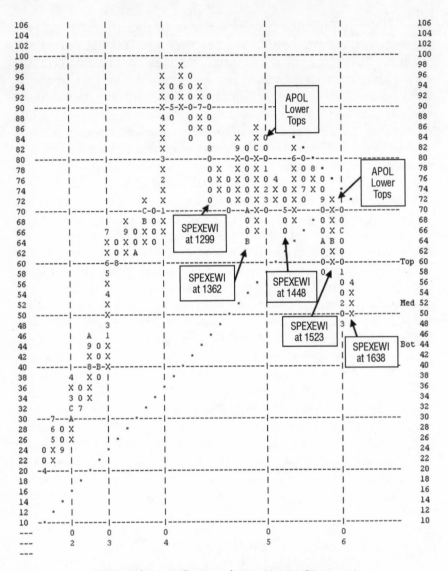

Figure 4.5   Apollo Group showing Negative Divergence.

especially true if the RS chart had previously been in a long column of O's down, either because the stock itself had been
shunned or because the sector as a whole had been out of favor.
Such instances can result in a long tail of O's on the RS chart. As

a result, to technically get a buy signal on the RS chart, the column of X's back up would have to travel a long way to break the previous column of X's. For this to occur, the stock will have likely already experienced a huge move to the upside. Therefore, after a Long Tail Down, it is acceptable to consider an RS reversal to X's as a buy signal of sorts, or at least a sign that the stock could be in the midst of a turnaround, and is worth you taking a closer look at the technical developments of that stock. I saw this situation many, many times years ago, which is why in the first edition of Point and Figure charting I discussed how the column was more important than the signal. Since then we have changed the charts to represent percent changes and the signals come more frequently now. So what I do is look at the RS chart to see if a signal is close at hand. If so I might wait for it to develop before I pile in. If the signal is not near then the change in column is enough for me to go ahead and buy given all other pieces of the puzzle fall into place.

A good illustration of this type of situation can be seen with Lockheed Martin (LMT). As you can see in Figure 4.6, LMT reversed up on its RS chart in April 2000 after a Long Tail Down. This was the first sign that changes were afoot for this defense contractor. Not too long after the RS reversal, LMT changed its overall trend to positive (in August 2000), and from then on it was "no looking back." But it wasn't until August 2002 that LMT gave a formal RS buy signal on its RS chart after having retraced the entire Long Tail Down of O's. The performance of LMT from April 2000 to August 2002 was staggering—the stock posted a gain of 185 percent while the market was down 20 percent. There were other such occurrences of this type of action in 2000. Stocks such as FMC Corporation (FMC), Emerson Electric (EMR), and Duke Energy (DUK) all reversed up (into X's) on their RS charts in late 1999 or early 2000, hinting that the NYSE type names were ready to move after having been overshadowed by technology stocks. These three stocks were up 40 to 50 percent each at the end of 2000. Not bad, considering what a tough year 2000 was.

With respect to RS changes in column to O's, you want to look at it exactly opposite as laid out in the preceding two paragraphs.

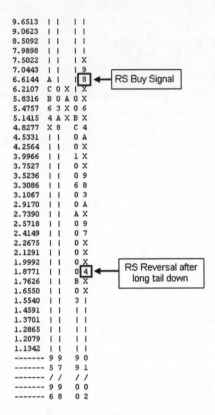

Figure 4.6 Lockheed Martin: RS reversal after Long Tail Down.

As mentioned before, overall weak RS stocks that reverse back to O's are dangerous, and in most cases should be avoided, or potentially shorted.

Strong RS stocks that reverse to O's suggest lower prices or possibly a period of consolidation for the stock, a breather if you will. At such time, positions in that stock could be lightened up, or possibly hedged by selling calls against the stock. This is especially something to note if the reversal to O's occurs after a long column of X's up, Apple Computer (AAPL) is a recent instance of this, which can be seen in Figure 4.7. AAPL's RS chart had shown dramatic outperformance for a couple of years, spiking up 29 straight boxes. But then in February 2006, the RS chart reversed

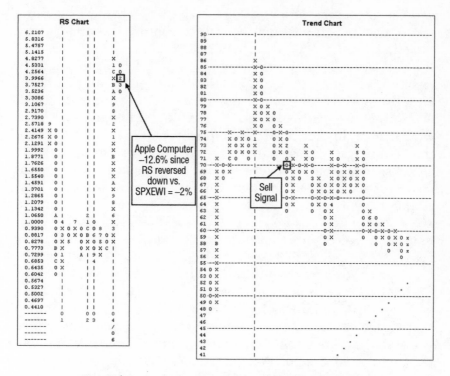

Figure 4.7   Apple Computer: RS reversal after Long Column Up.

to O's, suggesting the stock was starting to underperform the market; and that AAPL was going to take a breather after having been one of the best performing stocks in the S&P 500. While trying to catch its breath, AAPL so far has fallen 12.6 percent since the RS reversal to O's, while the SPXEWI has only dropped 2 percent.

Coming Full Circle with Relative Strength

In finishing our discussion on RS of a stock versus the market, we want to leave you with one last example, one that we believe is a textbook example of using RS with overall trend analysis. In other words, XM Satellite (XMSR) provides a great visual for how you can use both "absolute" and "relative" technical measurements together to position yourself to capture those large winning trades.

XMSR displays the importance of monitoring changes in trend, along with changes in relative strength—not only for entry in to a position, but also with respect to your exit. XMSR was a stock we featured in our "Daily Equity Report" on February 21, 2003. In that report, we brought to our clients' attention that XMSR had just recently violated its long-term Bearish Resistance Line; that its overall trend had changed back to positive after years of being in a downtrend. To boot, we wrote that XMSR had just given an RS buy signal in January, a month prior. Putting these two important factors together, we recommended to our clients that they buy XMSR. Over the next three years, XMSR gained 543 percent, dwarfing the SPXEWI's attractive gains of 69 percent. But things change, and you must watch for the evidence of change. As much as XMSR screamed that a positive turnaround was in the offing in early 2003, it shouted that things were likely to unravel in early 2006. After three years of being a positively trending, strong RS name, XMSR violated its Bullish Support Line in January 2006, thereby changing its overall trend to negative. The RS chart followed suit, giving an RS sell signal in the same month. XMSR was "tuning out" and was likely to underperform the market given these negative technical developments. XMSR promptly fell 49 percent compared to the market slipping a mere 3 percent. As with life, and the stock market, what goes around, comes around. Therefore, it is imperative to adapt to changes in such things as trend and RS (see Figure 4.8).

Examples of Peer Relative Strength Changes for Stocks

The evaluation and interpretation of the Peer RS chart is the same as the stock's RS chart versus the market. Similarly, we are interested in the most recent signal on the Peer RS chart, and current column the chart is in, be it X's or O's. Here, as well, the best combination for a Peer RS chart is to be on a buy signal and in a column of X's. Since Peer RS measures how a stock is doing relative

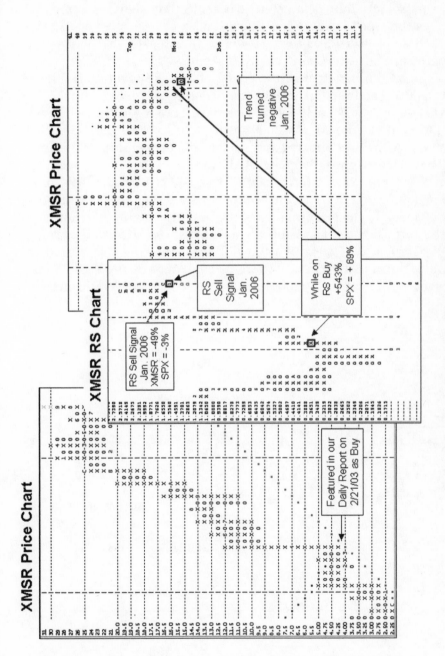

Figure 4.8 XM Satellite: Coming Full Circle with Relative Strength.

127

to its sector siblings, a positive Peer RS (buy signal) reading implies the stock is outperforming an index of its related peers. The purpose of Peer RS is to steer you to the stock(s) that will likely perform the best within any given sector.

A good illustration of the power of Peer RS involves Halliburton (HAL) and the Oil Service sector. As Figure 4.9 exhibits, HAL was on a Peer RS sell signal versus the DWA Oil Service Index (DWAOILS) from March 2000 until October 2002. This implied that HAL would underperform its sector peers during this time. That is exactly what we saw. HAL was down 59 percent over this two-and-half year stretch while the DWAOILS Index was only down 8.2 percent. As these numbers would suggest, Peer RS does not speak to the performance of the underlying group, but only to the performance of the underlying stocks compared to the group. By October 2002, Halliburton did an about-face and started to outperform its Oil Service peers, as evidenced by the Peer RS buy signal on October 21, 2002. After a period of underperformance,

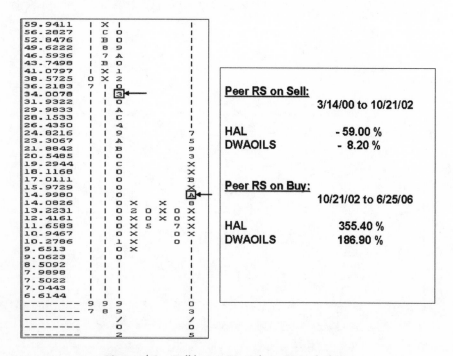

Figure 4.9   Halliburton Peer Relative Strength chart.

this change in signal now implied that HAL was ready to be one of the leaders of the group. The numbers confirm this—as of June 2006, HAL is up 355.4 percent while the DWA Oil Service Index is up a very respectable 187 percent. In sum, HAL is up almost twice that of the average Oil Service stock!

To take it a step further, let's look at the impact of not paying attention to Peer RS with respect to your stock selection. For this we will once again use the Oil Service sector. Toward the end of 2002, the Energy related sectors were showing clear signs of taking a leadership role. It was an area of the market that we recommend to our clients, suggesting they gain exposure. One such stock that presented itself as a viable candidate for purchase was Halliburton (HAL) for reasons mentioned earlier. But some may have said, "it doesn't matter what stock I buy in Oil Service." Well, it does matter as Figure 4.10 concludes. Let's hypothetically say that on a fundamental basis you had narrowed your OILS selection down to two names—Halliburton (HAL) and Tidewater (TDW). From there you may have said, "flip a coin" to decide which one to buy. That would have been a very bad decision. Instead, a glance at the Peer RS charts would have provided all the information you would have needed to make the final decision as to what stock to buy. In October 2002, HAL had given a Peer RS buy signal while TDW remained on a Peer RS sell signal (and in O's). This alone suggested TDW was and would continue to underperform its fellow OILS members, and that HAL was likely to continue to outperform. Through June 2006, these same Peer RS signals remained in force with HAL up 355 percent compared to TDW posting a gain of 63.3 percent. During this same period of October 2002 to June 2006, the DWA Oil Service Index was up 187 percent and the S&P 500 Equal Weighted Index was up 78 percent. So you see, it did matter which OILS stock you selected. HAL was up more than five times that of TDW. This is a simple example of how you can potentially choose the right sector to play, but not necessarily the right stock. Peer RS endeavors to guide you to the best in class, in this case to HAL rather than TDW. A good general rule, then, is to focus your buying on those stocks that have positive RS versus both the market and their peers. This will greatly help in narrowing the list of potential buy candidates down to a reasonable number. This points to the fact

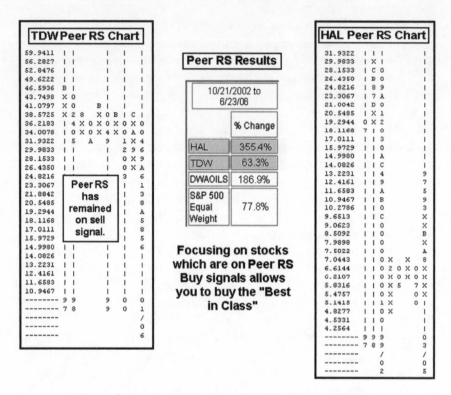

Figure 4.10   Peer Relative Strength: Halliburton versus Tidewater.

of what we are trying to do, in general, in this book. We're taking the fire hose of information investors are barraged with each day and rendering it down to the trickle of a garden hose. That's really the whole ballgame.

Peer RS becomes extremely beneficial when a sector rotates back into favor, as the example demonstrated. We all know that sectors rotate in and out of season just as vegetables and fruits do in the grocery store. Therefore, to achieve consistent returns over time, it is crucial to maneuver in and out of sectors as the indicators dictate. Can you imagine how well a clothing store would do all year if they didn't change their inventory to reflect the current or upcoming season? (We have numerous sector evaluation tools at our disposal to help guide us to the right sector(s) at the right time; we discuss these in more detail later.)

The Peer RS chart is quite valuable in this maneuvering process, specifically when it comes down to actually selecting the stock(s) you want to play within that sector. By identifying the stocks within the sector that are outperforming their peers, you are able to find the strongest of the group—and they are the ones most likely to perform the best as the sector strengthens. The Search/Sort function on our online database is extremely effective in handling this task. We have a favorite search that we conduct when trying to find the best stocks in a sector that has rotated back into favor. Let's assume that the Metals Nonferrous sector has just moved back into favor, and therefore is a sector that we want to gain exposure to; the search criteria would go as follows:

- All stocks that are on an RS buy signal versus the market, but allow for the most recent column to be either X's or O's.
- All stocks whose Peer RS chart is on a buy signal and in a column of X's.
- All stocks that are members of the Metals Nonferrous sector that are in a positive trend, trading above their Bullish Support Line.

The results of the query would give us a list of Metals Nonferrous stocks that have been outperforming the market over the longer term (denoted by the RS buy signal versus the market). With respect to the sector, we chose to have the stocks displayed to be on RS buy signals and in X's suggesting outperformance within their peer group on both a short-term and long-term basis (denoted by Peer RS buy signal and in X's reading). Last, only those stocks in a positive trend, showing absolute price appreciation over time would have made the cut, in addition to having met the strict RS requirements. This list of candidates could be narrowed down further by requiring the stocks to be fundamentally sound. With a couple of clicks of the mouse, this query would allow us to reduce the number of potential buy candidates down to a very reasonable number. A further technical review could then be administered to decide which stock(s) should be bought from this list. This process would pinpoint those stocks within the sector with the best RS, and as you have learned, it is these stocks that will likely lead the sector up as it strengthens.

Had you administered such a Search/Sort back in early 2003 when Metals Nonferrous was moving back into favor, Phelps Dodge (PD) would have made your final cut as a buy candidate. Yet, the venerable Alcoa (AA) would not have made the list. Although most investors may have felt better emotionally going with the well-known AA, it would have been a very bad decision. To this day, AA remains on a Peer RS sell signal, while PD continues to be on a Peer RS buy signal (given in late February 2003). Since that time, PD is up 374 percent while AA is only up 47 percent; and the DWA Metals Non-Ferrous Index (DWAMETA) is up 172 percent while the SPXEWI is up 82 percent. Phelps Dodge has been the leader and Alcoa has been the laggard, just as the RS implied.

Another application of Peer RS involves sector divergence. If you have representation in a particular sector, there may be times you should swap out of one name and into another because of a Peer RS change. Using the previous example, let's say you owned Alcoa (AA) in the Metals Nonferrous sector, and this sector continues to be an area where you want exposure. AA then gives a sell signal on its Peer RS chart, and the technical picture in general has deteriorated. One strategy would be to swap out of the Alcoa into a stock with positive Peer RS, such as Phelps Dodge (PD). This allows you to have sector representation in Metals Nonferrous, but realigns the token position to one with better Peer RS, which by definition has a better likelihood of outperforming the discarded Alcoa (see Figure 4.11).

As the Alcoa-Phelps Dodge example would suggest, emotional attachment to a stock because of its name or any other reason, can be detrimental to the overall portfolio's health, and ultimately can be a big drag on performance. This is why technical analysis, and in particular relative strength, is so powerful and unbiased—it concisely quantifies outperformance or underperformance. When a security moves into a laggard, underperforming position, you need to unemotionally detach yourself from it; sell it to make room for the leaders, such as PD in this example.

```
         PD Peer RS Chart                          AA Peer RS Chart
43.7498  |   |   | |       |   |   |      56.2827  |       |   |   |
41.0797  |   |   | |       |   |   |      52.8476  |       |   |   |
38.5725  |   |   | |       |   |   |      49.6222  |       |   |   |
36.2183  |   |   | |       |   |   |      46.5936  |       |   |   |
34.0078  |   |   | |       |   |   A      43.7498  |       B   |   |
31.9322  |   |   | |       |   |   X      41.0797  |       A   0
29.9833  |   | X | |       |   |   X      38.5725  |       X   0
28.1533  0 4 | C 0 |       |   |   X      36.2183  2   0   X   4
26.4350  0 X 0 B 0 |       |   2   9      34.0078  X   0   C   0
24.8216  1 X 0 A 1 |       |   1 0 X      31.9322  X   0   A   6
23.3067  0   8 X 2 |     A 0 X            29.9833  C   9   X   0
21.8842  |   6 X 3 |     X 5 |            28.1533  X   0   X   7
20.5485  |   0   0 2       X   8 |        26.4350  X   0   |   9
19.2944  |   | 5 B 0 7   2 0 X |          24.8216  4       |   0
18.1168  |   | 7 X 0 X 0 1 0 X |          23.3067  2       |   1
17.0111  |   | 9 X 4 X 0 X 5 | |          21.8842  1       |   5
15.9729  |   | A | 5   9 X | |            20.5485  X       |   7
14.9980  |   | | | A |   | |              19.2944  X       |   9
14.0826  |   | | |   | | |                18.1168  |       |   1
13.2231  |   | | |   | | |                17.0111  |       |   0
12.4161  |   | | |   | | |                15.9729  |       |   7
11.6583  |   | | |   | | |                14.9980  |       |   8
10.9467  |   | | |   | | |                14.0826  |       |   9
-------- 9   0   0 0     0 0 0            13.2231  |       |   0
-------- 8   0   1 2     3 4 5            12.4161  |       |   |
                                         11.6583  |       |   |
                                         10.9467  |       |   |
                                         10.2786  |       |   |
                                         9.6513   |       |   |
                                         -------  9       0   0
                                         -------  8       1   2
 Performance since PD Peers RS Buy from 2/27/2003 to 6/23/2006:   /       /
 PD = + 374%            SPX       = + 82%                         0       0
 AA = + 47%             DWAMETA = + 172%                          0       5
```

Figure 4.11   Peer Relative Strength: Phelps Dodge versus Alcoa.

Putting It All Together with Technical Attributes

Over the course of this chapter we have tried to impress upon you the importance of RS. As presented so far, we use two basic RS calculations for stocks. To that end, you have learned the definition and how to calculate and interpret these RS charts. Of course, the significance of each RS measurement by itself is notable, as you have seen from the previous examples; but the real power lies in bringing this information together in a succinct manner. Therefore, to facilitate a more concise representation of a stock's technical aspects, which includes RS, we developed what we call our "Positive Technical Attributes" reading. This, in essence, provides a summary of what you have learned so far, and provides a way to easily rank stocks on a technical basis.

DWA's Positive Technical Attributes reading (for a specific stock) is comprised of five criteria, yet there is a heavy emphasis on Relative Strength. They are as follows:

Positive Technical Attributes

1. A stock's RS signal versus the market (on buy signal)
2. A stock's RS column versus the market (in X's)
3. A stock's RS signal versus the peer group (on buy signal)
4. A stock's RS column versus the peer group (in X's)
5. Overall trend of a stock (Is it trading above the Bullish Support Line?)

There are five possible positive technical attributes a stock can have, as listed above. Strong stocks have at least three out of five of the criteria positive, and this is where your buying should be focused. Conversely, weak stocks, and typically ones to avoid, are those that have a Positive Technical Attribute reading of 0, 1, or 2 out of 5 (positive). In other words, strong stocks are those that are trending higher with superior RS; while weak stocks are typically those in a negative trend with poor RS. There are three charts to consult when determining what the Technical Attribute reading is for a stock—the Trend chart of the stock, the RS chart of the stock versus the market (SPXEWI), and the RS chart of the stock versus its peers (DWA Sector Index). As the list lays out, four of the five possible technical attributes are RS based—two are longer term in nature, dealing with the RS signals, and two are shorter-term based, dealing with the RS columns. In sum, the Positive Technical Attribute reading merely provides a quick, easy way to summarize the strength of a stock versus the market and the sector, in both an absolute and relative manner.

Although our DWA charting database provides the Positive Technical Attribute reading of each stock for you, an example of how the reading is arrived at may be helpful. For this we will return to Halliburton (HAL) because it affords an excellent illustration of how the Positive Technical Attribute reading can change, and how to arrive at what the reading is. As mentioned, we need to analyze three different charts to ascertain what the Positive Technical Attribute reading is for HAL, as shown in Figure 4.12. As this series of charts displays, HAL experienced

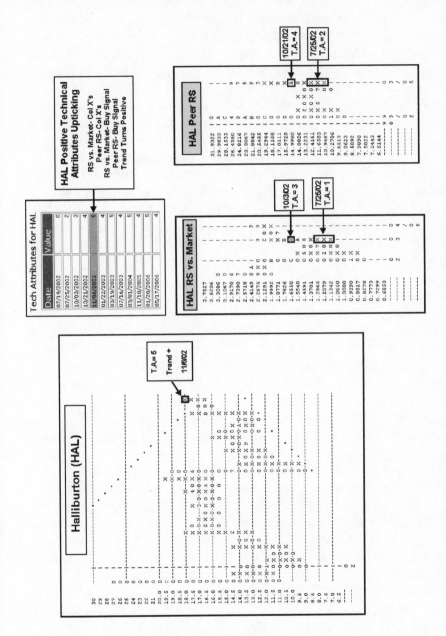

Figure 4.12 High Positive Technical Attribute Reading: Halliburton.

an orderly march from being a technically weak stock to becoming a technically sound stock, and therefore one to consider for purchase in order to gain Oil Service exposure in late 2002. Over the course of roughly four months, Halliburton upticked from a 0 for 5 status to a 5 for 5'er, which is the best reading a stock can have with respect to Positive Technical Attributes. The first improvement, not surprisingly, came from the shorter-term RS measurements—the column reading on both the Market RS and Peer RS charts. These two RS charts both reversed up into a column of X's on July 25, 2002, showing that HAL was starting to outperform both the market (SPXEWI) and the DWA Oil Service Index (DWAOILS) in the short term. This caused the Positive Technical Attribute reading to uptick to a 2 for 5 reading. By early October, Halliburton's RS chart versus the market gave a buy signal, causing the attributes to uptick further, to a 3 for 5 status. Shortly after that, on October 21, 2002, the Peer RS chart for HAL gave a buy signal, moving the Technical Attribute reading up to 4. In other words, within a few months HAL vastly improved on a relative basis, both short term and longer term and moved into a condition of outperformance. Within a couple of weeks (November 6, 2002), Halliburton penetrated its Bearish Resistance Line, thereby changing its overall trend to positive, and by doing so caused the Technical Attributes to once more uptick, to a 5 for 5 reading.

When we initially started this discussion on Technical Attributes, we stated that you should relegate your buying to those stocks whose Technical Attribute reading is 3, 4, or 5 for 5. But we do want to add a general rule of thumb to that statement— focus your buying on those stocks that are a 3, 4, or 5 for 5'ers AND are in an overall positive trend. The trend component assures that you are seeing, over time, absolute price appreciation, too. So in the case of HAL, strictly speaking, you would not have considered the stock for purchase until November 6, 2002, when the trend turned positive. Even still, the returns henceforth for HAL are dramatic, showing how robust the Technical Attribute ranking system can be. In sum, HAL stayed in an overall uptrend, with either a 4 or 5 (for 5) Technical Attribute reading from November 2002 until May 2006. During this time, the stock posted an extraordinary gain of 311 percent while the average Oil Service stock gained 194 percent and the market posted a return of 72 percent.

Just as the example of Halliburton shows how important it is to focus your buying on those stocks in a positive trend with a high Positive Technical Attribute reading, it is equally important to avoid (or sell short) those stocks trending negatively with a low Positive Technical Attribute reading (of 2 or lower). A case in point is Wal-Mart (WMT). This blue-chip stock has long been an institutional favorite, and additionally is one that is often found in many investors' portfolios. Throughout the late 1990s, you were rewarded handsomely for owning WMT, and the Technical Attributes supported such a posture. But lately, any long commitment to Wal-Mart has been a losing proposition.

Once again, this is where the Positive Technical Attributes could have been of great help, steering you away from this discount retailer when the indicators suggested it would be an underperformer. In Figure 4.13, the Technical Attributes are listed, chronologically, for Wal-Mart. Notice how on December 2, 2003, WMT's Positive Technical Attributes reading slipped to the unacceptable 2 for 5 level. Said another way, WMT was faltering on an RS basis, and was starting to trend negatively, and therefore was a stock to exit or hedge in some way. For whatever reason, supply had taken control of this stock—Wal-Mart had become its own "blue-light" special and no one was buying. This lack of demand for WMT's stock has persisted, as the Technical Attributes reading has stayed at either a 0, 1, or 2 for 5 for close to three years now. Translated, WMT has been an unacceptable investment on a technical basis since falling to a 2 in late 2003. The numbers support this stance—WMT has struggled lower by 9.3 percent, while the market (SPXEWI) has forged ahead 30 percent. This is a classic example of the need to separate your love or admiration for a company from an actual investment in the company's stock. The notion of marriage is that we enter into it with the intention of remaining faithful until "death do us part." But a stock is an investment—neither a commitment nor an attachment. A stock should not be held until "death do you part," but rather "until Technical Attributes do you part." I guess this suggests a stock can only be a bridesmaid, never a bride.

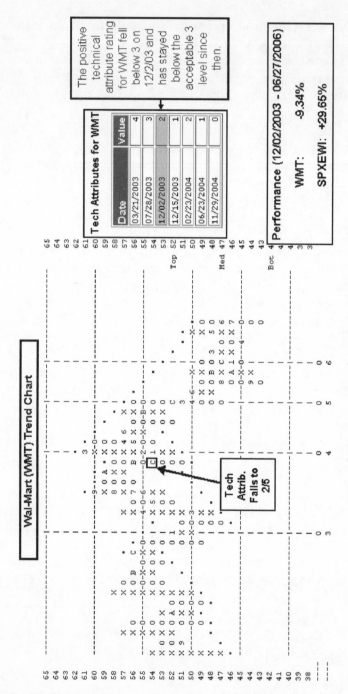

Figure 4.13 Low Positive Technical Attribute Reading: Wal-Mart.

Summary of Relative Strength

We believe RS to be one of the most robust and adaptable tools for analyzing a particular stock. As you have learned in this chapter, RS is a very simple concept and is easily calculated. Clearly though, this does not diminish its effectiveness. Instead, by definition and as the earlier examples attest, RS on a Point and Figure basis succinctly quantifies outperformance and underperformance. Stocks that exhibit positive RS are typically able to navigate the uncertain waters of the stock market much more easily than a stock with negative RS. By staying abreast of changes in Relative Strength, you are guided to new opportunities, while being steered away from danger. This enables you to capture the large winners, or positive outliers. Remember size does matter when it comes to your hard earned money. Of course, not every trade is going to result in outsized gains; in fact, the bulk of trades (such as 80 percent) will produce small gains or small losses, but the key is to avoid the large losing trades. Relative Strength, and more encompassing—Positive Technical Attributes, provide a means for doing just that. Bringing an absolute measurement (Trend), together with RS in a concise ranking or reading, as the Positive Technical Attributes provides, the stock selection process is streamlined, yet without compromise to performance. As said, long positions should be focused on those names that are in a positive trend that carry a 3, 4, or 5 for 5 Positive Technical Attribute reading, while those with a reading of less than 3 should be avoided.

Relative Strength has no bias; it tells you unemotionally what is really happening. By making RS a key component to your stock evaluation, you will increase your odds of success, and that's the best you can hope for. It's as simple as that.

POINTS AND FIGURES BY DORSEY, WRIGHT MONEY MANAGEMENT

Some months it seems like everything goes wrong. Your roof leaks in the rain, your refrigerator blinks out and turns your ice cream sandwiches into a sticky puddle, or your mailbox is filled with recall notices for your family car. It seems like trouble comes in bunches in the stock market too, but how often do things really go wrong?

Columbine Capital did a study on common return factors and their monthly failure rates. They considered a return factor to be a failure if, for that month, the bottom decile in the ranking outperformed the top decile in the ranking. So, for example, if the top dividend yielders had a terrible month while the no-yielders had a great month, the dividend yield factor would be considered a failure for that month. All of these return factors worked over time—this just tells you how often you can expect an out-of-pattern month. The time period studied was rather extensive: 1971 through early 2003 (or from 1990 in the case of estimate-driven factors).

In fact, dividend yield failed as a return factor 49.7 percent of all months. Price/book failed 43.8 percent of the time. Price/cash flow wimped out 38.4 percent of the months. Earnings yield was the best of the value factors and had a 37.4 percent failure rate. Earnings surprise was a little better at 36.9 percent. Among the best factors were estimate revision with only a 31.9 percent failure rate and price momentum—what DWA subscribers would call relative strength—at 27.3 percent. In other words, *of all of the return factors, relative strength is the most reliable,* with nearly three of four months showing strong stocks outperforming weak ones.*

These factors are, of course, primary inputs into our stock selection process at Dorsey, Wright Money Management. We are searching for strong stocks in strong sectors and the return factor failure rates are part of the reason we manage money the way we do. (The technical attribute ranking system, pioneered in Money Management and implemented beautifully by our database guru, Jay, allows you to find the outliers in each sector with ease.) Relative strength is just one more way to stack the odds in your favor. Used alongside risk management, you have a viable method for portfolio management.

---

*Relative strength is often lousy in January, when the "January effect" works in favor of the downtrodden stocks and against those that are relatively strong. Avoid using it at year end.

Chapter 5

ADVANCED RELATIVE STRENGTH CONCEPTS

In the previous chapter, we introduced the concept of Relative Strength (RS)—providing its definition, and a basic interpretation of an RS chart as it pertains to a particular stock. The overriding theme was to demonstrate to you the robustness and adaptability of RS and how this simplistic tool enables you to capture the large winning trades, while helping you to avoid the big losers. As you have learned, RS places you in the venues where out performance exists, while steering you away from areas of underperformance. In this next chapter we will show you how RS can be used in many different applications, not just as it pertains to individual stocks; and that these other applications provide great insights into where best to allocate your investment dollars.

The beauty of RS lies in its lack of complexity—it is merely a simple calculation of division, comparing one security or index to another. Because of this simple equation, the concept of RS can be applied across the entire spectrum of financial products. In essence, anything that has a price associated with it can be used in an RS calculation. Although this sounds so basic, it doesn't diminish its effectiveness in determining outperformance. In sum, RS can help to answer broad asset class allocation questions related to capitalization, style, fixed income, sector rotation, and even international exposure. Equally, RS permits you to pinpoint in a very refined aspect whether Pepsi (PEP) is a better choice over Coca-Cola (KO), taste buds aside; or whether Crude Oil is outperforming Copper. The point is, the power and transferability of RS is endless, and only limited by your imagination.

In the following discussions on the different RS uses, a common thread exists. The calculation, as alluded to earlier, is the same no matter what you are comparing—you just divide one security by the other and multiply by 100. As well, the plotting of the resulting RS reading is done using the same Point and Figure charting principles that were discussed previously, and with a uniform percent scaling method. The end result is the same—you focus your buying on those securities, sectors, indexes, or funds exemplifying the strongest RS, and sell or avoid those vehicles that display the weakest RS.

Sector Relative Strength

We first turn our attention to Sector RS because of its importance in the investment process. As you will learn throughout this text, it is our belief that sector rotation is the key to your overall success in the financial markets; an oft-referred study by Benjamin F. King (while at the University of Chicago) summarizes our reason for this posture:

> "Of a stock's move, 31 percent can be attributed to the general stock market, 12 percent to the industry influence, 36 percent to the influence of other groupings, and the remaining 20 percent is peculiar to the one stock."

In sum, 80 percent of the risk in any given stock is attributable to the market and sector risk, while only 20 percent is due to the actual stock itself; and, the majority of the 80 percent risk is due to sector influences. Not surprisingly, this is where Sector RS comes into the mix. It is a given, based on studies such as the one referred to earlier, that determining which sectors are in "season," or are in demand, is imperative. So what better way to establish this than with RS? Recall its definition: a way to quantify outperformance and underperformance. It stands to reason, then, that one of the very best instruments you can have at your disposal to help navigate the equity market is Sector RS. In essence, it is a tool that very easily helps you to analyze the greatest contributor to price fluctuation in a stock—sector risk.

The Sector RS reading measures how a particular sector is performing compared with the market in general. For example, Sector RS would measure how the Retail sector is performing versus the market. As suggested earlier, this allows you to ascertain which sectors are outperforming the market, while seeing which ones are "out of season," or underperforming the market.

Sector Relative Strength Calculation

The Sector RS calculation is the same as those previously discussed. Daily, using the closing prices, each DWA Sector Index is divided by the S&P 500 Equal-Weighted Index (SPXEWI), then multiplied by 100. The resulting readings are then plotted on each sector's respective RS chart. Recall that our DWA Sector Indexes were created for each broad industry group we follow. These DWA Sector Indexes are equal-weighted and include a nice mix of stocks with varying capitalization, unlike the exchange sector indexes, which tend to be more narrow and capitalization-weighted. An RS reading can be determined for an exchange sector index, such as the S&P Retail Index (RLX), and this is something we provide on our web site. But you must remember that in most cases, these exchange sector indexes are capitalization-weighted, and therefore their price is pushed around by only a few names. For example, with the RLX, Wal-Mart, Target, and Home Depot account for approximately 50 percent of the index's price movement.

Relative Strength of a DWA Sector Index versus the Market

$$\text{Sector RS Reading} = \frac{\text{DWA Sector Index}}{\text{S\&P 500 Equal Weighted Index}} \times 100$$

This calculation uses closing prices and is done on a daily basis. For example, we will calculate the Sector RS reading for two indexes, the DWA Retail Index and the DWA Drug Index.

DWA Retail Index is at 451 and the SPXEWI is at 1713:

$$\frac{451}{1713} \times 100 = 26.33 \text{ RS Reading}$$

DWA Drug Index is at 380 and the SPXEWI is at 1713:

$$\frac{380}{1713} \times 100 = 22.18 \text{ RS Reading}$$

DWA Retail Index has now risen to 473 and the SPXEWI is now at 1733:

$$\frac{473}{1733} \times 100 = 27.29 \text{ RS Reading}$$

DWA Drug Index has moved up to 383 and the SPXEWI is now at 1733:

$$\frac{383}{1733} \times 100 = 22.10 \text{ RS Reading}$$

In this comparative example, both of these sector indexes moved higher in price along with the market, but only the DWA Retail Index improved on an RS basis. Said another way, the DWA Retail Index outperformed the market, while the DWA Drug Index slightly underperformed the market. Groups that are exhibiting positive Sector RS versus the market are the ones to gravitate to when you're deciding which sectors to buy.

Sector Relative Strength Interpretation

When interpreting the Sector RS chart, the process is basically the same as outlined previously. In like fashion, we are concerned with the most recent signal on the RS chart, and the most recent column the RS chart is in. Given that Sector RS measures how a particular sector is performing compared with the overall market and that sector risk is the greatest contributor to price fluctuation in a stock, it is imperative to evaluate this on an ongoing basis. (We can't emphasize this point enough.) Those sectors exhibiting positive RS versus the market are the ones to focus on for new buying. Sector RS buy signals are given when a column of X's exceeds a previous column of X's. But of equal importance for Sector RS is what the most recent column is on the RS chart. This is the one slight difference in RS evaluation (compared with a stock's Market RS or Peer RS). When a sector index reverses up into a column of X's on its RS chart, we consider that to be a buy signal. Utmost attention is paid to column changes for Sector RS, because such a reversal will often be the beginning signs of a significant switch in sponsorship for the particular sector. We still regard the best reading for the Sector RS chart as being on a buy signal and in a column of X's, yet recommend exposure to a group if its RS chart is in a column of X's.

Probably the most valuable aspect of Sector RS is that it not only steers you to the sector(s) moving into favor, but keeps you invested in sectors that are market leaders, even if the sector(s) is considered overbought by other measures. To provide you with a little company history, this is one of the main reasons why we first started charting Sector RS. In 1996 to 1997, the best-performing sector was the Bank/Financial group. This sector had performed very well in 1995, after bottoming out in fairly oversold territory. The group raced to an extremely overbought condition, as measured by the sector Bullish Percent chart (which you will learn about in an upcoming chapter) by October 1995. Member stocks, such as Citigroup and Chase Manhattan recorded phenomenal gains during this time. Citigroup posted a 70 percent gain, while Chase Manhattan gained a remarkable 100 percent. But the upmove didn't stop there. Both Chase and Citigroup doubled in price during the 1996 to 1997 time frame. This is about the time when Sector RS became an integral part of our technical research.

We became less enthused with the Bank sector in late 1995 because, as stated, the group was overbought. Our cautious approach to new recommendations in the group was, in hindsight, a mistake. But as we always endeavor to do, we learned from our mistake and developed our Sector RS charts. In assessing the Sector RS for the Bank sector, we realized that the group had been outperforming the market, hands down! The Bank group sneakily ascended to top dog status despite being in the believed shadow of Technology stocks. The lesson here—simple mathematics, in the form of division, can quantify and pinpoint outperformance if you are willing to delve below the market's surface and evaluate the group's RS chart. In application, move to those sectors rotating into favor, stay with those sectors that continue to exhibit positive RS, and avoid those groups that turn negative on their Sector RS charts (reverse to O's or break a previous bottom). Bottom line, if you hope to outperform the market, you had better be invested in those sectors with the best RS.

Examples of Sector Relative Strength Changes

To display the sheer power of Sector RS, let's take a look at a couple of examples. To do so, we will return to two groups mentioned in the previous chapter—Telecom and Building. You will recall from that stock-specific discussion that AT&T (T) gave an RS sell signal in May 2000, along with the fallen angel, WorldCom. In other words, cracks were starting to appear in the cement with respect to Telecom and Technology after what had been an unprecedented, parabolic upmove in these stocks and sectors. But what is so amazing is how the Telecom Sector RS chart quantified all this information, telling you that not only were there cracks in the cement, but that the whole house was starting to crumble and collapse.

As Figure 5.1 reveals, the DWA Telecom Sector Index gave an RS sell signal in April 2000, when it reversed into a column of O's. But prior to that, this RS chart was in a column of X's from January 1998 until April 2000. In other words, the RS chart supported a bullish, overweighted posture with respect to the Telecom sector, all while the group was rocketing into the stratosphere. Yet before returning to earth, the RS chart warned you and told you to "get out"; to underweight or avoid the Telecom sector. Be it an individual stock, or an entire sector, notice how

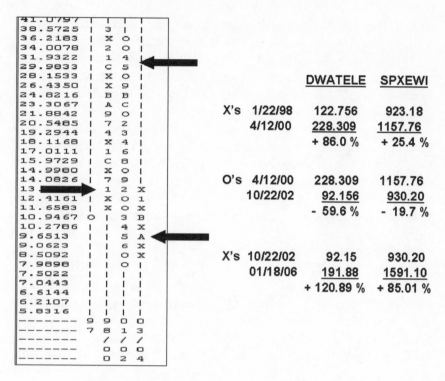

Figure 5.1   Sector RS: DWA Telecom Sector versus SPXEWI.

the RS chart positioned you to capture the large winner—indicating that Telecom was an area of outperformance from 1998 to 2000. The returns speak for themselves; the average Telecom stock, as measured by the DWA Telecom Index, posted a gain of 86 percent while in a column of X's, against a market return of 25.4 percent.

Conversely, when in O's, suggesting underperformance, the RS chart steered your focus elsewhere allowing you to avoid a loss of 59.6 percent for Telecom. Sector RS, therefore, provides a very important piece of information in the decision-making process. While in X's, you look to buy the best stocks within that sector— those with the high technical attribute reading that are in an up-trend, for example. But when in O's, you are avoiding the group, and concentrating on stocks in other sectors. Not only are AT&T and WCOM noteworthy examples of this, but it was evident across the group. We had mentioned that T basically doubled while on an RS buy signal in the late 1990s. But what about Nortel (NT) and Corning (GLW), two other very popular names during the Technology bubble? GLW was up an astounding 236 percent while on an RS buy signal during the 1998–2000 period, yet fell a mind-boggling 98 percent after giving an RS sell signal in 2000. Same story with Nortel; NT gained a very respectable 137 percent in the tech heyday, but then collapsed after its 2000 RS sell signal, dropping 97 percent. In sum, the carnage on a stock-specific basis continued from 2000 until the October 2002 bottom, yet the Telecom Sector RS chart forewarned us very early on that there had been a change in season—summer had turned to winter for Telecom.

But as the saying goes, "out with the old and in with the new." In 2000 to 2001, "new" literally meant the New York Stock Exchange-type stocks. Sectors such as Healthcare, Financials, Food and Beverage, and Building took the lead and assumed the role of outperformance in the market. Once again, the Sector RS charts were able to broadly summarize this change in leadership, guiding those willing to look into "new" sector opportunities. One such glaring, but much overlooked opportunity was in the Building sector.

We spoke of the RS improvement that we witnessed on an individual basis with respect to such stocks as Lennar (LEN), Toll Brothers (TOL) and Ryland Homes (RYL)—all members of the once-boring Building sector. Once again, though, the Sector RS chart provided a telltale sign that a positive change was afoot. The DWA Building Sector RS chart reversed up into a column of X's on January 10, 2001, revealing to us that this group had become an area of outperformance, and therefore was one to have long exposure. The Sector RS once again, in dispassionate fashion, told us and you the investor, when it was time to tactically maneuver into a "new" sweet spot in the market. The Building Sector RS chart remains in X's, and since giving the buy signal in January 2001, has registered a substantial gain of +155.5 percent compared to the SPXEWI gaining 39 percent, and a worst performance of –14 percent by the Nasdaq Composite (see Figure 5.2).

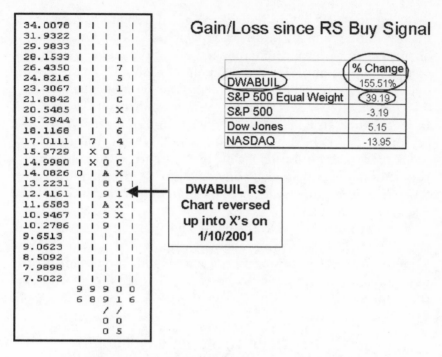

Figure 5.2   Sector RS: DWA Building Sector versus SPXEWI.

Sector Relative Strength Applied to Exchange Traded Funds

In short, Sector RS enables you to pinpoint those groups that deserve your investment dollars. One obvious course of action is to buy the stock(s) in a strong RS sector, which themselves possess positive RS versus the market and their peers. But due to the vast expansion in sector products via the Exchange Traded Funds (ETFs) there are now many ways to garner sector exposure, without having to buy index options to do so. Instead, Sector RS can be applied to a tradeable vehicle that represents an underlying sector index—you get a basket of stocks in a given sector with a single ETF purchase. This allows you to avoid single-stock risk, while also providing instant diversification in one simple transaction. A caveat to this strategy is the "weighting" issue. As mentioned early on, our DWA sector indexes are equal weighted, whereas the majority of ETFs are capitalization-weighted. Therefore, a couple of stocks can be responsible for the bulk of the move in an index, so it pays to be aware of the make-up of each ETF before buying one. We will cover ETFs in more detail in a later chapter.

One way to use Sector RS in conjunction with ETFs would be to merely buy an ETF based on the reading of a particular DWA Sector RS chart. In other words, if the DWA Healthcare Sector Index was in a column of X's on its RS chart, rather than buy a couple of individual stocks, you could buy a corresponding sector ETF, such as iShares Healthcare (IYH) or any of the other related ETFs now available.

Or why not just cut to the chase and analyze the actual RS of the ETF itself. If you think about it, this would provide a more "apples to apples" comparison—you would be measuring the exact RS of the vehicle that you are considering for purchase. And that is exactly what we do.

Sector ETF Relative Strength Calculation and Interpretation

On a daily basis, we calculate and plot RS readings for every ETF that trades. The calculation mirrors that of Sector RS on the DWA Sector Indexes, with one minor exception. Instead of having the S&P 500 Equal Weighted Index (SPXEWI) as the divisor, we use the Dow Jones Total Market Index that trades as an ETF itself under the symbol IYY. This benchmark is used as the divisor because it is capitalization-weighted and its approximately 1,600 members cut across large, mid and small-cap in asset class. In other words, it tends to reflect how the majority of ETFs are comprised. As a sidebar, there are new equal-weighted sector ETFs just being rolled out by State Street Global Advisors as I write this book. So when analyzing their relative strength, you may find it more useful to use the equal-weighted SPXEWI as the yardstick for the market.

In interpreting a Sector ETF RS chart, it is exactly the same as what we laid out with DWA Sector RS—you pay most attention to the current column the RS chart is in. As with a stock's RS reading, or a DWA Sector RS reading, the ETF's suggestion/posture of outperformance or underperformance can last for years on end. For example, the iShares Dow Jones Real Estate Sector Fund (IYR) has been in a column of X's, implying you should have long exposure to the sector, since May 2000—for over six years. In fact, the average stay in a column for an ETF RS chart is 500 days. In essence, it is an indicator that similarly allows you to verify, in a succinct manner, the long-term trend of a sector ETF. In sum, when the sector ETF RS chart is in X's, it represents demand for the sector relative to the market, or it is an area of outperformance. On the contrary, when the sector ETF RS chart is in a column of O's, it represents supply is in control of that sector relative to the broad market, or that it is underperforming and therefore one to avoid or underweight.

Examples of Sector ETF Relative Strength

There have been a couple of notable themes encompassing the financial markets over the past few years, namely Real Estate and Energy. Everyone has tried to call a top in the Real Estate market for years, yet as mentioned earlier, the RS chart for the IYR has been in X's for over six years, and has suggested exposure to that area of the market, and will so for as long as it stays in X's. When it changes to O's that is when you would want to back off with respect to investment in Real Estate, at least in using the IYR as the measurement. In essence, when in a column of O's, as it was from October 1995 to May 2000, it suggested there were better opportunities elsewhere. Let's recap the IYR's performance, using RS column changes as the inflection point:

IYR RS Chart in O's from October 1995 to May 2000

Stock	Symbol	Performance (%)
iShares Dow Jones Real Estate Sector Fund	(IYR)	37.17
iShares Dow Jones Total Market Index	(IYY)	141.94
S&P 500 Equal Weighted Index	(SPXEWI)	84.30

IYR RS Chart in X's from May 2000 to Present (July 2006)

Stock	Symbol	Performance (%)
iShares Dow Jones Real Estate Sector Fund	(IYR)	113.84
iShares Dow Jones Total Market Index	(IYY)	–2.17
S&P 500 Equal Weighted Index	(SPXEWI)	53.01

Another popular sector that has caught the public's eye has been Energy, or anything related to it such as Crude Oil, Oil Service, and Coal. But really it has only been in the past couple of years that mainstream media (and most investors) jumped on the energy train with respect to touting this sector as a potential investment gusher. But you guessed it, the RS chart allowed you to "strike oil" much sooner. As Figure 5.3 depicts, the iShares Dow

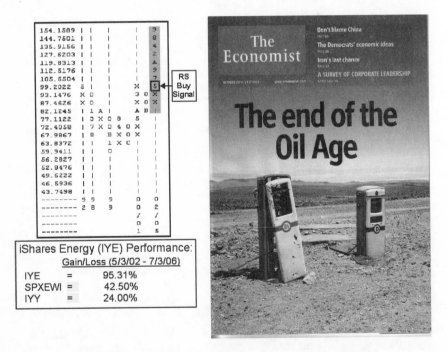

Figure 5.3   ETF Relative Strength: iShares Energy (IYE) versus IYY.

Jones Energy Sector Fund (IYE) reversed up into a column of X's on May 3, 2002, suggesting this sector would outperform the market for some time to come, and that it was a group that investors should commit to on the long side. Those that heeded this signal have been justly rewarded. The IYE, from May 2002 through June 2006, had posted a return of +95.3 percent, dwarfing the IYY's return of +24 percent.

What is all the more interesting, pertaining to Energy, is how mass media tried to sway the average investor out of Energy only a year and half into this positive RS condition. More specifically, *The Economist* magazine came out with a negative cover story on October 25, 2003, entitled "The end of the Oil Age," and depicted a desert condition with two dilapidated gas pumps. Mr. Jones would have seen this bearish cover story, and would have screamed "Get me out of anything related to Crude Oil!" Two and a half years later, the IYE RS chart is still impartially telling you to maintain exposure in the Energy sector (allowing you to capture a big winner), while Mr. Jones is still scratching his head about that magazine article.

Just as a sector ETF's RS chart will point us toward opportunity, as it did with Energy, it can serve to warn us of an impending problem. Such was the case with Technology in 2000. Our RS work identified, on many different levels that the "tech bubble" was bursting. Recall our discussions on AT&T and WCOM, and the DWA Telecom sector. In those instances, the RS charts revealed worrisome technical developments. This same phenomenon was witnessed in the ETF arena, too. In a broader respect, the RS chart of the iShares Dow Jones Technology Sector Fund (IYW) experienced a reversal into a column of O's on April 14, 2000. After having been in X's since September 1998, and what amounted to a monstrous rally, this RS chart was advising us that it was time to depart the broad Technology sector. All told, this was another example of how RS got us out of harms way. Surely, you can now guess what the magazine cover stories were like in April-May 2000. Yep, John Chambers' (CEO of Cisco Systems) picture was plastered all over *Fortune* and *Worth*, counseling you to "buy his stock." Thereafter, Cisco Systems stock price fell precipitously from 75 to 8.50, or roughly 88 percent!

Drilling Down: Subsector Relative Strength

Before leaving the topic of Sector RS, we want to briefly touch on one more aspect of it. In particular, we want to demonstrate to you how you can "drill down" below the surface of a broad sector, such as Energy, to pinpoint specific sub-sector strength. This can be extremely helpful when trying to determine where best to allocate your dollars within a given sector. As we have demonstrated, one way to do this is to merely buy a representative proxy (ETF) for a sector when the RS chart is in X's. Clearly, you would have provided considerable "alpha" to the portfolio had you listened to the Energy RS chart and bought the IYE. But underneath the broad surface of Energy there was a more compelling story.

There are subsectors that comprise each broad industry group, and in the case of Energy there is a subsector known as "Oil Companies—Secondary." Basically, this subgroup is made up of secondary oil companies—those that tend to be relegated to the backseat when compared to their ultra-large-cap siblings such as Exxon Mobil (XOM), Chevron Texaco (CVX) and British Petroleum (BP). All you have to do to see this submissive role is to check out the weightings of any of the broad Energy ETFs. For example, the IYE plays favorites with XOM, CVX; approximately 38 percent of the movement in the IYE is attributable to XOM and CVX. Yet it has been these secondary brothers and sisters that truly deserve the "gold star on the forehead."

Figure 5.4 brings this to light in a way as obvious as the little kid with her hand raised in class saying, "oh, oh pick me, pick me, please"! On February 24, 2003, the DWA DJ Secondary Oil Index reversed up into a column of X's on its RS chart (versus the S&P 500 Equal Weighted Index), advising you that it was best to pick Secondary Oil names such as Valero (VLO), Burlington Resources (BR), Occidental Petroleum (OXY), or Tesoro (TSO) for your Energy exposure. In other words, if you wanted alpha even within a particular group, they were going to give it to you. The returns have been staggering since the RS buy signal pinpointed outperformance in February 2003. For instance, VLO has vaulted 589 percent while TSO has gained a whopping 1295 percent. What makes this story compelling is that during this time the IYE put in a very respectable performance, gaining 145 percent,

```
29.9833  |  |        |        |
28.1533  |  |        |        |
26.4350  |  |        |        7
24.8216  |  |        |        1
23.3067  |  |        |        9
21.8842  |  |        |        8
20.5485  |  |        |        7
19.2944  |  |        |        6
18.1168  |  |        |        X
17.0111  |  |        |        2
15.9729  |  |        |        A
14.9980  |  |        |        9
14.0826  |  |        |        7
13.2231  |  |        |        6
12.4161  |  |        A        2
11.6583  |  |        9   O    X
10.9467  |  |        6   O    X
10.2786  |  4       4   B    |
 9.6513  |  A   O   X        |
 9.0623  |  X   O   X        |
 8.5092  |  X   7   |        |
 7.9898  O  |       |        |
 7.5022  |  |       |        |
 7.0443  |  |       |        |
 6.6144  |  |       |        |
 6.2107  |  |       |        |
 5.8316  |  |       n        |
-------     n   n   n        n
-------  O  1   2            3
-------                      /
-------                      O
-------                      6
```

RS for Secondary Oil Companies reversed up February 2003

Another affirmation of the small and mid cap outperformance over large cap; and important information for individual stock selection.

Performance of Secondary Oil Stocks vs. IYE

	02/24/2003 to 07/03/2006		
	Curr Value	$ Change	% Change
VLO	64.85	$57.20	589.34%
COG	46.99	$32.65	198.05%
CHK	29.47	$22.24	261.65%
OXY	103.14	$75.12	254.90%
SUN	67.87	$51.48	295.58%
TSO	71.72	$69.01	1294.75%
IYE	98.37	$57.68	145.36%
XOM	64.90	$28.15	82.79%
CVX	66.38	$30.55	94.85%
BP	71.37	$30.56	76.78%
S&P 500 Equal Weight	1647.14	$806.29	87.95%
S&P 500	1236.20	$447.61	53.76%
Dow Jones	10739.35	$3369.78	42.88%
NASDAQ	2037.35	$868.05	65.64%

Figure 5.4 Subsector RS: DWA Secondary Oil Companies Index versus SPXEWI.

yet XOM, CVX, and BP's returns were in line with the market, as measured by the S&P 500 Equal Weighted Index. The ultra-large-cap sector siblings provided very little with respect to outperformance. Now, you cannot argue that the Energy sector was the place to be, and to that end the IYE provided a fantastic venue for that one-stop shopping exposure. But without a doubt, for those willing to buy individual names, this Secondary Oil Companies subsector RS chart is a prime example of the benefit of "drilling down" in order to itemize specific areas of outperformance.

This particular use of RS can be applied to any subsector or mini-sector, with the calculation and interpretation of the chart being the same as that outlined with Sector Relative Strength. It allows you to find specific niches of strength, and therefore enables you to position yourself in that defined area. It is particularly useful when analyzing the very large broad industry groups such as Consumer Cyclical, Healthcare, Industrial, and Financial. In the case of Consumer Cyclical, for example, the RS has for years suggested that you should invest in the subgroup of Retail—Apparel, while telling you to shun Retail—Broadline. In sum, it would have pushed you toward names such as American Eagle Outfitters (AEOS) and steered you away from the likes of Wal-Mart (WMT). This is just one more arrow to put in your quiver when determining which sectors are in season, and which are not.

Relative Strength Applied to Asset Classes

Sports fans know that the three worst words a batter in baseball can recite to himself upon approaching the plate are "don't strike out." So it should be no surprise that "investing to avoid losing money" will be as hopeless an activity as "batting to avoid striking out." Put in investment terms, people crave safety—yet they desire high returns, so they invest in the stock market anyway. But how? By buying (and often holding) "safe stocks," or at least ones they perceive to be safe, such as General Electric (GE), Coca-Cola (KO), Wal-Mart (WMT), Merck (MRK), Intel (INTC), General Motors (GM), and Microsoft (MSFT). The problem is these stocks, on average, are down 38 percent in the past six years (since the Dow Jones Industrial Average peaked in 2000). The point of all this is, as an investor, you must take whatever returns the market is offering. Over the past six years, it hasn't been with the blue-chip, "safe" large-cap stocks. Instead, it has been elsewhere; and not surprisingly, RS has proven to be a viable tool with respect to asset class allocation, too. Remember, to the extent that you try to seek return where there is none, you create risk. In our opinion, it's actually less risky to go with the flow and follow the returns wherever they may be in the market; over the past six years it has been in the Small Cap segment of the market.

Relative Strength has yet another application—determining which asset class to overweight or emphasize. As alluded to earlier, RS has placed us in the right asset class for many years on end, and in particular has told us to steer our clients toward Small Cap for the past six years. In Figure 5.5 you can see this type of RS at work. In this example, we compare the S&P 600 Small Cap Index (SML) to the S&P 500 (SPX)—or David (small cap) pitted

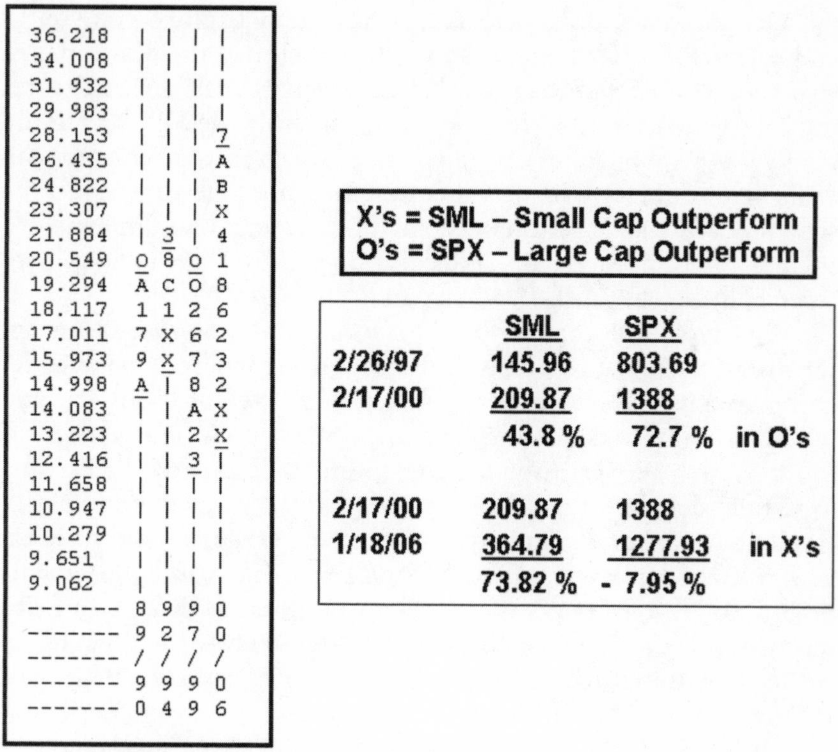

```
36.218   |  |  |  |
34.008   |  |  |  |
31.932   |  |  |  |
29.983   |  |  |  |
28.153   |  |  |  7
26.435   |  |  |  A
24.822   |  |  |  B
23.307   |  |  |  X
21.884   |  3  |  4
20.549   o  8  o  1
19.294   A  C  O  8
18.117   1  1  2  6
17.011   7  X  6  2
15.973   9  X  7  3
14.998   A  |  8  2
14.083   |  |  A  X
13.223   |  |  2  X
12.416   |  |  3  |
11.658   |  |  |  |
10.947   |  |  |  |
10.279   |  |  |  |
 9.651   |  |  |  |
 9.062   |  |  |  |
-------  8  9  9  0
-------  9  2  7  0
-------  /  /  /  /
-------  9  9  9  0
-------  0  4  9  6
```

X's = SML – Small Cap Outperform
O's = SPX – Large Cap Outperform

	SML	SPX	
2/26/97	145.96	803.69	
2/17/00	209.87	1388	
	43.8 %	72.7 %	in O's
2/17/00	209.87	1388	
1/18/06	364.79	1277.93	in X's
	73.82 %	- 7.95 %	

Figure 5.5   Asset Class RS: S&P 600 Small Cap versus S&P 500 Large Cap.

against Goliath (large cap). The calculation here is the same as instructed before, easy division:

$$\frac{\text{SML Price}}{\text{SPX Price}} \times 100 = \text{RS Reading}$$

The interpretation of the chart is similar to that of Sector RS, in that we place most importance on the current column. The investor should overweight Small Cap stocks at the expense of Large Cap stocks when in a column of X's (indicating outperformance), and should underweight Small Cap stocks when the chart is in O's (suggesting underperformance). As you can see, this particular RS chart has been in a column of X's since February 17, 2000—

for over six years. Simply stated, it has unmistakably told you to emphasize Small Cap stocks and to throw stones at Goliath (Large Cap stocks). The returns speak for themselves with the SML gaining 73.8 percent during the past six years while the SPX was in the red by 7.9 percent. Literally, one major switch in your portfolio six years ago would have made a monumental difference in the returns seen since then. Unfortunately, many investors stayed married to their Large Cap, blue-chip stocks, failing to live by the aforementioned phrase of "until RS do us part."

This type of RS can be used for more than just asset class determination. It is also helpful for discovering where to be with respect to style allocation—such as Value versus Growth, and whether or not to equal weight or capitalization weight your portfolio. With the explosion in the number of market ETFs now available, determining these types of RS can be useful and easily implemented. For example, you could put asset class and style together and compare the iShares Small Cap 600 Value (IJS) versus S&P 500 Growth (IVW). An RS chart comparing these two ETFs has instructed you (since November 2000) to favor the IJS. The returns are astounding:

Market ETF	Symbol	Gain/Loss since November 2000 (%)
iShares Small Cap 600 Value	IJS	+ 93.45
S&P 500 Growth	IVW	−22.54

By using RS to "tactically maneuver" within the confines of a traditional strategic asset allocation pie, you put yourself in a position to become a consistent hitter, and even hit an occasional home run, rather than going to the plate hoping you don't strike out!

Before moving on, I want you to take a minute to reflect on what we have discussed so far with respect to RS, and in particular I want you to recall the examples we have used throughout this chapter and the previous one. We talked about how the Technology stocks and related sectors gave RS sell signals in mid 2000, while at the same time the lesser-known Building stocks asserted themselves on an RS basis. We stated that Wal-Mart has been a low technical attribute stock for years, therefore suggesting poor relative strength, while American Eagle Outfitters has been soaring. Secondary Oil Companies have been a force to be reckoned with, while its ultra-large-cap brethren such as Exxon Mobil and Chevron Texaco have pulled up the rear in the Energy sector. The question is, "Do you see a pattern?" Remember the quote we referred to by Yogi Berra: "You can observe a lot just by watching." If you put all the pieces together, it should come as no surprise that Large Cap Growth has been the laggard on an RS basis. Surely the RS charts of the SML compared to the SPX and the IJS versus the IVW summarize this conclusion for you in a visual format, but when you have stocks such as Wal-Mart, Coca-Cola, AT&T, and Intel faltering, it should tell you something. I implore you to step back and "observe" what is going on. By observing, you will know. Therefore, knowing is believing, and believing gives you confidence.

Using Relative Strength to Determine International Exposure

We have all heard the phrase, or have read (to our kids) the book known as *Where's Waldo?* The book appeals to the reader, asking "Have you found Waldo yet?" The reader basically goes on a quest, wondering where in the world is Waldo, trying to determine what new place he has traveled to now. Well, I ask you in investment terms, "Do you know where in the world there is outperformance"? The answer once again lies with RS. Relative Strength can determine what new place should garner your attention with respect to your Global or International exposure.

In keeping with our earlier discussion regarding the standard strategic asset allocation pie, there is typically a slice or portion of the overall portfolio allotted to International. But often, this slice takes a back seat, as many investors just don't know how to go about making decisions dealing with the international markets. The good news is you have an investment map in the form of RS right at your disposal; this will not only tell you "where in the world" to be, but will also let you know if you should be cutting a bigger piece of the International pie (overweighting or underweighting your exposure to the Global markets).

To chart our International course, we use RS in a couple of different ways. First, we can compare the broad overseas markets to the domestic, U.S. market. This will tell us whether or not the overseas markets are exhibiting positive RS compared to the United States; and therefore prompt us to allocate more or less money to the global markets. Once we know whether or not to gain International exposure, we then can use RS to determine which regions or countries actually deserve our investment dollars. In this exercise, we would literally compare one region to another or one country to another—such as Europe versus Latin America or Japan versus China. The calculations, therefore, are the same as those previously learned—you are merely dividing one security by the other, then multiplying by 100.

Got Global? Measuring Overseas versus United States

It has only been recently that investors have gotten an appetite for foreign investment. But if you look at the RS chart of the EAFE Index versus the S&P 500, it would have petitioned you to travel abroad much sooner. The EAFE Index from Morgan Stanley Capital International is designed to measure the overall condition of the overseas markets—Europe, Australia, and Far East. There is an ETF benchmarked to this index, offered by iShares, that trades under the ticker EFA. Figure 5.6 reveals how the EFA has been flying first class for several years now, while the S&P 500 (SPX) has been in the coach seats. This RS chart reversed up into a column of X's on October 3, 2003, stating the EFA was outperforming the domestic market, and therefore deserved your attention, and your dollars. As long as the RS chart remains in X's, it implies you overweight your International equity exposure. Of course, you can merely buy the EFA to accomplish this; and in doing so you would have seized gains more than twice that of the SPX. Since the RS buy signal for the EFA, it has jumped 59.9 percent while the SPX has jet-lagged behind with gains of 23.7 percent. Moreover, just a year after this RS reversal to X's for the EFA, *The Economist* maga-

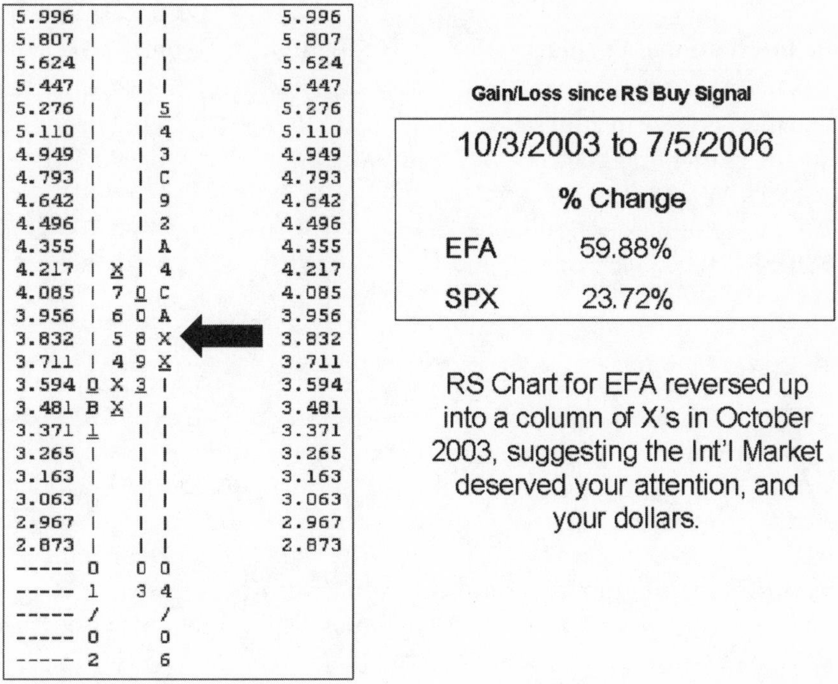

```
5.996 |    |  |          5.996
5.807 |    |  |          5.807
5.624 |    |  |          5.624
5.447 |    |  |          5.447
5.276 |    |  5          5.276
5.110 |    |  4          5.110
4.949 |    |  3          4.949
4.793 |    |  C          4.793
4.642 |    |  9          4.642
4.496 |    |  2          4.496
4.355 |    |  A          4.355
4.217 |  X |  4          4.217
4.085 |  7 0  C          4.085
3.956 |  6 0  A          3.956
3.832 |  5 8  X   ⬅      3.832
3.711 |  4 9  X          3.711
3.594 0 X 3 |           3.594
3.481 B X |  |           3.481
3.371 1    |  |          3.371
3.265 |    |  |          3.265
3.163 |    |  |          3.163
3.063 |    |  |          3.063
2.967 |    |  |          2.967
2.873 |    |  |          2.873
----- 0   0 0
----- 1   3 4
----- /   /
----- 0   0
----- 2   6
```

Gain/Loss since RS Buy Signal

10/3/2003 to 7/5/2006	
% Change	
EFA	59.88%
SPX	23.72%

RS Chart for EFA reversed up into a column of X's in October 2003, suggesting the Int'l Market deserved your attention, and your dollars.

Figure 5.6   Got Global? Measuring Overseas versus United States: EFA versus SPX RS.

zine boldly stated on its cover of October 2, 2004, "Scares Ahead for the World Economy." This provided us with all the more conviction that pulling the passport out and going Global was the right trip to take.

Where in the World to Be?

To delve a little deeper, RS can be very helpful in zeroing in on those areas or countries that are fueling the international economy. In other words, RS can tell us our precise travel itinerary. Granted, the EFA is an excellent and easy way to broadly allocate your global slice of money, but as the table below shows, there is alpha to be grabbed if you are able to pinpoint region or country outperformance:

International Region/Country	Symbol	Gain/Loss since October 2003 (%)
iShares MSCI EAFE Index Fund	EFA	+ 59.88
iShares S&P Latin America 40 Fund	ILF	+172.06
iShares Emerging Markets	EEM	+ 99.23
iShares MSCI Brazil Index Fund	EWZ	+186.40
iShares S&P Europe 350 Index Fund	IEV	+ 62.76
iShares MSCI Japan Index Fund	EWJ	+ 42.98
S&P 500	SPX	+ 23.72

When determining where you should travel to with respect to specific region or country, we use RS, but in a slightly different application. Of course one way to expose specific outperformance would be to compare each region or country to the EAFE Index, similar to evaluating a sector versus the S&P 500 Equal Weighted Index. But another way to establish this type of outperformance is by pitting a region or country against another—Europe versus Latin America, for example. We discuss this topic and its portfolio applications in greater detail in Chapter 10.

As you become skilled at plying the investment waters, you can additionally see how RS can help you to effectively reach distant shores; portfolio management need not be relegated just to U.S. soil. And when asked, "Where's Waldo?" you'll know the answer.

Mutual Funds: The Same Relative Strength Tools Apply

By definition, a mutual fund is an open-ended fund operated by an investment company that invests in a group of assets in accordance with a stated set of objectives. Two of the main benefits of a mutual fund are that it provides diversification and professional money management. The choice of funds available to the investor is staggering, including such types as sector, income, growth, fixed income, blend, tax-free funds, and so on. In many respects, a mutual fund is similar to an ETF, in that both are buying a basket of securities and provide diversification by doing so. But there are a few notable differences: ETFs are unmanaged while mutual funds are managed, yet ETFs are transparent while mutual funds do not readily expose their holdings; and ETFs typically have a lower expense ratio compared to the fees of a mutual fund. Each have their plusses and minuses, but differences aside, the mutual fund industry is still the behemoth in the "fund" marketplace with respect to assets under management, despite the progress seen in the ETF world.

Given this mammoth presence, it is worth spending a few minutes discussing how RS can be used with mutual funds. In a nutshell, the same RS tools you have already learned about can be applied to a mutual fund. The calculation is the same, too, in that you divide one security by the other and multiply by 100. For example, we calculate how a mutual fund is performing versus the market, as measured by the S&P 500 Equal Weighted Index (SPX-EWI). This basically provides you a measurement of outperformance or underperformance along the same lines as Sector RS. We use the SPXEWI instead of the IYY because most mutual funds are closer to being run on an equal-weighted basis, compared to most ETFs, which are skewed by their cap-weighted construction. The interpretation of a mutual fund RS chart is similar in that RS is said to be "positive" if the chart is on a PnF buy signal. But the best RS reading is when the chart is on a buy signal and in a column of X's. One difference in interpretation lies in addressing the volatility of the given fund. Sector funds are typically evaluated using the RS signal, whereas lower volatility broad asset class mutual funds are, as a rule, judged by the most recent RS column.

Mutual Fund Relative Strength Examples

In Figure 5.7, an RS chart of the Fidelity Select Energy Services (FSESX) mutual fund is shown. The applicability of RS is apparent here as well, as evidenced by the performance of FSESX versus the SPXEWI since its RS buy signal in March 2002. This particular fund has vaulted 125.8 percent compared to the S&P 500 Equal Weighted Index (SPXEWI) gaining 35.3 percent, and this return trounces the 9.3 percent gain of the cap-weighted SPX. (Note: The return of the FSESX does include dividends.) Relative Strength

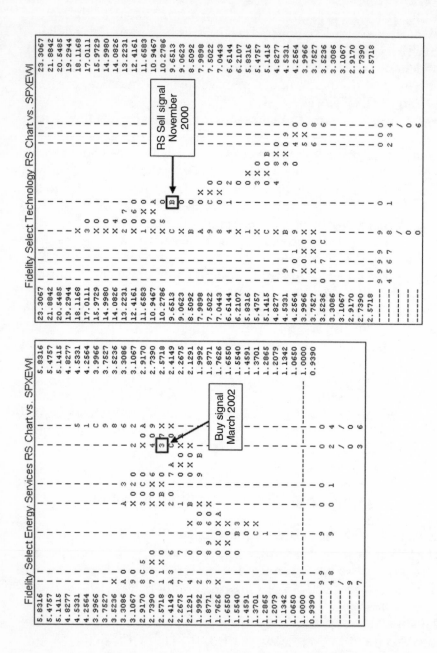

Figure 5.7 Mutual Fund Relative Strength Applied to Fidelity Select Funds.

works equally well in denoting suspected underperformance with mutual funds. In March 2000, the Fidelity Select Technology (FSPTX) fund reversed down into a column of O's on its RS chart versus the SPXEWI, providing the first warning sign that performance was starting to wane on the technology front. Then by November 2000, the RS chart recorded a Double Bottom sell signal. This was yet one more confirmation that the technology bubble had burst. To this day, the Fidelity Select Technology mutual fund remains on an RS sell signal, telling you that there have been better places to put your money. The performance numbers speak for themselves: FSPTX is down 45.6 percent since it gave the RS sell signal in late 2000; conversely, the SPXEWI is up 43.8 percent. For those that focus on a family of funds for sector rotation, you clearly see the need to incorporate RS into your evaluation process.

Mutual fund RS can be used in other ways previously discussed. For example, not only could you evaluate how the American Funds Growth (AGTHX) fund is doing relative to the market, but you could also assess how one fund is performing versus another, such as AGTHX compared to Dodge & Cox Stock (DODGX) fund. This would provide you with an RS comparison along the lines of Asset Class RS discussed earlier. In the case of AGTHX versus DODGX, the RS chart would tell you whether the large-cap growth fund has the upper hand, or whether the large-cap value fund deserves your investment dollars. Not surprisingly, this RS chart has indicated for years that the better play was buying DODGX, zeroing in on the outperformance of "value."

The Fund Score

With respect to mutual funds, we have devised a Technical Ranking Method, or Fund Score. This score is similar to the Positive Technical Attribute reading for stocks that was discussed in the previous chapter. Just as the Positive Technical Attribute reading provides a concise summary of a stock's technical picture, so does the Fund Score for mutual funds. In both cases, these ranking methods provide the investor a speedy way to work through and evaluate a large inventory of stocks or mutual funds.

The Fund Score, as a rating system, ranges from a reading of 0 to 6. The score includes the five basic Positive Technical Attributes, similar to how we rate stocks; yet the Fund Score also includes more parameters, which take into account chart patterns, moving averages, momentum, and percentile ranking for the fund versus several market and peer groups over several time periods. The Score uses proprietary weightings, but adds up to reflect one-third trend chart attributes and two-thirds RS attributes. Our Fund Score rating system is geared more toward evaluating the current market conditions, which differs from other mutual fund ranking systems that focus on a longer time period; and this longer period may not have pertinence, or can be inflexible for making beneficial investment decisions. In general, you want to focus your buying on those funds that have a Fund Score of 3 or higher. Of course, those funds that possess a Score of 5 or above are exhibiting phenomenal trend and RS characteristics, and should pique your interest most when working through and evaluating a large inventory of funds to purchase.

Stock versus Stock Relative Strength

Throughout this chapter, I have displayed for you a multitude of ways that RS can be used to help make investment decisions. Most of what we have covered so far has dealt with broader questions pertaining to asset class, style, sector, ETFs, and mutual funds. But now I want to show you how RS permits you to pinpoint in a very refined aspect whether one stock is a better choice over another, on a relative basis.

This type of comparison can be very helpful in a couple of ways. For example, you may have a fundamental list of stocks that you like to use as an inventory of ideas. Let's assume that you want to gain exposure to the Healthcare sector, and your fundamental list has two Healthcare stocks to choose from, but you only want to buy one. How do you choose which one to purchase? One simple answer would be to create an RS chart comparing the two stocks. By doing so, it would tell you, very matter-of-factly, which stock was performing better, giving you fodder to make your decision.

Also, stock versus stock RS is extremely beneficial when you are trying to narrow a list of strong technically sound stocks down to only a couple of names. For example, let's say that you wanted to purchase a Steel and Iron stock to take a Metals position. You have narrowed the list down to two stocks that both possess a 5 (for 5) Positive Technical Attribute reading. In other words, both have exemplary RS and trend characteristics. Which one do you buy? If you pit one against the other in an RS wrestling match, there will be a clear winner. The RS chart will quantify which one is outperforming the other, giving you the correct answer (of which to buy).

The Pepsi Challenge, Taste Buds Aside

The Pepsi Challenge in a formal sense has been an ongoing marketing promotion run by PepsiCo (PEP) since its introduction in 1975.* The challenge takes the form of a taste test. At malls, shopping centers, and other public locations, a Pepsi representative sets up a table with two blank cups, one containing Pepsi and one with Coke. Shoppers are encouraged to taste both colas, and then select which drink they prefer. Then the representative reveals the two bottles so the taster can see whether he preferred Coke or Pepsi. A taste test such as this will help you discern which cola pleases your palate, but it surely doesn't help you decide which cola company's stock deserves your money. Yet an RS chart is one way to see how investors are voting their wallet, regardless of taste buds. In Figure 5.8 you can see that since October 1999, Pepsi has had the upper hand compared to Coca-Cola (KO). PEP has "beat the Real Thing," handily outperforming KO, gaining 75.9 percent since 1999, while KO has fallen 14.4 percent. So while KO may possess the more dominant market share of cola drinkers, or may be your preferred soft drink based on taste, PEP has been more dominant in the stock market on a relative basis. PEP has been the "Joy of Cola" for investors.

A stock versus stock RS assessment can be helpful with specific purchase decisions, yet it can be very beneficial for those

* http://en.wikipedia.org/wiki/Pepsi_Challenge, www.pepsi.com.

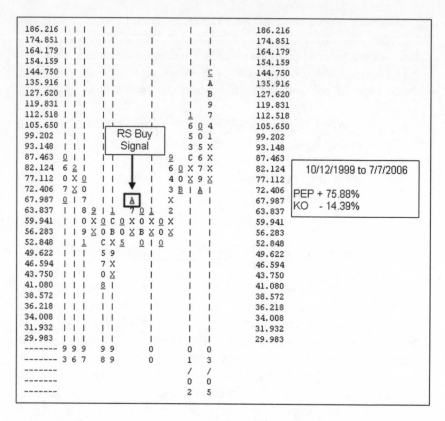

Figure 5.8   Pepsi Challenge: PEP versus KO Relative Strength chart.

traders or investors that like to construct "pairs trades." An advanced trading strategy such as this consists of buying one stock and shorting the other, and typically is done within one specific sector. So in using the RS information with respect to Pepsi and Coca-Cola, it would suggest that you buy PEP shares and short KO shares. The idea here is that you purchase the stock with the stronger RS, with the idea that it should rise faster than the stock with the negative RS. The best case scenario in this situation then is that the stock you buy goes up in price while the stock you shorted falls in price—such was the case with the Pepsi-Coke pairs trade. As a sidebar, in addition to a stock versus stock RS chart, other technical criteria can be brought into the equation when developing a pairs trade. For example, you can consult the Positive Technical Attribute reading for each stock, with the long side of the trade focused on a stock in an uptrend with a 3, 4, or 5 for 5 reading; and the short side geared toward a stock in a downtrend with a 0, 1, or 2 for 5 ranking.

Relative Strength Matrix Concept

In our previous discussions, we have suggested that RS is really nothing more than an arm wrestling match—pitting one opponent against the other such as Hulk Hogan versus Jesse "The Body" Ventura. The RS match determines which security gets its arm raised, declaring it the winner; ultimately, such a match shows where outperformance resides, and gives you important information to make your investment decisions.

DWA Relative Strength Chart Matrix

In an effort to constantly make our research better for our clients, we have taken this arm wrestling match concept and put it in the form of a big round-robin tournament. More specifically, we developed the RS Chart Matrix. In doing so, we created an RS chart for every sector against every other sector using our DWA Equal Dollar-Weighted Sector Indices. This allows us to identify the strongest sectors relative to all others. For example, the Aerospace sector would have 39 RS charts, one against Autos, Banks, Biotech, Buildings, and so on. In addition to the sectors, we also include an RS chart versus the S&P 500 Equal Weighted Index (SPXEWI). This means that each DWA Sector Index has a total of 40 RS charts. Realize it is still the same type of calculation: dividing the closing price of one DWA Sector Index by another DWA Sector Index. As well, the RS reading is still plotted on a uniform percent scale, but for these RS charts we use a smaller box size, or scale, than the standard. We wanted to "speed up" the charts in order to key off of signals rather than columns, but still not produce whipsaws.

But how do we possibly display and make sense of all of these RS charts? To do this we created the "DWA RS Chart Matrix." In this table, we placed the sector symbols horizontally across the top and vertically down the left side. The sector on the left side of the table is the numerator in the RS calculation and the denominator is defined along the top. As you move to the right of the symbol (numerator) the cells of the table are populated with the status of the RS chart versus the sector in the top row. "B" indicates the RS chart is on a buy signal and "X" indicates the RS is in a column of X's. An "S" indicates an RS sell signal and "O" indicates the RS chart is in a column of O's. Remember, an RS chart that is on a buy signal and in X's suggests that the sector on the left side of the table (numerator) is very strong and is outperforming the denominator on both a long-term and short-term basis.

All told, there are over 1,600 cells in this table or matrix. So how on earth can you "get your arms around" this huge wrestling tournament? To help quantify all this information, we implemented a simple ranking of the sectors. It is based on the total number of RS charts that are on a buy signal for a given sector. We tally the total buys for each sector and the one that has the most is ranked as #1. For the sector with the lowest number of buy signals, it is ranked as #41. If two or more sectors have the same number of buy signals, the tie is broken based on the one that has the most RS charts in a column of X's.

When applying this to your portfolio management, you obviously want to concentrate your buying on those sectors that are at the top of the matrix as they are the ones that are outperforming the most sectors. It is these sectors that have been able to win the most RS arm wrestling matches against their sector opponents. All told, the DWA RS Chart Matrix provides you another way to evaluate sector relative strength, and allows you to know which sectors to overweight, while also letting you know which sectors don't deserve your attention. A sample of the DWA RS Chart Matrix is shown in Figure 5.9; this matrix would suggest that you focus your buying on those sectors toward the top, such as Steel and Iron (STEE), Metals Nonferrous (META), Oil Service (OILS), and Transports Nonair (TRAN). Conversely, those sectors with the worst overall RS compared to other sectors would be Auto and Auto Parts (AUTO), Household Goods (HOUS), Media (MEDI), and Forest Products and Paper (FORE).

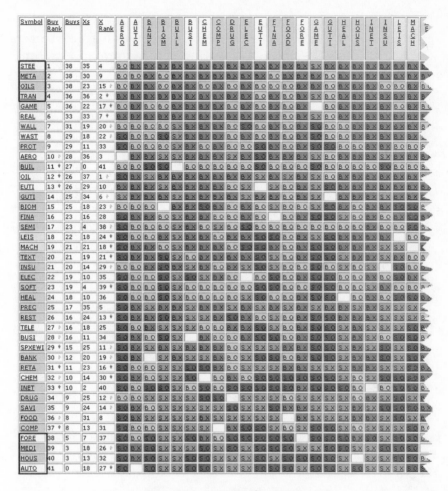

Figure 5.9   DWA RS Chart Matrix.

Stock to Stock Matrix

The DWA Matrix product, as outlined earlier, evaluates RS between multiple securities (sectors), rather than just against the market or one other index. We now want to take it a step further and enlighten you to how this same concept can be applied to a group of stocks. The goal here is the same—to identify from a group of stocks those that are the RS leaders.

For this style of matrix, the basis or starting point comes from creating an RS chart along the lines of the Pepsi (PEP) versus Coca-Cola (KO) RS chart, comparing the performance of one stock to another. Once again, the underlying calculation is the same in that we divide the closing price of one stock by another stock. The matrix in this case is sector specific, and is comprised of 20 to 25 representative stocks from a given sector. The member stocks are optionable and tend to be the larger cap or more well-known names from the group. For example, the Food, Beverage, and Soap sector matrix would include such stocks as PEP, KO, Archer Daniels Midland (ADM), Colgate-Palmolive (CL), Hershey's (HSY), Sara Lee (SLE), and so forth. To create the matrix, we literally create an RS chart of every stock in the list against every other stock. This allows us to identify the strongest stocks relative to the other 20 to 25 names. For example, Archer Daniels (ADM) would have approximately 20 RS charts, one against PEP, KO, SLE, CL, and so on. In addition to the stocks, we also include an RS chart versus the DWA Food Sector Index (DWAFOOD). All told, we have a Stock Matrix for every one of our 40 DWA sectors. This allows us to know at any given point, on a relative basis, what are the best-performing stocks in the Semiconductor group or the Biotech sector, for example.

The layout of each matrix is the same as that outlined with the DWA RS Chart Matrix; the RS signal of each chart is represented by a "B" for buy signal, an "S" for sell signal, with the "X" and "O" representing the recent column reading of each RS chart. Likewise, a similar ranking system is used to tally all of this RS data. Again, it is based on the total number of RS charts that are on a buy signal for a given stock, and the one that has the most is ranked as #1. For the stock with the lowest number of buy signals, it is ranked last, and appears at the bottom of the matrix. In the event of a tie, it is again broken based on the ones that have the most RS charts in a column of X's.

When using such a matrix for individual stock purchases, you undoubtedly want to focus your buying on those stocks that are at the top of the matrix as they are the ones that are outperforming the other member stocks. In Figure 5.10 the Food, Beverage, and Soap stock matrix is shown. Clearly, ADM should catch your attention because it resides in the top spot, followed by British

Symbol	Buy Rank	Buys	Xs	X Rank	ADM	BTI	BUD	CAG	CL	CPB	DEO	DWAFOOD	GIS	HNZ	HSY	K	KFT	KO	MO	PEP	PG	SLE	SYY	UN	Y
ADM	1	20	8	14		B O	B X	B X	B X	B O	B X	B O	B O	B X	B O	B O	B X	B O	B O	B O	B O	B X	B O	B O	[illegible]
BTI	2	18	13	5	S X		B O	B O	B O	S O	B X	B X	B X	B O	B O	B O	B X	B X	B X	B X	B X	B X	B X	B X	B
CPB	3	17	20	1	S X	B X	B X	B X	B X		B X	B X	B X	B X	S X	B X	B X	B X	B X	B X	B X	B X	B X	B X	[illegible]
DEO	4	17	13	6	S O	S O	B X	B O	B O	B O		B X	B X	B O	B O	B X	B X	B X	S X	B X	B X	B X	B X	B X	[illegible]
MO	5	17	12	8	S X	S O	B X	B X	B X	S O	B O	B O	B X	B X	B O	B O	B X	B O		B O	B X	B X	B X	B X	B
K	6	13	11	11	S X	S X	B O	B O	S O	S O	S O	B X	B O	B O	B X		B O	B X	S X	B O	B X	B X	B X	B X	[illegible]
CL	7	12	15	3	S O	S X	B X	B O		S O	S X	S X	B X	B O	S X	B X	B X	B X	S O	B X	B X	B X	B X	B X	B
PEP	8	12	12	9	S X	S O	B O	B O	S O	S O	S O	B X	B X	B O	S X	S X	B X	B X	S X		B X	B X	B O	B X	[illegible]
PG	9	11	4	18	S X	S O	B O	B O	S O	S O	S O	S O	B O	B O	B O	S O	B X	B O	S O	S O		B X	B O	B X	B
HNZ	10	10	17	2	S O	S X	B X	B X	S X	S O	S X	S X	B X		B X	S X	B X	B X	S O	S X	S X	B X	B X	B X	[illegible]
GIS	11	9	11	12	S X	S O	B O	B X	S O	S O	S O	S O		S O	B X	S X	B X	B X	S O	S O	B X	B X	B X	S X	B
KFT	12	8	5	17	S O	S O	B O	B O	S O	S O	S O	S O	S O	S O	B O	S X		B X	S O	S O	S O	B X	B O	B X	B
DWAFOOD	13	7	12	10	S X	S O	B X	B O	B O	S O	S O		B X	B O	S X	S O	B X	B X	S X	S O	B X	B X	B X	B X	B
HSY	14	7	11	13	S X	S X	B O	S X	B O	B O	S X	B O	S O	S O		S O	S X	S O	S X	B O	S X	B X	B X	B X	B
UN	15	6	2	20	S X	S O	S O	B O	S O	S O	S O	S O	B O	S O	S O	S O	S O	B O	S O	S O	S O	B X	B O		B
CAG	16	4	14	4	S O	S X	S X		S X	S O	S X	S X	S O	S O	B O	S X	S X	S X	S O	S X	S X	B X	B X	S X	B
BUD	17	4	13	7	S O	S X		B O	S O	S O	S O	S X	S X	S O	S X	S X	S X	B X	S O	S X	S X	B X	S X	B X	S
KO	18	4	8	15	S X	S O	S O	B O	S O	S O	S O	S O	S O	S O	B X	S O	S O		S X	S O	S X	B X	S X	S X	B
SYY	19	3	6	16	S X	S O	B O	S O	S O	S O	S O	S O	S O	S O	S O	S O	S X	B O	S O	S X	S X	B X		S X	S
WWY	20	3	4	19	S O	S O	B O	S O	S O	S O	S O	S O	S O	S O	S O	S O	S O	S O	S O	S O	S X	B X	B X	S X	
SLE	21	0	0	21	S O	S O	S O	S O	S O	S O	S O	S O	S O	S O	S O	S O	S O	S O	S O	S O	S O		S O	S O	S

Figure 5.10 Food, Beverage, and Soap Stock to Stock Relative Strength Matrix.

American Tobacco (BTI) and Campbell's (CPB). Those to avoid or consider as shorts would be names such as Wrigley's (WWY) and Sara Lee (SLE). Taking it a step further, by using this type of matrix in conjunction with the Positive Technical Attributes reading, you can easily stack the odds in your favor with respect to your individual equity positions.

This matrix concept can be applied to any number of universes. For instance, a matrix can be built to compare all sector ETFs to each other, or one that conducts an arm wrestling match between all the different commodities. The results will be the same—the matrix will identify those securities that are outperforming; it will tell you who has won the round-robin arm wrestling tournament.

Summary of Advanced Relative Strength Concepts

Throughout this chapter, we have tried to demonstrate to you the robustness, and more notably, the adaptability of RS; and how this simplistic tool enables you to capture the large winning trades, while helping you to avoid the big losers. You have hopefully learned that RS is not only useful for individual stock evaluation, but that it can be applied across a broad range of financial products. Moreover, the calculation is consistent across the board, as is the interpretation of the RS chart, with the overall goal being the same regardless of what you are measuring—to determine outperformance or underperformance.

The adaptability of RS is amazing in that it allows you to analyze so many different pieces of the investment puzzle. As discussed, RS is a must with respect to sector rotation, as this is where the majority of risk resides in any given stock. Not only that, a broad appreciation of where to tactically maneuver with respect to your strategic asset allocation pie can be accomplished with just a few RS charts. Basic, but important questions on Asset Class and Style can be easily answered with a glance at an RS chart. And new horizons can be traveled to, with greater confidence, by consulting RS charts on different regions and countries. Without a doubt, the possibilities are limitless.

In the end, these different RS applications provide great insights into where best to allocate your investment dollars. Put together, they create a dramatic and discernible picture; and from that, an understanding of what IS happening in the financial world. All told, the final result is the same—you focus your buying on those securities, sectors, indexes, or funds exemplifying the strongest RS, and sell or avoid those vehicles that display the weakest RS. Remember, as Yogi Berra used to say, "You can observe a lot just by watching."

Chapter 6

PRIMARY MARKET INDICATORS FOR GAUGING RISK

This chapter on the New York Stock Exchange (NYSE) Bullish Percent covers a critical area of investment strategy (see Figures 6.1a through 6.1c). It is critical that you grasp this concept thoroughly. This index is our main coach and dictates our general market posture. Since my first book was published, our experience with this concept has strengthened my conviction that this is the absolute best market indicator. This index, in combination with the Nasdaq Bullish Percent, has guided our decisions through the murky markets of 1999 and 2000 with flying colors, the bear market from 2000 to the end of 2002, as well as the bullish market we have had from 2002 through 2006. It continues to amaze me how effective this index is at alerting us to which team, offense or defense, is on the field.

It wasn't until January 1987 that I began to fully understand what the Bullish Percent Index was all about. That was the month my partner, Watson Wright, and I started Dorsey, Wright & Associates (DWA). Before that, I was director of options strategy at a large regional brokerage firm. Although my department was self-contained, in that we did our own research and never piggybacked off the firm's recommendations, we did use another outside service for our intermediate-term market outlook in addition to the Bullish Percent Index. I am an adamant believer in the KISS principle ("keep it simple, stupid"), from investing to running a company. When we started our own company, I wanted to

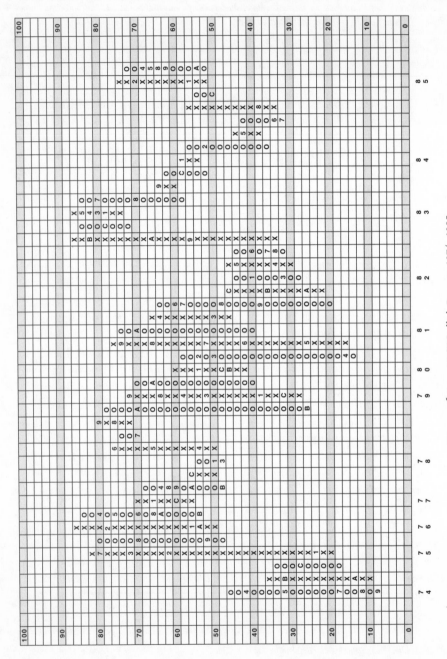

Figure 6.1a NYSE Bullish Percent, 1974–1985.

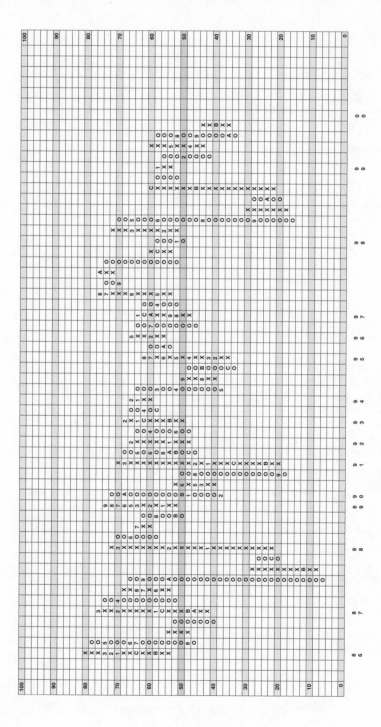

Figure 6.1b NYSE Bullish Percent, 1986–2000.

179

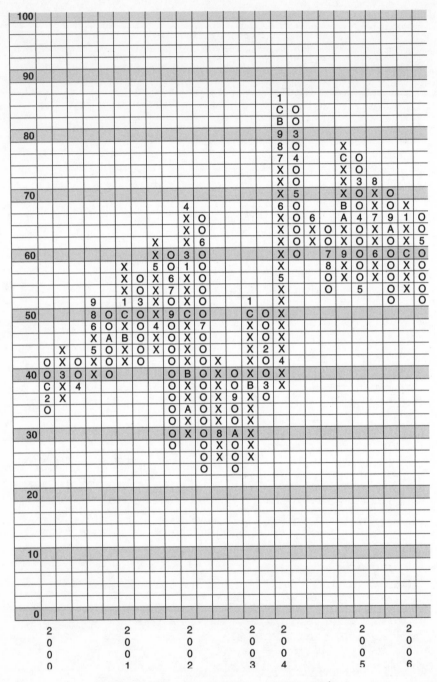

Figure 6.1c NYSE Bullish Percent, 2000–2006.

180

stick with the basics, and this continued to draw me back to the Bullish Percent concept I had used previously. What we found is that when the market in general had an upward bias, the call recommendations generally worked. When the general market was losing ground, the call recommendations did not work as well, but the put recommendations worked really well. In other words, we found that the first step in our game plan for investing was to determine the general direction of the market. Was the market supporting higher prices or not? It's kind of like the tide going in and out in a marina. When the tide goes in all boats are lifted. Conversely, when the tide goes out, all boats decline.

This concept has been numerically quantified by several studies including one by the University of Chicago and another described by Benjamin F. King in his book, *The Latent Statistical Structure of Securities Price Changes.* What these studies quantified is that 75 percent to 80 percent of the risk in any individual stock is in the market and the sector. Only 20 percent of the risk in any individual stock is related directly to that issue. Therefore, as we began building our business, we put tremendous credence in the Bullish Percent concept to tell us whether the tide was rising or falling in the market, and this guided our recommended strategies in the market. It is now 20 years later and I am even more convinced this is the right concept to guide our broad market posture. I have used this Bullish Percent concept now through every kind of market you can imagine in the past 20 years. We have successfully negotiated the crash and subsequent recovery of 1987, the recession and war in the Middle East during 1990 to 1991, the stealth bear market of 1994 and subsequent phenomenal bull market for the next several years, the bear market/Asian crisis of 1998, the bull market in indexes and bear market in stocks from 1998 to 2000, and the OTC meltdown of 2000, as well as the structural fair market or sideways market we have been in from 2001 through 2006. As the different types of markets have come and gone, I am even more impressed with how the Bullish Percent concept saw us through each market in fine form. Some markets are more volatile than others and require more vigilance, but they don't differ much from a football game. Some games are marked by many turnovers while others are marked by long periods of possession of the ball. Still other games are defined by how a certain team played defense. The stock market is the same way. Every game is different, but the process and rules of playing the game never change. It is imperative that you learn this concept well, and keep it in the forefront of all your market decisions. The Point and Figure method of analysis is not a science; it is, however, an art. The more you use the Bullish Percent concept, the better you will be at interpreting it and thus better at the investment process. Remember, you are an integral part of this whole program; nothing works without your involvement.

Do You Have an Operating System?

During the 1980s, the market pretty much went up. This decade made the reputations of many investment advisors and money managers, who then slipped back into obscurity in the 1990s. The decade of the 1990s ushered in a new breed of money manager. Many money managers in the 1990s had much in common with an eight-year-old snow skier—no fear. I remember financial television stations sporting fundamental analysts who had found new ways to evaluate companies that had no earnings, no hope of any earnings, and no real reason to even be listed on any exchange. This was one of the most amazing times I have seen in the stock market. If you asked an investor why he bought particular stocks, you would likely get the following response: "Because it's going up." Gravity eventually upsets a good thing, optimism quickly turns to pessimism, and those who were once considered heroes settle back to being mere mortals as their clients lose their shirts. I've seen this time and again during my career. As I write this, anything that smacks of oil or gold is, well, golden.

We primarily focused on the option stock universe in the 1980s, and to a lesser degree on the general market of stocks that did not have options attached to them. Stocks generally rose during this period, so the focus was on catching the next rising star. The 1980s were wild indeed. Things were popping, and the listed derivatives market was only about seven years old, having debuted in April 1973. By the time the 1980s rolled around, options derivatives were the fastest game in town. If I were asked to define that period with one word, it would be overleveraged. It seemed everyone had a stake in the game. By 1987, the game had gotten easy and everyone, it seemed, had become comfortable with the state of the market. Rising prices translated into easy money in options. Until October 1987, that is. Once again gravity exerted its influence, and in one day the air came out of the balloon. Today, with the Dow Jones at about 11,500, a similar drop to that of October 1987 would be the equivalent of falling about 2,600 points in a single day. Can you imagine the field day the media would have with that magnitude of a drop? And we've already been there, done that. One of the strategies that led to the one-day October 1987 decline was the misuse of put options that had a dampening effect on the options market. Put options can be viewed as insurance products. Buyers of puts are typically seeking insurance to hedge some market risk they are unable or unwilling to accept. The seller of puts on the other hand is contracting to provide the insurance the buyer is seeking. A put seller stands ready to purchase stock at a certain price for the life of the contract, no matter how far below that price the stock declines. This is similar to an insurance company insuring your car for the stipulated duration of the contract. The insurance company will make you whole if you have an accident. If cars never had any accidents, the insurance business would be the greatest business of all—good premiums and no risk. Because stocks rarely had accidents during the early 1980s, investors decided to enter the underwriting business. You know what happens when everyone thinks some investment is too good to be true—it generally is. Well, in October 1987, every stock on the stock exchanges had an accident the same day. The casualty companies of the stock market (put sellers) all went bankrupt. I am referring to the investors who sold those puts that, up until October, usually expired worthless. This expiration month, they didn't. From that day on, the options market changed.

This isn't anything new. It's been going on since the tulip craze in the 1600s. It happened again with Internet stocks in the late 1990s and early 2000. And I am sure it will happen in the future. You would think investors would learn from their mistakes or at least learn from history, but the conventional wisdom always seems to suggest that, "this time is different." Most investors make the same mistakes year in and year out. Their biggest mistake is operating in the markets without a logical organized method of analysis. I see it day in and day out. So much information is available today that investors are more confused than ever on how to manage their money. Most investors and brokers don't operate in the markets with a defining process, an operating system if you will. However, a select group of brokers have taken it upon themselves to see that they are well educated in this methodology. They have attended our Point and Figure Stockbroker Institute in Richmond, Virginia. These craftsmen brokers have a solid game plan for their customer that incorporates the strategies of wealth preservation and wealth accumulation based on the Bullish Percent concept and associated Point and Figure discipline.

If I could impress on you one fact, it would be that at least 75 percent of the risk in any stock is associated with the market and sector. If the overall market is not supporting higher prices, very few stocks you own, if any, will do well. In the past, I spoke at the Yale Club's annual Wall Street Night with Merrill Lynch's director of Investment Strategy, PaineWebber's director of Investment Strategy, Jim Rogers, Abbey Cohen, and some of Wall Street's top economists. In all, some of Wall Street's brightest people. The second year I was invited to speak I brought a chart I always use when I explain the Bullish Percent concept. This chart is a schematic of a football play we often see on TV during football games. This chart is my way of demonstrating how we view the market as a football game where the play shifts from offense to defense throughout the game. Once the other panelists had finished discussing the market's outlook, it was my turn. The first chart (Figure 6.2) I put up was a football schematic like the one John Madden writes on the TV screen with his grease pencil showing what just happened on the last play. This chart drove home the point I was trying to make that evening: The first thing an investor must know before investing any money is whether the offensive team or defensive team is on the field.

In a football game, two forces operate on the field at any one time, offense and defense. The same forces act in the marketplace. There are times when the market is supporting higher prices and times when the market is not supporting higher prices. When the market is supporting higher prices, you have possession of the ball. You have the offensive team on the field. When you have the ball,

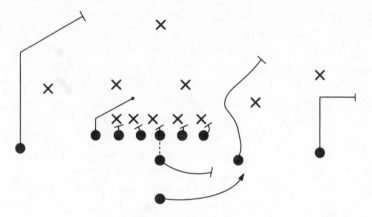

Figure 6.2 Game plan.

your job is to take as much money away from the market as possible; this is when you must try to score. During times when the market is not supporting higher prices, you have in essence lost the ball and must put the defensive team on the field. During such periods, the market's job is to take as much money away from you as possible. Think for a moment about your favorite football team. How well would they do this season if they operated with only the offensive team on the field in every game? They might do well when they had possession of the ball, but when the opposing team had the ball, your team would be scored on at will. The net result is your season would be lackluster at best. This is the problem most investors have. They don't know where the game is being played, much less which team is on the field. Let's face it, most American investors only buy stocks, they never sell short. The market is fair. It has something for everyone. It goes up and it goes down. The NYSE Bullish Percent signals when the environment is ripe for offense or defense. I want to stress that there is a time to play offense and a time to play defense. You must know which is which.

How the Bullish Percent Concept Developed

The need for a soulless barometer started with Earnest Staby in the mid-1940s. He was thinking about the market indicators in existence and determined there was a problem that needed to be addressed. He reckoned that if one were to look at any chart of the broad averages, whether it was a Point and Figure chart, bar chart, line graph, or candle chart, they all looked bullish when the market was at its absolute top, and conversely, they all looked bearish when the market was at its absolute bottom. He determined that we needed a soulless barometer that would guide us to become more defensive at market tops and more offensive at market bottoms. A contrary indicator if you will. Well, Earnest was not able to come up with this soulless barometer, but A. W. Cohen did in 1955.

What Cohen was trying to create was a market indicator that was bullish at the bottom and bearish at the top. Something that was totally contrary to how most investors operate in the market. Normal trend charts of indexes like the Dow Jones and the S&P 500 are always bullish at the top and bearish at the bottom. Thus, trend charts of market indexes invariably lead investors to buy at the top and sell at the bottom. Here's how the Bullish Percent concept works. It is contrary and goes against the prevailing wisdom. Most market pundits think the Point and Figure method is a trend-following system. It is not that at all in the initial stages of investment. What this method endeavors to do through the Bullish Percent Indexes is to buy stocks when they are washed out and virtually everyone has denied them. Kind of like a value investor might operate, not the other way around. Although once a stock does make a move off the bottom and starts a long-term uptrend, it can be bought along the way. But the method tries to initiate the buying of stocks when they might be considered value stocks whose momentum has recently turned up for the better. If a stock is moving up off the bottom, as it gains sponsorship at the price of, let's say, 40, it will likely be good at 45, 50, 60, or even higher. Remember stocks that are the first to double in a bull market are typically the first to double again. So this method of analysis is really a contrary investment style that turns into a trend-following style once the vast majority of stocks have moved off the bottom. Just because you did not catch a stock at the bottom doesn't mean you are out of the ball game. I have always wondered why a value investor would not incorporate technical analysis in his decision making process. The value player suggests that the stocks that he buys will eventually be recognized as a value by other investors and as a result will have their price bid up. What if no one sees it like the value player sees it? I'll tell you what will happen. The stock will go nowhere. Why not put the list of value stocks together and wait until the supply/demand relationship of the stocks begin to change where demand is in control. That would be an aces back-to-back trade, a whole lot better than Texas Hold 'Um Poker.

The NYSE Bullish Percent is simply a compilation of the percentages of stocks on the NYSE on Point and Figure buy signals. Think back for a moment to Chapter 3. A bullish chart is one where the last signal is a column of X's that exceeds a previous column of X's. If you simply thumbed through all the Point and Figure chart patterns of the stocks on the NYSE and counted the ones that were on buy signals, then divided by the total number of stocks evaluated, you would have the NYSE Bullish Percent reading for that day. A sixth grader could do it. We have computers that do the counting for us. Let's say there were 2,000 stocks on the NYSE and 1,000 of them were on Point and Figure buy signals. The Bullish Percent would be at 50 percent (1,000/2,000 = 50 percent). Each box constitutes 2 percent, and the vertical axes runs from 0 to 100 percent. That is the football field we are playing on. When the index is rising in a column of X's, more stocks are going on buy signals suggesting sponsorship is increasing in the market.

Think about what actually takes place if the index is in X's at 50 percent this week and over the next week rises to 52 percent. Changes in the index can only come from first signals that are given, not subsequent signals. What do I mean by first signal? Let's say XYZ stock is on a sell signal, bottoms out after declining, and then gives that first buy signal off the bottom. That signal turns the stock from bearish to bullish (see Figure 6.3). It is this first buy signal that is recorded. All subsequent buy signals are not counted—one stock, one vote.

To be sure you understand how this index can move from 50 percent to 52 percent, let's theoretically cut the number of stocks trading on the NYSE down to 100. Over the next week, 12 stocks experience a new buy signal like the one shown in Figure 6.3, and 10 stocks experience new sell signals. The net result

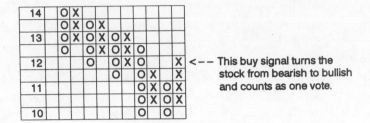

Figure 6.3   Bearish to Bullish pattern.

of the action for the week is net two new buy signals (e.g., 2 percent more stocks went on buy signals than went on sell signals). Remember that each box on the chart represents 2 percent, so a 2 percent net change in new buy signals allows the chart to rise one box. Think about the importance of what I just said. I get questions all the time about how this index correlates to the Dow Jones or the Nasdaq or the S&P 500. It doesn't correlate at all. These indexes are either price weighted or capitalization weighted. In the case of the Dow Jones, the highest price stock has the most votes. In the Nasdaq and S&P 500, the stocks with the largest capitalization have all the weight. It can take only a handful of stocks to move these indexes. Let's say IBM was bought out tomorrow 100 points higher than it is at today's close. Do you think it would have an effect on whether the Dow Jones rose or not that day? It sure would. The Dow Jones Average would rise today, but it would be only one stock that is causing all the action. If the top 20 highest capitalization stocks in the S&P 500 went up sharply one day, the S&P 500 would rise as well. Now, what does this type of action do to a basic chart of these indexes? It obfuscates reality, that's what it does. If IBM were bought out tomorrow 100 points higher than its close today, it would only count as one positive stock on the NYSE Bullish Percent Index. It would have virtually no effect on moving the index. It is important to keep the Bullish Percent separate in your mind versus indexes that are a measure of performance of a handful of stocks. The Bullish Percent is an assessor of risk in the market, not performance. This is the main difference.

Why Use the Bullish Percent
versus a Chart of an Index

One of our clients sent us an interesting article by James Surowiecki entitled, "The Financial Page Markets Always Outsmart Mavens" (from the *New Yorker*, October 9, 2000). That article had an interesting take on the markets and long-term capital management. That firm had bond trader John Meriwether and some of the smartest minds on Wall Street, yet the fund managed to blow up. The author compares the TV show *Who Wants to Be a Millionaire?* with long-term capital. The premise of the show is simple. Contestants pick one of four answers to a trivia question, with the value of each question getting greater until they reach the final million-dollar question. A contestant who answers a question wrong is out. The show gives contestants three "lifelines." If they are stumped on a question, they can use the lifelines to help them out. One lifeline is a 50/50, which takes away two of the wrong answers and leaves one correct and one wrong answer for the contestant to select from. Another lifeline is to call a friend to see if he or she knows the answer, and finally a contestant can poll the audience. To do this, each member of the audience keys in his or her choice for the right answer, then the computer displays what percentage of the audience voted for each answer. What the show's producers have found is that when the participant phones a friend for an answer, the person is right two-thirds of the time. When the contestant polls the audience, however, they are right nine times out of ten. So what gives here? Your super-smart friend is right less often than an audience of people who come from all walks of life and have diverse educational backgrounds.

In short, you are more likely to find right answers from a diverse group of people than from one person you deem to be extremely bright and well rounded. As Surowiecki says in the article:

Long-Term specialized in esoteric trading strategies, which meant that most of the time there were relatively few people it could trade with. If you want to buy stock in Cisco Systems, there are lots of folks out there who will sell it to you at a reasonable price. But if you want to buy, say equity volatility (don't ask), as Long-Term did, there are really only four or five dealers in the entire world who buy and sell this stuff. And they all know one another. These people may have been financial wizards, but, as *Millionaire* demonstrates, if you want to find the answer to a question—like "What's the right price for equity volatility?" you're better off asking a big, diverse group, rather than one or two experts.

Keep in mind that two of the principals of Comprehensive Capital are Nobel Prize Laureates.

You can test this phenomenon pretty simply with an old trivia game, "How many jelly beans are in the jar?" Surowiecki asserts in his article that a college professor does this with his classes and invariably the collective guess is within 3 percent of the actual number. At each of our Advanced Point and Figure Institutes, we conduct this experiment. We have an intern count out peanut M&M's into a large jar and write down the number. Then, the eight people in the office guess how many M&M's are in the jar. The results are essentially the same each time. In one of our latest Advanced Point and Figure Institutes, the average guess of the eight people who were teaching the seminar was 840. At the seminar, in which there were 80 attendees who all voted, the average guess was 1,398. Now, get this—the number of M&M's was 1,396! We found it absolutely amazing that the group came so close. We took all the guesses and applied the statistical concept of a bell curve to it. What we saw was a perfect bell curve. There were some outlying guesses but the collective guess was right on the money. Again, the larger the sample, the better the average guess.

Norman Johnson, a physicist at Los Alamos National Laboratory, quantified this hypothesis. He built a computer-simulated maze in which a person could navigate in numerous ways and tested people's ability to get through it. Johnson took the sample group and found what he called the "collective solution." In other words, he took the turn in the maze that the greatest percentage of people picked. This "collective solution" was just 9 steps long compared to an average of 34.3 steps the first time a person worked through the maze. Furthermore, he found the bigger and more diverse the group, the smarter the collective solution was. As

Surowiecki points out in his article, "The miracle of markets is that a hundred million ordinary people, just by going about their daily business, end up allocating resources much more efficiently than would five guys talking on the phone, no matter how smart those five guys are." Or as Michael Mauboussin, the chief investment strategist at Credit Suisse First Boston, puts it, "The market is smart even when the people within it are dumb." Does this speak in any way about the wisdom of the politicians we elect? Maybe the best way to solve world problems is through a collective vote of all Americans on the Internet. Hey, don't laugh; it might solve the hanging chad and dimple problems in Florida. I'll bet it could solve our energy crisis, too. The problem is it wouldn't get any incremental votes for politicians, so I'm sure it will never be tried.

Our Bullish Percent concept relies on the same approach as the jellybean, M&M, or maze tests. The larger and more diverse the sampling, the better or more accurate picture we get of risk in the marketplace. We view the Bullish Percent as "polling the audience" in the *Millionaire* show, while the most often quoted market indexes take the "phone a friend" solution. The audience members get it right more often than the phone a friend, and that is what we see with the Bullish Percent—it is better at assessing risk in the market than the indexes. Remember, it is the risk in the market we are assessing, not the market's performance. Each week when we calculate the Bullish Percent reading we are in essence polling our audience, which happens to be the NYSE (or OTC) stocks. This audience of about 3,000 for each market is better at assessing risk than the top 20 capitalized stocks in the S&P 500 or Nasdaq 100. Remember, the bigger the sample size, the more accurate a picture you get. Each week, we ask the stocks comprising the NYSE (and OTC) what is the correct level of the Bullish Percent. Should it be 50 percent, 70 percent, 30 percent, or somewhere else? It is then up to us to interpret the reading and decide what type of strategies we want to integrate.

Mechanics of the Bullish Percent

Let's go back to the mechanics of charting the index. We use the same three-box reversal to shift columns in this index as we do in the normal Point and Figure chart; however, we do not look for chart patterns in this index as we do in the individual charts that make up the index. We do, however, watch for Double Bottoms and Double Tops. I'll explain in a minute. Field position and the column you are in are the two most important considerations. Remember the only way to switch from one column to the next is through a three-box reversal. Since each box in the NYSE Bullish Percent is worth 2 percent, it would take a sum total of 6 percent net buy or sell signals to cause a reversal. Reversing from one column to the next is tantamount to losing or gaining possession of the ball.

The chart is made up of columns of X's and O's with the vertical axes running from 0 to 100 percent. We think of this as a football field consisting of 100 yards. There are two things we try to ascertain with this chart: (1) Who has the ball (offense/defense)? (2) What is the field position (current level from 0 to 100 percent)? If you colored the area above the 70 percent level in red and the area below 30 percent level in green, these would represent the two extremes much like the end zones of a football field. The higher the index climbs, the more overbought it becomes because more and more investors become fully invested, and those investors who are inclined to sell tend to hold off. The lower it drops, the more oversold it gets because more and more people who have an inclination to sell do, and those who have an inclination to buy hold off. When the index is rising in a column of X's, we say you have possession of the football. When you have possession of the ball you must run offensive plays. This is your time to attempt to score against your opponent, the stock market. When the index is declining in a column of O's, the market has the ball and your job is to try to keep it from scoring against you. The numbers in the boxes on the chart represent months of the year, so you can see the time spent in a column of X's or O's is generally a number of months, not weeks.

It is important to fully understand this index, so let's go back to our discussion about how the index rises and falls. It takes a net change in buy or sell signals to move the index. The minimum percentage move in the index is 2 percent to advance a box or decline a box. It requires a 6 percent net change between new buy and new sell signals to change columns. This 6 percent change is the critical part of how this index moves from column to column. Typically, I look at the index as a gauge of how many players are on the field. In July 1990, the Dow Jones was making all-time highs with the NYSE Bullish Percent Index at 52 percent. This showed that the Dow might have been at a new high but only 52 percent of the NYSE players were on the field. In other words, the NYSE Bullish Percent was at 52 percent and in a column of X's. One would have expected to see more than 52 percent of the stocks participating in the rally when the Dow was at new highs. This goes back to our discussion on how it only takes a few strong stocks to push and pull the index. A few weeks later, Iraq invaded Kuwait, and the same day the NYSE Bullish Percent reversed over into a column of O's, signaling investors had lost the ball once again. Those who heeded the signal avoided a major crunch in the market. The net result was the index declined to the 18 percent level in October 1990, which was the bottom. The first week in November the index reversed into a column of X's signaling investors had once again taken possession of the ball. Those who were willing to listen bought stocks right at the bottom. Those who preferred to listen to the news media were expecting a depression or worse. I am continually amazed with the accuracy of this index. It helps the investor understand the most important question in investing, "Who's got the ball?"

NYSE Bullish Percent Risk Levels

There are six degrees of risk in the index similar to the different signals a traffic light can give. A. W. Cohen felt if the index was rising in a column of X's and above the 50 percent level, the market was bullish. Conversely, if the index was declining in a column of O's and below the 50 percent level, the market was bearish. Earl Blumenthal fine-tuned the NYSE Bullish Percent to include 6 degrees of risk. Over the years of working with this index, I have found that field position and whether the index is in X's or O's is about as complex as you need to get with this concept. For this reason, I am leaving out the risk levels in this updated book. I have not found much use for them over the years, instead I have concentrated on column and field position.

Earlier I mentioned that we watch for two patterns—the Double Top and Double Bottom. It is significant that when the Bullish Percent goes into a period of weakness (reverses into O's) and then reverses up (into X's), rises to the previous level that caused the supply to come in, and exceeds that level (Double Top). We would give added value to this condition. Conversely, I would say the same thing with the Double Bottom. Don't try to think too deeply into it. Suffice it to say that when the Bullish Percent is in X's below 50 percent the field position is better than when in X's above 50 percent. When in O's, the field is worse above 50 percent level than it is below 50 percent. It's just logical. Keep it simple. Who has the ball and how is your field position? That is the most important guidance the Bullish Percent can provide.

Lessons from the Bullish Percent

As mentioned, my conviction in the Bullish Percent has only grown stronger through years of experience with different markets. In this new third edition, we have tacked on another five years of experience watching it guide us through even more market conditions and our own confidence level has just continued to build. You can gain this confidence level too by studying different market periods and how the Bullish Percent has reacted. If you take the time to read and study the market scenarios I am about to lay out, you will be miles ahead of the average investor in understanding how the markets work.

1987—The Crash

I discussed the crash of 1987 earlier because the NYSE Bullish Percent Index saved our company and would have helped any investor avoid the crash if he or she had been following it. We were only 10 months old at DWA and had just begun to acquire some clients. We had decided when we started the company that our main market indicator would be the NYSE Bullish Percent Index. That index was the soulless barometer we would hang our hat on. If it had worked so well since it was developed in 1955 by A. W. Cohen, and was well founded in the irrefutable law of supply and demand, why should we look any further? On September 4, 1987, the indicator reversed into a column of O's (Figure 6.4) and suggested we put the defensive team on the field. It was our Head Coach so we followed the signal without any reservation. From that day forward, our feature article in our "Daily Equity and Market Analysis Report" had to do with how to hedge a portfolio with options. The following month the market crashed, and I'll be the first to tell you we had no idea the decline would be so severe. Nonetheless, those who chose to follow our recommendations were prepared. The crash took no prisoners from our client base. This was a major confidence builder for us. We knew then, we were on the right track.

By the first week in November, the same indicator that had suggested defense on September 4, 1987, now suggested offense. This was just as tense as the sell signal the index had given us a couple of months earlier. All the newspapers, magazines, and TV shows were talking about depression, recession, 1929, no hope for Wall Street, and on and on. The media did their part in scaring investors, right at the time our Head Coach (NYSE Bullish Percent) told us to begin running plays. It was a great example of how the market looks ahead. The Bullish Percent Index reversed up into a column of X's and, once again, we knew of nothing else to do but follow it. Those who followed our recommendation to buy got back in right at the bottom. I must add there was no brilliance on our part for those calls on the market; it was the NYSE Bullish Percent that did it. We simply followed its guidance like football players follow the guidance of their coach. Ultimately, the most credit should go to the late A. W. Cohen for creating this index in 1955. Along the way, this method of analysis became a lost art that I revived in my first book.

After the crash, we put together a marketing piece consisting of excerpts from our report pre- and postcrash. This marketing piece, in essence, opened doors for us. From that day forward, the NYSE Bullish Percent has been the mainstay of our market indicators. I have written many articles on it, and each time I write about it I learn a little more. We have used this index to guide our intermediate market action for 20 years now. We have seen it work in bull, bear, and neutral markets. The more you learn about this index, the more confidence you will have in your day-to-day market operations.

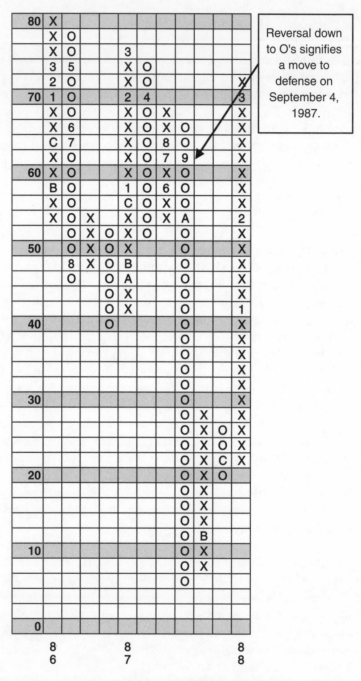

Figure 6.4 NYSE Bullish Percent: 1987.

1990—Kuwait Invasion

We really need to begin the discussion of the 1990's market by going back to 1989. In September 1989, the NYSE Bullish Percent hit 74 percent (Figure 6.5). Exceeding the 70 percent level put this important indicator into the red zone. In October 1989, everything changed. Six percent of the stocks on the NYSE moved from buy signals to sell signals and put the defensive team on the field. The initial move down carried the NYSE Bullish Percent down to 38 percent in a straight column of O's. By March, there was a slight reprieve. The NYSE Bullish Percent reversed up from March until August when, on the day of the invasion of Kuwait, the NYSE Bullish Percent reversed down into a column of O's, putting us back on defense. The thing about defense is you never know how bad it will be until it is over. For that reason, we always take the posture that it is better to preserve capital and lose opportunity than it is to lose money. Opportunity is easy to make up, but money is hard to make up. A 50 percent loss in a stock means you have to gain 100 percent just to get back to even. The NYSE Bullish Percent just continued to experience more sell signals and more sell signals until it was finally driven down to 18 percent in September. The Bullish Percent stayed at that level until November when it reversed up into a column of X's. I distinctly remember watching the financial news and hearing Alan Greenspan tell the American public that we were in a recession at the exact time our main market indicator was reversing up from oversold levels. The difference between economics and Wall Street is that economics reports on what is happening today, while the financial markets look ahead. The Bullish Percent was telling us that the recession was not just beginning, but rather it was nearing an end.

After the NYSE Bullish Percent reversed up from that 18 percent level to 24 percent, it rallied straight up to 70 percent. This is one of the few times the NYSE Bullish Percent has fallen to such an extremely low level and then rallied straight up to 70 percent. This is why we always take positions on any reversal from below 30 percent. Who knows when that move might end up going coast to coast? Usually we see an initial rally up off the bottom and then a retest that results in a higher bottom. When the

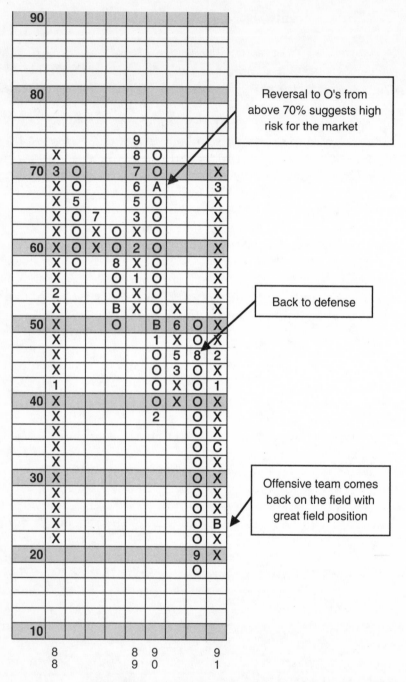

Figure 6.5 NYSE Bullish Percent: 1989–1990.

NYSE Bullish Percent reached 70 percent, the risk management process started all over again. This points out how the Bullish Percent is an oscillator and not a trend chart, and why you cannot compare it to an index like the S&P 500. Keep the concept of a risk assessor firmly in your mind as you evaluate this chart.

1994—Stealth Bear Market

The market of 1994 has been dubbed the "stealth bear market." The indexes were holding up, coming in even for the year, but the sector rotation in the market was unbelievable. As one sector was getting hit, another was recovering from its sell off; the effect of this was to cancel each other out in the broad market indexes. However, the individual stocks and many investors did not fare as well. The market during 1994 was one in which you came into the office and sat down and crossed your fingers that it wasn't your stocks that got taken out behind the shed and shot. The reality of the market was that 80 percent of the stocks on the NYSE were down 20 percent or more at some time during the year. The NYSE Bullish Percent was in a column of O's for eight months out of the year (Figure 6.6). That means for two thirds of the year we were playing defense. In 1994, the NYSE Bullish Percent started out the year at 66 percent. Is this good field position or bad field position to start out the year? Bad field position. By the end of the year, the NYSE Bullish Percent was at 32.1 percent. You might ask, "Why wasn't the Bullish Percent lower than 32.1 percent if 80 percent of the stocks were down 20 percent or more that year?" The reason is that many sectors bottomed at different points in time. Some sectors, like drugs, bottomed out in the spring; others like technology, bottomed in the summer, and yet other groups bottomed out in December. While some sectors were moving to sell signals, others were moving to buy signals, and those buy signals had the effect of canceling out some of the sell signals, thus keeping the NYSE Bullish Percent from getting down to a reading of 20 percent or lower. Nonetheless, what was the field position going into 1995? Good field position. In 1995, the NYSE Bullish Percent and other indicators had us playing offense for 70 percent of the year (36

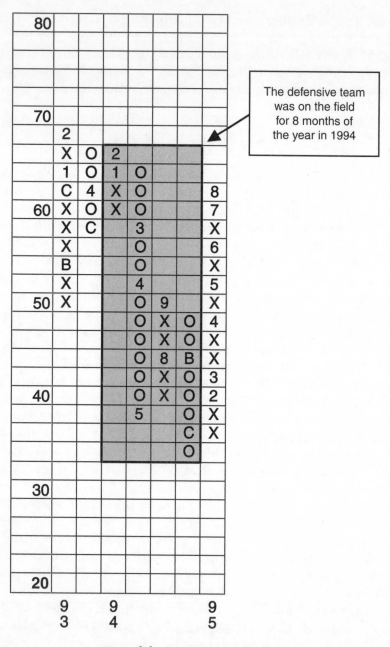

The defensive team was on the field for 8 months of the year in 1994

Figure 6.6 NYSE Bullish Percent: 1994.

weeks out of the year, the NYSE Bullish Percent was in X's), and certainly the market did quite well with the Dow Jones up 36 percent. In 1996, it was a similar story as the NYSE Bullish Percent was in X's 39 weeks that year, 75 percent of the time. The S&P 500 was up 20 percent that year. In 1997, the NYSE Bullish Percent was in a column of X's for 35 weeks or 65 percent of that year, and in general, it was another good year for stocks, except for the Asian crisis, which hit in October 1997. Before the market crumbled from the Asian crisis, the NYSE Bullish Percent gave us notice having reversed in O's from the 72 percent level. That reading of 72 percent was the highest for the NYSE Bullish Percent since 1987.

1998—Indices versus Stocks

The year 1998 showed another major change with respect to the NYSE Bullish Percent (Figure 6.7). What I find so interesting is that there are always different catalysts that seem to make the market rally or stumble, but that doesn't matter to the NYSE Bullish Percent. Those catalysts are always rooted in the supply-and-demand relationship in the market, and that is what the NYSE Bullish Percent is designed to measure. I'll never forget the 1998 market. By April of that year, the NYSE Bullish Percent had risen to 74 percent. We began to see selling pressure build up as more stocks were going on sell signals versus buy signals. A change definitely was in the offing. Reversals from above 70 percent are particularly concerning. On April 1, 1998, we wrote in our daily research report, "It Wasn't Raining When Noah Built the Ark." I saw this euphemism on the marquee of a Baptist church as I was going to lunch one day. I felt as if the Pastor had put it up there for me to read. We always keep our eyes on that marquee as we drive by because the Pastor of the church is incredibly creative with respect to his euphemisms. This one hit me right between the eyes because it was perfect with regard to what the market was on the verge of doing. We needed to have our professional clients begin to think about what they would do to protect their clients when this index moved to defense. Our intention was to get our clients to begin considering risk management/damage

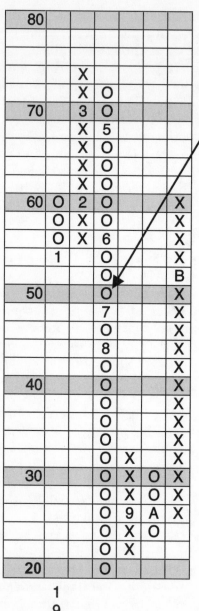

While the indices went to new highs, individual stocks couldn't even garner enough new buy signals to reverse the NYSE Bullish Percent up. This is typically a negative divergence.

Figure 6.7 NYSE Bullish Percent: 1998.

control—what to do when things go wrong. We could see the Bullish Percent was close to reversing to defense. It was like doing lifeboat drills on a cruise ship. The first thing you do when you embark on a cruise ship is participate in lifeboat drills that deal with what to do if the ship begins to sink. Our outlook was the same. Plan what to do if the market begins to sink so your portfolio won't go down with it.

By May 13, 1998, the NYSE Bullish Percent Index had reversed to a column of O's signaling defense. The index then marched straight down to 16 percent, which is an extremely washed-out condition. In July of that year, the Dow Jones rallied to all-time highs, as did the Nasdaq, NYSE, and S&P 500. The trend charts of these indexes looked very good, but the reality of the situation was that more sell signals were piling up while a handful of stocks pulled these indexes to new highs. It was as if the generals were in the battle but the soldiers had left the field. Those who followed the Bullish Percent Index were dead on the money, playing defense while others who followed the trend charts of these indexes were on the wrong road with the offensive team on the field. This "major" rally that took these indexes to new all-time highs only lasted two weeks. Shortly after the highs were made, the market caved in. Or, should I say, those indexes caved in. The market had been declining since April 1998. As mentioned, the Bullish Percent eventually went down to 16 percent before we experienced a reversal during the month of September.

2000—The Two-Sided Market

The year 2000 was interesting, indeed. The NYSE Bullish Percent had been making lower tops since its peak in 1998 at 72 percent, and by February 2000 the NYSE Bullish Percent had fallen to 32 percent, just above the green zone or low-risk level (Figure 6.8). Then in March 2000, the NYSE Bullish Percent reversed up on the exact same day that the OTC Bullish Percent reversed down into O's. We had a situation in which we went from offense to defense on the OTC Bullish Percent while going from defense to offense on the NYSE. In March, we also saw some of our other

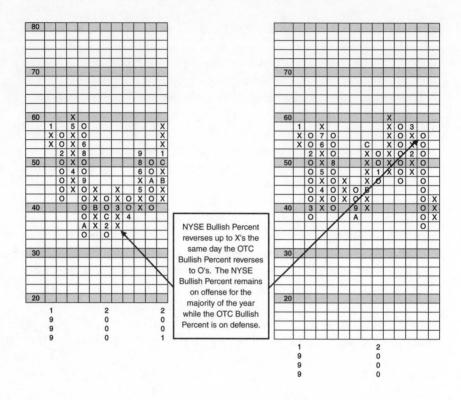

Figure 6.8   NYSE Bullish Percent: 2000.

Relative Strength (RS) indicators turning positive on the NYSE while turning negative on the OTC market. This call kept our clients underweighted in the OTC stocks and over weighted in NYSE stocks while most of the investing public was doing just the opposite and getting killed. As mentioned, the years 1995 to 1997 saw the NYSE Bullish Percent in a column of X's 70 plus percent of the time, keeping the offensive team on the field for those stocks for three quarters of the game. During 1998 and 1999, though, it was a different situation. During those years, the NYSE Bullish Percent was only in X's about half of the year. In other words, we had the ball for 50 percent of the game and the market had the ball for 50 percent of the game. That's why it was so hard to make headway in the NYSE stocks during 1998 and 1999. But in 2000, we saw a switch back to investors having possession of the ball for 75 percent of the time. Here is the reason for this. The RS of small-cap stocks overtook that of large-cap stocks. This was the first change in the market favoring small-cap issues in many years. Since the capitalization-weighted indexes are all driven by the handful of stocks with the highest capitalization, this change was imperceptible to the uninitiated. Over the previous years it was the big-tech names that drove the "market." Stocks like Microsoft, Sun Microsystems, Cisco, and the like were the locomotives that pulled the market up. Now it was the little guys, who never have any votes in the capitalization weighted indexes like the Standard & Poors 500 that were taking over the show. In fact, I remember in July 2001, I was on FOX *Cavuto on Business* when Neil Cavuto said, "Tom, everyone I talk to tells me they are losing money in the market. How can that be when over half the stocks that trade are up not down?" Well, this was a change in leadership in the market that the media totally missed. The media primarily looks at indexes like the S&P 500 and Dow Jones. If these indexes are going down, then in their eyes the market is not doing well, but in this situation the small-cap stocks were doing fantastic while the large stocks that generally pull the indexes up and down were losing sponsorship. The next five years through mid-2006 were marked by the advance of small-cap stocks.

During the dot-com craze, we saw an increase in the volatility of the NYSE Bullish Percent indicator, especially the OTC Bullish Percent. Some of this can be attributed to the advent of the Internet craze and technology stock proliferation. Over the past 50 years, there have been times when the index has only changed columns two times a year, like 2003 and 2004 when it changed direction four times. So far, five months into 2006, there is only one column of X's but volatility in this index is not unprecedented. From 1960 to 1965, the index averaged about six changes a year. That was during the close presidential race between Nixon and Kennedy. There was reason to believe there was voter fraud in that election. The Daley political machine was involved. During that span of years,

1960 to 1965, we witnessed the Cuban Missile Crisis, the Bay of Pigs incident, and the assassination of President Kennedy. The volatility in the NYSE Bullish Percent ebbs and flows. After the year 2000, when so many investors were absolutely and unequivocally wiped out as the Nasdaq dropped 50 percent from its high and that is over twice the percentage associated with a bear market, the volatility in the bullish percent charts came back to a more normal range. What we have learned is that volatility doesn't matter. Sometimes volatility increases significantly and other times it is less but the one constant is the Bullish Percent concept is still the best method of evaluating the markets, hands down!

9/11/2001

This is a day we will all remember. The day America was attacked by terrorists who hijacked and flew two airliners into the World Trade Centers. This act of terrorism caused the markets to collapse. The market did not open back up until September 17, 2001, and by September 21, a mere five trading days later, the Dow Jones Industrial Average had lost 1,543 points or 16 percent of its value. Many investors headed for the hills and sold everything that wasn't nailed down. Since this chapter is on the NYSE Bullish Percent, the question is "How did this index react during this sharp decline in the Dow Jones?" The answer can be found by just looking at the chart. You will notice that the NYSE Bullish Percent had us on the defense since June of 2001 (Figure 6.9). Any one who had taken the signal and was operating in a wealth preservation mode went through the attack in relatively great shape. The market had already been in decline when the attack happened. In reality, the attack actually created a bottom in the Dow Jones. It's major events like this that make investors "throw the baby out with the bath water" and often mark the bottom of the market. The problem is, who rings the bell that the bottom has been reached? For us the bell ringer is the NYSE Bullish Percent. On October 11, 2001, the NYSE Bullish Percent reversed up. What many investors thought would be a long-lasting market decline was only a one month phenomenon.

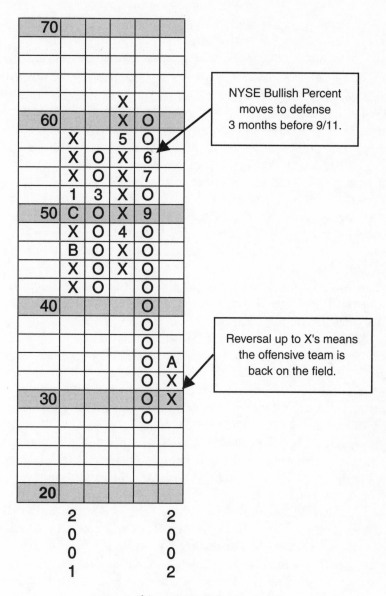

Figure 6.9 NYSE Bullish Percent: 2001.

2002—No Place to Hide

Just nine months after the NYSE Bullish Percent had reversed up from below the 30 percent level, in October 2001, our Main Coach was once again knocking at the door of the red zone (Figure 6.10). From the reversal up to X's in October 2001 at 34 percent, the NYSE Bullish Percent marched unwaveringly ahead and by April 2002 was at the 68 percent. You know, there's an old market adage that says "sell in May and go away" and what strikes me as I look at the chart of the NYSE Bullish Percent is the frequency of the numbers 2, 3, 4, 5 (for February, March, April, and May) when the NYSE Bullish Percent is nearing the red zone. Be that as is may, we defer to the chart and let it tell us when the time for defense is. In 2002, the time for defense was June 3rd. That is when the defensive team came on the field and boy did our team take a lickin' during the market's possession of the football. It seemed like the market scored against us at will. By July 23 the major indices were down 20 percent or more and the NYSE Bullish Percent had moved coast to coast, now residing at 24 percent; even lower than the 9/11/01 lows of 28 percent. In 2002, there was no place to hide as just about every stock took it on the chin. In fact a look at the DWA sectors during that time period show that 68 percent or 27 of the 40 sectors we follow were down 20 percent or more.

In August 2002, the NYSE Bullish Percent saw 6 percent of the stocks move from Point and Figure sell signals to buy signals and reverse this chart up into a column of X's and suggest that you bring the offensive team back on the field and the field position was ideal, below the 30 percent mark. The NYSE Bullish Percent had an initial move up to 42 percent and then reversed down into O's but this is not unusual (Figure 6.10). In the instances where the NYSE Bullish Percent has fallen below the 30 percent level and reversed up, we have seen the NYSE Bullish Percent reverse back down and make a higher bottom (or even level) in half of those occasions. But what is interesting is that while the major indices usually make new lows, the NYSE Bullish Percent makes a higher bottom. In October 2002, the NYSE Bullish Percent fell back to 24 percent to test and hold its July low levels while the Dow Jones moved through its lows like a hot knife through butter

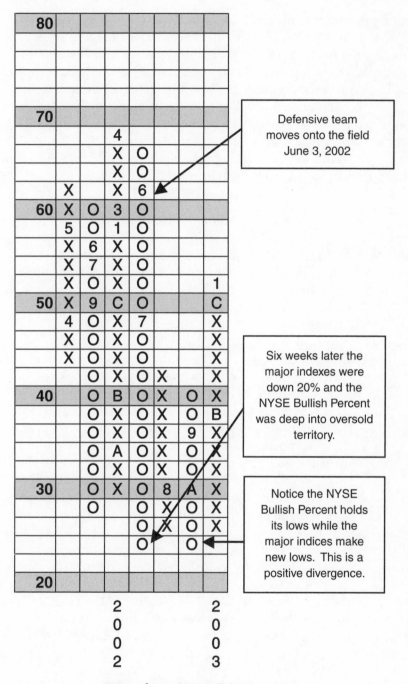

Figure 6.10 NYSE Bullish Percent: 2002.

falling past those July 2002 lows of 7532 to 7197. But because half of the time the NYSE Bullish Percent doesn't give us another chance, we have to start moving money back into the markets on that initial reversal up. Remember, since 1955 there have only been 18 instances where the NYSE Bullish Percent has moved below the 30 percent level. That's only about once every three years we get the opportunity to buy at very depressed levels. Of course, without a soulless barometer like the NYSE Bullish Percent, we would have no idea of when supply had dried up and demand moved back into the equation.

2003—Who Would Have Guessed

In March 2003, the NYSE Bullish Percent was residing at the 36 percent level (Figure 6.11) and as a nation we found ourselves heading into war with Iraq. Just as we were entering that war, the NYSE Bullish Percent was reversing up to a column of X's and putting the offensive team on the field as of April 2, 2003. The market in general was taking off quickly and conventional wisdom was that the rally shouldn't last too long. We were just coming out of three consecutive years of the S&P 500 posting losses (−10.13 percent in 2000, −13.04 percent in 2001, and −23.37 percent in 2002). Everyone's mentality was that this rally wouldn't last, we're in the middle of a bear market. But that kind of thinking can only get you in trouble. Think about this situation for a second. You pull a quarter out of your pocket and toss it in the air. You have a 50/50 chance of heads coming up. Now let's say that you toss that coin three times in a row and tails comes up each time. Does that mean you have a better chance of tails coming up again? No. However, our minds might fool us into thinking that was the case by weighting the most recent action more heavily. However, if you continued to toss that coin for say 500 times, I bet that you would find that heads comes up about 50 percent of the time and tails comes up about 50 percent of the time. In 2003, so many investors found themselves not believing their indicators because the recent market action had swayed their beliefs or the geopolitical situation made it seem implausible that the market could experience a rally.

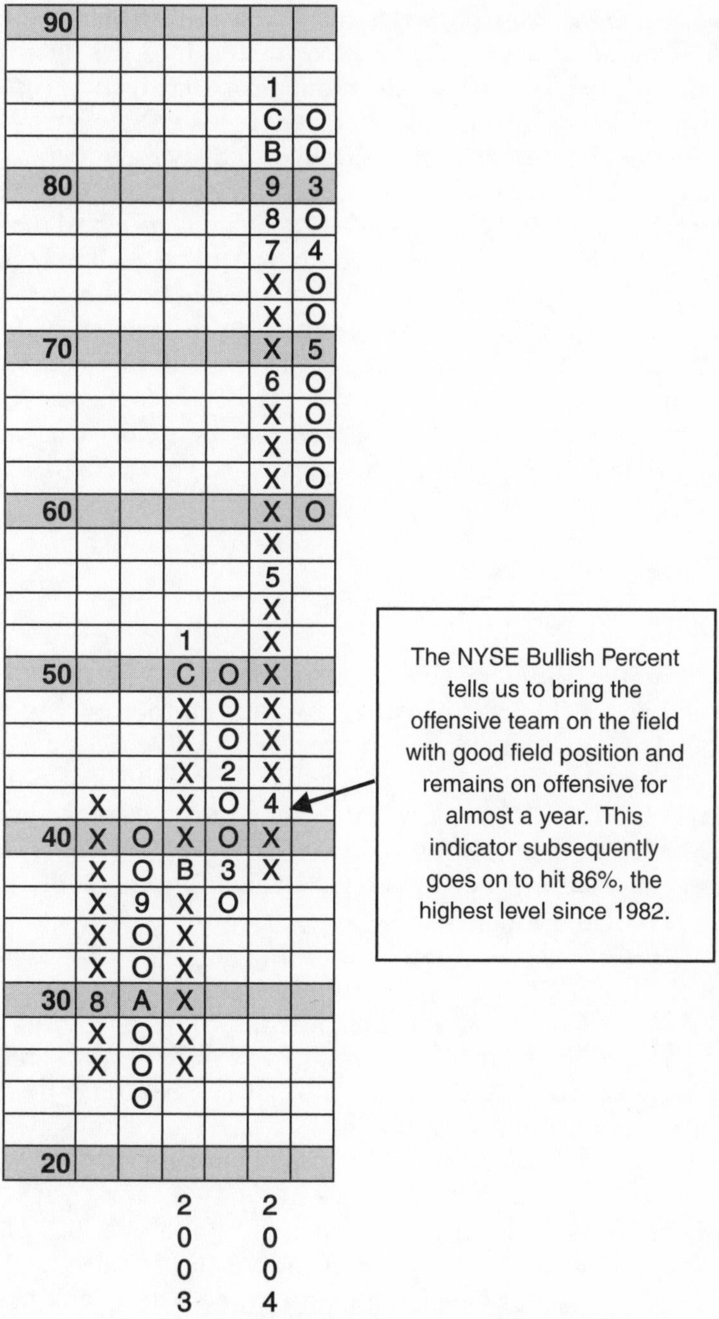

Figure 6.11 — Point & Figure chart (NYSE Bullish Percent: 2003)

Level	C1	C2	C3	C4	C5	C6
90						
					1	
					C	O
					B	O
80					9	3
					8	O
					7	4
					X	O
					X	O
70					X	5
					6	O
					X	O
					X	O
					X	O
60					X	O
					X	
					5	
					X	
				1	X	
50			C	O	X	
			X	O	X	
			X	O	X	
			X	2	X	
	X		X	O	4	
40	X	O	X	O	X	
	X	O	B	3	X	
	X	9	X	O		
	X	O	X			
	X	O	X			
30	8	A	X			
	X	O	X			
	X	O	X			
		O				
20						

Year labels (read vertically at base): 2003   2004

Callout:

The NYSE Bullish Percent tells us to bring the offensive team on the field with good field position and remains on offensive for almost a year. This indicator subsequently goes on to hit 86%, the highest level since 1982.

Figure 6.11 NYSE Bullish Percent: 2003.

What happened in 2003 was the NYSE Bullish Percent stayed in X's for almost a solid year not reversing into O's again until March of 2004 and the S&P 500 was up over 26 percent during that time while the S&P 500 Equal Weighted Index was up over 46 percent. The NYSE Bullish Percent rallied to 86 percent before it reversed into O's. That reading of 86 percent was the highest reading for the NYSE Bullish Percent since 1982. If you had asked me when the NYSE Bullish Percent reversed up in April 2003 if I thought it would go over 80 percent, I would have guessed not but that is one of the beauties of the system. It forces us to keep the offensive team on the field as long as we have the football. Just because this indicator nears the 70 percent level or even exceeds it doesn't mean you sell and move the defensive team on the field. What is does mean is that risk is higher at these levels so you ready the defensive team and select more conservative offensive plays.

2006

This actually brings us to the status of the NYSE Bullish Percent as I write this third edition. I want you to view the NYSE Bullish Percent chart from the top in 2004 at 86 percent to January 2006 (Figure 6.12). Actually, since the beginning of January 2006, the chart has only tacked on one more box but the Dow Jones is up 600 points through May 10. What you will see is a case where the generals are the only ones fighting the battle. The Dow Jones, in May, was within a hair of going to a new all time high and the cover of major financial periodicals flashed "Dow 12,000." As quickly as the Dow Jones had moved up to test those old highs, it has come down and actually reversed down into a column of O's putting the defensive team back on the field. When I look at the NYSE Bullish Percent that is producing lower tops as the Dow Jones neared a new high, it reminded me of another time in history—1987. This condition will be resolved one of two ways. Either the broad market begins to gain sponsorship and the Bullish Percent Index rises and broadens out, or we suffer a broad market decline. I just don't see it happening any other way. As you know by now, we don't predict, but it will be fun to watch

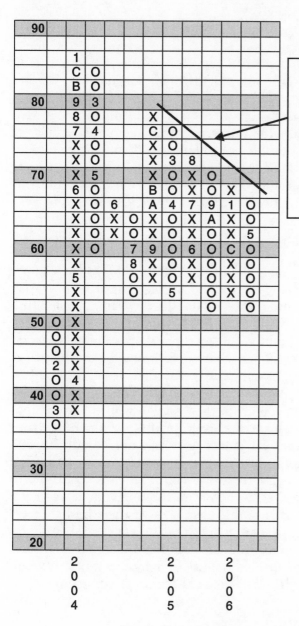

Notice the lower tops in the NYSE Bullish Percent. Where the reversal down to O's in May 2006 will lead, we don't know. What we do know is what team to have on the field at all times.

Figure 6.12   NYSE Bullish Percent: 2006.

how it unfolds. Depending on when you read this book, you might already know.

When the Bullish Percents get near or moves above the 70 percent mark, the availability of demand to push the market higher is diminished. An advisor calls their customer with a great idea. It's the newest widget-making company that will change the semiconductor industry. Your customer replies, "I love the idea. What should I sell to buy it?" If you sell a stock to buy another, supply and demand cancel each other out. One day you start to sell but decide to keep the cash from the sale in your bank account. You don't replace those sell tickets with buy tickets, and that's what causes the Bullish Percent to reverse down. It's like a pressure cooker when you're above 70 percent. The top on the pot is rattling with the steam underneath. One day the steam gets to be too much and the top blows off. We don't know what the cause will be. It may be the Asian crisis again or it may be another type of international crisis like the Iran nuclear bomb situation, or it's oil moving to $100 a barrel, or the Fed chairman raising interest rates and tightening the money supply. We never know what the cause will be. What we do know is that the risk is high at these levels and we must govern ourselves accordingly.

What does "govern ourselves accordingly" mean. It can mean many things to many people. For those of you who are professionals in the investment business, this is NYSE Rule 405: Know your customer. What is right for one person may not be right for another. There are many right answers. If you are unaware that the indicators are in high-risk territory, you might just continue to buy stocks with unbridled enthusiasm; the financial news media certainly will foster this enthusiasm. It's in their best interest that you remain enthusiastic about the markets. That way you keep tuning in. Most of us, though, would not take that tact. Here are some ideas that might make sense in market conditions when this index is at high levels. This is the type of commentary we provide in our daily reports:

- Do nothing.
- Tighten up stop-loss points. As stocks start to give sell signals, you ensure that you don't give back too much of your profits. You might choose to just take partial positions off the

table on the sell signal, but by doing that you have taken some defensive action.

- Take partial profits. One thing you might consider is selling a third of your position if you are up 30 percent or more. This gives you staying power with the rest of your position to handle a correction. The money you free up acts as a hedge and then you have that cash to reemploy once the indicators suggest you have a good buying opportunity again. As well, taking partial profits will keep one stock from becoming too large a portion of your portfolio.

- Sell calls against partial or total positions. This takes the sell decision away from you. You take in premium, which acts as a hedge against you, and you sell at the strike price. If the stock doesn't get called away, you keep the premium and can rewrite the calls. With this strategy, you must be willing to have the stock called away. If you are not willing to have the stock called away, then you're a closet naked writer.

- Buy protective puts on particular stocks. Let's say you own Exxon Mobil (XOM). The stock is at the top of its 10-week trading band, the weekly momentum just flipped negative, and the sector is extended and the next support is the 55 area with the stock currently trading around 65. You or your client might be willing to accept the risk down to 60 but after that want someone else to carry the risk. You might choose to buy a six-month-out put struck at 60. That gives you (or the client) the right but not the obligation to sell his stock at 60 anytime between now and expiration no matter where XOM is trading. If the stock does in fact fall, you can always take the profits on the put and hold the stock, too.

- Buy protective puts on a portfolio. Ask anyone if he or she owns a put and the answer would likely be no. Ask the same people if they own a home or a car and you get a resounding yes. If you own a home or a car, you own a put. You own insurance on your home and car. Every six months, you send the insurance company a check to protect you for the next six months should there be an accident. Many people have portfolios worth more than homes and yet they don't even think to buy insurance on their stocks should there be an accident in the market. Let's say you have a portfolio worth

$250,000 of blue chip names. Your client says he can handle a 5 percent drop in the market but after that he wants some insurance. The S&P 500 (SPX) is currently trading at 1265. A 5 percent drop in that index would bring it down to 1200. One way to hedge the portfolio is to buy puts on the SPX struck at 1200. Each put that you buy protects $120,000 (1200 times 100) of the portfolio. To hedge a $250,000 portfolio, you would buy 2 puts. The price you pay for the puts is like the car insurance premium you pay every six months to your insurance company. You hope you don't have to use it but if you do, you're sure glad you have it. Also, you don't have to buy protective puts on the whole portfolio. You can hedge just a partial portfolio.

- Buy only half positions here and average in the other half on a pullback. This allows you to at least get your foot in the stirrup in case we don't get a pullback. If the stock does pull back, then you can average in lower.
- Buy calls or leaps on stocks you want to own. Let the premium you pay be your stop-loss point and come back at expiration and see how you stand. The important thing to remember here is not to over leverage. If you normally buy 500 shares, only buy 5 calls; don't over leverage by buying 15. Keep the rest of the money in a money-market fund.
- Buy an Exchange Trade Fund (ETF) that holds the stock you are interested in owning. It will give you more diversification with less volatility. Let's say you are interested in buying a particular oil stock. You can buy an ETF that is simply a basket of oil stocks. This way instead of buying one fish, you buy the whole school of fish.

There are lots of ways to take a more defensive stance. What makes you different from the competition, or other investors, is you have a game plan. You have a soulless barometer to tell you what plays to run.

This is the type of research we put out each day. We try to make sense of the indicators. We never anticipate the anticipators; however, when we see changes in the offing, we discuss what to do if the event does in fact take place. We always try to have the moves we would make in the chess game laid out for us ahead of time so that we don't act like a deer in the headlights when the change does take place.

Every few years, the NYSE Bullish Percent gives us some real opportunities by declining below the 30 percent level. It doesn't happen every year, but when it does, be prepared to buy. The last time it was below 30 percent was in 2002. It's now 2006. Could we be in for a great opportunity with the index working its way back down below 30 percent this year and on this reversal down into O's? Depending on when you are reading this book, you might already know. But like I have said many times in this book, we don't anticipate. We change the players on the field when this indicator tells us to.

The OTC Bullish Percent Index

The OTC Bullish Percent Index is important because of the plethora of high-tech, over-the-counter stocks we deal with each day. Chartcraft began the OTC Bullish Percent in 1981, and the same rules of reversals, box sizes, 70 percent high risk, and 30 percent low risk all apply to this one as well. On our web site (www.dorseywright.com), we now have Bullish Percents on virtually every country that has a stock exchange in the world—from Tel Aviv to London to Australia to Shanghai you can follow the same concept on any country.

The OTC Bullish Percent Index is a compilation of the percentage of Nasdaq stocks that are on Point and Figure buy signals (see Figure 6.13). The OTC Bullish Percent Index can give you a great deal of insight into what the technology stocks are doing. In 1982, the small stocks bottomed out much earlier than the large-cap stocks. By the time the big-cap stocks were ready to go in August 1982, the small stocks were already up 70 percent. The chart is read the same way as the NYSE Bullish Percent Index. When the index is rising in a column of X's, you have the football and should be running plays (buying stocks). Conversely, when it is in a column of O's, the OTC market has the football and you should be more concerned with defense (protecting your portfolio). The best sell signals come from above the 70 percent level and the best buy signals come from below 30 percent. Much of the time the truth lies somewhere in the middle. Notice also the OTC Bullish Percent bottomed at the 22 percent level three years in a row, 2000, 2001, and 2002. Since 2003 we have also seen the OTC Bullish Percent make lower tops, like the NYSE Bullish Percent, but we have also seen it make higher bottoms. Like the NYSE Bullish Percent, the OTC Bullish Percent hasn't seen the 30 percent level or lower, the green zone, since 2002 so it's due. This Bullish Percent Index can be an important clue when evaluating the risk in the market.

The Nasdaq or OTC stocks have become much more important than they were years ago. When I was a broker in the 1970s, these stocks were considered poison. They were the lowest rung of the ladder and always considered high risk. Now we have Nasdaq stocks in the Dow Jones. Some of the largest cap stocks that trade are in the Nasdaq. I must say though, they are still volatile and in many cases are not suitable recommendations for investors who have a low risk tolerance. In the latter part of the 1990s, many investors who barely understood the mechanics of investing had totally overleveraged their whole portfolios with Internet stocks. The media as well as Wall Street analysts had convinced them these stocks could only go up. In the end, many investors lost over half of their retirement funds in these "never decline" stocks. Closely watching the markets is a great education in investor psychology.

From 2000 to 2002, most of those stocks didn't go up, they blew up. I'll tell you something else. Just go back and view some of the recommendations by Wall Street fundamental analysts on these Internet stocks when they were at their absolute highs. You will break out in a cold sweat when you see the adoring reports at the top. I'll bet Google still has them archived. Goldman Sachs took the stock Ask Jeeves Inc. (ASKJ) off their recommendation list after the stock dropped from 59 to 4. That's only a 93 percent decline from recommended to off recommended. They rated it Market Performer. I guess if the market moved up 20 percent from there, ASKJ would have risen 20 percent. Of course, at 4, that would be 80 cents (ASKJ was acquired by IAC/InterActiveCorp in 2005.) During this same time, Goldman took E-Toys off its recommended list when the stock declined under 1. This is why the technical analysis coupled with fundamentals is so important.

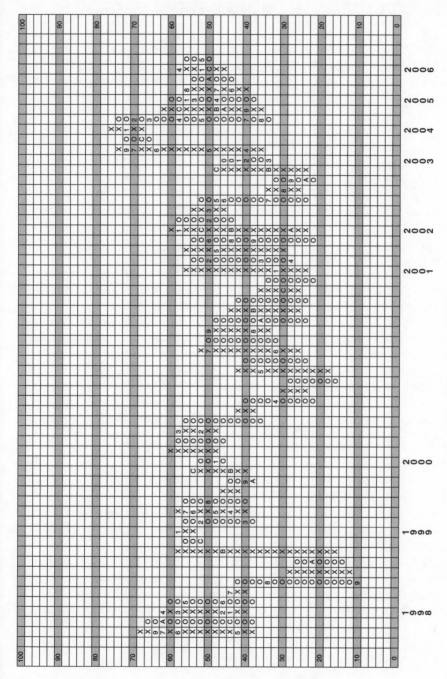

Figure 6.13 OTC Bullish Percent.

219

We are trained from birth that obedience to proper authority is right and disobedience is wrong. That essential lesson fills parental lectures, the schoolhouse, children's books, Sunday school lessons, and is carried forward in the legal, military, and political systems we encounter as adults. Notions of submission and loyalty to legitimate rule are accorded much value in our society.

In many cases it makes great sense to comply with the wishes of properly constituted authority. Those in authority often have superior knowledge and judgment.

However, problems can arise if we stop thinking for ourselves and blindly trust the authorities. Furthermore, what if the authority is misguided? Let's consider an example from a facet of our lives where authority pressures are visible and strong: medicine. Physicians possess large amounts of knowledge and influence in the vital area of health and hold the position of respected authorities. The medical establishment has a clearly terraced power and prestige structure and various health workers understand that the MD sits at the top. Yet, even with these knowledgeable authorities calling the shots, the application of medicine still has its challenges. A study done in the early 1980s by the U.S. Health Care Financing Administration showed that, for patient medication alone, the average hospital had a 12 percent daily error rate! A decade later, things had not improved: According to a Harvard University study, 10 percent of all cardiac arrests in hospitals are attributable to medication errors. Commenting on those examples, Robert B. Cialdini, PhD points out in his book, *Influence,* problems arise when those lower in the hierarchy stop thinking for themselves. In his book, Cialdini cited the strange case of the "rectal earache" reported by two Temple University professors, Cohen and Davis. A physician ordered eardrops to be administered to the right ear of a patient suffering pain and infection there. But instead of writing out completely the location "right ear" on the prescription, the doctor abbreviated it so that the instructions read, "place in R ear." Upon receiving the prescription, the duty nurse promptly put the required number of eardrops into the patient's . . . well, you can probably guess where!

Cialdini, also cited an experiment conducted on five classes of Australian college students, in which a man was introduced as a visitor from Cambridge University in England. However, his status at Cambridge was represented differently in each of the classes. To one class, he was presented as a student; to a second class, a demonstrator; to another, a lecturer; to yet another, a senior lecturer; to a fifth, a professor. After he left the room, each class was asked to estimate his height. It was found that with each increase in status, the same man grew in perceived height by an average of a half-inch, so that as the "professor" he was seen as two and a half inches taller than as the "student."

Wall Street has seemingly crowned a multitude of authorities. Some may justly deserve our attention, others do not. It is worth asking ourselves who or what has the most influence on our investing decisions. Is it the CEO of the company in which we are considering investing, our firm's chief investment strategist, a market commentator, or other authority figure? Is their influence on our decisions due to their status or to their ability to add real value?

For the technician, there is only one authority: the almighty price! In price there is knowledge. Objectivity is key to investing and price is only influenced by supply and demand for the stock. Price determines trend and RS and is, in our estimation, *the* legitimate authority.

Chapter 7

SECONDARY MARKET INDICATORS

The first edition of this book was published in 1995, and the second edition was published in 2001. I felt it was time for a third edition because we have continued to develop and apply the Point and Figure theories and further the development of other indicators to enhance our interpretations of the markets. These other indicators dovetail beautifully with the long-established Point and Figure indicators. With these new indicators, we still use the Bullish Percent concept. We simply apply this concept to the other aspects of a stock's technical attributes that we find essential. I think about it like the dashboard of your car. You'd never be successful in reaching your journey if you didn't keep your eyes focused on the road ahead, which for us are the NYSE and OTC Bullish Percents, but you do need to consult the gauges on your dashboard to make sure the car is performing the way it should be. You probably find that you most often glance at the speedometer, but periodically you glance at the temperature gauge to make sure the car isn't running to hot suggesting something might be wrong with the engine internally. You keep checking the gas gauge and your RPMs. These gauges are akin to the secondary indicators we are going to discuss in this chapter.

All our indicators are kept on our web site (www.dorseywright .com) so you can refer to them in real time as you read this book. The Internet has truly revolutionized how we maintain and present our charting and portfolio system. It doesn't seem that long ago we kept all these charts by hand. Each day before the advent of our computerized charting system with five analysts, we updated 2,500 charts by hand. Once we were able to computerize this process, getting our analysts to stop the hand charting was like pulling teeth. They loved seeing the stocks they updated. Every day each analyst rotated the book he or she updated to another analyst. This way in one week, each analyst saw firsthand 2,500 charts. We did this for a decade before the Internet became popular. Then we were limited to sheer people power with respect to the number of indicators we could develop, but today's technology has allowed us to limit ourselves only to our imaginations with respect to the way these indicators can be applied to different markets.

While we have added a number of indicators to our repertoire, we are still very mindful of the fact that you have to keep it simple. Once a concept is developed and tested, it is then applied to each market, NYSE, ASE, Nasdaq, sectors, mutual funds, international markets, and even fixed income. But one thing you can be assured of: We never gravitate from the underlying principles of the methodology—supply and demand; they define our work. We have no need to search for any other concept. We are, however, always looking for other ways to apply this same concept. It's like the hub of a wheel. This hub is the Point and Figure method of analysis with all the associated indicators. From this hub, we attempt to extend as many spokes as we can without ever leaving the concepts that define our company. Many investors make the mistake of trying to follow too many indicators or jump from one to another when one doesn't seem to work. Just about everywhere you turn there is another indicator that someone assures you will make you rich. Just go to the chat rooms on the Internet and you will be hit with a barrage of information and indicators that will both confuse and obfuscate the picture. The "real deal" is the irrefutable law of supply and demand. There is nothing else that causes price change.

In the previous chapter, we discussed our most important indicators—the NYSE and OTC Bullish Percent Indexes. Now that you understand the Bullish Percent concept, it can be applied to a multiplicity of different areas with differing time frames. The NYSE and OTC Bullish Percents are our long-term coaches, but within long-term trends it is important to identify underlying currents and shorter-term trends as well. First, we'll start off with a look at some of the secondary Bullish Percent indicators, then our other equity indicators, and end with a review of applying these indicators to the mutual fund markets.

Other Equity Indicators

Bullish Percents

Recall the NYSE and OTC Bullish Percent concepts you just read about in Chapter 6. We can apply this Bullish Percent concept to other indices. Three other Bullish Percents that we review daily in our work are the Bullish Percent for the Optionable Stock Universe (BPOPTI), the Bullish Percent for the S&P 500 (BPSPX) and the Bullish Percent for the Nasdaq Non-Financial (BPNDX). Let's outline a couple of important tenets about these Bullish Percents. Some of this is a review from the previous chapter but it's such important information that it doesn't hurt to have another review.

All of these Bullish Percents are equally weighted meaning one stock, one vote. The charts measure the percent of stocks that are on a buy signal on their Point and Figure trend chart. Take the BPNDX, for example; there are 100 stocks in this universe. Let's say that 50 stocks are on buy signals. This would result in a reading of 50 percent (50/100) on the BPNDX.

No matter what Bullish Percent you are looking at (BPNYSE, BPOTC, BPSPX, etc.) they are all a measure of risk; it is not a measure of performance. That is, the BPSPX measures the risk in the S&P 500; the BPNDX measures the risk in the Nasdaq Non-Financial universe; and so on.

Similar to the BPNYSE, these two Bullish Percent charts are charted in the same manner in that the "field" extends from 0 to 100 percent, and the same lines of demarcation exist. The 70 percent level and above is considered the high-risk area, and the 30 percent level and lower is considered the low risk area. Each box is worth 2 percent, and the 3 box reversal rule still applies. Therefore, if we are in a column of X's at say 60 percent, it would take a 6 percent change in the reading to reverse the chart back into O's, which in this example would be a move to 54 percent.

If the Bullish Percent is in a column of X's, this means that we have the ball and are on offense. If the Bullish Percent is in a column of O's, this means we have turned the ball over to the opposing team (the market) and it is time to put the defensive team on the field. However, having the ball at the 30 percent level is much different than having the ball at the 70 percent level.

The two most important considerations when using these Bullish Percent charts are field positions (whether the reading is 30 percent, 40 percent, 50 percent, etc.) and what column the chart is in (X's or O's). Risk is considered on the high side of the ledger above 50 percent and on the low side below 50 percent.

The Optionable Bullish Percent is a good intermediate term bullish percent that we follow closely. The reason we like this bullish percent is that it is made up of over 2,500 stocks that trade options. We don't plot the option prices but rather we plot the Point and Figure charts of all stocks that have listed options on them. This is a nice cross section of stocks without one sector influencing too much of this Bullish Percent. For instance, financial-related stocks comprise about 20.6 percent of the stocks listed in our NYSE Bullish Percent calculation but only 11 percent of the Optionable Bullish Percent calculation. The technology sector is also a great example. Technology-related stocks only account for about 3.3 percent of all stocks in our NYSE Bullish Percent and over 21 percent of all stocks in the OTC Bullish Percent but in the Optionable Bullish Percent, technology related stocks are 15.6 percent of the universe. Often changes in the Optionable Bullish Percent will precede changes in the NYSE Bullish Percent so we do take into consideration this Bullish Percent's calculation in our assessment of the overall risk in the marketplace. The one time we did not find the Optionable Bullish Percent useful was in 2000. That was because the NYSE and OTC stocks were moving opposite one another and the Optionable Bullish Percent found itself gyrating around the 50 percent mark for most of the year.

Now let's take a look at some of the nuisance of the smaller Bullish Percents. While the calculation of the Bullish Percent for the S&P 500 and the Nasdaq 100 is the same, these indexes have fewer stocks than our broader markets like the NYSE and OTC, so what you will find is that these charts do move much faster. Since 1998, the NYSE Bullish Percent has seen 38 column changes while the S&P 500 Bullish Percent has had 66 column changes. We also want to stress that these Bullish Percents are not designed to be used as trading or timing tools for the Exchange Traded Funds (ETFs) associated with these indices. The primary reason is that the S&P Depository Receipts SPDR (SPY) and the Nasdaq 100 Shares (QQQQ) are both cap weighted, meaning that one stock can carry more than one vote while the Bullish Percents are a one stock one vote indicator.

Take the S&P 500 Capitalization-Weighted Index. The highest capitalization stocks in the index carry all the weight. Those stocks are in the top 40. Say for instance institutions sold out general stocks in their portfolios and moved to the largest capitalization stocks as a safe harbor in a market storm. This would put added buying pressure in those top 40 stocks that in turn would pull the S&P 500 Capitalization-Weighted Index with it. So you end up with a bull market in capitalization-weighted indexes and a bear market in stocks in general. This happened in 1998 and in reverse in 2000. It's incredibly interesting when you understand how the game is played. So, the Bullish Percent concept is a measure of risk in the market and not to be used as a trading signal generator. It is not a measure of absolute price movement. To evaluate the overall trend of an index ETF, always consult the ETF chart. Let's look at an example.

In Figure 7.1 we see a Bullish Percent chart for the S&P 500 with two areas highlighted, April 2002 and January 2005. In both of these instances the reversal down into O's by the BPSPX suggested that risk was increasing in these stocks. I like to think about risk in the markets like I think about risk in driving my motorcycle. I used to have a group of financial-related professionals from all over the country ship their bikes out to the Southwest each year. We would then spend a week riding together, taking in the beautiful scenery, and in general have a great "City Slickers" experience. Having done this trip for a number of years, I've ridden through all types of weather. On a perfect day the sun is shining, it's about 75 degrees, and it's just our group out there on the open road. Those days I find myself a little more relaxed at the wheel. I can really take in the picturesque landscape. On a couple of these trips though, the weather was our enemy. One year we were riding in freezing temperatures, blowing snow, and visibility was next to nothing. This was no time to be relaxed at the wheel. I had to concentrate intently, hold the handlebars with a tight grip, and slow down. All of these things I did to compensate for the fact that the conditions were not ideal. We still successfully made it from point A to point B, but the trip wasn't as enjoyable, and the risk of an accident was higher. The Bullish Percent concept is like our weather forecast. Can we expect the trip to be easy and pleasant, or is it

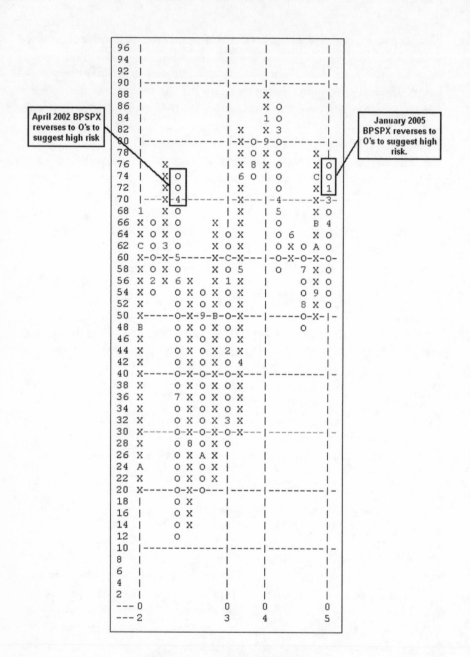

Figure 7.1 S&P 500 Bullish Percent.

228

going to be a trip that is likely to encounter a number of potholes? Somehow we stopped doing this trip. Now I take my wife with me on a trip out west. I love it in New Mexico and Arizona. Maybe in the future I can get a group to start up the biking trips again.

By looking at Figure 7.1 we can see that in both April 2002 and January 2005 the S&P 500 Bullish Percent reversed down into O's suggesting that risk was increasing. The next step in the process we take is to review our holdings to see which still have strong technical pictures, as these are likely to be held in the portfolio. If any holdings have started to exhibit weak technical pictures like sell signals, violating Bullish Support Lines, or giving Relative Strength (RS) sell signals, these will be the first candidates for potential

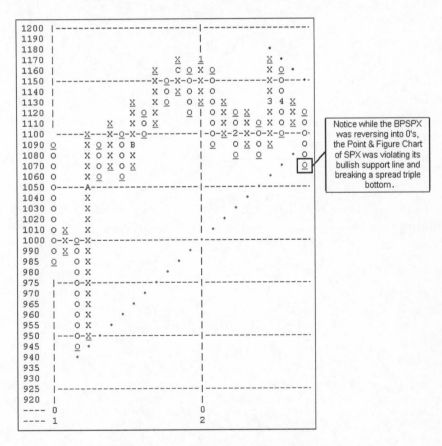

Figure 7.2   S&P 500 Point and Figure chart: 2002.

sales. Let's assume for a minute that in both instances, April 2002 and January 2005, we owned the SPDR S&P 500 ETF (SPY) which replicates the movement of the S&P 500 Capitalization-Weighted Index (SPX). In Figure 7.2 from April 2002, we see that the S&P 500 Bullish Percent reversal down into O's was accompanied by a chart

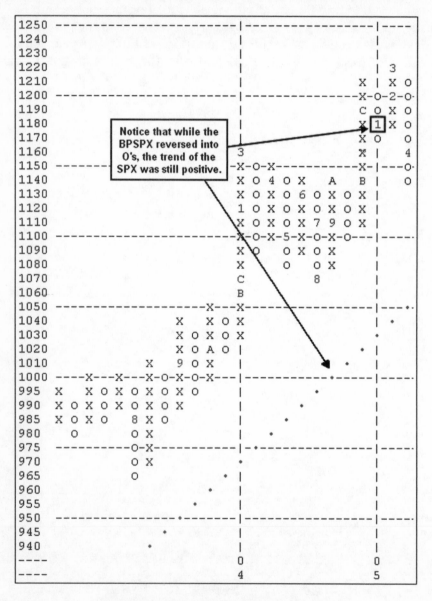

Figure 7.3 S&P 500 Point and Figure chart: 2005.

pattern from the SPX that was also breaking down, making lower tops, and in general showing that supply was coming into control. The defensive action we take with a picture like this is much more stringent. By contrast, in Figure 7.3 we see that in January 2005 the trend chart of the S&P 500 remained above the Bullish Support Line and on a buy signal. The defensive action required here is less stringent. For instance, you might choose not to reduce your equity exposure as much as when the S&P 500 chart is negative.

Other Equity Indicators

The Percent of Stocks above Their Own 10-Week Moving Average Index

This index has one of our most important short-term market indicators. It should be used in conjunction with the High-Low Index. As its name implies, the Percent of 10 is simply made up of the percentage of stocks on any index you are evaluating that are trading above their own 10-Week Moving Average (see Figure 7.4). We keep this indicator for both NYSE and OTC stocks and each sector as well. It is as important to keep abreast of the short-term trend of the overall market as it is to keep abreast of the long-term trend. We use the same grid with this index that we use with the Bullish Percent Index. The vertical axis has a value of 2 percent per box and runs from 0 to 100 percent. The best sell signals come when the index rises above the 70 percent level, then reverses down below that critical level. In cases like this, there is a very high probability that the broad averages have begun a short-term correction. This is significant because the short term often spills over into the long term. Conversely, the best buy signals come when the index declines below the 30 percent level then reverses back up. In the case of the buy signals below 30 percent, the index does not have to cross that level on the upside to be valid.

What about changes between 30 percent and 70 percent? For example, say the Percent of 10 reverses up from below 30 percent changing the prevailing risk level to a short-term buy signal. The index then rises to 58 percent where it encounters supply and reverses into a column of O's. In this case, we defer to the broad Bullish Percents. If the NYSE Bullish Percent were still in X's in this case, we would conclude that demand is still in control of the

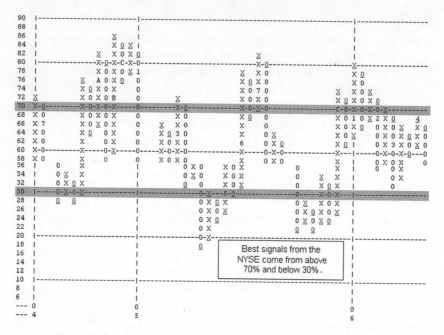

Figure 7.4   NYSE Percent of Stocks above Their 10-Week Moving Average.

market, but a short pause that refreshes in the market could be expected. Overtime we have found that the most important signals from this indicator tend to come from those changes in the Red and Green Zones, above 70 percent and below 30 percents, and particularly when the index gives a buy signal.

This index is of great benefit when you are planning your trade. Investors, however, should never use the Percent of Stocks above Their Own 10-Week Moving Average Index as their sole indicator in making new stock commitments. Rather, it is used to help us with play selection. The NYSE Bullish Percent tells us which team is on the field, offense or defense, and then depending on the position of the short term indicators, the Percent of Stocks above Their Own 10-Week Moving Average, and the High-Low Index discussed next, we can get a better idea of which plays to run. For instance, let's say the NYSE Bullish Percent is in X's but the Percent of 10 has reversed into O's and fallen below the 70 percent level. This would tell us that the risk in the market is now a little higher, so perhaps buying 300 out of your 500 share position would compensate for that increased risk. Or maybe buying an ETF instead of an individual stock would work better for you. In both plays we are still maintaining long exposure, just the manner in which we do it adjusts for the fact the short-term indicator is in a column of O's.

The High-Low Index

This index is another short-term indicator that we use in conjunction with the Percent of 10. Again, just as with the Percent of Stocks above Their 10-Week Moving Average, we keep a High-Low Index on both the NYSE and OTC stocks. If you wish, you can calculate this indicator yourself. Just take the daily NYSE (or OTC) highs divided by the daily NYSE (or OTC) new highs plus the new lows. Then take a 10-day moving average of this number and plot that figure on a grid exactly like the Percent of 10 (see Figure 7.5). The vertical axes will extend from 0 to 100. We evaluate it the same way as the Percent of 10. The two critical levels are 30 percent and 70 percent. Buy signals come from reversals up from below 30 percent. Sell signals come from reversals from above to below 70 percent. Buy and sell signals can also come by exceeding a previous top or bottom, respectively. Reversals from above 70 percent suggest that there is a trend change from more stocks making new highs to more stocks making new lows. Conversely, when the index reverses up from below 30 percent, it tells us the number of stocks making new lows is drying up considerably.

There are a couple of other things we want to point out about this indicator. First, to get a good feel for the risk in the short term, we place the greatest emphasis on the signals when the two short-term indicators are moving in tandem. Second, the High-Low can go above 70 percent and remain above that level for some time, even months at a time. Second, this indicator can really move to extremes, hitting 90 percent or higher and also falling to 10 percent or even lower. Third, when the NYSE High-Low Index goes below the 10 percent level, it is a sign of a very washed-out market. Think about it for a second. To get to 0 percent we would have to see 10 consecutive days of no stocks hitting new highs. Reversals up from 10 percent are usually good buying opportunities. Figure 7.6 shows the times the NYSE High-Low Index has been below 10 percent.

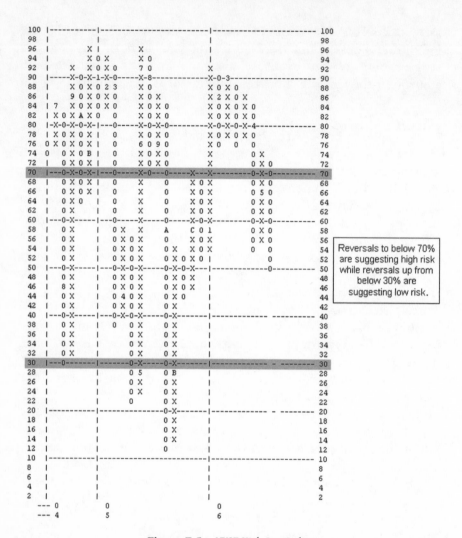

Figure 7.5   NYSE High-Low Index.

The Percent of Stocks Above Their 30-Week Moving Average Index

The NYSE Percent of Stocks above Their 30-Week (150 Day) Moving Average is a longer-term indicator for the NYSE universe of stocks. As its name suggests, this indicator measures the percent of stocks that are trading above their 30-Week Moving Average. Let's say that the 30-Week Moving Average of a stock is 50. If the stock's price is above 50 we say that it is above the 30-Week Moving Aver-

Date	Moved Below 10%	Dow Reading	Low Reading	Dow Reading	Upside Reversal	Dow Reading
March, 1980	3/6/80	828.07	0.9%	800.94	4/10/80	791.47
September, 1981	8/31/81	881.46	2.0%	849.98	10/7/81	868.72
June, 1982	6/7/82	804.03	5.5%	795.57	6/24/82	810.41
February, 1984	2/17/84	1148.87	7.5%	1134.21	2/28/84	1157.14
May, 1984	5/29/84	1101.24	5.3%	1124.35	6/11/84	1115.61
July, 1984	7/18/84	1111.64	5.5%	1096.95	8/2/84	1166.08
October, 1987	10/20/87	1841.01	0.7%	1938.33	1/4/88	2015.25
January, 1990	1/31/90	2590.54	8.9%	2590.54	2/7/90	2640.09
May, 1990	5/2/90	2689.64	9.7%	2689.64	5/7/90	2721.62
August, 1990	8/15/90	2748.27	3.4%	2613.37	9/18/90	2571.29
November, 1994	11/23/94	3674.63	5.4%	3746.29	12/21/94	3801.80
August, 1998	8/31/98	7539.07	4.2%	7615.54	9/23/98	8154.41
October, 1999	10/21/99	10297.7	7.7%	10302.1	10/29/99	10731.8
July, 2002	7/24/02	8191.29	7.5%	8264.39	8/5/02	8043.63

Figure 7.6   NYSE High-Low Index times below 10 percent.

age. Once we do this for all the stocks in the NYSE (we also do it for the Nasdaq market), we plot the percent of stocks above their 30-Week Moving Average on a grid from 0 percent to 100 percent. Like the other indicator charts that we follow, there are two lines of demarcation on the chart, the 70 percent level and the 30 percent level. The 70 percent level and above is the red zone or high-risk area. The 30 percent level and below is the green zone or low risk area. Like the NYSE Bullish Percent, the 30-Week does not get to either of these extreme levels very often, much less to very overbought or oversold conditions of 80 percent or 20 percent. The NYSE 30 has reached the 80 percent level 14 times since 1970. Typically, the 80 percent level has only been seen in very strong markets in which almost all stocks rally.

There is another interesting phenomenon about the NYSE 30-Week that we want to bring to your attention. Dan Sullivan of the *Chartist* found that when the Percent of 30 goes above 80 percent and then falls below 60 percent it will see 40 percent before it sees 80 percent again. This has happened 14 times and on each time the 80-60-40 percent rule has worked. When this phenomenon has happened, it has occurred before important, often severe, corrections in the market. For instance, in October 1982, the Percent of 30 went above 80 percent and then fell below 60 percent in August 1983, which was the beginning of a year-long decline in the market, carrying the NYSE Bullish Percent below 30 percent before another lift off in the market in 1984. The Percent of 30 also saw this action, above 80 percent, below 60 percent, in April 1987 before the Crash of 1987. It was also a very early warning of the 1998 crash. Figure 7.7a is a list of each time the NYSE 30-Week has seen the 80-60-40 phenomenon occur as well as the corresponding Point and Figure chart in Figure 7.7b. For the last two times this indicator saw the 80-60-40 phenomenon.

The Advance-Decline Line

The Advance-Decline Line is a nonprice measure of the trend of the market. It is based on the number of issues advancing and declining

Date Above 80%	Fell Below 60%	Fell Below 40% Before 80%?	Ultimate Low
December, 1970	May, 1971	Yes - July, 1971	November, 1971 - 12%
March, 1972	April, 1972	Yes - June, 1972	October, 1972 - 28%
January, 1975	August, 1975	Yes - August, 1975	September, 1975 - 26%
February, 1976	June, 1976	Yes - October, 1976	November, 1976 - 38%
April, 1978	October, 1978	Yes - October, 1978	November, 1978 - 8%
July, 1980	December, 1980	Yes - February, 1981	September, 1981 - 10%
October, 1982	August, 1983	Yes - February, 1984	May, 1984 - 20%
January, 1985	August, 1985	Yes - September, 1985	September, 1985 - 34%
March, 1986	July, 1986	Yes - September, 1986	September, 1986 - 30%
March, 1987	April, 1987	Yes - October, 1987	September, 1987 - 2%
February, 1981	August, 1991	Yes - February, 1994	December, 1994 - 24%
July, 1997	December, 1987	Yes - July, 1998	August, 1998 - 12%
May, 2003	April, 2004	Yes - May, 2004	August, 2004 - 34%
November, 2004	March, 2005	Yes - May, 2005	May, 2005 - 40%

Figure 7.7a   NYSE 30-Week Moving Average 80-60-40 Rule.

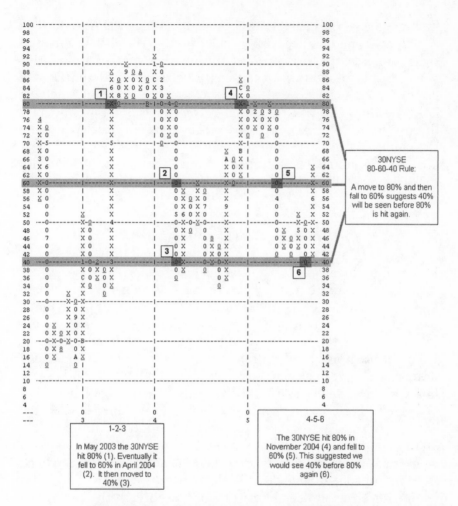

Figure 7.7b NYSE 30-Week Moving Average 80-60-40 Rule.

and not on the price of these issues. Every day, the difference between the issues advancing and the issues declining is calculated. If more issues advanced than declined, the difference is added to the preceding day's total; if more issues declined than advanced, the difference is subtracted from the previous day's total. We keep Advance-Decline Lines for the NYSE, ASE, and Nasdaq markets. We look at the Advance-Decline indicators in two ways. First, we look to see if the level is above that of 10 days ago. If it is, then we say that market's Advance-Decline Line is positive on a short-term basis. Second, we look at a Point and Figure chart of the Advance-

Decline Line. If the chart is on a buy signal, we say the Advance-Decline for that market is positive longer term. If the chart is on a sell signal, we say the Advance-Decline for that market is negative longer term. In addition to looking for Double Tops and Double Bottoms on the chart, we also take into account High Pole and Low Pole Warnings. We like to look at Advance-Decline Lines because they, like the Bullish Percent, give each stock one vote. While the Dow Jones or Nasdaq Composite may be going down what are most of the stocks doing? The Advance-Decline Lines give us insight into the "true market" and not just an index of 30 stocks or so.

Average Weekly Distribution

Regression to mean—it's a natural progression that we all go through in our lives. Just the other day I was on my way to Washington, DC, from Richmond, Virginia. The two-hour drive north was going quite smoothly. There was relatively no traffic, no police running radar, and the weather was sunny. The conditions were right to make good time, so I pushed the envelope and ended up speeding. I get just outside of Washington, DC, and don't you know it, an accident. Darn, foiled again. I had just been regressed to mean. Have you ever gotten too big for your britches? Come on, be truthful. We all at times become too full of ourselves and all of a sudden we get figuratively slapped down. We get regressed to mean. Something happens to make us aware we are getting a little out of control and we settle back to normal.

It's life's way of keeping nature in the center of the curve. In a particular field there might be a certain number of rabbits. As they begin to reproduce, their numbers grow geometrically. The more rabbits in one particular field mean the available food supply decreases as a percentage for each rabbit. The rabbits reproduce until starvation kills some off. This is life's way of regressing the rabbits back to normal for this field. Then, the over abundance of rabbits in the field attracts more wolves to the area. The wolves in the area cause the population to regress past the mean to the endangered side of the equation. The wolves leave because their food supply is gone, and the cycle begins again. This is how the stock market works.

One of the best ways to graphically represent this movement back and forth to mean is with the 10-week trading band. We all remember the bell curve concept from our college Stats 101 class. Given a set of data, we can construct a range, which is depicted as a bell curve. There are six standard deviations to the bell curve (Figure 7.8). Three standard deviations to the left are considered 100 percent oversold. Three standard deviations to the right are considered 100 percent overbought. The middle of the curve is normal and most of the time stocks reside within one standard deviation of normal. For each stock and index, we can take 10 weeks worth of data and create a bell curve. When a stock gets to the overbought side of the curve, it will typically move back to the middle. There are two ways a stock or index can get back to the middle of the curve. First, the stock can fall in price and move back to the middle of the curve. Second, as time passes, the stock can stay relatively the same in price and the curve shifts. Conversely, when a stock or index gets oversold, you will typically see it move back to the middle in one of those two ways. As a general rule, you will see strong RS stocks trade between the middle and the top of their trading bands. Most of the time you will see weak RS stocks trade between the bottom and the middle of their trading bands.

Since every stock in the DWA universe is plotted on its 10-week trading band or bell curve, we can obtain a calculation of where the average stock lies on that bell curve. This chart is called the Weekly Distribution (WD) chart. What the WD chart does is take a simple average of where all the stocks are on their

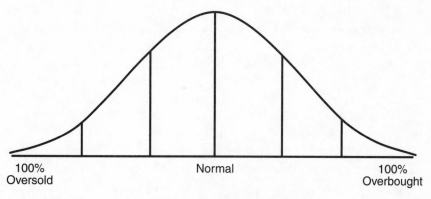

100%
Oversold

Normal

100%
Overbought

Figure 7.8 Bell Curve—Normal Distribution.

10-week trading band. For instance, if there were two stocks in our universe, one at –100 percent (100 percent oversold) and one at 100 percent (100 percent overbought), then the average would be 0 percent. Using the symbol WDALL you can access this chart at any time on the DWA system.

If a stock were three standard deviations above normal, it would be considered 100 percent overbought. Conversely, if a stock were three standard deviations below normal, it would be considered 100 percent oversold. The middle of the curve or normal is considered 0. These three areas depict the range of the 10-week trading band where the top is 100 percent overbought, the bottom is 100 percent oversold, and the middle is the 0 percent point, or the middle of the statistical bell curve. So, if we were to see a reading on the Average WD chart of 0 percent, this would mean that if you were to flip through individual stock charts by hand, what you will find is that the average stock is going to reside at the middle of its trading band. A reading of 0 percent means that the average stock is neither overbought nor oversold as nature has regressed the stock back to mean. A reading of 50 percent, for instance, would mean that the average stock is 50 percent of the way between the middle of the trading and the top of the trading band.

Looking at the Weekly Distribution for All Stocks, see Figure 7.9, especially over a period of years, we can get a feel for when the average stock, and thus the overall markets, are a little high and due for a pullback or a little low and due for a bounce. We have found that this chart tends to reside between the 50 percent (overbought) and –40 percent (oversold) levels. When the average stock is up in the 30 to 50 percent overbought territory, we tend to see near-term pullbacks in the market as stocks have rallied in a condition like this. Conversely, we have seen market bottoms come when the indicator is approaching the –40 percent level. As a sidebar, to get to levels of –70 percent or more the drop in the market must be extreme, swift, and severe like July 2002 and September 2001, for instance. The Weekly Distribution for All Stocks chart is a secondary indicator to the Bullish Percents, the Percent of Stocks Above Their 10- and 30-Week charts, and the High-Low Indices, but we find this chart especially helpful in gaining an overall perspective of the market on a near term basis. We should also note that the WD chart is available for sectors as well. The format for this chart is WD, and

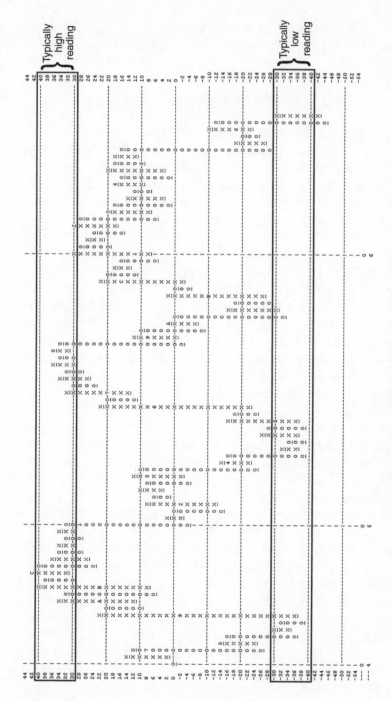

Figure 7.9 Weekly Distribution Reading for All Stocks.

241

the first four letters of the DWA sector. For instance, WDBIOM would be the WD chart for the Biomedics/Genetics sector.

Summary of the Indicators

Now let's stop for a second and allow this discussion to seep in, because I know that we have covered a lot. We have talked about several different concepts and indicators that can be applied to the NYSE and Nasdaq markets as well as to sectors. Each week to keep this information straight in my mind, I sit down and fill out the Market Indicator Summary form shown in Figure 7.10. We do the same type of exercise on our web site, but I still find that writing something by hand is especially helpful. It just makes what is going on in the market more real when you write it down instead of just looking at it on the computer screen.

Once I have the Market Indicator Summary form filled out, I evaluate it. You would be surprised that there are very few changes. Making changes in the overall bias of the indicators we have outlined here is like moving an aircraft carrier, not a jet ski. But when those changes occur, it is important to heed them and take action where necessary. If you become very comfortable with these indicators and the types of strategies you want to employ when changes do occur, you won't have the "deer in the headlights syndrome." You will intuitively understand what used to baffle you. Someone once said, "lack of decisiveness has caused more failures than lack of intelligence or ability." I think this is so true of investing and in life.

I have just recently taken up golf and am absolutely enthralled with the game and trying to improve. Those of you who play golf have probably read some of Robert J. Rotella's works. He was the director of sports psychology at the University of Virginia and is a consultant to many professional golfers; he also writes extensively about golf. One of Dr. Rotella's tips that stayed with me was, "It is more important to be decisive than to be correct when preparing to play any golf shot, particularly a putt." Life on Wall Street means that you will not be correct every time. However, you must not let that keep you from sticking to your game plan, and you must not allow yourself to second-guess your tactical moves. One of the problems with pursuing perfection is hunting for the perfect method.

Indicator Sheet for 6/3/02

Indicator	X	O
NYSE Bullish Percent		62%
OTC Bullish Percent		46%
Optionable Bullish Percent		50%
S&P 500 Bullish Percent		58%
NASDAQ 100 Bullish Percent		29%
NYSE 30 Week Moving Average		64%
OTC 30 Week Moving Average		44%
NYSE 10 Week Moving Average		42%
NYSE High-Low Index		74%
OTC 10 Week Moving Average		32%
OTC High-Low Index		46%
Advance-Decline Lines		Neg.
Weekly Distribution for All Stocks		−12

Notice all the indicators were in columns of O's

Indicator Sheet for 4/2/03

Indicator	X	O
NYSE Bullish Percent	42%	
OTC Bullish Percent		34%
Optionable Bullish Percent	40%	
S&P 500 Bullish Percent	42%	
NASDAQ 100 Bullish Percent	50%	
NYSE 30 Week Moving Average	50%	
OTC 30 Week Moving Average	48%	
NYSE 10 Week Moving Average	64%	
NYSE High-Low Index	60%	
OTC 10 Week Moving Average	56%	
OTC High-Low Index	62%	
Advance-Decline Lines	Pos.	
Weekly Distribution for All Stocks	−8	

Notice almost all of the indicators were in columns of X's

Sample Sheet

Indicator	X	O
NYSE Bullish Percent		
OTC Bullish Percent		
Optionable Bullish Percent		
S&P 500 Bullish Percent		
NASDAQ 100 Bullish Percent		
NYSE 30 Week Moving Average		
OTC 30 Week Moving Average		
NYSE 10 Week Moving Average		
NYSE High-Low Index		
OTC 10 Week Moving Average		
OTC High-Low Index		
Advance-Decline Lines		
Weekly Distribution for All Stocks		

Figure 7.10   Indicator Summary table.

Trying a new system each week will not get you to your goal. It requires remaining focused on one method and maintaining consistency and discipline. You may find that Fibonacci numbers, Gann angles, or astrology work for you, and that is fine. But once you find the method that you are comfortable with, you must stick with it. We find the Point and Figure method works the best for us, because it is firmly cemented in something we can easily understand and

know is true—the irrefutable law of supply and demand. If you begin
to second-guess your play book, you are doomed to lose the game.
Take those principles you have practiced and implement them when
the time comes. Remain true to yourself, win, lose, or draw. Nothing
is right every single time but the objective is to be more right than
wrong and to stack as many odds in your favor as possible.

When you are evaluating the form in Figure 7.10 each week,
think about some of the scenarios that might occur. If there are
more indicators in X's and rising for each market, then I know I
have the football and can run plays. If the indicators are in X's but
all near the 70 percent level, then I know the risk is high and I
need to make sure the defensive players are well rested and ready
to come on the field at a moment's notice. If the majority of the
indicators are in O's and falling, that tells me we have a weak market and I should continue to employ wealth preservation strategies. If the indicators are in O's but all below 30 percent, then I
need to begin formulating shopping lists of ideas to begin buying
once the indicators reverse up. What you will find is that some indicators move faster than others, and when major changes in the
market occur, it is like a puzzle coming together. When you dump
out a puzzle on a table, it is a hodgepodge of pieces. Once you get
those corner pieces in place and the border set, however, the picture becomes much clearer. That's the way the indicators work.

Mutual Fund Indicators

As we pointed out at the beginning of this chapter, you can apply
the Bullish Percent to any grouping of stocks; you can do the
same thing to a universe of mutual funds. If you recall from Chapter 2, when plotting a mutual fund chart, we use three different
scales for varying levels of sensitivity. Because of this fact, mutual fund Bullish Percents are maintained using three different
sensitivity levels for each group. The short-term Bullish Percent
reads the short-term charts for each fund using relatively small
box sizes to pick up more net asset value (NAV) action and can be
used by anyone who needs to take advantage of that short-term
reading. The intermediate version is less sensitive and each fund
is measured using its intermediate chart, which uses larger box
sizes to filter out more NAV action, and this indicator can be used

by all investors as the to bullish or bearish nature of the fund market. The long-term Bullish Percent uses very large box sizes to filter out even more action and presents the long-term investor with something to give guidance as to the major long-term areas of support and resistance for the fund. Figure 7.11 is a picture of the Intermediate Term All Equity Mutual Fund Bullish Percent.

The longer term the Bullish Percent is, the less activity. All three Bullish Percents can still be useful in your analysis though. I like to think about the varying nature of these Bullish Percents like a weather forecast. You can look at tomorrow's forecast, the seven-day forecast, or you can take a look at the entire season's projection for say rainfall. You will notice all of the same principles about Bullish Percents you have already learned to apply— X's mean offense and O's mean defense and field position analysis is important. Something else you'll notice about mutual fund Bullish Percents is that they tend to move to greater extremes, often hitting 10 percent and 90 percent, especially the shorter term Bullish Percents. Once you learn the application of the Bullish Percent concept, you can apply it to any universe—the S&P 500, mutual funds, or even foreign markets.

Other unique indicators in the mutual fund arena include additional moving average indicators. The 40-Week Bullish Percent is just like a 10-Week or 30-Week Bullish Percent but this indicator measures the percent of funds in a group that has its NAV trading above its 40-Week Moving Average, which is another way to say the 200-day moving average. Many technicians look at the 200-day moving average of the markets and individual equities so it is a fairly important measurement of the health of price movement over time. It is helpful to know where this average is especially if the fund's trend line is too far away to be of immediate importance. The moving average is an invisible trend line, if you will, that is always relevant and you can use it to make trending evaluations.

Another longer term moving average indicator for mutual funds is the 1040 Bullish Percent. This measures the percent of funds that have their 10-Week Moving Average above their 40-Week Moving Average. Another way to look at this is whether the fund has its 50-Day Moving Average above its 200-Day Moving Average. If so, that would be considered a "buy signal" in the Bullish Percent calculation. Funds that have this characteristic are considered to be positively trending and vice versa.

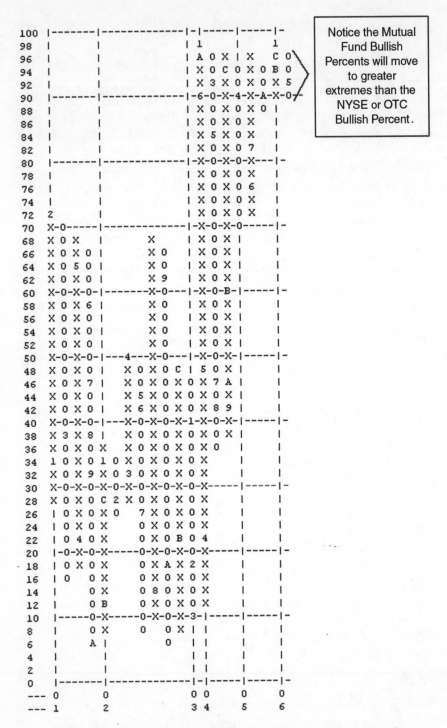

Figure 7.11 Intermediate Term Bullish Percent for All Equity Mutual Funds.

Intended Use	Symbol	Group	Type
Short-Term Analysis	BMPU0	All Equity Funds	BP - Short-Term
	TWMU0	All Equity Funds	10 Week
	MOMU0	All Equity Funds	Weekly Momentum
Intermediate Analysis	BPMU0@2	All Equity Funds	BP - Intermediate
	40MU0	All Equity Funds	40 Week
	30MU0	All Equity Funds	30 Week
Long-Term Analysis	BPMU0@3	All Equity Funds	BP Long-Term
	PTMU0	All Equity Funds	Positive Trend
	1040MU0	All Equity Funds	10 Week/40 Week

Figure 7.12   Mutual Fund Indicator Summary Table.

At our web site (www.dorseywright.com), you can find the most extensive technical research available on mutual funds in the world. Above is a recap of the absolute mutual fund indicators followed on our web site. Figure 7.12 is categorized by an investor's time frame. Those investors sensitive to the short-term fluctuations of the markets need to pay attention to the short-term indicators. Investors that have more of a buy and hold objective can use the long-term indicators to evaluate their funds and more tactically manage their portfolios. We tend to find the intermediate indicators to be the area of emphasis for us.

POINTS AND FIGURES BY DORSEY, WRIGHT MONEY MANAGEMENT

Save more money. Everyone wants to know the answer to the question "How to get Rich?" but no one wants to believe that the answer may be as simple as saving more. Perhaps Americans are simply averse to saving and therefore living beneath their means. In fact, judging from the data on consumer debt, many Americans are busy living beyond their means.

Putnam's new study, mentioned in October 2005's *Wall Street Journal*, suggests that savings may be the key to building assets. Putnam studied the retirement savings plan of "Joe," the prototypical 401(k) investor, over a 15-year period. Joe started off earning $40,000 in 1990, received 3 percent annual pay increases, and finished off 2004 earning $60,500 annually. Joe put 2 percent of his salary in his 401(k) each year.

Scenario 1 has Joe invested with a conservative asset allocation which never changes, and somehow (probably much like most investors) Joe manages to pick out bottom-tier mutual funds. He ends up with $39,700 after 15 years.

Scenario 2 gives Joe a crystal ball. He has the same conservative asset allocation, but this time Joe buys all of the best-performing funds. In this scenario, he ends up with $42,000 after 15 years. In other words, after 15 years of saving, he's $2,300 ahead because of better investment performance.

Scenario 3 makes Joe double his salary deferral to 4 percent a year, but still sticks him in the crummy funds. In this case, Joe ends up with $79,500 after 15 years. Doubling his savings has doubled his wealth.

There's no doubt that Putnam spun the story to encourage larger 401(k) contributions, some of which would undoubtedly end up in some of their funds. The truth is that savings counts for a lot more early in the game, when the absolute size of the pool of funds is small. Joe's 401(k) contribution of $1,210 for 2005 (2 percent of $60,500) is relatively a lot bigger when his capital base is $4,000 than when it is $100,000. As the capital grows, the investment performance does become more critical. With a $100,000 account, a 10 percent year in investment performance has the ability to add a lot more value than Joe boosting his contribution rate to 4 percent.

Savings, it seems, is particularly important when you are starting out. When the asset base is small, incremental savings can make a big difference in how fast it grows. Joe's case is a good example of that, as were the Beardstown Ladies. For a young or new investor, it's most important to get them motivated to save and build some capital. Worrying about which fund to buy or the return of one fund versus another really isn't the point.

Once the pool of capital becomes larger, the focus should shift to investment management. It's not that savings isn't still important—it's just that a good return on the portfolio can add more value than additional savings. I've never seen a rule of thumb mentioned, but just from looking at Putnam's example, something like the greater of $100,000 or 10× the annual contribution rate might be a reasonable threshold at which to start paying more attention to investment performance.

Chapter 8

SECTOR ROTATION TOOLS

Sector Analysis with Bullish Percent Indexes

The same Bullish Percent concept that is applied to the NYSE, OTC, Mutual Fund, and International markets can be applied to sectors within the market. In fact, on our web site we have created Bullish Percent Indexes for every viable stock exchange in the world from Malaysia to Portugal. This application expands our ability to separately evaluate the pieces of the puzzle. The puzzle is the whole market, made up of many sectors. We look at these sectors as the pieces of the puzzle. Sector analysis is probably the most important consideration when investing. Sectors are like the schools of fish you might have seen on the Discovery Channel. These schools dart quickly in one direction or the other, but what is amazing is how a whole school of fish moves perfectly together on each turn, as if some sixth sense tells each individual fish what the group is about to do. Sector rotation tends to behave the same way. Economic stimuli that would have an effect on a particular sector tend to affect all the stocks underlying the sector causing them to move in unison. Sector analysis is one of the most important yet least analyzed parts of the market. We place tremendous emphasis on sector rotation in our daily work. I have said in previous chapters that about 75 percent of the risk in a stock is associated with the market and sector, and only 25 percent is stock-specific risk. Stocks don't just jump about with no rhyme or reason. Moves tend to be orchestrated like the Boston Philharmonic.

Another analogy keeps coming to mind. I picture a herd of wildebeest romping across the African plains. They move in unison, first in one direction, then another. A few of the herd get out of sync, but the majority tend to move together. Sectors operate the same way. Wall Street tends to follow the actions of the herd. First the sector's supply demand relationship changes and more informed buyers begin to cause the stocks in that particular sector to rise. As the sector moves up, other institutions are alerted that the move is on, and they climb on board. Eventually, the mainstream financial media catch wind of a sector move underway and begin to write articles about how the industry has made a turnaround and should have clear sailing ahead. This draws in the individual investors just in time to catch the top. By the time the articles appear in magazines about how great the industry is, almost everyone is in who wants to be in leaving little available demand to force the industry up much further. The last group in is the unsuspecting public, who use newspapers and magazines as their primary source of stock market research. *Time* magazine has a cover story about XYZ Company rated "Company of the Year." Mr. Jones, who sees this major statement on the cover of this mainstream magazine, calls his broker and buys the stock, virtually drying up the last available demand for the sector. Everyone is now in who wants to be in. The magazine cover signaled maximum saturation of positive information about this company. At this point, all it takes is the slightest selling pressure to start the downturn because there are no buyers left. With little demand left, it only takes a small amount of supply to turn the situation around. Once the public is in, virtually no one is left to do the buying. Remember that prices move as a direct result of supply-and-demand imbalances. If there are no more buyers left to cast their vote, supply, by definition, must take the upper hand. The sector then begins to lose sponsorship and moves to an oversold condition where everyone who wants to be out of the sector is out, and the whole process starts anew. It's actually beautiful how these natural rhythms evolve. When you think of the seasons changing, or the produce in the supermarket coming in and out of season, think of sector rotation as I do.

I mentioned magazine covers. Watch them carefully. The next time you are in the airport, look at the magazine rack and see if you can find a widely read magazine that makes a major statement on its cover about some sector of the market—something like "The Banking Industry Is in Trouble." If you find one, buy the magazine and keep it. Actually, just keep the cover. Normally, the trend in that sector will continue to move for a couple of months in the direction the cover suggests, as the last Joneses buy their shares. Give that sector eight months, and you will find its behavior has a high probability of being opposite of that suggested on the magazine cover. The reason for this is that the covers stirs Mr. Jones and Ms. Smith into action and while all the Joneses and Smiths are busy reacting, the sector moves in the forecasted direction. Once these investors are in and the door slams behind them, there is no more buying or selling pressure (whichever the cover suggests) left to sponsor the sector. The forces of supply and demand slowly begin to change, optimism turns to pessimism or visa versa, and the sector takes the opposite tack. Try it—you will be amazed. It's simply human nature.

To put some quantitative research on why sector rotation is so important in stock selection, I want to discuss an interesting study we did at Dorsey, Wright & Associates (DWA). In this study, we had four hypothetical investors invest $10,000 starting in 1990; each had a different set of investment rules. The first investor used a buy-and-hold strategy. The second timed the market. The third and fourth investors both used sector timing. The study looks at each one of the theories from 1990 to 2005.

Mr. Buy and Hold started with $10,000 and just bought the S&P 500 and held that original investment through thick and thin; his account grew to $35,322. That is certainly not a bad return, about 8.2 percent annualized and the portfolio hit its peek in 1999 and still hasn't recovered to those levels yet, six years later. He did what we call "ride them up and ride them down." The next investor, the market timer did even better though. For the purposes of the study, Mr. Market Timer was omnipotent enough to know every month when the S&P 500 was up and stayed invested for those months; and when the S&P 500 was going to show a loss for that month, he was not invested. Keep in mind we know no one has this ability in the real world. Using these rules, Mr. Market Timer turned his $10,000 into $440,290! The third investor was Mr. Good Sector Timer. Like, Mr. Market Timer, Mr. Good Sector Timer was omnipotent about the fate of sectors in the marketplace. Every year he consulted the crystal ball and knew exactly what sector was going to be the best performer for the coming year. By putting his money into the best performing sector each year, his account swelled from the original $10,000 to $3,656,168 by the end of 2005. This was spectacular performance to say the least. Finally, the last investor was Mr. Poor Sector Timer. This poor soul didn't have fate on his side and invested in the worst performing sector each year. His portfolio had dwindled to $260 by the end of 15 years. You can graphically see these results in Figure 8.1.

While all these investors are fictitious and certainly no one would ever be able to have the 100 percent accuracy that Mr. Market Timer and Mr. Good Sector Timer had, the study points out that market and sector timing are extremely important in investing. Being able to identify strong sectors and weak sectors can enable one to gain an advantage over just buying and holding

Year End	Buy and Hold Strategy	Perfect Market Timing	Buying the Best Performing Sector	Buying the Worst Performing Sector
Beginning	$ 10,000	$ 10,000	$ 10,000	$ 10,000
1990	$ 9,344	$ 12,253	$ 11,271	$ 5,499
1991	$ 11,802	$ 17,334	$ 18,135	$ 5,550
1992	$ 12,329	$ 19,694	$ 22,435	$ 4,676
1993	$ 13,199	$ 22,256	$ 27,604	$ 4,334
1994	$ 12,996	$ 26,028	$ 33,864	$ 3,567
1995	$ 17,429	$ 35,092	$ 51,487	$ 3,978
1996	$ 20,960	$ 45,198	$ 69,935	$ 3,859
1997	$ 27,460	$ 67,962	$ 105,078	$ 4,215
1998	$ 34,783	$ 103,921	$ 282,008	$ 3,151
1999	$ 41,575	$ 140,880	$ 753,836	$ 2,605
2000	$ 37,359	$ 168,486	$ 1,176,587	$ 885
2001	$ 32,487	$ 208,068	$ 1,315,424	$ 404
2002	$ 24,896	$ 248,911	$ 1,363,173	$ 248
2003	$ 31,463	$ 333,023	$ 2,058,938	$ 266
2004	$ 34,293	$ 388,507	$ 2,726,652	$ 270
2005	$ 35,322	$ 440,290	$ 3,656,168	$ 260

Note: Buy & Hold and Market Timing based on S&P 500; Sector performance based on Dow Jones Sector Indices

Figure 8.1   Buy and Hold versus Market Timing versus Sector Timing.

without regard for sector rotation. One doesn't even have to be close to getting every sector move correct to outperform the buy-and-hold theory.

When evaluating sectors, you must be a contrarian. You must find the courage to buy stocks in sectors that are out of favor. You must avoid the crowd. This is extremely difficult as it goes against human nature. We tend to gravitate to the crowd. You go to your neighborhood supermarket, it's payday and you are sure the store will be crowded. When you arrive at the store, you see that a major incident of sorts has captured everyone's attention. There is a major crowd around this incident. Do you go with the crowd to see what is happening or do you take advantage of an empty store while the other shoppers are crowded around the incident outside? The sector Bullish Percent indexes force you to go into the store and shop while you can with no interference. You will be able to have your pick of the best produce, best meats, not wait in line at the deli, and have first choice in the marked-down meat section. On top of that, you will be able to check out with no line and all because you went against the crowd.

That contrary view of things is exactly what Earnest Staby was talking about in the mid-1940s. As mentioned earlier, trend charts always look most bullish at market tops and most bearish at market bottoms. The Bullish Percent Indexes force you to be more negative at tops and more positive at bottoms. Once you see more than 70 percent of the stocks underlying the market or a sector go on buy signals, you are in a condition where just about everyone is in who wants to be in. When translated into supply and demand, it simply suggests that the availability of demand has been spent. If this is the case, then an investor should be less enthusiastic about buying stock in the market or that sector when the index is at 70 percent or higher. When the index is near the 30 percent level or lower, it's time to put your buy list together.

When I was a stockbroker, I went with the crowd. It was easier to do business that way. Even though I was at a major brokerage firm with highly paid fundamental analysts who were literally hit or miss (you never knew which), my primary source of research was the *Wall Street Journal* and *Barron's* weekly financial newspaper. When those didn't yield enough ideas, I listened to the broker next to me pitching a stock. All of us got ideas the same way, and as you may have already guessed, the process was lackluster at best. Our training back then was basically in sales and not much else. It really hasn't changed much since then either. Now the emphasis for many stockbrokers is on raising money and giving it to a "professional manager" to manage, knowing full well that over 75 percent of all managers and mutual funds never outperform the broad averages. The broker's place in this equation is to manage the manager and manage the customer relation for a fee. He primarily performs a middleman function. For the most part, computers perform this function as they do in most any other business. Somehow I seriously doubt this type of fee for the middleman function will rise in the future. What is a broker to do, though? Most brokers have no plan of action one way or the other. Don't get me wrong, there are many craftsmen out there indeed; and many of them subscribe to the Point and Figure method of managing accounts. These people bring major value to the table. The investor's job is to find a broker who has a solid game plan that includes not only buy strategies but also sell strategies. I assure you, you will not find one by going to a branch office of any firm and asking for the broker of the day. Good stockbrokers who have all the skills to manage the money themselves are a rare breed these days. When you find one, stick with that broker. If you need one, just e-mail us (DWA@dorseywright.com), and we can supply the name of a craftsman who lives near your area. Most of our clients understand the concepts in this book and use them in their daily market operations. There are still no guarantees but I assure you, I would want a broker who at least had the principles of this book firmly in mind. This is his operating system, just like Windows XP. There is no question about it; wealth is still created in the stock market. But as we also found out in 2000 to 2002 the market is the fastest place to lose wealth if your portfolio is not managed properly. The year 2000 was a real eye-opener for most investors. Recently, I had a Sunday morning call at my home from an independent broker in New Jersey who decided he would be better off having the Money Management arm of DWA handle a number of his accounts. The market had just taken the wind out his sails. Not only had it taken a strong understanding of Point and Figure Technical Analysis to negotiate that market from 2000 to 2002, it also took a good understanding of how to use the options product to help manage the volatility and risk of the markets.

We run Bullish Percent calculations on numerous sectors as well as international sectors. International sector rotation is becoming increasingly more important as we shift to a total global society. In Chapter 6, we discussed the NYSE Bullish Percent Index in detail. The same principles apply here. You might think these concepts are universally known, but they aren't. It's still a lost art. There use to be a TV show called *The Street*. I was totally surprised that on the show they shouted over the broker's intercom, "The Point and Figure Charts are now updated." It really floored me when I heard this. How did Hollywood ever learn about the Point and Figure concept and feel it was important enough to create an audio that all the viewers of the program could hear? I was so surprised because very few individuals or professionals understand these concepts. After reading this book, you will join a very elite group of investors I often call the SEAL Team 1 of Wall Street. You would be hard-pressed to find a broker, outside our client list, who understands this philosophy and has reached what we would call craftsman status. The reason is simple, it takes some education and dedication to understand it, and most investors and professionals are not interested in going that extra mile to become a true craftsman. A good friend of mine, Dave Winder is a Master Plumber. He told me it takes four years to become a craftsman plumber. Why would the business of investing take any less time? Those of you who are reading this book are a rare breed indeed. You are learning a lost art.

Everything you learned in Chapter 6 on the Bullish Percent Index applies here, so I'm not going to rehash the discussion. If you find you do not understand this concept thoroughly, go back to Chapter 6 and reread it. Sectors employ the same concept, but the number of stocks in the sector universe is smaller than that of the New York Stock Exchange (NYSE) or Nasdaq universe. Because of the smaller number of stocks in sector Bullish Percents, they tend to move faster than the NYSE Bullish Percent. To construct a statistically valid Bullish Percent, a sector should have a minimum of 100 stocks. If you have less than 100 stocks, then one stock's buy or sell signal could move the Bullish Percent more than 6 percent. The best way to get a handle on using this concept as well as other indicators for sectors is to take an example and go through it. Let's take a look at a sector Bullish Percent chart and outline on the chart where the pertinent changes took place.

Electric Utility Bullish Percent

In Figure 8.2, you can see the Electric Utility Bullish Percent. Many people would regard this as a sleepy sector, not worthy of consideration because "it doesn't move enough." That really is not the case at all. This sector, like others, has provided good opportunities over the years. In 1994, the Electric Utility Bullish Percent chart fell to 24 percent. This is down into the "Green Zone," "Promised Land," or "oversold" territory. The fall to 24 percent had come after the Electric Utility Sector Bullish Percent reached as high as 94 percent in February 1993 and then reversed down in December 1993. The reversal down in December 1993 into O's suggested that you bring the defensive team on the field with respect to electric utilities. In your portfolio, you would have wanted to examine the electric utility stocks you owned on a fundamental and technical basis. If the individual stock had deteriorated on either account, then action was warranted. Remember that a reversal down from above 70 percent puts the sector on defense and suggests high risk. If you owned electric utility stocks in December 1993, you had a high-risk position in your portfolio. To mitigate that risk, you would have several choices. You could set a stop-loss point at which you were not willing to give back any more. You could have taken partial profits off the table thus reducing your exposure to the sector. You could have bought protective puts on your electric utility positions giving you the right to sell that stock at a specific price at a specific time in the future. Again, the whole point would be to reduce risk in an otherwise high-risk sector. You will read in the Fixed Income Indicator chapter that at the same time the Electric Utility Bullish Percent was reversing down, the fixed income indicators were also giving major sell signals in November 1993. Do you see how this is all coming together, and the pieces of the puzzle begin to fall into place? Well, the Electric Utility Bullish Percent fell all

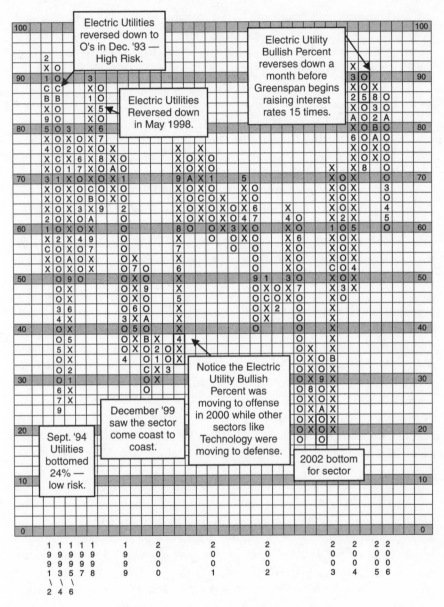

Figure 8.2   Electric Utilities Bullish Percent chart.

the way down to 24 percent by September 1994. Sometimes, sectors fall in a straight line and other times they move down like a staircase with each rally producing lower highs and each sell-off producing lower bottoms. From the February 1993 high in the PHLX Utility Index (UTY) to the September 1994 low, the UTY was down 27.5 percent. That's a utility index, mind you, down 27.5 percent!

Now continuing forward in time, in January 1995, the Electric Utility Bullish Percent chart reversed up to X's meaning we bring the offensive team back on the field with respect to the sector. As well, the bond market indicators were beginning to give buy signal, the first since the November 1993 sell signal. This information would have suggested you evaluate your fundamental inventory of electric utility stocks and find those stocks controlled by demand to initiate new positions in. You could have also bought calls on the PHLX Utility Index (UTY) or purchased a utility ETF allowing you to buy a school of utility fish instead of owning just one fish. Just as there are numerous ways to be defensive, there are numerous ways to be offensive, too. Another simple strategy you might consider when a sector reverses up from a low level is to buy not just one name within that sector, but two. This can be advantageous for a couple of reasons: First, when a sector is reversing up from an oversold condition and has some other factors going for it, we overweight that sector. Let's say typically you take a 5 percent position in a sector. If the sector Relative Strength (RS) is strong and things are lining up well for the sector, then you might take an 8 percent position. By purchasing two names in the sector, it allows us some extra flexibility when we feel the indicators warrant scaling back in the sector. Second, it seems like Murphy is always hanging around the corner. The electric utility stock you choose to buy would be the one with some type of noose around its neck that doesn't allow that stock to rally while the rest in the group take off like a rocket. Think about Microsoft (MSFT) in the software sector. From April 2003 to April 2006, the general markets were in a rising trend with the S&P 500 up 54.5 percent during that time. Individual sectors were also doing well. The DWA Software (DWASOFT) sector made a nice recovery from its 2000 to 2002 decline of about 56 percent, to rally 118 percent during the next three years. If the software sector was up 118 percent, it would make sense that the largest software company in the world with sound fundamental numbers would participate. However, Microsoft was only up 10.8 percent. Of course utilizing peer RS can help you avoid this situation but sometime having two individual picks within a sector can help smooth out any mistakes along the way.

Just as the move down in 1993 for electric utilities was very sharp and steep, the upmove for electric utilities in 1995 was powerful. The sector Bullish Percent rallied from 30 percent on the reversal up into X's straight up to 80 percent. During this time frame (January 1995 to March 1996), the PHLX Utility Index (UTY) was up 21.7 percent. This was a good move for a "slow" sector like electric utilities, and that return doesn't include any dividends.

Let's continue to look at the Electric Utility Bullish Percent chart for the year 1998. In March 1998, the sector Bullish Percent was at 90 percent, near those 1993 highs of 94 percent. Now look at that chart again and say out loud whether you think this is a high-risk or low-risk time to buy electric utility stocks. It's a high-risk time. With a reading above 70 percent on a Bullish Percent chart, it tells us that most of the people who want to be in the sector are already in. The availability of demand to continue to push the sector higher is extremely limited. In May, the sector Bullish Percent reverses down to O's and falls to 66 percent by September. Then in October 1998, the electric utility sector reverses up to X's at 72 percent. The sector is back in X's, but the field position is 72 percent. What would you do? Would you go out and enthusiastically buy electric utility stocks the way you would when the sector is reversing up from below 30 percent? You probably would not. In fact, I'm sure after reading this book you definitely would not. A sector Bullish Percent may be in a column of X's, but the field position may not be good; have patience, it will come back to a better level. They all do. Or, if you have to have a presence in that sector, take just partial positions, not full positions. By January 1999, the Electric Utility Bullish Percent was back into a column of O's at 72 percent. It resulted in a drop to 28 percent.

The Electric Utility Bullish Percent is no different than any of the DWA sector Bullish Percents, from small sectors like precious metals to large macro sectors like energy or technology. After you finish reading this case study on the Electric Utility Bullish Percent, go to our web site (www.dorseywright.com) and get another sector Bullish Percent chart and do this exact same exercise. The more charts you look at and analyze, the higher your confidence level will get in this methodology. Now, let's pick up again with the Electric Utility Bullish Percent chart in Figure 8.2 with the end of the year 1999. During the year 1999, the Electric Utility Bullish Percent fell from 70 percent down to the 28 percent level. That move from October 1998 to the December 1999 lows saw the PHLX Utility Index (UTY), fall 28 percent. In January 2000, the Electric Utility Bullish Percent was reversing up to X's at 34 percent, great field position. Like the NYSE Bullish Percent, often times a sector will retest its lows after reversing up from such a low level. The electric utility sector made a higher bottom in March 2000, and in April 2000, was back in X's at 38 percent. Think about this a second. The electric utility sector was reversing up to X's right when technology sectors were giving RS sell signals. The sector was the best performing in 2000, up over 40 percent while the Nasdaq Composite was down almost 40 percent for the year. When one door closes, another window opens, but we have to keep our eyes open to those new opportunities. I love good peaches in the summer. But come fall, you can rarely find a peach and when you do it is hard as a brick. In the fall, I start buying apples that are at their peak, crisp and juicy just like I like them. Sectors rotate in and out of season just like the produce in the supermarket does. Successful portfolio management means that you are in tune with these rotations by watching the Bullish Percent charts. Embrace sector rotation in your portfolio, don't try to fight it. In the year 2000, the electric utility sector was the best performing group, up about 40 percent in the face of a Nasdaq Composite down 50 percent from its highs.

By the end of 2000, the Electric Utility Bullish Percent had moved back into the Red Zone above 70 percent and then reversed down into a column of O's. As you are already catching on, this suggests to us high risk in the group. By looking at the history of the Electric Utility Bullish Percent chart you will see that the move in this sector has generally run out of steam when the sector Bullish Percent gets into the upper 70 percent range or beyond. At these levels a prudent thing to do would be to begin scaling out of Utility positions and take partial profits off the table. Set stop-loss points so you make sure those hard-earned profits don't turn into losses.

Let's follow on to the top in September of 2000 and subsequent reversal down to 18 percent by 2002. These were tough times in the market. The average stock was getting hit pretty hard. In fact, most investors lost large chunks of their retirement portfolios and still to this date in 2006 have not made it up. The "buy and hold" type clients are down in equity over the last eight years. We are nearing a lost decade for many investors.

But let's get back to the bottom in the Electric Utility Bullish Percent in 2002. This was a major bottom and like it often happens, the index reverses up; profit taking sets in as most investors simply can't believe the sector is actually rising. The next reversal up gets the attention of the institutions and the move is on. The index ratcheted itself up from 18 percent to a top of 92 percent in 2004. This was the highest level for the Electric Utility Bullish Percent in 12 years, since hitting that level in early 1992. During the rise in the Electric Utility Bullish Percent from 2002 to 2004, Greenspan was lowering interest rates like there was no tomorrow. Housing markets were rocking and everyone thought they had found a "free lunch." Actually there was for a while. The real rate of interest rates, taking the interest rate and subtracting inflation was below 0 percent.

All things must come to an end and it was clearly signaled by this Bullish Percent index in May 2004, with a reversal down into O's at 86 percent. Looking back now, I wish I had sold my condominiums in Florida on this date. There is an old real estate adage: "You can buy more real estate in a day than you can sell in a lifetime." I'm finding that out to be true. I'm starting to see the wisdom of the "rent it all and own nothing" camp. In retrospect, it signaled that rates were about to go on the rise. On June 29, 2004, Fed Chairman Greenspan began raising rates and raised them 15 times. Today, May 2006, the Fed is still raising rates. The Electric Utility Bullish Percent is in O's and has been since October of 2005. This is very interesting how this market is playing out. Here's my guess. The new Fed Chairman Bernake continues raising short-term rates until the Electric Utility Bullish Percent drops below 30 percent and reverses up. Once this happens, the

Fed will be finished raising rates and the market will be ready for a sustained move on the upside. Depending on when you read this, you might already know how it played out. It's like a great mystery, like the game Clue. The murderer turned out to be Colonel Mustard in the Library with the Candlestick. In reality, I never predict, it's only for fun. When the indicators change, I change. Never anticipate the anticipators.

Sector Bell Curve

The Sector Bell Curve is one tool we use to get a good perspective of the overall market's relative position on a Normal Distribution. You probably know this as a bell curve. There are basically just two things we know from the study of economics or statistics that we can apply to the stock market. First, supply and demand governs all price change. Embrace it! When there is more demand than supply, the price will rise and conversely when there is more supply than demand, prices will fall. We depict the supply and demand in the marketplace by recording the price (the net of all supply and demand) of a stock in a logical, sensible, and organized manner, the Point and Figure chart. Second, we have the statistical concept of the bell curve with an overbought, oversold, and normal level.

One way we use the bell curve concept is to take the different sector Bullish Percent charts we follow and plot them on a bell curve. This is a concept you will never learn in a university. For that matter, you will never learn any of the concepts in this book at a university. Now read carefully: Every sector will always trade between 0 percent and 100 percent because every stock in the sector can either be on a buy signal (100 percent), on a sell signal (0 percent), or some combination thereof. Typically, we publish the sector Bullish Percent readings in a vertical format with the Y-axis on the left going from 0 percent to 100 percent like that of the Electric Utility Bullish Percent in Figure 8.2. With the Sector Bell Curve, we take the vertical axis and make it the horizontal axis. Then, the first four letters of each sector Bullish Percent (for ease of identity) are plotted on the curve (Figure 8.3). If the sector abbreviation is in upper case, then the sec-

Average Level: 65.64

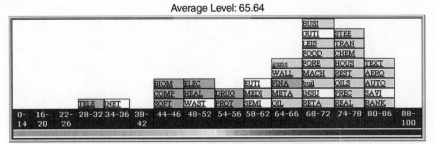

Note: Uppercase denotes column of Xs for the Bullish Percent Chart.

Figure 8.3 April 2002 Sector Bell Curve.

tor Bullish Percent chart in question is in X's on its own Bullish Percent Index, and moving to the right of the curve. Lower case letters indicate the sector Bullish Percent is in O's and moving to the left of the curve. Plotting each of the sectors on a bell curve in this fashion gives us a composite picture of the risk in the market. Sometimes, as in April 2002, the curve will get very skewed to the right-hand side indicating an overbought market. To start off the year in 2005, the bell curve of the 40 DWA sectors was also quite overbought and skewed to the right-hand side. We all know how the market of 2002 played out and even in 2005, while the major indices closed up for the year, those gains came after the bell curve had corrected back to a more neutral time. When you see a bell curve like that pictured in Figure 8.3, it usually suggests a "bad moon rising."

Sometimes, like December 1994, October 2002, or March 2003, the bell curve will get very skewed to the left-hand side indicating an oversold market (Figure 8.4). Pictures like this don't happen very often, only once every couple of years on average. Most of the time, a correction will take the bell curve from an overbought position down to what I call a Normal Market were most of the sectors are huddled around the middle of the curve. This is what happened from May 2006 to June 2006. This market is still in the process of resolving itself and so far the NYSE Bullish Percent remains in O's so we'll have to see how far down it goes. This last strong decline has taken the NYSEBP from 68 percent to 43.5 percent at this writing.

Sector Bell Curve for 10/15/2002
Average Level: 27.11

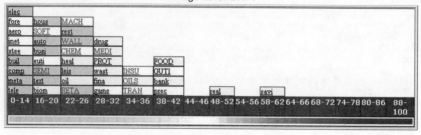

Sector Bell Curve for 3/17/2003
Average Level: 34.90

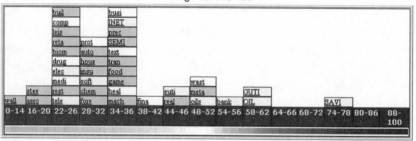

Figure 8.4   Oversold Bell Curves: October 2002 and March 2003.

The Sector Bell Curve of February 2000 was interesting and unusual. In the February 9, 2000, curve, there are some sectors, mostly NYSE denominated, on the oversold, left-hand side of the curve (Figure 8.5). On that same curve, we see that on the right-hand side, it is populated by technology stocks, mostly OTC or Nasdaq denominated. In general, if you limit yourself to buying

Average Level: 44.77

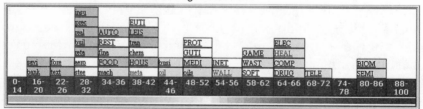

Note: Uppercase denotes column of Xs for the Bullish Percent Chart.

Figure 8.5   February 2000 Sector Bell Curve.

in sectors that are bullish and around 50 percent or lower, it would have forced you to buy when the risk is low and be more defensive when the risk is high. In this case, it was clear the risk was in the OTC/Nasdaq issues, not the NYSE issues, which is two-thirds small cap. By July 2001, the move was on. The Nasdaq technology issues were slammed and the small-cap issues that had already experienced their bear market in 1998 were ready to rock. In fact, I was a regular on FOX News *Cavuto on Business* during this time. Neil Cavuto, who I think is the best on the air today, asked me a pointed question: "Tom, all I hear from investors is how they are losing money in the market when more than 50 percent of the stocks that trade are up not down." This is what the bell curve was telling us at the time. Buy NYSE and avoid technology which was then primarily populated with Nasdaq issues. My answer to him was that the small-cap stocks have already taken the baton in this relay race and the leadership had changed. Indexes like the Dow Jones and Nasdaq were definitely declining because they are capitalization weighted. The stocks that underlie these indexes were rising. What an interesting time in the market this was. We saw it coming because we subscribe to the Yogi Berra School of Investing where he once said: "You can observe a lot just by watching." We watch a lot. So by regularly viewing the Sector Bell Curve you will see an excellent composite picture of risk in the market. There are many people who think the Point and Figure method of analysis is only a trend-following system. It isn't. This Bullish Percent concept developed in 1955 forces an investor to do things that are unnatural. It forces him to buy when things look the worse and sell or defend the portfolio when things look the best. The financial media has a vested interest in keeping viewer so they typically present only one side of the market, the good side.

Favored Sector Status

Now, let's bring another piece of the puzzle into the equation— Relative Strength (RS). As you read in Chapters 4 and 5, RS is an integral part of our work. Starting in the mid-1990s, we began to take a much closer look at incorporating a RS overlay to the Bullish Percent work and here's the reason. We might have two Bullish

Percent charts that looked almost identical. Both had corrected from overbought territory above the 70 percent mark down to oversold territory below the 30 percent level and reversed up to X's. Positions were taken in both sectors and one vastly outperformed the other. A look at the bell curve of October 2002 in Figure 8.4 shows that restaurants (REST), retail (RETA), software (SOFT), and telecom (TELE) all were down into oversold territory and by the end of October 2002, all four of these sectors were in X's with great field position. A look at performance 15 months later at the end of 2003 shows that all four sectors performed well, but software and telecom returns nearly doubled those returns of REST and RETA (Figure 8.6). From a portfolio management perspective, how could we better ascertain the potential magnitude of movement from sectors? We've found RS to be an invaluable tool and specifically the Favored Status ranking.

The concept behind the Favored Status ranking is to marry RS readings with the Bullish Percent concept we know works so well. We began keeping the charts that comprise Favored Status in 1997, so these charts are not very long, but we have certainly seen their value in the last 10 years time and time again. Let's think back for a second about an individual stock evaluation. If I

Sector	Return: Oct. 2002 to Dec. 2003
DWA Telecom Sector	64.44%
DWA Software Sector	81.64%
DWA Retail Sector	34.59%
DWA Restaurant Sector	38.03%
S&P 500 Equal Weight Index	44.19%
S&P 500	25.53%

Figure 8.6   Favored versus UnFavored Sector Return Comparison.

were thinking about buying a stock some of the basic things I would want to see is that first the stock was trading in a positive trend or on I-95 North. Next, I would want to see that the stock had good RS versus the market long term and short term. It would make sense then that if these are general attributes of a stock I would want to buy that before I invested in a particular sector of the market, I would want to focus on those sectors where more stocks were moving to positive trends and showing good RS versus the market. This is the genesis of the indicators we use to determine Favored Status ranking. Each ranking alone is a valuable tool but the Favored Status ranking really gives life to these individual indicators. The four criteria we use to assign a Favored Status ranking for sectors is as follows:

1. Sector Relative Strength
2. Percent Positive Trend
3. Percent Relative Strength in X's
4. Percent Relative Strength on buy signals

Let's now take a more detailed look at each of the four criteria used to determine Favored Status ranking.

Sector Relative Strength

In Chapter 5, you learned about sector RS. Specifically, for each DWA sector an equal weighted index is created. Just like a stock, a daily RS calculation is performed and then plotted on a Point and Figure chart. To quickly review, the daily RS calculation is the price of the index divided by the S&P 500 Equal Weighted Index and then multiplied by 100 to provide a reading. The reading is then plotted on a Point and Figure chart. When the sector RS chart is in X's, we can assume that group has a higher probability of outperforming the market than underperforming the market and vice versa. We will be well rewarded for focusing our investments in those sectors whose RS charts are in X's. If you're not completely comfortable with the RS concepts, go back to Chapters 4 and 5. Before you can fully grasp how we apply RS to sectors, you need to be comfortable with how individual equity RS is calculated. It's like learning anything else, you probably won't get it all on the first reading. Utilize the exercises, review the concepts, pull up some examples on your own at our web site. This will take you miles into your journey of becoming a craftsman.

Percent Positive Trend Chart

The Percent Positive Trend (PT) chart measures the percent of stocks within a particular market or sector trading above their Bullish Support Lines. So let's say there are 100 stocks in a sector and 50 of them are trading above their Bullish Support Lines. This would give us a reading of 50 percent. If this number is increasing, it tells us more stocks in the sector or market are turning to positive trend charts and supporting higher prices. Conversely, if we see a net 6 percent change of stocks that were in positive trends now in negative trends, it speaks volumes about the change in trend for the sector to negative. It is this battle between the two trends that eventually causes one or the other to win the match and reverse. It is the reversal that warrants our attention.

As outlined earlier, whenever we initiate a new position, we try to stack as many odds as possible in our favor and one of the primary things we look at is "What is the overall trend of the stock?" We want to focus our buying on those stocks trading above their Bullish Support Line. In the aggregate, we want to focus on those areas of the market that are showing more and more stocks moving to a positive trend or trading above their Bullish Support Line. We can easily see whether this is happening by looking to the PT chart of an overall market or a sector. Like any other Bullish Percent chart, if this chart is in X's we say it is positive and if this chart is in O's, we say it is negative.

Percent Relative Strength in X's

Another important attribute we want to see in any stock we purchase is that the RS chart is in a column of X's, showing the stock is currently outperforming the market. Taking the same logic of the PT charts, we want to focus on those areas of the market that are showing more and more stocks in a column of X's on their RS charts. Within each industry group, we calculate the number of stocks whose individual RS charts are outperforming the market on a shorter term basis. Though RS signals on average last two years or more, a change in columns on the RS chart can last several months, we find it very useful to evaluate stocks based on their RS chart's most recent column. If the RS chart is in X's the stock is outperforming on a nearer term basis; if it is in O's, it is underperforming the market on a nearer term basis.

This RSX percentage is also plotted on a grid from 0 percent to 100 percent, like the PT indexes, and when this indicator is in X's and moving higher, it suggests that area of the market or sector is performing better than the market on a shorter term basis. We refer to these charts in-house as RSX charts because we use the prefix RSX before the market or sector symbol to call up the chart on our web site. For example, RSXTELE is the percent of stocks in the telecommunications sector that have their RS charts in a column of X's. When evaluating the RSX chart, because it can move the fastest of all the Favored Status indicators, we look at the *signal* on the chart. We place the most emphasis not on what column the chart is in but rather is it on a buy or a sell signal, a Double Top or a Double Bottom.

Percent Relative Strength on Buy Signals

The Point and Figure RS buy and sell signals are long term in nature, lasting on average two years. Within a market or an industry group, we calculate the percentage of stocks whose RS charts are on buy signals. This percentage is then plotted on a grid from 0 percent to 100 percent. When it is in a column of X's and rising, it means more stocks underlying that sector are getting stronger versus the market on a long-term basis. This indicator is much slower moving than the Percent RS in X's and the Percent Positive Trend. When changes in the Percent RS on buy signals (RSP charts) do occur, however, they are important. For instance, the RSPOTC chart reversed down in April 2000, and this was yet another sign that this area of the market was in for a rough ride. Not surprisingly, the RSP charts for the telecommunications, software, Internet, and other technology sectors were also reversing down into O's in the spring of 2000. When you think about what this is telling you it is quite astonishing. When a sector's RSP chart reverses for instance into a column of X's that is telling us that 6 percent of the stocks in that sector have gone from a RS sell signal to a RS buy signal and the tide has shifted from these stocks underperforming the market to these stocks outperforming the market. Since the average RS signal last about two years, reversals on these charts are major statements about a sector's likely future performance.

Let's quickly summarize again the indicators that go into determining a sector's Favored Status. The following are the four indicators we use to evaluate sectors on an RS basis:

1. *Sector RS Chart:* Look at the Column.
2. *Sector Percent Positive RS (RSP) Chart:* Look at the Column.
3. *Sector Percent RS Chart in X's (RSX) Chart:* Look at the Signal (Buy or Sell).
4. *Sector Percent Positive Trend (PT) Chart:* Look at the Column.

For each sector, we evaluate each of these indicators and give the sector a 0 to 4 score. If all four of the indicators were positive, the sector would get a score of 4. If none of the indicators were positive, that is, all of the charts were in O's or on a sell signal in the case of the RSX chart, then the Favored Status score would be 0. When the majority of these indicators are positive, that sector should be a market leader and it is where we would concentrate most of our new money going into the market. Once the sector no longer has the majority of indicators in its favor, then we must begin to think about defensive strategies. New positions in sectors where the majority of indicators are not positive suggest we should expect trading rallies only, not market leadership qualities. Once we have established the score, we then assign the sector a Favored Status according to the following template:

Favored Sector: 3 or 4 indicators positive
Average Sector: 2 of the indicators positive
Unfavored Sector: 0 or 1 of the indicators positive

I think the concept of Favored Sector will come alive with an actual example. We'll use the software sector from October 2002 that we discussed at the beginning of this chapter to start with. Let's take a look at the four charts that make Favored Sector status in Figure 8.7 and just count off what is positive. The first chart is the DWA Software Index RS chart (DWASOFT). Notice that this chart is in a column of X's so that is one positive. Next, we can take a look at the Percent Positive RS for Software (RSP-SOFT). This chart has also just recently reversed up to X's so we have another positive for the group and we're up to 2 positive scores for the sector. Moving on, the Percent of RS charts in X's for software (RSXSOFT) is on a buy signal. Remember for this chart we look to see whether it has exceeded a previous column of X's or not. In this case, the last signal was in fact a buy so we have another positive for the group. Our Favored Sector score is now up to 3 for the sector. The final chart to evaluate is the Percent Positive Trend for Software (PTSOFT). This chart is also in X's so we add another positive to the score and we can say that the software sector has 4 out of 4 of its Favored Sector Status indicators positive and thus it is a Favored Sector.

What this tells us is that the software sector has a higher probability of being an outperforming sector of the market than a sector with an Unfavored Sector status, like the retail sector. From the same time, October 2002, here's how the Favored Sector Status charts for the retail sector stacked up:

Retail Sector Relative Strength Chart	Column of X's
Retail Percent Positive Relative Strength Chart	Column of O's
Retail Percent Relative Strength Chart in X's	Sell Signal
Retail Percent Positive Trend	Column of O's

If we count up the score for the retail sector, we come up with only 1 out of 4 positive and that makes the retail sector an Unfavored group. In October 2002, both the retail and the software sectors were reversing up to X's on their Bullish Percent charts but a further investigation into the groups, another overlay of analysis if you will, and we see that software is a Favored Sector with strong RS and retail is an Unfavored Sector with weak relative strength. Which are you going to overweight? The Favored Sector of course. And, it pays off. For the next 15 months, the retail sector is up 34 percent while the software sector is up 82 percent.

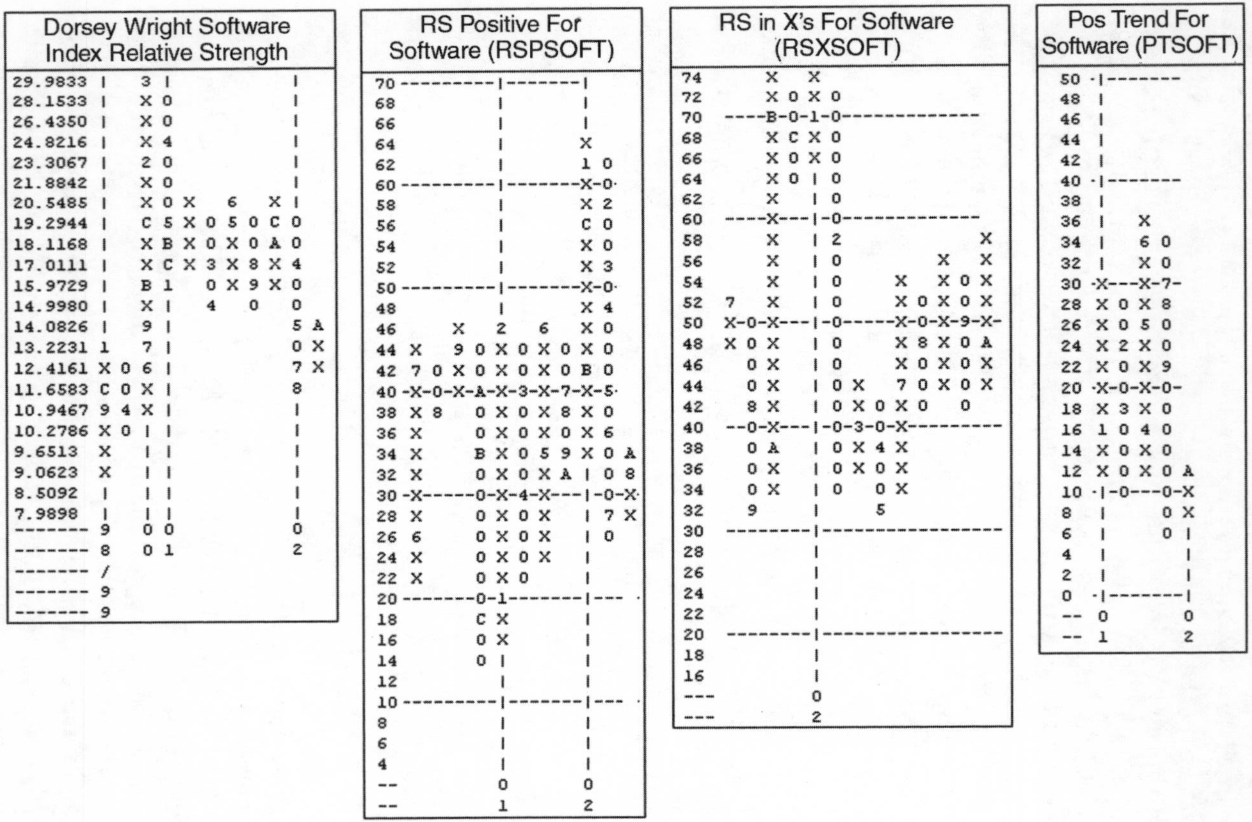

Figure 8.7 Favored Sector Status Evaluation for Software in October 2002.

272

I learn best by actually doing so let's take a minute here and look at three sectors and you write down what the Favored Sector score for each sector is:

	Tele	Oil	Drug
Sector Relative Strength	In O's	In X's	In O's
RSP Chart	In X's	In X's	In X's
RSX Chart	Sell Signal	Sell Signal	Sell Signal
PT Chart	In O's	In X's	In O's
Favored Sector Score	_____	_____	_____

The first sector in the exercise is the telephone (TELE) sector. This sector only has a score of 1 as the only indicator positive is the RSP chart. With a score of just 1 we would consider the telephone sector to be Unfavored. Do you know when this reading is from? April 2000. Had you been utilizing this methodology in 2000, you would have known to underweight this sector or eliminate it entirely from your portfolio. Let's look at the next two sectors as they are taken from the same time, April 2003. You should have come up with a score of 3 for the oil sector as its Sector RS chart, RSP chart, and PT chart are all considered positive. This would make the oil sector Favored. The drug sector is an entirely different picture. The score for this sector is only 1 as the RSP chart is the only indicator positive. Thus, the drug sector is an Unfavored group. So how did they perform? Over the next 18 months, the S&P 500 Equal Weighted Index, our benchmark, was up 47 percent. The oil sector did in fact perform better, up 66 percent while the drug sector was the underperformer, only 23 percent. I hope that you are seeing all types of applications for this type of analysis in your investing. It doesn't matter whether you are a short-term trader or a long-term investor, we all want to be in the right places at the right time and that means sector rotation is a key component of your analysis.

We knew intuitively at DWA that the Favored Status work added a tremendously important tool to our analysis but we wanted to put some actual numbers to this work so the DWA Money Management team went to work on a comprehensive analysis of the Favored Status tool they helped develop and bring to life. The results were quite astounding and confirmed something we had already seen work so many times for us in the past.

In the study, each of the 40 DWA sectors were considered from early 2003 to mid-2006. (A previous study was down from 1997 to 2003 and the results were similar.) Each day the sector is assigned a Favored Sector status reading. For the purposes of this study, those sectors whose status is Average remained classified at the previous classification rating it held. For example, if a group was Favored and then dropped to Average status, we considered it to still be Favored. In order for that group to fall to an Unfavored status, the sector score would have to be 0 or 1. To remove the effects of the market, all of the returns are calculated relative to a benchmark, the Value Line Arithmetic average that is also an equal weighted index like the DWA sectors index used for performance figures. On average, Favored sectors outperformed Unfavored Sectors by 5.9 percent per trade. As we have previously discussed, the performance of your outliers can really affect portfolio returns. In our study, the top 10 percent of all trades in Favored Sectors shows the spread over Unfavored Sectors to widen to 14.1 percent and the bottom 10 percent of all trades shows an Unfavored Sector lagging by an average of 6.4 percent. Another important part of the study was to look at the length of the signal because the Favored Status indicators are designed to be more of an intermediate to longer-term measure of RS. The average length of time a sector remains either Favored or Unfavored is about six to seven months with 10 percent of all observations lasting a year or more. Doing studies such as this show us that a systematic, disciplined application of the Point and Figure tools to investing help improve your investment results. Will this mean that every time you buy a Favored Sector you will have a winning trade? No. But more often than not, you will find that the Favored Sector is one of the large outsized winners.

Summary

At this point in the book, I imagine your mind is racing with ideas of how this methodology can be incorporated into your current investment process. As we have pointed out before, this methodology is an operating system similar to Windows XP that allows your computer to run programs. The great thing about the methodology is that once you have the operating system, the choice of which programs and what you want to accomplish on the computer is up to you. Throughout this chapter, I hope that you've learned the processes can be applied to a variety of different investment styles from trader to long-term buy and holder to increase your odds of success and that's all we can ask of ourselves in the market—stack as many odds in our favor as possible and then manage the position.

Part Two

THE POINT AND FIGURE METHODOLOGY —A COMPLETE ANALYSIS TOOL

Chapter 9

FIXED INCOME INDICATORS

One of the most important themes in the market to keep close track of is the fixed income area. Fixed income is always battling the stock market for investor's dollars. Fixed income is considered the stable part of an investor's portfolio while the stock side is considered the volatile side. By combining them, the risk is mitigated considerably. In fact, in our money management division one account we manage is a model that combines stocks with strong Relative Strength (RS) and a bond side of the portfolio that makes up about 40 percent of the total. At this writing, the model has not had a losing year going back to 1997 in our back test. The one thing we endeavor to do with respect to the fixed income indicators is to determine if the probability is that interest rates are likely to rise or fall. This is one part of the equation that if we could be dead right on our expectation, we would own the world in very short order. Since we still come to work each day, this is not a perfect science. However, I have never seen any other methods that can bring you closer to the right answer than what we do with our charts. In 1994, the indicator we used back then was the Dow Jones 20 Bond Average. Dow Jones maintained the average and we then plotted a Point and Figure chart of it. Eventually, Dow Jones gave up keeping the index and we began to be the keeper of it. As time went on, the data we got became less reliable and we eventually discontinued maintaining the chart and picked up another bond index, the Dow Jones Corporate Bond Index, which has been just as robust. Looking at signals in history can give us a grasp of how these indicators operate and when the Dow Jones 20 Bond Average was in existence, it was fantastic. When it was on a buy signal. You could darn near take it to the bank that rates would fall and bonds would rise.

Let's look at just one example of a signal given by the Dow Jones 20 Bond Average. In January 1995, the Dow Jones 20 Bond Average gave a buy signal saying that we would see higher bonds and lower rates. By June, bonds had taken off, following this indicator had you on the right side of the equation. Take a look at a story by Suzanne Wooley from *BusinessWeek* (June 19, 1995):

Hang on: More Surprises on the Way

Bond funds did a dramatic about-face from 1994, when virtually every category of bond fund was in negative territory. But in the first half of 1995, every category sported positive returns. Only two fund groups—short-term world income and government adjustable-rate mortgage—failed to generate a return of more than 8 percent. Government bond funds investing in Treasuries took the top slot, with an 11.5 percent average return, boosted by the powerful rally in the bond market. But many government bond fund managers, having built up more conservative positions in short and intermediate maturities in the wake of last year's market rout, didn't participate in much of the rally. World bond funds came in second, gaining 10.2 percent.

I thought for a second how we had been long bonds since January 1995 because our bond indicators had given a buy signal. Then I thought about all those high paid, and I mean high paid, bond analysts and traders who missed the whole move. What were they looking at or evaluating that caused them to be totally opposite the trend in bonds? As I have said, we subscribe to the Yogi Berra School of Investing: "You can observe a lot just by watching." The charts are silent, yet all knowing. All you have to do is watch and have faith. There is an old saying, "Those who know, don't speak, those who speak don't know." The charts don't speak. They are there for your observation and typically the signals are long term in nature.

So let's get into the most important chart we keep on interest rates, the Dow Jones Corporate Bond Index, which is what I consider as the modern day version of the Dow Jones 20 bond Average we use to follow years ago. This index is comprised of 96 investment grade issues that are divided into the industrial, financial, and utility/telecom sectors. As well, they are further divided by maturity with each of the sectors represented in the 2, 5, 10, and 30-year maturities. All issues are equally weighted and strict rules for liquidity, rating, and issuers are applied. The index is reviewed monthly and maintained by Ryan Labs. We use the price return value for the index, instead of the total return index, because a total return index will have a positive bias and we feel that evaluating the index itself is more appropriate for our needs of determining strength or weakness in the corporate bond area. Recently, I was called by a broker, a client of ours. He asked me what I thought about interest rates. The first thing I looked to was the Dow Jones Corporate Bond Index to get a good feel for the current interest rate environment. All you have to do is look at Figure 9.1 and you will see that in October 2005 the index not only gave a sell signal but also penetrated the long-term Bullish Support Line. That was the moment it was clear that interest rates were going to rise and bonds decline on a long-term basis. One chart spoke volumes to us months ago. Here we are in June of 2006 and rates are still rising. When will they stop rising? Once this index bottoms and gives a Double Top buy signal.

As you can see in Figure 9.1, the Dow Jones Corporate Bond Index (DJCORP) is longer term in nature—this chart goes back to 1996. If we want to get a nearer term outlook, we can adjust the box size down. Recall that the smaller the box size, the more movement and thus the shorter term in nature. When evaluating the DJCORP chart, we look at buy and sell signals as well as High Pole and Low Pole Warnings. That is, when the DJCORP is on a buy signal, it suggests higher bond prices and thus lower rates. Conversely, when this chart is on a sell signal it suggests lower bond prices and higher rates. A High Pole warning is defined as a "pole" of X's up more than 3 boxes than the previous X column. The warning comes when the index falls more than 50 percent of the number of boxes up in the pole.

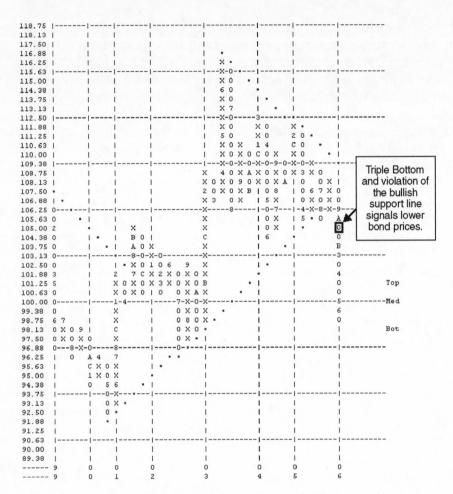

```
118.75 |-------|-----|-------|------------|------------|-------|---------|----------
118.13 |       |     |       |            |            |       |         |
117.50 |       |     |       |            |            |       |         |
116.88 |       |     |       |            | •          |       |         |
116.25 |       |     |       |      X •   |            |       |         |
115.63 |-------|-----|-------|------------|---X-0-•----|-------|---------|----------
115.00 |       |     |       |      X 0   • |          |       |         |
114.38 |       |     |       |      6 0   •             |       |
113.75 |       |     |       |      X 0   | •           |       |
113.13 |       |     |       |      X 7   |   •   |     |
112.50 |-------|-----|-------|------------|---X-0------3--------|---------|----------
111.88 |       |     |       |      X 0      X 0      X •       |
111.25 |       |     |       |      5 0      X 0      2 0 •     |
110.63 |       |     |       |      X 0 X  1 4        C 0   •   |
110.00 |       |     |       |      X 0 X 0 C 0 X     X 0    • |
109.38 |-------|-----|-------|------------|---X-0-X-0-X-0-9-0-X-0-X-----•--------------
108.75 |       |     |       |  X    4 0 X A X 0 X 0 X 3 X 0   |
108.13 |       |     |       |  X 0 X 0 9 0 X 0 X A | 0    0 X |
107.50 •       |     |       |  2 0 X 0 X B | 0 8   | 0 6 7 X 0
106.88 | •     |     |       |  X 3   0 X   | 5 X   | 0 X 0 X 0
106.25 0---•---|-----|-------|------------X-----8------|-0-7---|-4-X-8-X-9---
105.63 0     • |     |       |        X          | 0 X   | 5 • 0   A
105.00 2       •     |       |        X          | 0 X   | •       0
104.38 0       |  •  |   B 0 |        C          | 6     •         0
103.75 0       | • | A 0 X   |        X          |     • |         B
103.13 0-------|-----|---8-0-X-0--------X---------|---|----|---------3----------
102.50 0       |     |  | • X 0 1 0 6   9   X     | • |    |         0
101.88 3       |     |  2   7 C X 2 X 0 X 0 X     •          |      4
101.25 5       |     |  X 0 X 0 X 3 X 0 X 0 B   • |         0        Top
100.63 0       |     |  X 0 X 0 | 0   0 X A X   • |         0
100.00 0-------|-----|-----1-4-----|----7-X-0-X---•--------|-------|---5---------Med
99.38  0       |     |  X          0 X 0 X   •    |        6
98.75  6 7     |     |  X          0 8 0 X •      |        0
98.13  0 X 0 9 |     |  C          0 X 0 •        |                 Bot
97.50  0 X 0 X 0     |  X          0 X • |        |
96.88  0---8-X-0-----8-------|-----0-•----|------------|-------|---------|----------
96.25  |  0   A 4    7        | • •       |
95.63  |     C X 0 X |   •    |
95.00  |     1 X 0 X       •  |
94.38  |     0   5 6     •  |
93.75  |-------|---0-X-|------------|------------|-------|---------|----------
93.13  |     | 0 X •   |
92.50  |     | 0   •   |
91.88  |     | • |     |
91.25  |     |   |     |
90.63  |-------|-----|-------|------------|------------|-------|---------|----------
90.00  |       |     |       |
89.38  |       |     |       |
------ 9       0     0       0            0            0       0
------ 9       0     1       2            3            4       5       6
```

Triple Bottom and violation of the bullish support line signals lower bond prices.

Figure 9.1   Dow Jones Corporate Bond Index.

Let's say for instance that the pole of X's up was 10. If the DJCORP were to fall 6 O's, that would cast a shadow on the last buy signal. The Low Pole Warning is the exact opposite with the warning, of potential improvement, would be when the reversal up to X's exceeds more than 50 percent of the O's down in the pole. The DJCORP index is robust in its design and diversification and the ability to follow its components gives us a heads up with regard to its underlying strength or weakness. The 2-year, 5-year, 10-year, and 30-year charts that comprise this index are all available on the DWA web site using the following symbols: DJCORP02YR, DJCORP05YR, DJCORP10YR, DJCORP30YR.

In addition, we also follow its sector components the industrial, financial, and utility sectors. These sectors are also broken down into 2-year, 5-year, 10-year, and 30-year maturities and we follow these charts as well. These maturities for each of the sectors are combined to create a total index. Evaluating these components helps to shed some light on the status of the DJCORP as well as these broad industries. For example, in early February 2002, the utility/telecom component went to a sell signal across the board and stayed this way until mid-August 2002. I like to go back and evaluate this time in the market because it was a watershed of stock declines. There have actually been several of these periods since the first edition of this book including a four-week period of May—June 2006, when two trillion dollars was lost in the market on a global basis. Let's go back to 2002 for a moment. The weakness in the utility component in July 2002 was substantial, especially when compared to the industrial and financial components, and it was this weakness that lead to the sell signal in the DJCORP in July 2002. It also was an indication of the marketplace's view of the creditworthiness of this sector. It is interesting now we look back to 2002 that the long-term trend line did not break on this reversal and sell signal in 2002. It continued its rise to its top of 116.25 where it began to produce a long-term series of lower tops. Each time the bond index rose, it somehow was unable to get as high as it was previously. It shows that interest rates were in a battle between higher rates and lower rates. It's a time where the economy is in transition, in this case to higher rates. Notice how the index produced lower tops right down to the trend line break and sell signal in October of 2005. This was the point it was clear that we could expect a long-term series of rate hikes by both the fed and the market itself. It was not until May of 2006 that investors began to believe this change was happening. In one month, global investors lost $2 trillion in equity. This bond index clearly showed that rates were on the long-term rise with the trend line break. The next piece of the puzzle was to figure out how this would impact equities. This is why we have the Bullish Percent Indexes you have already read about to signal when the equity play is either on or over. It is interesting that in November 2005, we put the offensive team on the field for equities while rates were rising. It is not unusual to see rates and equities rise at the same time. This remained the case until May 2006. The run in equities was fantastic during that period but when the NYSE Bullish Percent went to defense the play was over and the down move happened so fast that most investors were caught unaware. Our clients were not, however. We rang the bell in time to play defense before the carnage set in.

In addition to the Dow Jones Corporate Bond Index (DJCORP), we have a number of indicators to measure the treasury markets. Sometimes the best thing to do is just go to the source. For us, that means looking at the supply-and-demand picture. Just as we can chart the supply-and-demand relationship for equities, we can also do it for the fixed income market. We can chart bond futures, fixed income Exchange Traded Funds (ETFs), yield indices, and inverse bond funds. When bonds are rising, we will see positive patterns for both the bond futures and fixed income ETFs. If bonds are rising, that means that rates are falling so conversely we will see negative patterns from the yield indices, which measure rates themselves, and from the inverse bond funds. The exact opposite picture will develop when rates are rising. That is, we will see the yield indices showing positive patterns and a positive trend along with the inverse bond funds. If these charts are positive, by definition, the chart patterns of the bond futures and the fixed income ETFs will be giving negative Point and Figure patterns and generally trading below the Bearish Resistance Lines. Figure 9.2 is a summary of the most frequently used Point and Figure chart by the DWA analysts for you to keep and periodically review to get a good grasp on the interest rate environment we are currently in.

As you can see from Figure 9.2, we look at bond futures, yield indices, fixed income ETFs, and inverse bond funds to get a composite picture of the trend of rates—not the financial media. Just as we presented in seminars and training classes, magazine covers can be great contrarian indicators. For example, in June 2004, the *Economist* cover said the following; "Back to the 1970s: Inflation Returns, Worldwide." The cover also had a very dramatic picture—a large platform, high-heeled shoe, reminiscent of the 1970s. But

Bond Futures	Yield Indices
- Muni Bond Continuous Chart – MB/ - T-Notes Continuous Chart – TY/ - T-Bonds Continuous Chart – US/ - Commodities under the Database Tab	- 13 Week Treasury Bill (IRX) - 30 Year *Yield* Index (TYX) - 10 Year Note *Yield* Index (TNX) - 5 Year Yield Index FVX
Fixed Income ETFs	**Inverse Bond Funds**
- iShares Lehman 20+ Yr. Treasury Bond (TLT) - iShares Lehman 7–10 Yr. Treasury Bond (IEF) - iShares Lehman 1–3 Yr. Treasury Bond (SHY) - iShares GS $ InvesTop Bond Fund (LQD) - iShares Lehman Aggregate Bond Fund (AGG) - iShares Lehman TIPS Fund (TIP)	- Rydex Juno (RYJUX) - Profunds Access Flex Bear High Yield (AFBIX) - Profunds Rising Rates Opp Inv (RRPIX) - Profunds Rising Rates Opp 10 Inv (RTPIX) - Potomac Contraband Fund Inv (PCBDX)

Figure 9.2 Interest Rate Sensitive charts.

the Point and Figure chart at the time shows that the 10 Year Yield Index (TNX) had given a Double Bottom sell signal at 45.50 in July 2004, and this began a series of lower tops and lower lows for the TNX over the next year. In fact, during the next year, the TNX fell 13 percent, not rose. The Point and Figure chart is an excellent resource on the supply and demand nature of rates just as it is for equity prices. Let's look at another example.

In Figure 9.3, we compare the 30 Year Index (TYX) beside the iShares Lehman 20+ Year Treasury Bond (TLT). It shows in September 2004 that long-term rates had just violated a Bullish Support Line and turned to a negative trend. This tells us that rates are on I-95 South. Not surprisingly, a look at the TLT chart shows that it had just violated the Bearish Resistance Line and moved to I-95 North. Understanding the interest rate picture can have implications across everything you do. In your 401k, it might prompt you to take a closer look at the bond funds available for positive pattern.

This trend stayed in effect essentially a year, until October 2005 (see Figure 9.4). In October 2005, the 30 Year Yield Index moved from being on I-95 South to I-95 North. This means that long-term rates are in an intermediate term uptrend and consequently, long-term bonds are in an intermediate term negative trend. When evaluating fixed income ETFs and yield indices, we like to follow the trend primarily but there are certainly times in which the support

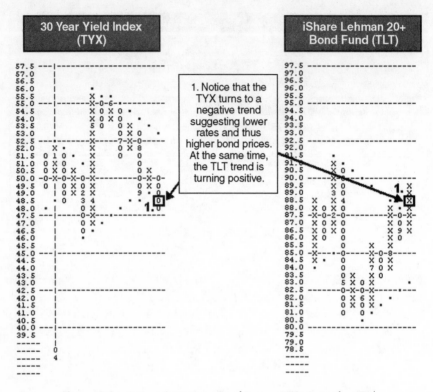

Figure 9.3 Interest Rates versus Fixed Income ETFs: September 2004.

or resistance line is too far away. In this instance, either a subsequent line should be drawn, or more emphasis is placed on the signal than the trend. We should note here that the iShares are ETFs and can be bought and sold just like stocks. The only way to play the Yield Indices is through the options market with calls and puts. Again, being aware of the interest rate environment can be helpful for a variety of reasons. Let's say you were purchasing a house. Knowing that interest rates were rising might suggest you get a fixed rate mortgage instead of an adjustable rate.

In investing, there are numerous truisms that don't in fact hold a lot of water. They are truisms that are sometimes true and sometimes not. For instance, it has been said that falling rates are good for the stock market. However, during the year 2000, the 30 Year Yield Index fell 15 percent and the S&P 500

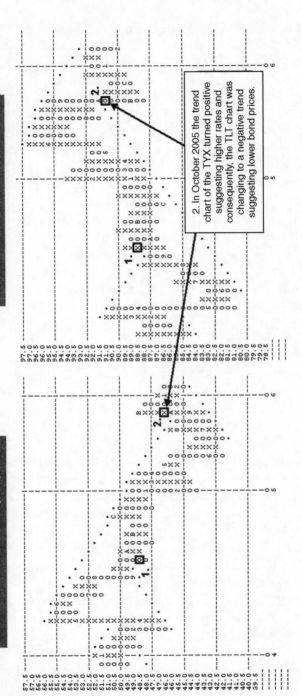

Figure 9.4 Interest Rates versus Fixed Income ETFs: October 2005.

fell 10 percent. In 2002, the 30 Year Yield Index fell 12 percent and the S&P 500 fell 23 percent. Conventional wisdom would say that in a rising interest rate environment, the long end of the curve would be the most volatile and thus the most risky. This isn't always the case. The 5 Year Yield Index moved to a buy signal in 2004, well before the 30 Year Yield Index did in October 2005. The 5 Year Yield Index is up substantially more than the 30 Year Yield Index since April 2004, and thus the short end bond ETF, the iShares Lehman 1 to 3 Year Bond Fund, has underperformed the long end, the iShares Lehman 20+ Year Bond Fund.

It reminds me of the following Zen story (source: http://www .rider.edu/~suler/zenstory/zenstory.html):

> After 10 years of apprenticeship, Tenno achieved the rank of Zen teacher. One rainy day, he went to visit the famous master Nan-in. When he walked in, the master greeted him with a question, "Did you leave your wooden clogs and umbrella on the porch?" "Yes," Tenno replied. "Tell me," the master continued, "did you place your umbrella to the left of your shoes, or to the right?" Tenno did not know the answer, and realized that he had not yet attained full awareness. So he became Nan-in's apprentice and studied under him for 10 more years.

In the end, the market will do what it wants to do. Our job is to listen and be aware of the market's movements by examining the charts and then taking the appropriate actions.

At this point in the book, you have really learned all of the concepts there are to know. It's just a matter of applying those concepts to different areas of the market. For instance, let's take the RS tool that is applied to individual equities and apply it to the fixed income markets. Using this dynamic tool, we can compare the fixed income markets to the equity markets and within the fixed income markets, we can find out those areas with the weakest and the strongest relative strength. For this comparison we will use the iShares Lehman Aggregate Bond Index (AGG) to the S&P 500 (SPX). The iShares Lehman AGG is a measure of a broad spectrum of different types of bonds as well as maturities and quality so it is a good overall picture of the bond market. In the RS chart we will use a smaller scale than the traditional equity chart so we can still look at the buy and sell signals for guidance as to when we want to overweight fixed income in the portfolio. The gray shaded areas are when this RS chart is on a sell signal and the denominator, the S&P 500, should outperform. The lightly highlighted area is when the RS chart is on a buy signal and suggests the numerator, the AGG, should outperform. As with most RS charts, once a trend is established, it tends to last several years. And you see that the RS chart has aptly guided us with respect to the weighting of fixed income versus equities in the portfolio. From November 2000 to July 2003, this RS chart was on a buy signal and the AGG was up 23 percent, while the S&P 500 was down 25 percent. Once the chart moved to a sell signal, one would have lightened up their fixed income positions in the portfolio and added to their equity positions. Since moving to a sell signal, the AGG is down about a percent while the SPX is up almost 30 percent (see Figure 9.5).

Another concept that you've learned about that can also be applied to our fixed income fund analysis in the same manner as analysis on the equities funds is the Bullish Percent. We chart the bond fund prices using the Point and Figure method and then use the basic Bullish Percent method where we measure bond mutual fund charts for buy signals just as we do for stock and equity funds. Figure 9.6 is an example Bullish Percent for the group All Fixed Income funds (BPMU99), which covers over 3,000 distinct bond portfolios. This indicator tells you the percent of the entire fixed income fund universe that is on a buy signal on their default trend chart. (We also have Bullish Percents on subcategories of the fixed income universe.) The back and forth action from X's to O's is interpreted the same way that you would interpret a stock bullish percent. In Figure 9.6, you will notice the BPMU99 chart reversed into O's in October 2005. That was also when the trend of the 30 Year Yield Index we discussed earlier moved to I-95 South. Do you see how these pieces of the puzzle are coming together?

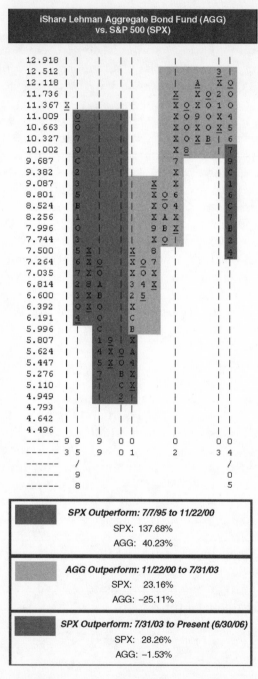

Figure 9.5 Fixed Income versus Equities.

```
100 |-----|-------|-----|-|---|---|----------·
98  |     |       |     | 6 |   |
96  |     |       |     | 5 0 |   |
94  |     |       |     | 3 0 |   |
92  |     |       |     | 9 7 |   |
90  0-----|-------|-----|-X-0-|---|----------·
88  0     |       |   X | 8 0 X |
86  2     |       1   X 0 X 0 3 0 |
84  3     |       X 0 X 0 X 0 2 0 |
82  0 X   |       C 0 X B X 0 X 4 |
80  5-X-0-|-------X-4-8-0-X-0-X-0-|----------·
78  0 X 0 |       B 5 X 0 X 0 X 0 |
76  6 X 0 |       A 0 X 0 X 0 X 0 |
74  0 X 0 |       9 0   0 X 0 X 0 |
72  0 X 0 |       X     C 7 0 X 0 |
70  0-X-0-|-------X-----0-X-0-1-0-X----------·
68  0 X 0 |       X     0 X 0 X 0 X 0
66  0 X 0 |       8     0 X 0 X 0 X 0
64  0 X 0 |       X     0 X 0 X 0 X 3
62  0 X 0 |       X     0 X 0 X 0 X 0
60  0-X-0-|-------X-----0-X-0-X-0-2-0--------·
58  0 X 0 |       X     0 6 0 X 0 X 0 9
56  0   0 |       X     0 X 0 C 0 1 0 6 0
54  |   8 |   X   7     3 X 0 X 0 A 0 X 0
52  |   0 |   4 0 X     0 | 0 X 5 9 0 X A
50  |---0-C---3-0-X-----|-|-0-X-0-8-4---0----·
48  |   0 X 0 X 5 |     | | 0 B 0 X     0
46  |   9 B 0 X   |     | | 0 X 0 X     0
44  |   A X 1     |     | | 0 X 0 X     0
42  |   0 X       |     | | 0 X 0 7     B
40  |---0-|-------|-----|-|-0-9-0-X-----0----·
38  |     |       |     | | 0 X 0 X
36  |     |       |     | | 8 X 0 |
34  |     |       |     | | 0 |   |
32  |     |       |     | | | |   |
30  |-----|-------|-----|-|---|---|----------·
28  |     |       |     | | | |   |
26  |     |       |     | | | |   |
24  |     |       |     | | | |   |
--- 9     0       0     0 0   0   0
--- 8     0       1     2 3   4   5
--- /
--- 9
--- 9
```

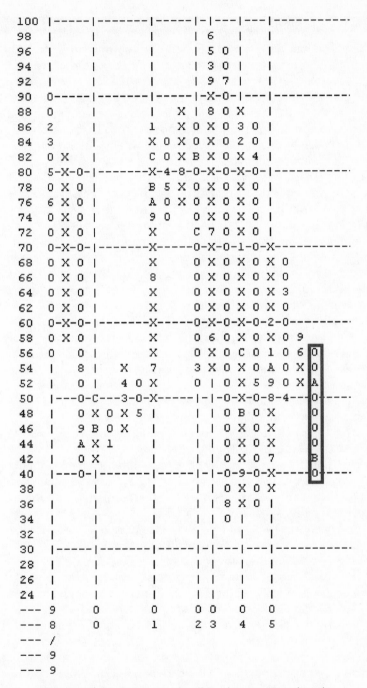

Figure 9.6 Bullish Percent for All Fixed Income Mutual Funds.

291

Anything you can do, I can do better. Those words from an old Irving Berlin song encapsulate the current status of the battle of man and machine. According to a recent article in the *New York Times* ("Maybe We Should Leave That Up to the Computer," July 18, 2006), professor Chris Snijders of the Eindhoven Institute of Technology is convinced that computer models can do a better job making decisions than humans. He even issued a challenge to any company willing to have its humans compete against his computer models.

Scientists have known for a long time that mathematical models generally perform better than humans on a variety of complicated tasks. According to the article, studies have shown that models can better predict the success or failure of a business start-up, the likelihood of recidivism and parole violation, future performance in graduate school, various medical diagnoses, picking the winning dogs at the racetrack, and credit scoring. You can add to that list playing chess, as no human player, including a couple of World Champions, has been able to defeat one of the silicon monsters in a match for several years.

Yet, each time I see one of these articles, I always think to myself that they haven't got it quite right. The articles always somehow imply that computers make better decisions than people, without fully incorporating the notion that humans simply wrote a computer program to reflect the knowledge that they already possessed. What's really happening is that computers are much more efficient at executing the decisions that knowledgeable humans might make under ideal circumstances.

In the case of the early chess programs, continuous improvement from feedback was critical. The first generation of programs played horribly and was beatable by low-level players. As programmers got more guidance from chess masters and learned better ways to reflect the knowledge that expert human players already had, the programs got stronger and stronger. Humans, as many of us know from experience in the office, often don't take feedback well, and/or don't incorporate it going forward! But chess programmers used the feedback and now a $50 CD that will run on any desktop can wipe the floor with a regular player.

The second big advantage computers have is their consistency in making decisions. Really, it's just that they are consistent and humans tend to be inconsistent. Computer models do not have psychological hang-ups stemming from childhood trauma. Models do not get emotional, tired, hungry, or cranky, but people do. This is very apparent in a chess program. You can set up an inferior position for it to play from, but rather than panicking or giving up, it will continue to grind away and often will be able to draw or even win against a human. When money is involved, people definitely get emotional, so there is a big advantage for computers in financial modeling.

The traditional knock on computer modeling is that it can't recognize when conditions have changed. (Actually, humans aren't very good at that either!) If the model doesn't adapt as conditions change, it can be thrown for a loop when the underlying data distribution changes. Developing a model that is adaptive is important to overcoming that hurdle.

We tried to utilize the advantages of computerized modeling and to minimize the disadvantages when we developed the Systematic RS portfolios. We feel the consistency of executing the strategy improves the performance. To minimize the problems, the stock selection is based on relative strength, the best adaptive tool we know. The portfolios are designed to change as market themes change. It might just be the tool you need to move your business to the next level.

Chapter 10

UTILIZING THE EXCHANGE TRADED FUND MARKET

Timing Is Everything

It is said that timing is everything. In my life, I certainly have found this to be true. I remember my early navy days and how just four short months changed my life. I joined the navy with the express purpose of entering Underwater Demolition (UDT) and then move on to SEAL Team I. Out of Boot Camp, I was told I had to first go to my duty station, Naval Air Squadron VP31, and then apply for Underwater Demolition. I did so and was accepted. Fortunately for me, I was stationed just down the road from the UDT training school while I waited for the next class to start. Since I was a Red Cross Water Safety Instructor, the squadron personnel department placed me in Air-Crew Training. They had been waiting for a Water Safety Instructor to come through for months by then. I was immediately placed in the Deep Sea Survival Instructors group. My duties were to teach pilots, who were heading to Vietnam, how to survive in the ocean if they had to abandon their plane over the ocean.

As an enlisted man, the position as a Deep Water Survival Instructor was as good as it could get. So, when my Underwater Demolition Class was about to begin, I decided to postpone the class for the second half of my enlistment if the Squadron would allow me to stay in my survival instructor position. The Squadron was perfectly happy to have me stay on so the die was cast. I simply put on hold my desire to become a U.S. Navy SEAL until my last two years of enlistment. Well, all good things must come to an end, and my first two years of shore duty were rapidly expiring. I had a choice—go to sea or go back to Underwater Demolition Class. I chose UDT/SEAL training.

I was accepted to class again after spending three months getting in shape for the entrance test a second time. I ran into a little administrative wrinkle though. Since I waited for the second half of my enlistment to attend class, the navy required I extend my enlistment by four months to qualify for having two full years of naval duty following the end of training. Since I had made a commitment to go back to college at the end of my enlistment, I decided not to extend. As I look back in retrospect, this was a major turning point in my life. I was transferred to Vietnam on an Aircraft Carrier already positioned in the South China Sea. In fact, they flew me out to the ship on a mail plane. Experiencing an arrested landing on an aircraft carrier that was under full steam in the middle of an ocean is an experience I'll never forget.

I spent the next two years both at sea and on shore in San Diego. When I was honorably discharged from the navy, I immediately went back to college. I'm sure, had I chosen UDT, I would not have gone back to college and would more than likely own a dive shop in some part of the world. It's interesting how life is full of choices. I made the right choice for me and went back to college, but at the same time I lost an opportunity to test myself that few others have. Soon after graduation and a short stint as a production supervisor at a winery, I found employment on Wall Street as a stockbroker at Merrill Lynch. One decision, not to extend my enlistment for four months, profoundly affected how my life turned out. Timing is everything.

During World War II, the United States was cut off from rubber produced in Southeast Asia just as demand for the rubber was increasing significantly. Do you know what happened? We made synthetic rubber through a large national effort to both increase the output and quality of this rubber. Here is the clincher though. After the war, we went right back to natural rubber even though we had weaned ourselves off it by creating high quality, synthetic rubber. Why would we do that? It doesn't make sense. We had already broken away from the addiction to Southeast Asian rubber, but we went right back. The reason is simple; we just weren't ready as a society for synthetic rubber. Many years later we gravitated back to synthetic rubber, but only when we were ready as a society to accept it. The war accelerated the process of substitution beyond what was natural. After the war we settled back to the natural curve.

It's like the technology gap. New technologies emerge while we fight tooth and nail to hold on to the old guard. I remember my company had to drag me away from WordPerfect to begin using Microsoft Word when the quality of Word was already superior to WordPerfect. I wanted the old technology I was used to. Look at the resistance that electricity met when Thomas Edison first developed it. People cried about the demise of the candle industry, not the acceptance of this new source of light. And, so it is with financial products. They have a time and a place and until the time is right, substitution for the new will be slow coming.

History of Exchange Traded Funds

I remember my first thoughts on securitizing a basket of stocks came from working with the PHLX Gold & Silver Index. I knew early on, before Exchange Traded Funds (ETFs) hit the market, their viability, as an investment vehicle, was undeniable. I remember vividly my conversations at the time with Joseph Rizzello, head of product development and marketing at the Philadelphia Stock Exchange (PHLX). The Philadelphia Stock Exchange is one of the most progressive and forward-thinking exchanges in America. In 1983, the PHLX had just come out with a new product, options trading on indexes. It was truly a revolutionary idea developed by Joseph Rizzello who was then the head of marketing at the PHLX. Joseph was also one of he real thinkers on Wall Street. Much like the first commodity-based ETF was in gold, the first index options traded were on the PHLX Gold & Silver Index (XAU). This was the first product of its kind where an investor could simply make an investment in an option on an index of stocks in a particular sector, rather than having to focus on one stock itself.

At the time, the index was priced around the $600 level, and the options were naturally very expensive as well. That would be tantamount to trading options on a $600 stock. It hit me one day that the real product was not the options that traded on this index, but rather the ability to buy the index itself. Having been a stockbroker in the past, I knew exactly what would have made the most difference in my business, and it would have been the ability to buy the index, a basket of stocks with a common theme. What the PHLX needed to do was split the XAU 10-for-1, making it a $60 per share index and then securitize it. In other words, trade the XAU as a $60 stock, a stand-alone product. Then, add the options for those who were so inclined.

I knew in my heart that this had to be a fantastically successful product. It was as clear as a bell to me. I went to Joseph Rizzello, who was a close friend of mine. He concurred. It would be a huge undertaking to create a product like that. It would be expensive to accomplish and it was very forward thinking, maybe in fact, too forward thinking for the time.

Nothing happened with that idea for the XAU. But Joseph Rizzello and the PHLX did come out with a product called CIP, Cash Index Participation units, on the S&P 500 (SNP) and Dow Jones (BIG). These were theoretical baskets of stocks that acted like an index portfolio. You owned the unit in perpetuity and had cash-out provision once a quarter. If the cash-out provision was drifting away from the net asset value, those long the unit could ask for the net asset value of the unit. This prevented short sellers from manipulating the value of the unit. Because you owned the unit, when any components went ex-dividend, you would collect the dividend by debiting the short sellers and crediting those long the unit. The Cash Index Participation unit (CIP) could also be margined.

It was a fantastic product, but doomed from the start. I traveled all over the country with the PHLX holding seminars to packed houses. I mean packed houses of 500 to 600 brokers and professionals. The investment world wanted this product. But, it was doomed because the futures exchanges decided to sue for the product. They suggested that the product was a futures contract and should come under their purview. This lawsuit resulted in a famous ruling called the Easterbrook Decision. The judge ruled in favor of the futures exchanges. While this instrument had all the elements of a security, it also had an element of futurity. Therefore, the courts ruled in favor of the futures exchanges. The futures exchanges, after winning the lawsuit, simply took the product and shelved it—"Dead on Arrival."

That decision spurred the workings of the ETF that we now have in our arsenal of trading tools, but it came from an unlikely source. The Toronto Stock Exchange came to the PHLX to learn how the CIP was created. The Toronto Stock Exchange created the first ETF called TIPS (Toronto Index Participation Units), which traded on the Toronto Stock Exchange. Following the debut of the TIPS, the AMEX created the SPDRs (SPY) and now we have numerous vehicles to invest in that have the same characteristics as the CIP we first traveled the country marketing. Once again, timing was everything. Like the final development of synthetic rubber I discussed earlier, this time society was ready and willing to accept the product.

Today's Exchange Traded Fund Market

The ETF market exploded in the late 1990s with the popularity of the SPDRs and the QQQs, representing the S&P 500 and the Nasdaq 100, respectively. Merrill Lynch then introduced the HOLDRs and Barclay's burst onto the scene with the most comprehensive listing of index-based, sector-based, and international ETFs named iShares. Sector Select SPDRs are available and other companies like Vanguard, well known for its vast mutual fund offerings, have been entering the scene. Since then we have seen more ETFs introduced including Powershares, which are more philosophy-based rather than index-based, and the most recent ETFs introduced have been commodity-based ETFs, more subsector ETFs as well as more equal weighted sectors.

Before we get into the ins and outs of using technical analysis to trade and invest in ETFs, let's start out with some basics. There are a couple of different types of structures to the ETFs but the basic premise is this vehicle allows us to buy a package of stocks as just one vehicle, much like a mutual fund. ETFs are different from mutual funds because ETFs do not trade at Net Asset Value (NAV). However, traders on the floor will arbitrage the stocks underlying the ETF if a price disparity develops. They are also different from mutual funds because they trade throughout the day. You can buy and sell anytime during the day using stop-loss orders and limits just like you would with a commodity or a stock. Also, like stocks, and commodities, ETFs can be sold short. Many ETFs have options allowing for other strategies like the covered write and other methods to gain long or short exposure. ETFs are also transparent. That is, most mutual funds do not list their current holdings and weightings (there are a couple of exceptions to that including the Rydex Funds). On any day, you could go to the web site of the ETF in question, and find the current holdings and the weighting. This is very important in the evaluation of the ETF as you will learn a little later in this chapter. Below we have listed some web sites you will find helpful in learning more about ETF structures and what's available as you begin to use this product in your investments and trading:

www.ishares.com
www.vanguard.com
www.powershares.com
www.rydexfunds.com
www.currencyshares.com
www.spdretfs.com
www.holdrs.com
www.ftportfolios.com
www.proshares.com
www.vaneck.com
www.wisdomtree.com
www.bldrsfunds.com

The ETF landscape is changing so quickly that we aren't going to list every ETF available right now, but at our web site (www.dorseywright.com), we have the most comprehensive list of ETFs available with all of the Point and Figure technical analysis tools you see for stocks also applied to the ETF universe. Part of the analysis is a series of worksheets with holdings for each ETF categorized by market asset class, sector, or international area. This allows you to compare similar ETFs for nuances in their construction. In addition to the Point and Figure chart of each ETF, we also have available Relative Strength (RS) charts, technical fund scores for ETFs, the ability to create customized box size charts on ETFs, and you can search our database of ETFs based on technical criteria to quickly find exactly what you are looking for. DWA provides the most comprehensive "Productivity Tool" for ETF investing in the world on the Internet. We also do weekly reports for numerous ETF providers such as iShares, Vanguard, Rydex, State Street Global Advisors, and Powershares.

Exchange Traded Fund Evaluation: Know What Is Inside

With any ETF, the most important consideration when determining whether to buy or sell, and how to manage a position, is to examine the ETF chart you are purchasing or selling. Some ETFs have a long enough history to evaluate the chart itself but in those cases where there isn't enough history on the chart of the ETF, we examine the underlying index. You see, every ETF is designed to track an index and generally the index will have at least three years worth of history, and in most cases many more. The job of the ETF provider is to make sure the ETF you purchase actually replicates the performance of the index and they do a great job at it. For instance, the iShares COMEX Gold Trust (IAU) began trading in February 2005, so that's as far back as our Point and Figure chart goes. However, the IAU is designed to track the price of London Gold Fixed PM whose symbol on the DWA web site is UKGOLD. To get a longer-term perspective on this ETF, it would be entirely appropriate to look at the chart of UKGOLD for guidance as well as the chart of the IAU.

Another question we often get is, "what is the best ETF to purchase when the Bullish Percent Index chart (our most important risk evaluator) reverses up?" The short answer to that question is that there is none. But I want to explain why. If you recall from Chapter 6 on the NYSE Bullish Percent, this type of indicator is a one stock—one vote indicator. This approach is different from the way indices are typically composed. There are three basic ways indices are composed. One method is to price weight. In price weighting, the higher the price of the stock, the more weight it carries. This is the way the Dow Jones Industrial Average is priced. Another way to weight an index is by capitalization. That is, the larger capitalized the stock (shares outstanding times price), the more influence it has on the index. This is the most common way to weight indices and ETFs. With this type of weighting, just a handful of stocks can control the vast majority of an indices' move. You will see this in our example in just a minute. Finally, we can weight an index equally. That is, each stock gets an equal vote. This is the way the DWA sector indicators and Bullish Percents are constructed. The universe of equal weighted ETFs is expanding. The first was an equal weighted index on the S&P 500 brought to the market by Rydex and the symbol is RSP. The way the RSP and the SPX moved from 2000 to 2006 was like the difference between day and night. The equal weighting effect on the RSP caused this index to significantly outperform the same S&P 500 index that was capitalization weighted. In other words, this divergence in performance points up the fact that in the market we sometimes have a bull market in stocks and sometimes have a bull market in indexes. The latter is generated by the capitalization weighting of the index.

In 1998, we were in a bull market in indexes. The top handful of stocks in the S&P 500 pulled the index to new highs while the smaller stocks that have little weight underlying this index were going down. Conversely, in 2000 the opposite happened. The small-cap stock university caught fire while the big stocks that typically push and pull the capitalization indexes turned cold as winter. This had the effect of making the market look like it was in a bear market but in fact more stocks were going up than down. This is why it pays to have an operating system in your head to understand the mechanics of the market. The Point and Figure method of analysis is the operating system that we have found most effective and easy to learn. Remember, in the stock market things aren't always what they seem. This is especially true of the young media reporters who have been around Wall Street for only a few years since they graduated college with a degree in journalism. One more ETF I wanted to mention that was equal weighted is the First Trust Nasdaq 100 Equal Weighted Index^{SM} Fund (QQEW). As we write this book, a number of sector ETFs are being introduced on an equal weighted basis. You know, it might be a good thing to securitize our whole DWA sector lineup because our Bullish Percent Indexes are all based on this universe. At present, most ETFs are capitalization weighted, and therefore it's very important to analyze the chart of the ETF you are actually buying and then evaluate the top holdings of that ETF. You might find that the highest percent holdings in the ETF are in one stock. This would affect how you view that sector. A great example of this would be the drug sector. A look at the Dorsey, Wright & Associates Drug sector shows there are 151 stocks currently in this group. That means each buy or sell signal in the group can affect the Bullish Percent by about .67 percent. However, a look at the broad iShares Dow Jones Healthcare Index (IYH) shows an index very skewed toward just a couple of names. Pfizer (PFE) and Johnson & Johnson (JNJ) each have over a 10 percent weighting. If these two stocks were in a Bullish Percent Index with a 10 percent weighting a piece, and each were to move to a buy signal from a sell signal on its Point and Figure chart, that would mean the drug Bullish Percent could jump 20 percent in a day. Because of this fact, we use the DWA Bullish Percent chart to alert us to a change within a sector or market's risk level, but we never just blindly buy a similar sector ETF, it must have good technical merits on its own.

What you find under the hood of the ETF is what will generate the move. Learn to look under the hood when evaluating the investment merits of any ETF. In Figure 10.1, we compare the iShares Dow Jones Financial Service Sector (IYG), Vanguard Financials (VFH), and KBW Bank ETF (KBE). The top 10 holdings in the IYG and the KBE are both over 50 percent while in the VFH, the top 10 holdings account for only 38 percent so this one is more equally weighted. A closer inspection at the actual holdings and you'll see that Citigroup (C) accounts for 7.66 percent of the movement in the VFH while accounting for 11.72 percent in the IYG. This doesn't make one ETF better than another, but rather you just need to be aware of the weightings when considering how the ETF will fit into your overall investment strategies.

iShares Dow Jones U.S. Financial Service Sector (IYG)		Vanguard Financial (VFH)		KBW Bank ETF (KBE)	
C	11.72%	C	7.66%	JPM	10.10%
BAC	10.43%	BAC	6.78%	BAC	10.03%
JPM	7.19%	AIG	4.67%	C	9.89%
WFC	5.24%	JPM	4.67%	WFC	9.05%
WB	4.48%	WFC	3.42%	WB	4.76%
MER	3.54%	WB	2.93%	USB	4.42%
MS	3.02%	MER	2.20%	WM	4.31%
GS	2.88%	MS	1.95%	BK	3.73%
AXP	2.85%	GS	1.93%	STI	3.47%
USB	2.72%	AXP	1.88%	STT	3.38%
Top 10 Wt.	54.07%		38.09%		63.14%

** Holdings as of approximately 3/31/06.

Figure 10.1   Sample Financial ETF Comparison.

If C is one of the strongest stocks in the sector, then the IYG or the KBE would be a good choice for purchase as they have higher weightings in C. However, if C has a weak chart pattern compared to other financial stocks, the VFH would make more sense. Or, perhaps you have a large holding in C and wish to hedge that position by shorting an ETF. Then using the IYG would be the logical choice. This is also where RS tools can come into play, and RS charts could be made comparing the IYG, to the VFH to KBE, similar to the RS matrixes seen earlier in this book.

With respect to International ETFs, you will find that some countries are more skewed toward certain sectors than others. In Figure 10.2, we have highlighted just a couple international ETFs to show you how the movement of a particular sector can influence an international ETF. The iShares MSCI Switzerland Index Fund (EWL) is very heavily weighted in the pharmaceutical sector, which has been an underperformer compared to other sectors, such as energy and basic materials. Both the iShares MSCI Austria Index Fund (EWO) and iShares MSCI Brazil Index Fund (EWZ) have weightings of about 20 percent and 50 percent, respectively, in these two groups while iShares MSCI Malaysia Index Fund (EWM) has no significant weighting in either of these groups. The returns from each of these ETFs reflect those sector weightings. From December 31, 2003, to March 31, 2006, Sweden and Malaysia were up 42 percent and

iShares MSCI Switzerland Index Fund (EWL)		iShares MSCI Malaysia Index Fund (EWM)		iShares MSCI Austria Index Fund (EWO)		iShares MSCI Brazil Index Fund (EWZ)	
Pharm. & Biotech	25.39%	Banks	22.55%	Energy	19.71%	Materials	26.28%
Diversified Financial	16.14%	Food Bev & Tobacco	12.53%	Telecom Services	15.48%	Energy	24.79%
Food Bev & Tobacco	11.67%	Consumer Services	12.19%	Banks	14.26%	Banks	18.84%
Materials	11.44%	Utilities	10.97%	Materials	13.61%	Telecom Services	7.63%
Insurance	8.67%	Transportation	9.66%	Real Estate	13.44%	Utilities	7.00%
Consumer Durables	6.07%	Telecom Services	8.46%	Capital Goods	9.12%	Food Bev & Tobacco	5.73%
Capital Goods	5.49%	Capital Goods	8.43%	Utilities	8.42%	Capital Goods	3.00%
Healthcare Eqp/Svc	5.09%	Diversified Financial	3.49%	Transportation	2.74%	Transportation	1.68%
Banks	2.78%	Media	2.55%	Insurance	1.87%	Retailing	1.02%
Commercial Services	1.95%	Auto & Components	2.51%	Diversified Financial	1.17%	Household Products	0.83%
	94.69%		93.34%		99.82%		96.80%

* Top Ten Sector Weight

* Note all data is through approximately 3/31/2006.

Figure 10.2 Sample International ETF Comparison.

16 percent, respectively, while Austria and Brazil were up 133 percent and 135 percent, respectively. You can't forget to look under the hood of ETFs, both domestically and internationally. There are ways to logically and sensibly go about the investment process. This does not guarantee profits but it does guarantee you are doing the proper homework before you make a move and we have found that over time this is the key to out performance, plain and simple.

Exchange Traded Funds Trend Chart Evaluation

One of the first and foremost means of evaluating an ETF is just to look at its trend chart. Just like a stock, or any index, ETFs are plotted using intraday high and low prices. All of the same charting rules apply—columns of X's and O's alternate, at least three X's or O's in a column, and so on. The only real change for an ETF chart is that we most often use a smaller box size since ETFs are baskets of stocks and they tend to move a little slower than individual names. Once an ETF gets into the $50 range or higher though, we find that often times a 1 point per box chart, the default scale, works just fine. Again, one of the great things about the SmartChart function at www.dorseywright.com is the ability to make the boxes any size you want to create a chart with the volatility you desire.

As we have outlined in previous chapters of this book, we take a top down approach to investing. That is, we first evaluate the overall market to determine whether it is supporting higher prices or not. Or, which team is on the field? If the offensive team is on the field, as dictated by the Bullish Percents, we will generally look to initiate long positions as we are in a wealth accumulation mode. Conversely, if the defensive team is on the field, we will generally be employing plays that preserve wealth. Or to look at it another way, a rising or falling tide generally carries boats. Once we have determined our outlook on the overall market, then we will look to sectors for opportunities. Next, we go to our inventory. For more and more professionals and investors, a significant portion of that inventory is the ETF universe. There are currently over 350 listed ETFs as we write this and more are coming to the market everyday so using an ETF universe, you can almost guarantee that you'll have access to just about any area market segment. The final step of our game plan is to evaluate the individual security to be purchased using tools such as trend, chart pattern, and RS and then use the Point and Figure charts to manage the trade. What are we going to do if things go right and what are we going to do if things go wrong?

Let's take a look at an example of how an ETF might just fit into your investment process. We'll paint a picture from history and outline the landscape in April 2003. The NYSE Bullish Percent was reversing up to X's at the 42 percent level. This put the offensive team back on the field with good field position. Next, if we reviewed the sectors, one which has emerged is the biotech sector. The DWA Biomedics/Genetics sector reversed up to X's from below 30 percent, the optimum buy level. In addition, the sector's RS was turning positive and the sector had a Favored status. All in all, the technical indicators were suggesting offense for both the market and the biotech sector. Now comes the time to evaluate whether to buy an individual name or the whole school of fish. A look at the Point and Figure chart of the iShares Nasdaq Biotech Sector (IBB) in April 2003 shows it violating the Bearish Resistance Line in March at 51 and subsequently going on to break a Triple Top at 53 in April (Figure 10.3). In planning the trade, we want to know what we will do if things go right and what we will do if things go wrong. So entering this trade, we would want to use a violation of the Bullish Support Line as our stop. Going into the trade, that stop or hedge point would be at 48.50. The IBB subsequently stayed above this support line until October when it violated it at 69.5. This would be our clue that the underlying supply and demand relationship was starting to shift in IBB and positions needed to have the risk managed in some fashion. Most ETFs are now getting options listed, too, so this opens a vast array of risk management tools from purchasing puts as protection against declines to selling calls and many more strategies that unfortunately we won't have enough time to discuss in this book. We could probably devote a whole book to this new ETF product that is the most significant development I have seen in my financial career.

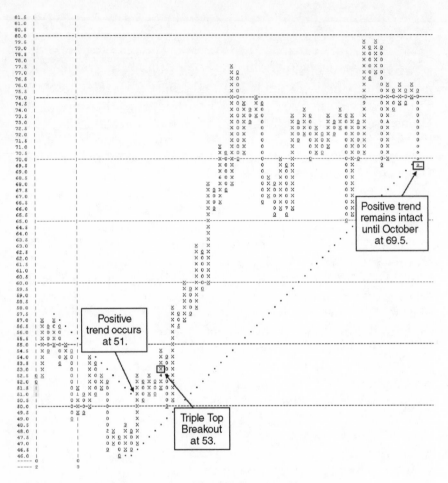

Figure 10.3   iShares NASDAQ Biotechnology Index Fund.

ETF Relative Strength

As you have gathered by now, RS is a very important tool in our work. It tells us where we should be and when we should be there. It smoothes out the rough edges of the buy and sell signals and allows us to step back and see the big picture. When I think about relative strength, I recall the Zen story of an old man who accidentally falls into the river rapids leading to a high and dangerous waterfall. Onlookers feared for his life.

Miraculously, he came out alive and unharmed downstream at the bottom of the falls. People were amazed he had lived and asked him how he managed to survive. The old man replied, "I accommodated myself to the water, not the water to me. Without thinking, I allowed myself to be shaped by it. Plunging into the swirl, I came out with the swirl. This is how I survived." You should allow yourself to accommodate to the market not the other way around.

If we just let the market tell us what it is doing and we adapt ourselves, we'll come out fine. When we try to make the market accommodate us, that's when the trouble begins. This is probably where the old Wall Street adage, "the market can remain irrational much longer than we can remain solvent" comes from. Thinking back to 2000 in the equity markets, large-cap stocks were all the rage. It's where all the money flowing into funds was going. But those well versed in reading the tides and currents of the river, that is understanding the Point and Figure work, knew that in February 2000, the small-cap stocks moved back in favor. Instead of trying to fight the current, go with it and change where you are investing. Since that change, to the end of the first quarter 2006, the S&P Small Cap 600 (SML) is up 88 percent while the S&P 500 (SPX) is down 7 percent. There are ETFs available for both the small-cap and large-cap universe of stocks from a variety of different ETF providers. I once coined a phrase "never anticipate the anticipators." Never forget this. Wall Street research is famous for anticipating the anticipators not to mention the news media.

Or, if you had wanted to buy large-cap stocks for whatever reason, it was best to purchase the S&P 500 on an equal weighted basis instead of a cap weighted basis. Again, the RS chart alerted us to this switch in May 2000. That move has meant the difference between being profitable and unprofitable from May 2000 to March 2006 in large-cap stocks. And you know what? Most investors and the media have no idea there is an S&P 500 equal weighted index that can be bought just like stock. The S&P 500 Equal Weighted Index is up 50 percent while the S&P 500 Cap Weighted Index is down 11 percent and ETFs are available on both weightings of the S&P 500. Is that not amazing? Both are S&P 500 indexes but one is up 50 percent and the other down 11 percent.

Wouldn't you want to be dealing with an advisor who was well versed in this? So in the Zen philosophy, trying to fight the water would make it much more difficult to survive the turbulence. You must accommodate yourself to the markets, not the other way around.

The same RS calculations that we perform on stocks and indexes can be applied to all ETFs, helping us to determine when the tide is coming in and when it is going out. Again, there are a couple of distinctions with a RS chart of an ETF. With a RS chart of an ETF, we look most closely at the column of the RS rather than the signal because these are baskets of stocks and move a bit slower than an individual name. An individual stock can move around, maneuver in and out of traffic like a sports car, while an ETF will keep moving with the traffic, like a big semi-truck. Let's go back to the iShares Dow Jones Financial Services Sector (IYG) and look at its RS chart. On this RS chart we see that there are three columns going back to 1992. The RS charts of ETFs are designed to capture major trends and not each wiggle in a sector. In fact, in a sample study of 18 sector ETFs going back to 1992, the average length of time a sector ETF spent in either a column of X's or O's was 624 days at this writing. That's just shy of two years so again you can see that the RS tool is longer term in nature and well suited for investors. Of course traders will also want to be aware of RS as the largest magnitude of movement usually comes from those areas with the best relative strength. But back to our chart of the IYG; let's examine each of these column changes in a bit more detail. The first column of X's is from December 30 1992 to October 6 1998. As long as this RS chart was in a column of X's it suggests that we have an overweighted exposure to the financial services area of the market. During this time, the IYG was up 185.1 percent compared to only 137.4 percent for the iShares Total Market Index (IYY), our benchmark. The IYG subsequently moved into a column of O's for almost two years. During this time, the IYG performed just slightly worse than our benchmark, up 39 percent compared to the IYY's return of 43.8 percent. When a RS chart reverses into O's, it doesn't mean the sector has to fall off a cliff and decline significantly. In fact, most often the sector does just what the IYG did—underperform slightly. But why would you want to be overweighted in a sector that has a high probability of slightly underperforming or even underperforming significantly? Once the RS chart of the IYG moved back into X's on May 23, 2000, that told us we wanted to beef up our exposure to financials. Since this column of X's has been in effect, the IYG is up 40.9 percent compared to the IYY's return of –3.7 percent. Think about this for a second. What if you had moved money from ETFs that were starting to reverse into O's in May 2000, mostly technology, and into those ETFs moving into X's? (See Figure 10.4.)

Utilizing a universe of about 20 ETFs, we went back and did a case study on a sector rotation strategy using ETFs and specifically the iShares universe. In our study, to be included in the portfolio, the RS chart had to be in a column of X's. Then, the portfolio was equally weighted among those ETFs whose RS charts were in X's. The only time the portfolio would be rebalanced was when there was a change in relative strength. We wanted the *market* to tell us when to rebalance the portfolio, not just the calendar. So let's say there were 10 sector ETF RS charts in X's. Each ETF would receive a weighting of 10 percent. The portfolio would remain unchanged until there was an RS change.

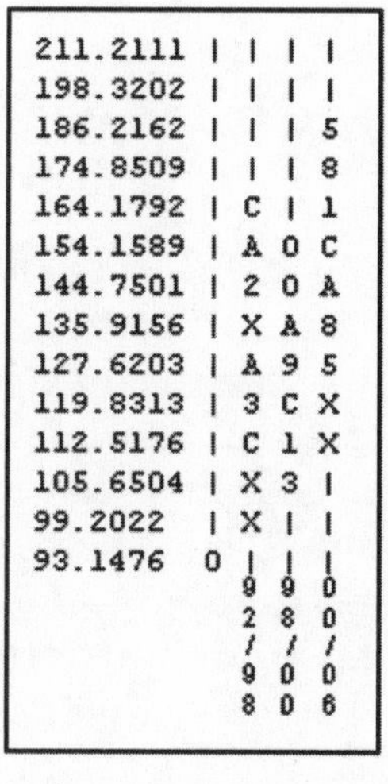

```
211.2111 |  |  |  |
198.3202 |  |  |  |
186.2162 |  |  |  5
174.8509 |  |  |  8
164.1792 |  C  |  1
154.1589 |  A  0  C
144.7501 |  2  0  A
135.9156 |  X  A  8
127.6203 |  A  9  5
119.8313 |  3  C  X
112.5176 |  C  1  X
105.6504 |  X  3  |
99.2022  |  X  |  |
93.1476  0  |  |  |
            9  9  0
            2  8  0
            /  /  /
            9  0  0
            8  0  6
```

Status		IYG/IYY Returns
Column of X's:	12/30/92 10/06/98	185.1% / 137.4%
Column of O's:	10/06/98 5/23/00	39.0% / 43.8%
Column of X's:	5/23/00 6/23/06	40.9% / –3.7%

Figure 10.4   iShares Dow Jones Financial Services Index (IYG) Relative Strength chart.

This might be for one month or six months. Then, let's say that an RS chart reversed into O's. That position would be sold and each position reset back to a weighting of 11.1 percent now that there were only 9 members of the portfolio; kind of like resetting your trip odometer on each segment of a road trip. Over the 12 year test period; this portfolio has outperformed the broad market averages nicely. Through the first quarter of 2006, this sector rotation-based strategy is up 355 percent, while the IYY is up 210 percent, and the S&P 500 is up 185 percent.

Probably the most telling time of this portfolio is the 2000 market that put a damper on so many investors' hopes of retiring early or having a better retirement than they ever hoped by being overweighted in technology and not having a sell discipline. In March 2000, the portfolio was 100 percent in technology in three ETFs—iShares Dow Jones Technology Sector (IYW), iShares Dow Jones Internet Sector (IYV), and the iShares Dow Jones Telecom Sector (IYZ). Over the next two months the portfolio completely transformed itself. The first to come out was the IYV, which had been in the portfolio since August 3, 1999. Then the financial and chemical sectors moved into the portfolio as their RS charts reversed up. Next, we saw the IYW come out of the portfolio on April 14, 2000, after having been in the portfolio since September 25, 1998. The IYW was up 188 percent from the time it come into the portfolio to the time it came out. Then, two weeks later the IYZ's RS chart reversed down into O's, and that meant it come out of the portfolio. Over the following two-week period, sectors like utilities, real estate, financials, and healthcare were rotated into the portfolio. By May 2000, the portfolio had a 0 percent weighting in technology (Figure 10.5). iShares sponsors DWA to update this strategy each week on our professional web site along with a similar rotation strategy for international ETFs. You can clearly see what a powerful tool you have in RS and the virtually endless possibilities of how you can take this concept and create a managed portfolio strategy around it. And, you know, keeping it simple is usually best. There is nothing complicated about this strategy. Could you do things to optimize the portfolio? Sure. But even just a straightforward approach like this can help keep the odds of success in your favor.

March 2000 Portfolio:	iShares Dow Jones Internet Sector (IYV)
	iShares Dow Jones Technology Sector (IYW)
	iShares Dow Jones Telecom Sector (IYZ)

March 29th 2000:	iShares Dow Jones Internet Sector (IYV)	RS Rev Down *
April 3rd 2000:	iShares Dow Jones Financial Sector (IYF)	RS Reverses Up
April 12th 2000:	iShares Dow Jones Chemical Sector (IYD)	RS Reverses Up
April 14th 2000:	iShares Dow Jones Technology Sector (IYW)	RS Rev Down *
May 2nd 2000:	iShares Dow Jones Telecom Sector (IYZ)	RS Rev Down *
May 10th 2000:	iShares Dow Jones Energy Sector (IYE)	RS Reverses Up
	iShares Dow Jones Utilities Sector (IDU)	RS Reverses Up
	iShares Dow Jones Real Estate Sector (IYR)	RS Reverses Up
May 23rd 2000:	iShares Dow Jones Healthcare Sector (IYH)	RS Reverses Up
	iShares Dow Jones Fin'l Services Sector (IYG)	RS Reverses Up

May 2000 Portfolio:	iShares Dow Jones Financial Sector (IYF)
	iShares Dow Jones Chemical Sector (IYD)
	iShares Dow Jones Energy Sector (IYE)
	iShares Dow Jones Utilities Sector (IDU)
	iShares Dow Jones Real Estate Sector (IYR)
	iShares Dow Jones Healthcare Sector (IYH)
	iShares Dow Jones Fin'l Services Sector (IYG)

* The IYV had been in the portfolio since 8/3/99 and was up 77%, the IYW had been in the portfolio since 9/25/98 and was up 118%, and the IYZ had been in the portfolio since 11/26/97 and was up 62%.

Figure 10.5 Conservative iShares Sector Manager—2000 Snapshot.

Advanced ETF Relative Strength

The RS concept is so transferable and the comparisons you can do are almost unlimited, but I wanted to give you an idea of some of the ones we find especially helpful by first taking a look at the international markets. As we pointed out in Chapter 5, we can do an RS chart of the broad international markets to the U.S. markets to help determine "where in the world" you want to invest. But just as we do more in-depth analysis of the U.S. markets, we can also do the same for international markets. There are currently over 30 international ETFs listed on the U.S. exchanges and trading in U.S. dollars. On the international area of our web site, you'll also find a complete list of all the international ETFs denominated in Euros but we'll stick to the international ETFs listed on the U.S. exchanges for the purposes of this example. I highly recommend you get to know these international ETFs because this broadens your horizons in investing globally. With today's Internet, you can trade in any country you wish. I currently have accounts open for online trading in Indonesia, Portugal, and Australia. My account at www.DIF.pt (change the language to English) allows me to trade all European stocks from one location and all ETFs from this location whether they are international or domestic. I hold U.S. Bonds as collateral for the account simply as an added safety factor, but over the years I have not seen a real need for this. It is the best trading platform I have seen and you can execute our Sector Rotation Models on the site automatically even if you are an individual investor. Generally, our models are primarily for professionals who then invest in them on individual investors behalfs. Okay, let's get back to the U.S. side of the equation. So let's say that you've done an RS chart of the U.S. markets versus a broad international index like the MSCI EAFE Index and it suggests the international markets are favored over the U.S. markets. Okay, now what? Throughout the world, some areas are going to be stronger than others and the best way we've seen to determine the strength across the entire globe is through a simple RS chart.

Figure 10.6 is a comparison of the iShares Latin America 40 Index (ILF) to the iShares MSCI Japan Index (EWJ). When this chart is on a buy signal, it suggests the ILF should outperform the EWJ. Conversely, if this chart is on a sell signal, it would suggest that we would want to own Japan over Latin America. The RS chart of the ILF versus the EWJ moved to a buy signal on November 19, 2002, and remains on that buy signal as we write this. It's been three and a half years since that signal has been given and the ILF is up 257 percent while the EWJ is up 97 percent. Both have far exceeded the returns of the U.S. markets as the S&P 500 is only up 39 percent during the same time but clearly the ILF was a better place to be with your international allocation.

Taking this concept a step further, we can construct a DWA International Matrix (Figure 10.7 on p. 316) to give us a snapshot of strength in the international markets. This Matrix is essentially the culmination of a large arm wrestling tournament. In our

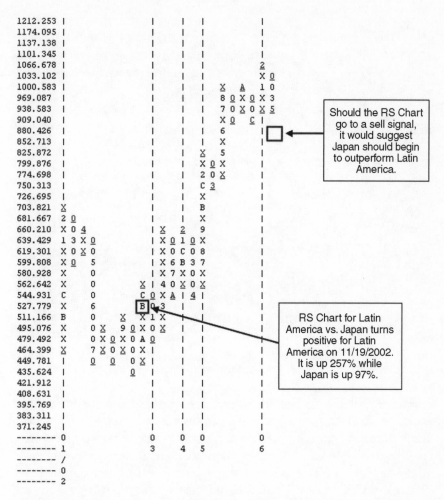

Figure 10.6 iShares Latin America 40 Index (ILF) versus iShares MSCI Japan Index (EWJ).

tournament, every international country arm "wrestles" another country until every country has been wrestled. To determine the winner of the tournament, we merely count up the "wins" or RS buy signals for each country and then rank the countries with the one with the most wins at the top of the matrix. With about 30 international ETFs in the matrix, you want to focus your investments in those that are outperforming at least half of the total

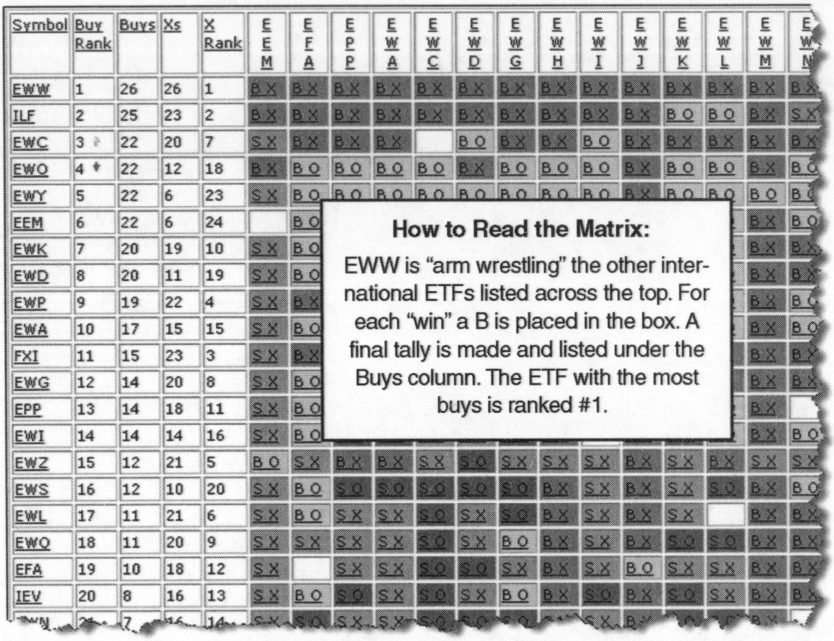

Symbol	Buy Rank	Buys	Xs	X Rank	E E M	E F A	E P P	E W A	E W C	E W D	E W G	E W H	E W I	E W K	E W L	E W M	E W N
EWW	1	26	26	1	BX	BX	BX	BX	BX	BX	BX	BX	BX	BX	BX	BX	BX
ILF	2	25	23	2	BX	BX	BX	BX	BX	BX	BX	BX	BX	BO	BO	BX	SX
EWC	3	22	20	7	SX	BX	BX	BX		BO	BX	BX	BO	BX	BX	BX	BX
EWO	4	22	12	18	BX	BO	BO	BO	BO	BX	BO	BO	BO	BX	BO	BO	BO
EWY	5	22	6	23	SX	BO	BO	BO	BO	BO	BO	BO	BX	BO	BO	BO	
EEM	6	22	6	24		BO										BX	BO
EWK	7	20	19	10	SX	BO										BX	BX
EWD	8	20	11	19	SX	BO										BX	BX
EWP	9	19	22	4	SX	BX										BX	BO
EWA	10	17	15	15	SX	BO										BX	BO
FXI	11	15	23	3	SX	BX										BX	BX
EWG	12	14	20	8	SX	BO										BX	BX
EPP	13	14	18	11	SX	BO										BX	
EWI	14	14	14	16	SX	BO											BO
EWZ	15	12	21	5	BO	SX	BX	BX	SX	SO	SX	SX	SX	BX	SX	BX	SX
EWS	16	12	10	20	SX	BO	SO	SO	SO	SO	SO	SX	BX	SX	SX	SO	BO
EWL	17	11	21	6	SX	BO	SX	SO	SO	SO	SO	BX	SX	BX	SX		BX
EWO	18	11	20	9	SX	SX	SX	SX	SO	SX	BO	SX	BX	SO	SO	BX
EFA	19	10	18	12	SX		SX	SO	SO	SX	BO	BX	BO	SX	SX	BX
IEV	20	8	16	13	SX	BO	SO	SX	SO	SX	BO	BX	SO	BX	SO	SX	BX

How to Read the Matrix:

EWW is "arm wrestling" the other international ETFs listed across the top. For each "win" a B is placed in the box. A final tally is made and listed under the Buys column. The ETF with the most buys is ranked #1.

Figure 10.7   iShares International ETF Matrix.

universe. Utilizing the International Matrix concept (you can't imagine the computer power it takes to do this), we have conducted some studies creating a portfolio out of these principles. The portfolio holds five international ETFs in an equal weighted manner. An ETF can fall out of the portfolio by losing significant RS against the field. That ETF will be replaced, not rebalanced, with the next highest ranked ETF in the matrix not currently in the portfolio. The back test on this portfolio only dates to 2002 but the results are impressive with the portfolio returning 145 percent and the MSCI EAFE Index (EFA) up 62 percent and the S&P 500 (SPX) up 11 percent thru the first quarter 2006.

This portfolio is designed to point out RS across the world, and does not take into account absolute price declines. In other words, if the market goes down, this portfolio will likely move lower too but should outperform over the long term on a relative basis. In markets like April through June 2006, we found the high RS international ETFs were extremely volatile. We came into this period up 28 percent for the year. The decline in the world markets was so severe we lost 25 percent of those gains in a heartbeat. Once the markets stabilized we shot back up 10 percent but what a ride that was. Over two trillion dollars of equity was lost worldwide during this period. The U. S. markets were just as volatile. When the plug is pulled on the world markets there is nowhere to hide. The strong RS snapped back fast however when the dust settled. So, to manage the absolute price risk, you'll want to use things like the Bullish Percent and actual trend chart patterns to help manage that portion of the risk. Remember, RS is just that, *relative*. It does not speak toward absolute performance unless you are a delta neutral investor where you would go long one and short the other. International markets definitely have volatility. That ride I discussed earlier was like riding the bull "Bodacious" in a rodeo. That bull has put more professional bull riders in the hospital than all the other bulls combined. It's not unusual to see these markets move 5 percent to 8 percent in just a week's time. Professional DWA clients have access to the DWA International ETF Manager with weekly updates as iShares sponsors this portfolio on the web site.

Yet another way to analyze the ETF market is versus the mutual fund market. In any given year, over 80 percent of the mutual fund managers don't outperform the S&P 500. If that is the case, why should you pay for active management of that fund when you purchase an ETF for a much lower expense ratio? There are fund managers that can and do outperform their benchmarks and the extra fee is well worth it. Furthermore, those managers that outperform the indices change from year to year. A broad observation about this type of outperformance is that when the benchmark, small caps, growth, value, and so on is a leading asset class, the harder it is for the active manager to outperform his or her benchmark and you're probably better off with the ETF. The reverse is also true—when the benchmark is an underperformer to most asset classes, the greater likelihood you can find a manager who is in fact adding value. Let's look at an example how you can use the RS tools to determine whether the active manager is worth the fee.

Phoenix Capital Growth (PHGRX) invests with a Domestic Growth style so we would want to do a RS chart of the PHGRX versus a Domestic Growth ETF like the iShares S&P 500 Growth Index Fund (IVW). If the RS chart were on a buy signal, it would tell us that the manager(s) of Phoenix Capital Growth were adding value over the index. If the RS chart were on a sell signal though, it would tell us that we would be better off in the index itself. By looking at the RS chart in Figure 10.8, we see that the RS chart is on a sell signal. That signal was given on March 27, 2001. Since that RS sell signal, the fund is down 20 percent while the IVW, its peer index, is only down 1.4 percent. If I wanted to invest in a large-cap growth fund that had a higher probability of outperforming the IVW I might look at something like the American Funds New Economy (ANEFX). This RS chart moved to a buy signal on August 19, 2003 (see Figure 10.9). So let's say that we like the American Funds family and this was our inventory we were working from. Prior to August 19, 2003, instead of purchasing the New Economy Fund, we were instead using the IVW for our domestic growth exposure. Once that RS chart moved to a buy signal, we would call up the New Economy fund from the farm team and substitute him on the field for the IVW, essentially putting him on the bench. Making that simple substitution on our mutual fund team, we enhanced our performance tremendously— the ANEFX is up 36.7 percent compared to the IVW only being up

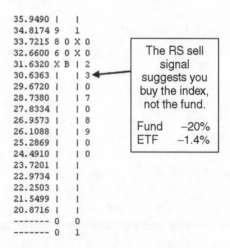

Figure 10.8 Phoenix Capital Growth (PHGRX) versus iShares
S&P 500 Growth Index Fund (IVW).

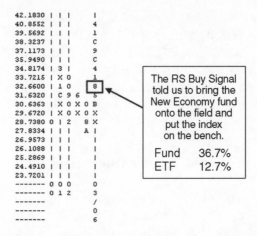

```
42.1830  | | |      |
40.8552  | | |      4
39.5692  | | |      1
38.3237  | | |      C
37.1173  | | |      9
35.9490  | | |      C
34.8174  | 3 |      4
33.7215  | X 0      1
32.6600  | 1 0    [ 8 ]
31.6320  | C 9 6    5
30.6363  | X 0 X 0  B
29.6720  | X 0 X 0  X
28.7380  0 | 2    8 X
27.8334  | | |    A |
26.9573  | | |      |
26.1088  | | |      |
25.2869  | | |      |
24.4910  | | |      |
23.7201  | | |      |
-------  0 0 0      0
-------  0 1 2      3
-------             /
-------             0
-------             6
```

The RS Buy Signal told us to bring the New Economy fund onto the field and put the index on the bench.

Fund   36.7%
ETF   12.7%

Figure 10.9   American Funds New Economy (ANEFX) versus iShares S&P 500 Growth Index Fund (IVW).

12.7 percent. This is so interesting. I get goose bumps every time I think about these concepts we have created. DWA is all about adding value to the investment process and we have come a long way with our RS work.

Here's another example in the small-cap growth area. As we have outlined before in this book, the small-cap area of the market has been the place to be since February 2000. Over the past six years, funds have been emerging and falling against its peer in the area, the iShares S&P Small-Cap 600 Growth Index Fund (IJT). On July 13, 2005, the Winslow Green Growth Fund (WGGFX) moved to a RS buy signal versus its peer group. That told us to expect this fund to begin to outperform the IJT. At the same time, the MFS New Discovery Fund (MNDAX) remained on a RS sell signal versus the IJT. So, if in July 2005 I was looking to add some small-cap growth exposure to my portfolio, I would prefer to buy the WGGFX over the IJT and certainly the IJT over the MNDAX. In the last 11 months, the WGGFX is up 8.4 percent, while the base index is up 3.55 percent, and the MNDAX, the weak RS chart, is only up 2.76 percent. These RS charts are extremely powerful for anyone using mutual funds and at our web site, you can easily click the "Peer RS" button and the chart is already done for you. As well, you can harness the power of technology and search our entire database of funds to cull out those with a particular peer RS characteristic. For professional using mutual funds and ETFs to populate their asset allocation strategy, this is a tool you cannot live without. It would be like trying to build a house without a hammer. It's all there for you at the DWA web site.

What Does the Future Hold?

Where is the future of ETFs? We think it is only going to continue to expand. Just as we were writing this book, the first inverse and leveraged ETFs have been introduced. I saw this coming in 1982 and, in my opinion, we are only in the first foot of a 26-mile marathon. DWA will be in the forefront of this product as we were in 1982 when I went to Joseph Rizzello at the PHLX with the idea of securitizing their indexes and trading them instead of the options. As well, currencies ETFs have just been introduced. These new ETF products really open a door to risk management for individual investors that previously was only open to institutes. Cash management takes on a whole new meaning now. In fact, it can now become a profit center. The ETF product is certainly a tremendous leap forward for our industry but it is the analysis of the product that will make them a viable alternative to an investor's portfolio. Like investing in general, you must have an operating system firmly placed in your mind before any information about the investment process can effectively be evaluated. It is the analysis we do in the ETFs that make an index something that is truly special and one of the most viable investment tools one has today. With the Point and Figure methodology's robust, adaptive nature, you will be armed with the tools you need to evaluate any ETFs on the market. For instance, we have developed a model based on RS for the currency ETFs as a way to manage the cash side of your asset allocation. Manage cash? You bet you can—now with flair. Just think about holding cash in Euro's instead of dollars when the RS chart suggested you do so. You can now with ease thanks to Rydex's efforts in bringing out ETF's on currencies. We welcome all ETFs. The more the merrier for us and this form of analysis.

POINTS AND FIGURES BY DORSEY, WRIGHT MONEY MANAGEMENT

According to the *Wall Street Journal* (June 14, 2006), the Dow Industrials are down 8 percent since May 10. And it's not just the United States. Some of the strongest foreign markets have been knocked down much harder. For example, Brazil (–21.3 percent), India (–28.1 percent), and Russia (–29.0 percent) have all dropped much more sharply. What's more, the correction has happened relatively quickly, which tends to get investors especially nervous.

The irony of a correction in the market is that it can't stop going down until everyone "knows" it's going lower. The entire purpose of a correction is to shake out the weak holders. In this sense, a correction is a healthy part of the market cycle. You can't make any money in a crowded trade, and Mr. Market knows that. So he will do whatever he needs to make investors dump their shares. If investors are already nervous, Mr. Market knows that a 5 to 7 percent pullback will shake them out. If investors are supremely confident, Mr. Market realizes it will take a bear market to make the weak holders let go. Your goal is to hang on and not be shaken out.

Instead of facing a correction with dread, look at it as an opportunity. The Chinese sage, Fu His, wrote that "a situation only becomes favorable when one adapts to it." Instead of using all of your energy resisting the situation, look at it as an opportunity to display your risk management skills, and when it is over, as an opportunity to buy at lower levels.

Here's the most important thing of all: Once you have a risk management plan in place, stay the course. Risk management can take many forms. It can be done with sector rotation, through raising cash, or hedging, or a combination of these things. Other common methods of risk reduction are diversification and strategic asset allocation. Decide what works for you, and then stick to it.

Risk management should not be done on the fly. The danger of not sticking to your preset risk management plan is well illustrated by the famous Dalbar studies on investor returns. Almost every advisor is familiar with the Dalbar study that shows how investors do not exactly optimize their returns by getting nervous and managing risk by emotion rather than a carefully thought-out plan. According to a story in *Investment News* (June 12, 2006), from 1986 to 2005, investors in the S&P would have realized a return of 11.9 percent annually, if they had just been able to sit on their hands. However, after analyzing fund flows, Dalbar was able to determine that the average investor actually earned just 3.9 percent annually. In fact, investors have demonstrated, in aggregate, that they can't even sit still when they already have a "risk management plan" in place. Dalbar suggests that asset allocation funds, balanced funds, lifestyle, life cycle, and target date funds are all effective ways to make investors more disciplined. Yet the evidence doesn't really bear them out on this count. The average asset allocation investor made only 3.3 percent annually, even worse than the 3.9 percent of the twitchy investors who were yanking their money in and out of the market. It's apparent that asset allocation investors, despite going into funds that were more conservative and supposedly managed their risk to begin with, were *still* jerking around with their accounts trying to avoid losses!

It's not that the market itself is beating their brains out—investors are doing it to themselves. And why is it happening? According to Dalbar, most investor mistakes are made in attempting to avoid loss! This is a perfect example of the "karma boomerang" effect where having a fear of something can actually "cause" the feared consequence. Managing risk is a good idea, but believing you can somehow eliminate it—which is what investors secretly desire—is nuts. Dalbar concludes that "actions driven by aversion to loss are the *primary causes of losses* among mutual fund investors." (my emphasis)

In other words, the more you fear risk and loss and try to run away from it, the more it will seek you out! There needs to be an explicit recognition that even with a risk management plan in place, whether through sector rotation, raising cash, hedging, or whatever, drawdowns are an inevitable and healthy part of the market cycle. Face it—accept that you might lose some money in a correction. It happens. It's not a big deal if you are managing your risk the way you had planned. It's only a problem if the losses are uncontrolled and your emotions get involved.

Client education about risk and risk management is absolutely central to long-term investing success. In the market, risk is not a matter of being careful on an individual basis. Risk happens. If you're in the market at all, you're subject to it. The root cause of investor problems comes from not understanding what risk is, and specifically, not accepting what *your* risk is. Dalbar points out that a "good understanding of risk produces more prudent behavior." This is true, but it will never happen in real life. Studies in psychology point out that human beings are not wired to take risk. People take risk or put themselves in risky situations *because they don't think it is a risk*. Investors (and people generally) are overconfident and imbued with a belief that "it won't happen to me." Ben Roethlisberger wasn't planning to bounce his face off a windshield. Instead, he thought, "if I'm careful, it won't happen to me." If he felt there was a risk, he would have certainly worn a helmet, or maybe even not been on a motorcycle in the first place. This is an example of *not* having a good understanding of risk, and not having any kind of risk management plan in place.

When the market corrects, implement your prearranged risk management plan. Recognize that corrections are healthy for the market and use the opportunity to display your skills. Handled properly, corrections might end up proving very beneficial for your business.

Chapter 11

EVALUATING THE COMMODITY MARKET FOR OPPORTUNITIES

It was October 19, 1987, another typical Monday morning, we prepared for the normal call volume of questions on which stock to buy, which to sell, what sector to consider, and all the other typical questions professionals in the brokerage business mull over each day. We had already shaken off the hundred or so points the previous Friday. That was about all we expected for the correction, in fact we even bought into it. I bought call options on the OEX (S&P 100) that Friday expecting a nice snapback trade on Monday. That Monday morning didn't experience the snapback though, the selling pressure continued from Friday's session. It never backed off all day. We watched in amazement as the Dow Jones Industrial Average fell 22 percent in one day. There was only one other day that saw more carnage in one day than October 29, 1987, and that was December 12, 1914, when the Dow Jones fell 24 percent. In today's numbers as I write this book, a 22 percent decline in the Dow Jones would be 2,431 points. Can you imagine the field day the media would have with a number like that? Heck we've already been there, done that, and got a T-Shirt. But the *New York Times* would probably lead in the feature article with a title "Chicken Little's Revenge." Well, that day changed our life at Dorsey, Wright (DWA). You see we were in essence the only outsourced Options Strategy firm on Wall Street. When Watson and I started DWA, we simply moved the Options Strategy Department I developed and managed for Wheat First Securities, down the road. Following this fateful day in October, I knew the options business would never be the same again. Some firms were rumored to go under because of options exposure. We immediately moved away from options and puts as the locomotive for DWA, to the Point and Figure Technical Analysis we had done for so many years. I also knew we needed an alternate source of income. Commodities were a natural extension for us so I created a commodity report and sold it to Interstate Securities who had one of the best commodity departments on Wall Street. They were located in Atlanta, Georgia. It was simple to me. Commodity prices are governed by the irrefutable law of supply and demand, making it a seamless application for our Point and Figure work. I look at most things in both life and business in the most simplistic of terms. Copper is, quite simply, a hunk of metal. Cocoa is simply a bean that grows, primarily, in the Ivory Coast, and from time to time the locusts will come and wreak havoc. Coffee is similarly a bean that Juan Valdez and others cultivate down in Colombia. By the same token, IBM is simply a stock that moves about on the New York Stock Exchange, its price governed by supply-and-demand imbalances. What makes the movement of Cocoa's price different from the movement of IBM's price? One could offer that there are no cocoa CEOs to be carried out of their offices in handcuffs for various improprieties. There are no claims of corporate malfeasance thrust upon Live Cattle. But in terms of what causes a change in price, there is nothing different between a share of IBM and a contract of coffee. IBM is to cocoa, as coffee is to copper, and so on.

At the time I had never seen a soy bean, or a cocoa bean, or even a coffee bean that wasn't ground already. Armed with the Point and Figure chart, I was an expert in their price movement just the same. I knew that if there were more buyers than sellers willing to sell gold, the price of gold would rise. Conversely, if there were more sellers than buyers willing to buy gold, the price would decline. If supply and demand for gold was in perfect balance, the price would remain the same. There is nothing else to consider.

Still, it turned out to be the right product at the wrong time. The stock market was in the middle of a 20-year bull market, while commodities were amid a 20-year bear market. The report we had created didn't take off as we would have hoped; it was, quite simply, 13 years early. The stock market instead began to make up all the ground it lost in that one Black Monday and was on its merry way by year end. Commodities went back to being the red-headed stepchild of investing once again.

Had we hung our hat on this single product, or any single product really, we would have ended up in Wall Street's graveyard, as Mr. Hamilton suggests. The beauty of Point and Figure is that it is adaptive to any free market, and while the commodity business was ready to contract significantly for the next 13 years, the Point and Figure Technical Analysis skill we had developed for many years prior to starting DWA was applicable to many other facets of Wall Street.

There was one more act to the commodity show before we allowed it to atrophy back in 1987. There was a hedge fund manager in Europe who was a client of ours on the equity side. I talked to him one day and told him his temperament was more suited to commodity trading. I offered him our commodity report for free so that he could get familiar with trading commodities on paper before venturing into the real world of platinum, pork bellies, and currencies. This began a long and intriguing story at DWA, much of which I can only look back upon and shake my head. It took this client about three months to get used to commodities and then one day I received a call from him, "Tommy, I'm ready." I replied, "Ready for what?" Unabashedly he offered, "Commodity trading." Well, the rubber hit the road that second, and I was immediately called upon to advise this large, very nimble, hedge fund on commodity trading, and I had never traded the first commodity in my life. I had a disciplined methodology and an operating system to fall back on, but very little else at that time.

I set this client up with an Introducing Broker to clear through and we were off and running. If you can recall the last time you sat down to watch the Kentucky Derby, the horses are all in the gates, the bell rings, the commentator then offers heartily, "and they're off." Well, that was us. This hedge fund manager had the intestinal fortitude of a gladiator. We started trading 500 lots of currencies at a time. A five-hundred contract position in something like the Euro today is still a massive position, over 62 million Euros worth of leverage. At that time I either didn't, or couldn't, fully conceptualize the scope of these positions; it was simply colossal like King Kong holding Ann Darrow in his hand. The commodity was King Kong and I was Ann Darrow. Come to think of it, I don't think we ever had a calculator that would quantify that amount of leverage back then, so we just didn't get the full flavor of the risk we were taking. Today, I would break out into a cold sweat with a position that size, but back then we did it, did it regularly, and didn't flinch. At any one time, we could be long and short a combination of currencies totaling $250 million in value. Buying 600 gold contracts for this client became commonplace. At this writing, each contract controls 100 ounces, or $50,000, worth of gold. Six hundred contracts is then $30 million in leverage. Still, this client didn't even breathe heavy with a position of this magnitude, and so eventually, neither did I. While my experiences trading currency futures 500 lots at a time makes for a good story, the comfort I feel today in the commodities market is far more a function of simply having a logical, disciplined approach toward managing risk to fall back on. I feel as comfortable trading commodities as I do stocks, I still don't know what a soybean or a cocoa bean looks like, but I have been very successful trading them over the years nonetheless.

We would suggest that you familiarize yourself with some of the basics of commodity trading, such as hours of trading, contract sizes, and other environmental influences. All of this information is readily available on the Internet, much of it on our web site, or in various other commodity books. We won't rehash that work, but will rather focus specifically on why this asset class might add value to your investment game plan, and on using the Point and Figure tools to develop a disciplined trading plan for commodities. We also won't focus on only futures contracts as the vehicle for commodity exposure as there are many commodity-related vehicles that are present in today's markets outside that of strictly futures contracts. I think you will be both amazed, and delighted, to see the various instruments available to you in today's market.

Futures Contracts

It was in the 1840s that Chicago became a commercial center where farmers and dealers could meet to deal in "spot" grain. At the time, it was simple to exchange cash for immediate delivery of wheat. This was the point in time when railroads, telegraphs, and the McCormick reaper provided a confluence of both supply and widespread demand. The reaper lead to exponentially greater wheat production, while the railroads and telegraph allow farmers of the Midwest to sell their wheat to dealers who then shipped it all over the country. Where previously the farmer was at the mercy of a city with very few storage facilities for such a supply of wheat and the limited availability of dealers (demand) standing ready to purchase his crop, the technology of the time allowed for both supply and demand to establish a more liquid equilibrium.

This liquidity allowed the futures contract to evolve toward essentially what we know it to be today: farmers (supply) and dealers (demand) committing to future exchanges of grain for cash. Then as today a farmer can agree with the dealer on a price to deliver to him 5,000 bushels of wheat at a point in the future; the end of December, for example. As with any free and open market, the price goes up and down depending on the supply /demand relationship of wheat, which could be influenced by any combination of weather, soil conditions, or a change in eating habits.

Trading Futures Contracts

While we'll discuss a number of different market vehicles in this chapter, we'll begin with commodity-based futures contracts, and the statement that they are first and foremost about trading; not investing. Most people (other than hedgers) trade commodities for the purpose of profiting from relatively short-term swings either directly or by investing with a commodity trading advisor or in a commodity pool. In the latter case, the commodity trading advisor or commodity pool operator does not invest in commodities either; he trades commodities for the purpose of profiting from relatively short-term swings. Why does this make a difference? Because the shorter your time horizon, the more critical it is to select the correct entry point and the more important it is to pay attention to the technical characteristics (as opposed to the fundamental characteristics) of a stock or commodity. Always remember that following trends and near-term Point and Figure signals are imperative for those using futures contracts because both the leverage and the time horizon make this of paramount importance.

Using Spot Charts

Spot refers to a cash market price for a physical commodity that is available for immediate delivery. The Spot Month is basically the futures contract month closest to expiration, and is also referred to as the "nearby delivery month," or simply "near-month" contract. A continuous chart uses the current nearby futures contract price data, continually rolling to the next near month as the earlier one expires. So, the price of a futures contract at expiration and the cash or spot price of the underlying asset must be the same, because both prices refer to the same (physical) asset. By consulting a spot or continuous chart, you will be provided perspective as to what the longer term trend of a given commodity is, thereby directing your overall trading posture. Spot charts are useful for establishing a posture on individual commodities, as well as commodities as an asset class, both of which we will examine in this chapter.

The spot or continuous charts are generally considered long term in nature. For instance, the NYMEX crude oil (CRUDE) chart reflects the spot price of West Texas Intermediate light sweet crude and has maintained a generally positive technical picture since early 2002. We'll revisit the merit of trend lines in a moment, but clearly the price action of crude oil has trended nicely since 2002, creating an advantageous backdrop for the commodity trader willing to explore exposure there. Over the years, we have found it very helpful to follow spot charts for gold, crude oil, and copper. These specific commodities all carry notable importance on an economic basis, so close monitoring of them can serve you in more ways than one. London Gold (UK-GOLD) is a chart that we have been keeping since 1987, posting it by hand for many of those years. The chart is now available on our web site under the ticker UKGOLD. In essence, this chart is the London Gold PM Fixing. Copper is another commodity we tend to follow very closely. Copper, like gold or crude oil, is often considered a barometer of economic (industrial) health. I like to view both the spot chart as well as the future I intend to trade. It just provides more perspective (see Figure 11.1).

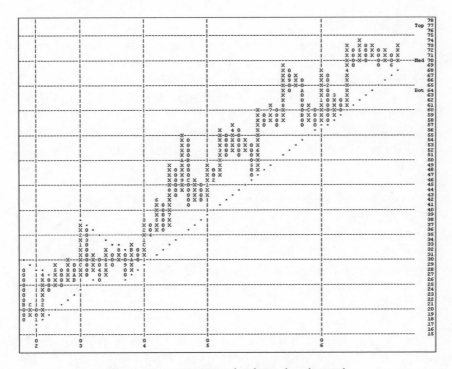

Figure 11.1   NYMEX Crude Oil P&F chart (CRUDE).

Trend Lines

So whether we are talking about shares of IBM or bushels of corn, one of the main premises of technical analysis is that prices tend to trend. Therefore, one of the main purposes of a chart is to help in the identification of the overall trend of a given vehicle—and to then play the direction of that trend for as long as it stays in force. Just like stocks, there are two main trend lines that are used: the Bullish Support Line (BSL) and the Bearish Resistance Line:

1. Bullish Support Line:
   - Also known as the Uptrend Line.
   - Suggests the commodity is recording higher prices.
   - The Bullish Support Line is always a 45-degree line, which is upward sloping to the right.
   - In an overall uptrend, your trades should be limited to long positions.

Drawing this Uptrend Line is very easy—once the first buy signal is given, off the bottom or after a period of accumulation (moving sideways), you then go to the lowest-reaching column of O's in that pattern on the chart and begin drawing the trend line by placing a mark in the box directly below the lowest O. You then move up and over a box and place a second mark, and repeat this process which will result in an upward sloping 45 degree angled line—this is your Bullish Support Line:

2. Bearish Resistance Line:
   - Also known as the Downtrend Line.
   - Suggests the commodity is recording lower prices.
   - The Bearish Resistance Line is always a 135-degree line, which is downward sloping to the right.
   - In an overall downtrend, your trades should be limited to short positions.

As a general rule of thumb, if a commodity is trading above its Bullish Support Line, in an overall uptrend, your trades

should be limited to long positions. This is hard to do sometimes. There are times when a shorter term trend line can allow
you to fine-tune a position, which we will discuss later, but your
overall bias—long or short, will be determined by whether the
commodity is trading above or below its Bullish Support Line. A
violation of the Bullish Support Line, coupled with a sell signal
(recall the discussion on chart patterns) on a commodity chart is
quite simply a "call to action." It is a sign that you must change
your current course of action with that particular commodity.
Long positions, generally speaking, should be sold or some type
of protective action should be taken; as well, short positions
could then be considered. That's the interesting thing about
commodity trading that is unlike stock trading. Once a commodity proves you are wrong in the direction of the trade, you
can close it and execute an opposite trade going in the proper direction as dictated by the price action. By adapting your posture
to the overall trend, you can let your winners run, staying with
and catching a long-term trend. Or should a trend change, it allows you to, more importantly, cut your losses short. Over time,
this is one of the keys to success in trading both stocks and commodities. (See Figure 11.2.)

Chart Patterns

Chart patterns such as the basic Double Top and Double Bottom break, as well as more developed patterns like the triangle
or catapult formation, were discussed in depth earlier in this
book. These patterns are simply a record as to whether supply
or demand is winning the latest battle in price, and they are as
applicable to commodity trading as they are to stocks. Bullish
patterns within a positive trend are a strong signal to be long a
futures contract, and bearish patterns within a negative trend
are strong signals to sell short a futures contract. Signals that
are counter to the prevailing trend (buy signals within a bearish
trend, or sell signals within a bullish trend) are most often used
as stop loss points, which will be discussed shortly, but are
rarely used to establish a new position. A sell signal that is

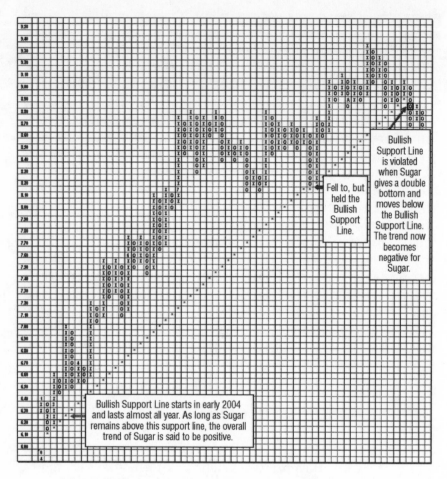

Figure 11.2　March 2005 Sugar Contract (SB/H5).

given within a positive trend (counter trend) is typically a sign of consolidation or a pullback toward the next significant level of support, but not of a long-term change in direction. Such a condition is most likely to produce a move toward a previous bottoming area or long-term trend support, and can simply provide an opportunity to reenter the position at lower prices. When trading futures contracts, focus on entering positions

that are on buy signals within positive trends or shorting con-
tacts that are on sell signals below trend. These are the situations that present the greatest probabilities for success in
commodity trading.

A look at the Gold Continuous Chart (GC) over the past few
years shows numerous buying opportunities when implement-
ing the concepts recently discussed in this chapter. There were
a number of occasions where we witnessed gold prices retrace
to its long-term Bullish Support Line only to hold support and
give a Point and Figure buy signal, this happened in February
2002 at $328, again in June 2005 at $448, in November 2005 at
$480, and still again in June 2006 at $592. As well, pattern
recognition proved profitable over the years by identifying the
Bullish Triangle patterns that were completed in August 2003
at $380 and April 2006 at $640, each of which foreshadowed
moves higher of more than 10 percent in the price of gold in
short order. (See Figure 11.3.)

Risk Management

Risk is basically the amount and probability or possibility of in-
curring a meaningful loss (of capital), or series of losses. There
are several types of risk inherent to trading commodities.

Avoidable risk is risk which can be reduced or eliminated
without any reduction or compromise in reward. A couple examples of this type of risk would be trading an illiquid market, and
not properly diversifying your commodity portfolio. Illiquid markets can provide a great deal of slippage and bad fills on trades.
Diversification typically will serve to reduce risk.

Unavoidable risk is risk which cannot be reduced or eliminated. In other words, there will always be some risk involved in
trading commodities, stocks, or any investment for that matter,
given that there is an expected return or profit.

Controllable risk is risk that can be reduced or mitigated as
a function of your entry and exit points. This will be dealt
with in more detail in our discussion on stop-loss points, and
risk-reward.

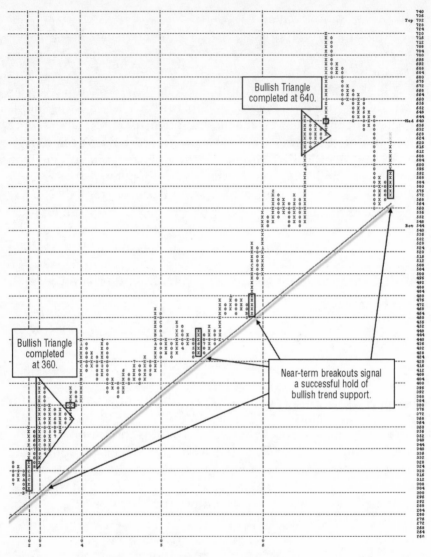

Figure 11.3 Gold Bullion Continuous chart (GC/).

As mentioned, with any investments, and in this case with commodity trading, there is risk involved. To a large extent, you can reduce or mitigate your risk with smart risk management techniques. Truly, over the long haul, it is proper risk management that will be the key to your success in commodity trading. You must always be aware of the risk you are taking on any given trade—the risk of loss. Being aware of your risk is important, as is defining that risk in our experiences.

Stop-Loss Points

Stop-loss points are a key element of risk control. Recall our definition of risk—the probability of significant loss of capital. One of the best ways to provide a control mechanism on risk is through the use of a stop loss. That is why we always determine where we are getting out before we even get in (to a trade). So to determine if the risk is acceptable on any given trade, you must know what you will do (and where you will do it), if things go wrong. At DWA, we must deem the risk to the stop (the potential loss) acceptable before we place the trade. But then once that trade is executed, our approach dictates that a stop order be placed GTC (good til cancelled). This serves a couple of purposes. One, you don't have to constantly watch each tick of trading, for fear of missing your exit point. Two, it removes much of the emotion from the trade. Having a predetermined exit strategy (a GTC stop) can protect you from large losses because you can't procrastinate or rationalize staying in a losing trade that has negated your reasons for entering. Avoidance of severe losses, truly, is the key to success in any trading. Using a stop-loss point reduces the possibility of a severe loss. In fact, there has been plenty of research conducted on this subject, with the results showing that the key to a successful trading program is the size of your winners versus the size of your losers, not the number of winning trades versus the number of losing trades. So cutting your losses short, while letting your winners run is really what it's all about. This is why a trend-following system based on Point and Figure analysis can be so helpful in achieving this goal.

To that end, how do you know where to place stops using PnF? If the entry point is where risk is low and the potential reward high, then the exit point (stop loss) is where the risk is high and the potential reward low, or increasingly uncertain. So, where would risk be high and potential reward uncertain?

Turning to the PnF chart, it would be where the commodity will break a significant bottom or violate its trend line—basically, a point at which the chart suggests supply has won the battle, not necessarily the war but at least the battle, and therefore suggests you no longer want to be long the commodity. In Figure 11.4, we provide you with two such stop loss examples. The main point to remember is that you should always have an exit strategy for each and every trade you enter. The beauty of using the Point and Figure chart is the ease with which you can determine this exit point, or stop, and then the fact that you may design a trade with a defined risk up front. As well, the PnF chart allows you to raise (or lower) the stop as the chart unfolds. This serves to reduce risk further as price action develops in your favor, allowing you to protect a profitable trade and its related gains.

In general, sell signals given above trend suggest the potential for a meaningful breather for the commodity, while sell signals that involve a violation of trend suggest a structural change in the supply-and-demand relationship for that commodity. So while a near-term sell signal for a commodity that occurs within a positive trend may setup a re-entry point at lower prices in the near future, a violation of trend suggests that any trade in that commodity in the near future will likely be in the opposite direction.

Relative Strength with Commodities

We now want to turn our attention to the application of Relative Strength (RS) within the commodities realm. When interpreting an RS chart, there are two main points to determine—the most recent signal given on the chart, and the current column. In other words, was the last signal given on the RS chart a buy signal (a previous top broken) or a sell signal (a previous bottom broken)? As well, is the chart currently in a column of X's or a column of O's? So go back to our discussion of chart patterns.

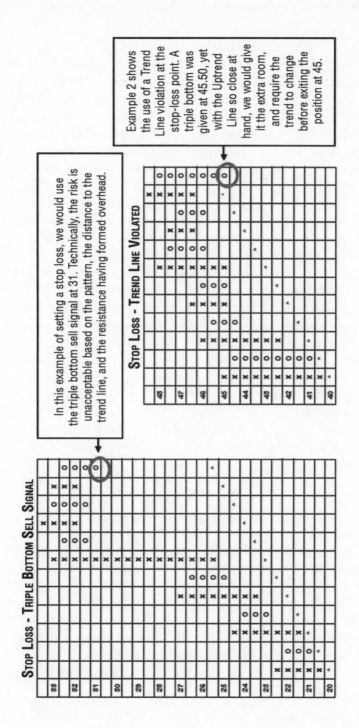

In this example of setting a stop loss, we would use the triple bottom sell signal at 31. Technically, the risk is unacceptable based on the pattern, the distance to the trend line, and the resistance having formed overhead.

Example 2 shows the use of a Trend Line violation at the stop-loss point. A triple bottom was given at 45.50, yet with the Uptrend Line so close at hand, we would give it the extra room, and require the trend to change before exiting the position at 45.

Figure 11.4 Setting Stop-Loss Points: Trend Stops versus Signal Stops.

We first want to ascertain if the RS chart is on a buy or sell signal. This will demonstrate the long-term implications for the underlying commodity. If that last signal on the RS chart was a Double Top, the RS is said to be "positive"; if the last signal on the RS chart was a Double Bottom, then RS is "negative." Positive RS implies outperformance, while negative RS suggests underperformance. In measuring RS on a shorter-term basis, we want to focus on which column the RS chart is in. If the current column is X's, the commodity is said to have "positive" RS on a short-term basis; if in O's, the short-term RS is "negative." Ideally, you want to focus your buying on those commodities exhibiting positive RS, while avoiding or shorting those commodities that are exhibiting negative RS. With stocks we most commonly employ RS charts that compare the stock to the S&P 500 Equal-Weighted Index, whereas the Continuous Commodity Index (UV/Y) is the closest counterpart among commodity-based indexes. In sum then, the strongest RS reading is one in which the most recent signal on the RS chart versus UV/Y was a buy signal and the most recent column is in X's.

Copper is an interesting example of RS. The RS chart for copper continuous (HG/) remained on a sell signal versus the Continuous Commodity Index (UV/Y) for three years from March 2000 through March 2003, suggesting this particular commodity was most likely to underperform a more diversified allocation toward commodities. Over that time, copper not only underperformed on a relative basis, but copper prices actually fell 2 percent during a period where raw material prices generally rose by 7 percent. That's not to say that a commodity trader couldn't have produced short-term gains in copper futures over that time, but the bias was for copper to lag other commodities. Upon seeing a change on the RS chart, however, it was clear that something had changed within that dynamic and that copper was ready to enter a period of likely outperformance. The results since March 2003 have been dramatic as copper prices have inflated 300 percent from March 2003 through June 2006, versus a gain of only 61 percent in the commodity index. See Figure 11.5.

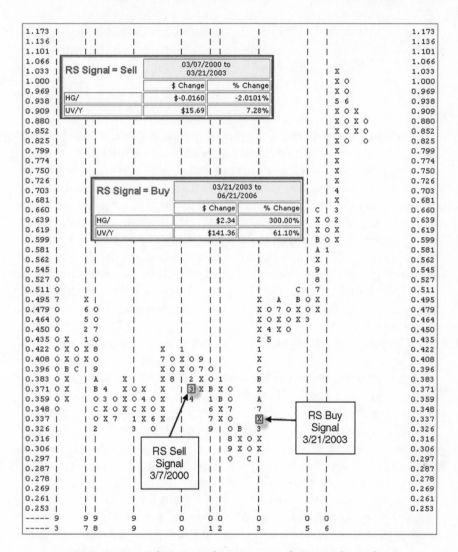

Figure 11.5   Relative Strength: Copper versus the Commodity Market.

The key to consistent success is to use chart patterns, trend lines, spot and continuous chart evaluation, and RS together to arrive at the best decisions for your commodity trading. You want to focus long exposure on strong trends, bullish patterns, and areas that are most likely to outperform the broader commodities market, while short exposure should be concentrated upon just the opposite to stack the odds in your favor.

Support and Resistance

One of the keys to trading commodities on a technical basis is being able to properly analyze the technical condition of the underlying commodity. Support is basically a level where the commodity begins to gain buying pressure and significantly slows it's decline. Conversely, resistance is a level at which a commodity loses buying pressure and selling pressure takes over. It's the point where the commodity begins to slip back. As a general rule of thumb, scale into purchases on pullbacks close to support; or scale into short sales on rallies to resistance, provided your macro analysis of trend, relative strength, chart patterns, and so on has already been completed and corroborates your posture.

The Soybean Meal, July 2005 chart is a good example of resistance and support. In particular, Bean Meal displays why you must recognize where significant resistance lies before embarking on a trade. Notice in early January 2005 that a Triple Top buy signal was given at 169. Technically speaking, you could have drawn a short-term Bearish Resistance Line from the December peak at 172, so the move to 169 would have violated this downtrend line, suggesting you could have considered a long posture. But such a trade would not have been in your best interest. Here's why. Evaluating Bean Meal more closely, you would have seen that formidable overhead resistance resided at 172—a level that it retreated from three previous times. This information might have prevented you from initiating a position. (See Figure 11.6.)

Price Objectives

We've discussed the concept of price objectives earlier in this book and they are by no means a guarantee as to where a given commodity will rise or fall anymore than they are for a stock, but it does similarly provide a guideline as to where you might expect to see prices travel. These price objectives provide a useful component in ascertaining the risk versus reward of a given

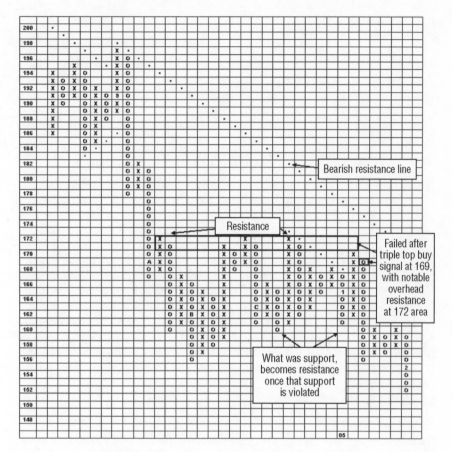

Figure 11.6 July 2005 Soybean Meal Contract (SM/N5).

trade, particularly so after seeing a significant technical breakout in one direction or the other. To assess a risk-reward scenario for any trade we need to both define the reward potential
of a trade as well as the risk we are exposing ourselves to in any
given position. The approach is no different than it is with
stocks, an example of which can be seen using the horizontal
price objective after witnessing a "Big Base Breakout" on a chart
of a commodity futures contract.

Big Base Breakouts

In keeping with the premise of a horizontal count, the bigger the base, the larger the price objective; or said another way, the bigger the base, the bigger the potential move (or "bang for your buck") up out of the base. You would not want to be a buyer of a commodity when it has rallied up to resistance, but instead want to see it penetrate that key resistance. The only exception to this would be if you are merely trying to trade the "range" of a base—meaning you buy on the pullback to the bottom of the base (support), and sell on the rally to overhead resistance (or the top of the base); such a posture would be considered more of a short-term trading tactic. Generally speaking, the greater upside potential is found on seeing a commodity break through a major resistance level. July 2005 sugar futures provided such an opportunity on breaking out of a sizable base in late-2004. The base, which took three months to develop in this case, allowed us to generate a horizontal price objective and more effectively quantify the risk-reward parameters of a long position in sugar, which produced an advantageous scenario for the commodity trader in this example. (See Figure 11.7.)

Changing Box Size

When analyzing a commodity on a technical basis, your main tool is the actual trend chart of the commodity. Often, the commodity chart will progress in a very orderly fashion, showing a series of higher tops and higher bottoms (if in an uptrend), or a consistent series of lower tops and lower bottoms (if in a downtrend). But there are times when a commodity will experience a straight spike up (or down) in price, resulting in an extended condition with no apparent support (or resistance) at hand. This can be troublesome for a pair of reasons—no viable stop loss point is apparent for managing risk, nor are any pullbacks shown to allow for potential new entries into the commodity.

This is where a change in box size can be useful. When necessary, reducing the box size on the chart can be a very helpful method to employ in order to gain insight as to levels of support and resistance, areas of consolidation, potential entry levels, and viable stop loss points. If the default box-sized chart appears or-

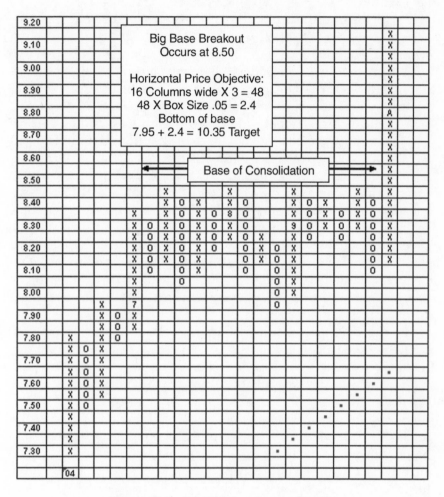

Figure 11.7 July 2005 Sugar Contract (SB/N5).

derly use that chart. If on the other hand the chart seems to be very slow in reacting to price change, that is only a few columns on the chart, it would make sense to lower the box size and speed up the chart. It's very helpful to look at lower box-sized charges as well as longer-term higher box-sized charts. It can only help. Lets look at a chart of the Euro FX December 2004 (ECZ4) chart as an example of a chart with no discernable resistance or near-term support. The Euro FX, December 2004 contract (ECZ4) broke out of a big base in mid-October at 1.245. This was a strong buy signal, and one that we actually took in our in-house commodity investment account. The Euro quickly spiked straight up to 1.283 without a breather. The chart obviously displayed an extended condition, with the contract well above any near-term support. At this point, new entries would have been tenuous given the lack of near-term support or a viable stop-loss point. This is where bumping the box size down, cutting it in half from .005 per box to .0025 per box, could help with the management of trading the Euro. By doing this, the chart exhibited a textbook shakeout pattern that wasn't apparent on the .005 per box chart. Therefore, had you consulted the smaller box-size chart, you were afforded an entry point on the reversal up from the shakeout pattern, and a very reasonable risk with a stop-loss point of 1.2625. The smaller box size also gave you a slightly tighter stop-loss point of 1.317 if you adjusted that stop point as the chart developed, as that is where it broke a Double Bottom to give its first sell signal. (See Figure 11.8.)

In the end, as a result of bumping the box size down, you could buy the December Euro at 1.275 on the reversal up from the shakeout pattern, whereas no reasonable entry level presented itself on the default chart. In this example, the risk of not consulting the smaller box-size chart was one of opportunity risk rather than capital risk, but buying the December Euro at 1.275 and selling at 1.317 resulted in a sizable profit of $5,312.50 per contract. Not only that, but gaining exposure to that trade came at a risk of only $1,875, which would have been the loss resulting from buying at 1.275 and selling at 1.2625; the initial stop-loss point. Rather than totally missing out on the trade, an enviable risk-reward scenario presented itself by simply changing the scale and consulting the more sensitive chart.

Momentum

We've discussed the use of Point and Figure signals for near-term guidance and the use of support and resistance lines for long-term guidance. Weekly momentum is what we would call a secondary indicator and one that we turn to for guidance in terms of intermediate-term price direction. We keep both monthly momentum and daily momentum calculations, but with commodi-

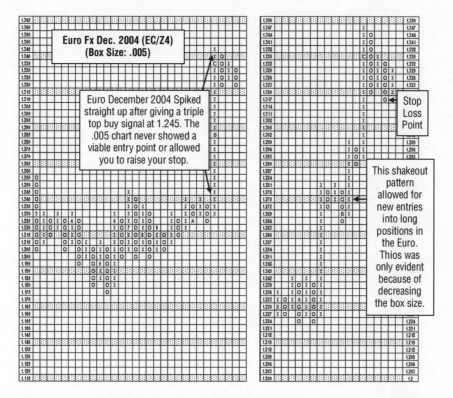

Figure 11.8 December 2004 Euro Fx Contract (EC/Z4).

ties specifically we rely most heavily on the weekly momentums. Weekly momentum tables are constructed using a one-week and five-week moving average that is exponentially weighted and smoothed. When the shorter-term average (one week) is above the longer-term average (five week), the momentum is "positive" and we would expect to see strength from the commodity (or at least a pause if in a downtrend). When the one-week moving average falls below the five-week moving average, it represents a turn to "negative momentum" suggesting weakness in the commodity, or at least a breather if in a strong uptrend. Momentum becomes most useful once you have established your overall posture on the commodity (as a function of trend, chart pattern, risk-reward, etc.), which is why we refer to it as a secondary indicator. (See Figure 11.9.)

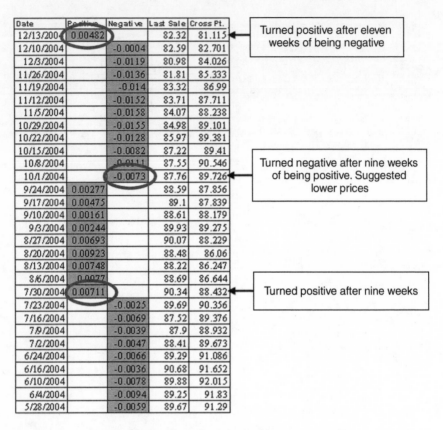

Date	Positive	Negative	Last Sale	Cross Pt.
12/13/2004	0.00482		82.32	81.115
12/10/2004		-0.0004	82.59	82.701
12/3/2004		-0.0119	80.98	84.026
11/26/2004		-0.0136	81.81	85.333
11/19/2004		-0.014	83.32	86.99
11/12/2004		-0.0152	83.71	87.711
11/5/2004		-0.0158	84.07	88.238
10/29/2004		-0.0155	84.98	89.101
10/22/2004		-0.0128	85.97	89.381
10/15/2004		-0.0082	87.22	89.41
10/8/2004		-0.0111	87.55	90.546
10/1/2004		-0.0073	87.76	89.726
9/24/2004	0.00277		88.59	87.856
9/17/2004	0.00475		89.1	87.839
9/10/2004	0.00161		88.61	88.179
9/3/2004	0.00244		89.93	89.275
8/27/2004	0.00693		90.07	88.229
8/20/2004	0.00923		88.48	86.06
8/13/2004	0.00748		88.22	86.247
8/6/2004	0.00077		88.69	86.644
7/30/2004	0.00711		90.34	88.432
7/23/2004		-0.0025	89.69	90.356
7/16/2004		-0.0069	87.52	89.376
7/9/2004		-0.0039	87.9	88.932
7/2/2004		-0.0047	88.41	89.673
6/24/2004		-0.0066	89.29	91.086
6/16/2004		-0.0036	90.68	91.652
6/10/2004		-0.0078	89.88	92.015
6/4/2004		-0.0094	89.25	91.83
5/28/2004		-0.0059	89.67	91.29

Turned positive after eleven weeks of being negative

Turned negative after nine weeks of being positive. Suggested lower prices

Turned positive after nine weeks

Figure 11.9 U.S. Dollar Index Weekly Momentum table.

Moving beyond Trading

Commodity Market Indexes

There are four commodity market indexes that we turn to when evaluating the general picture for the commodities market. You may consider these to be the Dow Jones Industrial Average of commodities, and similar to stock market indexes each commodity market index is constructed a little differently. The one we have focused on the most over the years is what is now labeled the Continuous Commodity Index (UV/Y). This is an equal-weighted index of 18 commodities that has actually been around since the 1950s, though under a different name. The CRB Futures Index was originally designed to reflect, in a dynamic fashion, the broad trends in overall commodity prices and to serve as a price measurement for macro-economic analysis. In 2005, the Reuters/Jeffries CRB Index (CR/Y), considered the standard in the industry, made its tenth major revision since first being calculated by the Commodity Research Bureau back in 1957. This revision, however, caused the index to move away from equal-weighting its components and instead began overweighting the more heavily produced raw materials. And so it was that the Continuous Commodity Index (UV/Y) came into existence, essentially carrying the torch passed on by the "old CRB Index." This gives us an equal-weighted commodity index that is diversified across all major commodities.

The Goldman Sachs Spot Return Commodity Index (GN/X) has become a favorite among institutions as a premier global commodity benchmark for measuring investment performance in the commodity markets. The GN/X is currently composed of 24 commodities that meet certain liquidity requirements and are weighted by the world production quantities; and the index is rebalanced annually. So for use as an economic indicator, the appropriate weight to assign each commodity is in proportion to the amount of that commodity flowing through the economy (i.e., the actual production or consumption of that commodity). The GN/X is not only a valuable commodity index to use for economic analysis, but it is also tradable via futures contracts on the Chicago Mercantile Exchange (CME), and exchange-traded notes (ETNs) on the NYSE.

The Dow Jones-AIG Commodity Index (DJAIG) was established in July 1998. Originally, it was only available as an OTC product, but then the CBOT introduced futures contracts on the Index, making it easier to invest in this commodity index as an asset class. The DJAIG is composed of futures contracts on 19 different exchange-traded physical commodities and uses a combination of liquidity and production data to determine its component weightings. Like the GN/X, the DJAIG is rebalanced annually. Unlike the GN/X, which has close to 73 percent of its weight in energy, no related group of commodities may constitute more than 33 percent of the index. As well, no single commodity may constitute less than 2 percent of the index. The DJAIG is also available in an exchange-traded note (ETN) that trades on the NYSE. (See Figure 11.10.)

	Goldman Sachs Commodity Index GSCI	Dow Jones AIG Commodity Index	RJ/CRB Index	Continuous Commodity Index
Crude Oil	31.56%	12.78%	23.00%	5.88%
Brent Crude Oil	14.91%			
Unleaded Gas	8.76%	4.05%	5.00%	
Heating Oil	8.23%	3.85%	5.00%	5.88%
GasOil	4.49%			
Natural Gas	5.81%	12.32%	6.00%	5.88%
Aluminum	2.97%	6.85%	6.00%	
Copper	4.24%	5.88%	6.00%	5.88%
Lead	0.24%			
Nickel	0.97%	2.66%	1.00%	
Zinc	1.09%	2.70%		
Gold	1.88%	6.22%	6.00%	5.88%
Silver	0.24%	2.00%	1.00%	5.88%
Platinum				5.88%
Wheat	2.34%	4.77%	1.00%	5.88%
Red Wheat	1.02%			
Soybean Oil		2.77%		
Orange Juice			1.00%	5.88%
Corn	2.18%	5.87%	6.00%	5.88%
Soybeans	1.40%	7.77%	6.00%	5.88%
Cotton	0.79%	3.16%	5.00%	5.88%
Sugar	1.82%	2.97%	5.00%	5.88%
Coffee	0.58%	2.93%	5.00%	5.88%
Cocoa	0.19%		5.00%	5.88%
Live Cattle	2.15%	6.09%	6.00%	5.88%
Feeder Cattle	0.64%			
Live Hogs				
Lean Hogs	1.48%	4.35%	1.00%	5.88%
Energy	**73.76%**	**33.00%**	**39.00%**	**17.64%**
Industrial Metals	**9.51%**	**18.09%**	**13.00%**	**5.88%**
Precious Metals	**2.12%**	**8.22%**	**7.00%**	**17.64%**
Agriculture	**10.32%**	**30.24%**	**34.00%**	**47.04%**
Livestock	**4.27%**	**10.45%**	**7.00%**	**11.76%**

Figure 11.10   Commodity Index Weightings.

It is important to stay abreast of the specific weightings within commodity indexes, as their price action can be greatly affected by one group in particular, such as Energy in the case of the GN/X. Not only can these indexes provide knowledge on a macro-economic basis, but as we've mentioned, both the Goldman Sachs Commodity Index and Dow Jones AIG Index can be traded as an asset class via their individual futures contracts, open-end mutual funds, or ETNs. The later providing access to this asset class much in the same manner as S&P Depository Receipts (SPY) provide access to the S&P 500 as a large-cap equity asset class. Given this, you want to keep in mind how these vehicles will correlate with other asset classes as well as specific groups within the commodity realm. (See Figure 11.11.)

Dow Jones AIG Commodity Index

(data based on monthly returns)

Correlations	5/31/06
Dow Jones-AIG Commodity Index Total Return	1.00
GSCI Total Return Index	0.89
Goldman Sachs Crude Oil Total Return Index	0.74
S&P 500 Index	0.09
Lehman Aggregate Index	0.00
MSCI EAFE Index	0.23

Goldman Sachs Commodity Index

(data based on monthly returns)

Correlations	5/31/06
GSCI Total Return Index	1.00
Dow Jones-AIG Commodity Index Total Return	0.89
Goldman Sachs Crude Oil Total Return Index	0.87
S&P 500 Index	0.01
Lehman Aggregate Index	0.04
MSCI EAFE Index	0.14

Figure 11.11   Commodity Index Correlation Example.

Invest in Commodities as an Asset Class

Diversification

There are many sound reasons for adding commodities to your investment process, not the least of which being a time-tested lack of correlation between stocks and commodities. This will be discussed in more depth later in this book, but sufficed it to say that this lack of correlation gives investors a valid way to diversify assets by using the commodities market. The more common approach toward diversification is to allocate funds toward large-cap stocks, small-cap stocks, international stocks, and so on to achieve an overall portfolio allocation. However, this is a task much easier explained than implemented, as many "diversified" investors found out the hard way in 2002, when nearly every area of the equities market finished solidly in the red. It was particularly obvious in that year that simply spreading money around different regions or style boxes is not true diversification, but that was because everyone was losing money. The truth is that it is simply a fallacy of composition to assume that foreign stocks are not correlated to U.S. stocks, or that small-cap stocks are in no way correlated to large cap stocks. A "diversified" portfolio of some of the largest, most widely held, mutual funds in existence can still fall prey to a deceivingly high correlation with the S&P 500. (See Figure 11.12.)

A tremendous benefit that commodities can provide to an account is true diversification; which is to say diversification by means of a noncorrelated asset. Diversification is something to consider within your "commodity" asset class, as it can reduce "avoidable risk." One way to provide diversification in your commodity account is to trade different markets. It is important to keep in mind that diversification increases with more markets, but it does so at a decreasing rate as more and more markets are added. The added diversification provided by tangible goods, such as agriculture or petroleum, is rooted in the premise that these goods are impacted by different factors than stocks or bonds. That doesn't mean that when stocks are going down, commodities will always go up, but it does mean that if they both go down it is likely for very different reasons, which is as

Correlation to the S&P 500 for 2005 3 Year Range			
	Value	Blend	Growth
Large	Amer Funds Washington Mutual Inv 0.96	Vanguard 500 1	Amer Funds Growth Fund of America 0.97
	Dodge & Cox Stock 0.93	Fidelity Magellan 0.99	Fidelity Capital Appreciation 0.95
Mid	T. Rowe Price Mid Cap Value 0.91	Fidelity Mid Cap Stock 0.91	Fidelity Aggressive Growth 0.9
	Goldman Sachs Mid Cap Value 0.83	Vanguard Extended Market 0.88	T. Rowe Price New Horizon 0.88
Small	Scudder Dreman Small Cap Value 0.73	Amer Funds Small Cap World 0.83	Van Kampen Small Cap Growth 0.72
	Vanguard Small Cap Value Index 0.77	Fidelity Low Priced Stock 0.84	Aim Opportunities 0.81
Global		Amer Funds New Perspective 0.96	
		Dodge & Cox International 0.87	
Bonds		Pimco Total Return Bond −0.24	
		Federated Bond 0.08	

Equal Weighted Port Avg Equity Correlation	0.88

Strategic EQ Weighted Port	%
	100
Large	60
Mid	7.5
Small	7.5
Global	25
Estimated EQ Weighted Correlation	0.934

Figure 11.12 Portfolio Correlation Example.

far as diversification is meant to go. As evidence, it is worth pointing out that there have only been two years since the Goldman Sachs Commodity Index was established (1970) that both stocks and commodities have been down in the same year (see Figure 11.13).

Inflation

The second valid reason to consider commodities as part of a portfolio is as a hedge against inflation. Typically, when inflation rises, the cost of both producing goods and borrowing funds increases, each of which can have a negative impact on stock and/or bond investments. Commodities, however, can benefit in this environment, as rising prices for raw materials (which are commodities after all) benefit the investor who owns a mutual fund invested in these same raw materials.

Period End	SPX Comp Total Return Value	SPX Comp Total Return Percent Change	GSCI Value	GSCI Percent Change
1/31/1970	10,000	-	10,000	-
12/31/1970	11,224	12.24	11,309	13.09
12/31/1971	12,832	14.32	13,693	21.08
12/31/1972	15,262	18.94	19,502	42.43
12/31/1973	13,004	-14.8	34,120	74.96
12/31/1974	9,559	-26.49	47,602	39.51
12/31/1975	13,122	37.27	39,404	-17.22
12/31/1976	16,220	23.61	34,706	-11.92
12/31/1977	15,021	-7.4	38,305	10.37
12/31/1978	16,001	6.52	50,412	31.61
12/31/1979	18,958	18.48	67,457	33.81
12/31/1980	25,113	32.47	74,933	11.08
12/31/1981	23,870	-4.95	57,691	-23.01
12/31/1982	29,013	21.55	64,351	11.56
12/31/1983	35,557	22.56	74,824	16.26
12/31/1984	37,788	6.27	75,609	1.05
12/31/1985	49,777	31.73	83,180	10.01
12/31/1986	59,068	18.67	84,881	2.05
12/31/1987	62,170	5.25	105,061	23.78
12/31/1988	72,495	16.61	134,411	27.94
12/31/1989	95,486	31.69	185,865	38.28
12/31/1990	92,501	-3.11	239,906	29.08
12/31/1991	120,685	30.47	225,186	-6.14
12/31/1992	129,878	7.62	235,147	4.42
12/31/1993	142,969	10.08	206,157	-12.33
12/31/1994	144,858	1.32	217,072	5.29
12/31/1995	199,300	37.58	261,209	20.33
12/31/1996	245,050	22.96	349,800	33.92
12/31/1997	326,807	33.36	300,592	-14.07
12/31/1998	420,189	28.57	193,134	-35.75
12/31/1999	508,654	21.05	272,160	40.92
12/31/2000	482,339	-9.11	407,531	49.74
12/31/2001	407,392	-11.88	277,394	-31.94
12/31/2002	317,341	-22.1	366,341	32.07
12/31/2003	408,388	28.69	442,234	20.72
12/31/2004	452,791	10.87	518,642	17.28

In 35 years there have only been two instances where both stocks and commodities have finished the same year in negative territory.

	SPX	GSCI
Average Annual Returns since 1970:	12.9	14.6

Figure 11.13   Non-Correlated Comparison: Goldman Sachs Commodity Index versus SPX.

In such an environment, when inflation may or may not be led by rising energy prices, an investor may seek a commodity investment less correlated with crude oil at times, and more correlated to a broader investment in raw materials. Currently, the most evenly diversified option among commodity-based indices that are traded via open or closed-end funds is the Dow Jones AIG Commodity Index.

Opportunities for Capital Appreciation
—The Exchange Traded Funds

In recent years, we have seen a growing number of market vehicles begin trading that allows access to the commodities market on an exchange-traded basis. Both broad-based commodity index products have been introduced, as well as focused products that allow participation in individual commodity markets. In either case, these exchange-traded products allow investors to gain access to these markets without the leverage of commodity-based futures contract. For instance, Barclay's Global introduced the iShares COMEX Gold Trust (IAU), which is an exchange-traded fund that is indexed to the price of gold. One share of IAU represents ownership of $\frac{1}{10}$ of an ounce of gold bullion that is actually held in a vault. If gold is valued at $600 per ounce; one share of IAU will trade at roughly $60 per share. For an investor to gain exposure to 100 ounces of gold, he must buy $60,000 of IAU. This is contrary to an investment in gold futures contracts where one gold contract represents 100 ounces of gold but requires only an initial margin requirement of $3,000 to be met on purchase. That, in essence, is how future contracts create such leverage. A 10 percent move in the price of gold would represent a 10 percent change in value for IAU shares ($6,000 fluctuation on a $60,000 investment), but a 200 percent move relative to that $3,000 initial investment in the futures contract. (See Figure 11.14.)

Most exchange-traded commodity vehicles are created similarly, allowing dollar-for-dollar exposure to a commodity index or individual commodity market. The analysis for buying or selling these funds is no different than that described previously for entering a futures contract; it is primarily the leverage that is different.

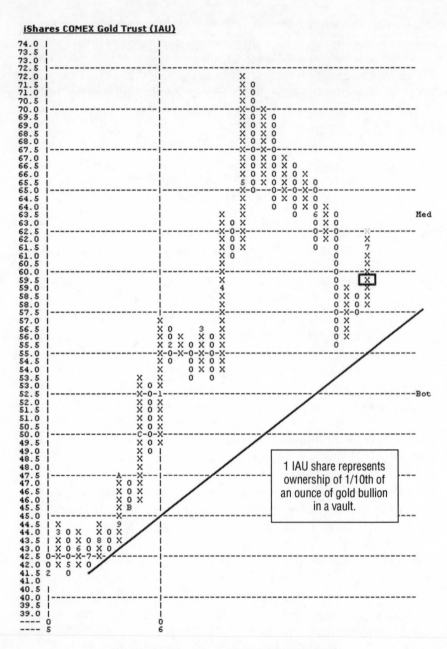

Figure 11.14 iShares COMEX Gold Trust (IAU).

354

Ticker Symbol	Fund Title	Fund Type	Fund Description
SLV	iShares Silver Trust	ETF	Represents ownership in 10 ounces of Silver Bullion
IAU	iShares COMEX Gold Trust	ETF	Represents ownership in 1/10th of an ounce of Gold Bullion
GLD	StreetTracks Gold Trust	ETF	Represents ownership in 1/10th of an ounce of Gold Bullion
DBC	Deutche Bank Commodity Index	ETF	Represents ownership in DBLCIX, an Index comprised of 6 commodities
GSP	iPath Goldman Sachs Commodity Index	ETN	Represents ownership in DJAIG, a diversified commodity Index
DJP	iPath Dow Jones AIG Commodity Index	ETN	Represents ownership in production-weighted GSCI Index
USO	United States Oil Fund	ETF	Designed to replicate, dollar for dollar, price movement of Crude Oil
QRAAX	Oppenheimer Real Asset Fund	Mutual Fund	Primarily tracks GSCI, production-weighted, heavy in Energy
PCRIX	Pimco Real Return Fund	Mutual Fund	Primarily tracks DJAIG, diversified commodity exposure
RYMBX	Rydex Commodity Fund	Mutual Fund	Primarily tracks GSCI, production-weighted, heavy in Energy

ETF, Exchange Traded Fund
ETN, Exchange Traded Note
Mutual Fund, an Open-End Mutual Fund

Figure 11.15 Commodity-Based Index Funds.

The existing commodity-based open-end (mutual funds) and exchange-traded products available as of this writing are found in the attached table, a list that will no doubt grow substantially in the coming years if the bull trends in commodity indexes remain in tact (Figure 11.15).

Summary

By this point in our journey, we hope that at a minimum we agree on two things, the first of which being that simply having a set of rational tools at your disposal is quite helpful in deciphering the commodities markets, and second, that none of these tools need be hoes, pitchforks, or McCormick's famous reaper. Rather, while remaining attentive to a few key ingredients, which pertain to any commodity, we can begin to train ourselves to find consistent opportunity in the futures market.

POINTS AND FIGURES BY DORSEY, WRIGHT MONEY MANAGEMENT

Daniel Goleman, in his book *Emotional Intelligence,* distinguishes between intellectual intelligence and emotional intelligence. Our intellectual intelligence is a function of the IQ we were born with and how that intellectual intelligence is cultivated. Emotional intelligence, according to Goleman, includes self-awareness and impulse control, persistence, zeal and self-motivation, empathy and social deftness. His book goes over many examples of people who, intellectually speaking, are brilliant. He cites many examples of these people doing really stupid things, due to a lack of emotional intelligence. One such example is as follows:

Exactly why David Pologruto, a high-school physics teacher, was stabbed with a kitchen knife by one of his star students is still debatable. But the facts as widely reported are these:

Jason H., a sophomore and straight A student at Coral Springs, Florida, high school, was fixated on getting into medical school. Not just any medical school—he dreamt of Harvard. But Pologruto, his physics teacher, had given Jason an 80 on a quiz. Believing the grade—a mere B—put his dream in jeopardy, Jason took a butcher knife to school and, in a confrontation with Pologruto in the physics lab, stabbed his teacher in the collarbone before being subdued in a struggle.

A judge found Jason innocent, temporarily insane during the incident-a panel of four psychologists and psychiatrists swore he was psychotic during the fight. Jason claimed he had been planning to commit suicide because of the test score, and had gone to Pologruto to tell him he was killing himself because of the bad grade. Pologruto told a different story: "I think he tried to completely do me in with the knife" because he was infuriated over the bad grade.

After transferring to a private school, Jason graduated two years later at the top of his class. A perfect grade in regular classes would have given him a straight-A, 4.0 average, but Jason had taken enough advanced courses to raise his grade-point average to 4.614—way beyond A+. Even as Jason graduated with highest honors, his old physics teacher, David Pologruto, complained that Jason had never apologized or even taken responsibility for the attack.

The question is, how could someone of such obvious intelligence do something so irrational—so downright dumb? The answer: intelligence has little to do with emotional life.

Goleman argues that just as intellectual intelligence can be changed by experience and education, so too can emotional intelligence be learned and improved. Goleman proposes a number of methods for improving emotional tendencies that decrease the quality of life one enjoys. Such methods include catching worrisome emotional episodes as near their beginning as possible. With practice, people can identify the worries at an earlier and earlier point in the anxiety spiral. People also learn relaxation methods at the moment they recognize the worry beginning. One's mind can also be trained to more thoughtfully consider the consequences of different emotional responses.

The same principles apply to portfolio management. Unmanaged emotions lead investors to sell their winners too quickly, hold on to their losers too long, and overtrade. Academic intelligence alone does not lead to great investment results. It comes down to a question of execution. Do we have enough intellectual intelligence to develop a winning investment strategy? If not, more research and extensive testing is required. Then, do we have enough emotional intelligence to execute?

Part Three

APPLY THE POINT AND FIGURE METHODOLOGY TO YOUR INVESTMENT PROCESS

Chapter 12

PORTFOLIO CONSTRUCTION AND MANAGEMENT

Thus far, in the book we have dissected the puzzle and examined each piece separately. Let's take a few moments and succinctly sum up the investment process. Think of this method of portfolio management as an operating system. This operating system is not unlike the operating systems one might download on a computer. A computer can do absolutely nothing until it has an operating system, like Window's, installed on its hard drive. Even the newest comer to the computer world knows this universal truth. Investing is no different. In fact, everything in life is a software program of sorts that is installed in your mind (hard drive) and you are in essence the sum total of the software programs running on your mind's hard drive. To be successful at investing, you need some way of evaluating the firehose of information available on the subject of investing. You need some way of constricting that firehose of information down to the trickle of a garden hose. This whole book is in essence the operating system we have found to be the most logical, easy to understand, sensible, and organized method of constructing and managing your portfolio. In the end, you must have accumulated more money than the market and the government can take away from you or you have failed in your quest for a sound retirement. Isn't that what we are all ultimately striving for? At the end of the road, we need more dollars in our account than when we started. We are more or less aggressive in this endeavor at various points in our life.

I want this chapter to be more of a cool down period. So sit back, relax—you have already done the heavy lifting. Let's just briefly look at some of the steps that were covered in detail in the book to summarize the overall game or operating system if you will. Remember there is a CD Study Guide along with this book to help you solidify the concepts presented here. Here you will find all of the important concepts reinforced along with study questions. The CD was purposely constructed with a number of examples, and investment situations, for each topic. These examples and tests are designed to help you take the concepts you learned in the book and apply them to real-life situations that you are likely to experience when investing real money.

One of the best ways to learn how to use the Point and Figure method is to practice with real examples. Whenever we conduct our Point and Figure Institutes, we always teach a particular section then do some practice examples relating to the section just covered. We culminate the seminar with several practice exercises, and in some instances a full case study, incorporating all the concepts taught at the institute. Therefore, as you finish reading this book, which is like attending a Dorsey, Wright Point and Figure Institute, it is fitting to do some practice examples that bring all the information together. One of the things I recommend is that you get a sheet of paper and just write down the pros and the cons for the stock. Create a checklist with two columns, one positive and one negative, as well as a comments column. Then as you examine each of the attributes of the market, sector, and stock, put it in the positive or negative column. Your evaluation sheet would look something like this:

	Positive	Negative	Comment
Market			
Sector			
Sector RS			
Trend			
Relative Strength			
Peer Relative Strength			
Pattern			
Price Objective			
Stop loss point			

Continue to do this exercise whenever you evaluate a position. It's like the notes you took in college. Writing it down helps to remember it. Once you feel comfortable with evaluating a stock you are ready to visit our web site. The DWA Internet site makes this easier because with the click of a computer mouse, will see an evaluation sheet automatically completed for you on your stock of choice. As well, the *Point and Figure Charting, Third Edition* CD has a section entitled "Resources." Here you will learn about the resources available at www.dorseywright.com to help make the implementation and study of the Point and Figure methodology as seamless as possible. So sit back and relax. Let's talk concepts with a step-by-step discussion of constructing and managing a portfolio.

Steps for Constructing an Investment Portfolio

Step 1. Evaluate the Broad Market—Who's Got the Ball?

Evaluate the market to determine whether it is supporting higher prices or lower prices. Any type of business comes down to supply and demand—it's that simple. I don't care whether we are talking about the oil market, iPods, golf courses, lemonade stands, or the stock market. Simply said, when there are more buyers than sellers willing to sell, price will move higher. When there are more sellers than buyers willing to buy, price will move lower. When supply and demand are in equilibrium price must remain the same. In the end, there is nothing else. The reason that the price of produce in the supermarket changes is the very same reason the prices on Wall Street change. The Point and Figure methodology is just a logical, sensible organized way of recording that supply and demand relationship. It simply arranges the information in a way that makes sense to the viewer. When demand is in control of the market we want to focus on wealth accumulation strategies and when supply is in control of the market, we want to focus on wealth preservation strategies.

The indicator that tells us whether supply or demand is in control of the market is the Bullish Percent. This is kept on a variety of markets but the two most important are the NYSE and the OTC. We consider these indicators our main coaches. The first thing I do each morning is check this indicator to see what team the coach is telling me to put on the field. I often log on at night to see how the Bullish Percents did before I go to bed. From there, I'll pick my individual stock plays. Here are just some of the plays from our playbook, segregated by field position. Use this as a starting point for developing your own playbook.

Market Indicators Oversold—Reward Greater, Lower Risk

Offense, in X's	Defense, in O's
Aggressive offense	Reduce defensive posture
Offensive sectors (BP in X's)	Build shopping list of ideas
More volatile sectors can be bought	Reduce exposure to defensive sectors
Buy ETFs to gain market exposure quickly	Liberal stops for strong RS positions
Buy stocks	Tighten up buy stops for short positions
Buy leaders and laggards on breakouts	Trim or take profits in shorts
Consider bottom fish plays	Take profits on long put positions
Liberal stop-loss points	Trim positions in inverse funds
Increase volatility	
Buy calls	
In-the-money covered writes	
Sell puts	

Market Indicators Middlin' between 30 and 70 Percent

Offense, in X's	Defense, in O's
Offensive posture	Defensive posture
Focus on strong RS sectors	Reduce equity exposure
Focus on sectors whose BP is in X's	Raise cash
Sell laggard stocks on rallies	Hold strong RS sectors
Focus on high tech attribute stocks	Sell weak RS sectors
Buy on pullbacks	Hold strong RS stocks
Use trend line stop loss points	Sell laggards (weak RS)
Buy ETFs	Use trend line stop loss points
Covered writes	Inverse funds to hedge
Bull spreads	Protective puts to hedge
Covered combinations	Bear spreads

Market Indicators Overbought—Risk Greater

Offense, in X's	Defense, in O's
Reduce offensive posture	Aggressive defense
Increase exposure to defensive sectors	Decrease volatility
Trim sectors whose BP moves to O's	Raise cash levels
Trim offensive positions	Reduce exposure to offensive sectors
Sell any weak RS positions	Sell stocks on breakdowns (PnF sell)
Buy ETFs instead of specific stocks	Tighter stops
Add defensive positions	Buy protective puts to hedge
Tighter stop loss points	Buy inverse funds to hedge
Buy calls as stock substitute	
Buy protective puts	

Step 2. Evaluate the Sectors

Seventy-five to eighty percent of the risk in any particular stock, ETF, or fund is the market and the sector. Because of this, we take a top down approach when evaluating the market. Once we have determined the stance of the overall market, we move to individual sector evaluation. We are simply moving from the whole to the parts. Numerous internal and other academic studies have shown that over time a successful sector rotation strategy is paramount to portfolio success. Never deviating from the basic laws of supply and demand, we rely first on the Bullish Percent concept to tell us which sectors are on offense and which are on defense. Like the blobs in a lava lamp, you'll generally find that at any one given time, some are down at the bottom, some are at the top and have been hot for a while, and others are huddling in the middle of the lamp. The beauty of the Bullish Percent concept is that once you understand it, its easy to apply to different market segments. In some cases most sectors will be huddling together in the middle and there are no great opportunities and other times there will be an overabundance of opportunities. That's life on Wall Street. Simply stated, make the best of what you have.

To increase our odds even further with respect to sector rotation, we will overlay the Bullish Percent concept with a Relative Strength (RS) reading. This allows us to stack yet one more thing in our favor. We try to keep our focus on those sectors with the strong RS. This allows us to identify major themes and turning points in the market. Typically, these themes last for several years. Where so many investors go wrong is they don't believe that the stock that has been strong can continue to stay strong. There's an old stock market adage that says the first stocks to double in a bull market usually double again. Or, as Sir Isaac Newton would say, "things in motion tend to stay in motion." The Point and Figure charts, Bullish Percents, and RS indicators will let us know when an investment theme is coming to an end. Having a sell discipline allows us to be comfortable owning those winners and letting them run. One of the fundamental truths to portfolio success is to cut your losses short and let your winners run.

Step 3. Creating an Inventory

There are many right answers in investing and all too often I see investors and brokers alike try to get their arms around too large of a universe of investment vehicles. My dad taught me "life's a cinch by the inch, life is hard by the yard." Take it inch by inch. In the DWA database we follow over 7,000 domestic stocks, 15,000 mutual funds, almost 400 ETFs, and over 25 exchanges across the world encompassing 3,000 international stocks. I don't throw out these figures to overwhelm you but rather to point out the importance of determining your inventory. Do you like mutual funds? Pick a couple of fund families you believe in and concentrate on those. Maybe as an advisor you like working with money managers. Compile a list of managers whose management style you like and they will become your inventory. Maybe the ETF product is what appeals to you. There is a terrific universe of those available. Do you prefer to work with individual stocks? If so, start with a fundamental inventory. I feel more comfortable working with a list of fundamentally sound stocks. I know full well a fundamentally sound stock can act like a "cat" or a "dog" at any time because supply and demand imbalances are the only economic concept that drives price change, but I still feel more comfortable with a list of stocks that appear to have no fundamental cracks in their armor. The point is you take that firehose of products available to you and take it down to the trickle of a garden hose. It's easier to take a sip from a garden hose than a fire-hose. Once you have your inventory established, you can use Point and Figure methodologies outlined in this book to enhance the portfolio strategies you are already using. Just keep everything in perspective. This is not a science. It's simply best to operate in a logical, organized manner. That's the key to success.

Step 4. Evaluate and Monitor the Point and Figure Technical Picture

Once your inventory is established and culled down to a reasonable number that gives you a cross section of exposure to asset classes and sectors, evaluate the technical's of each stock (ETF, fund, manager, etc.) in the inventory to answer the question, "What to buy and When to Buy it, and what you will do if all these plans go your way and what you will do if these plans do not go your way." It is essential you know this and you write it down for the future. It helps to go back and reevaluate exactly what you did and why you did it. Our computer systems can answer this question in a matter of 2 seconds. I am continually amazed at where we have come technologically over the last 20 years. Twenty years ago we did it all by hand. Today, we have even taught the computer to evaluate any investment vehicle from stocks to bonds to ETFs, then explain in writing what it saw, what it recommends doing with the position, and alternative ideas. I have been involved in the thought process on these technological advancements over the past 20 years and I'm continually amazed at where we are today at being able to provide such a great productivity system to you the investor. It's hard to figure where technology goes from here but I know we are only limited to our ability to communicate and these technologies continue to expand on a daily basis. Here's an example of our ability to communicate. We held a technical analysis and option strategy seminar in Kuala Lumpur, Malaysia, at a prominent hotel, while we taught from our offices here in Richmond, Virginia. That's technology.

Once a position is established, continually monitor the position for signs of impending change in the trend or RS of the stock. This is a pretty simple step but an important one. You must evaluate all your portfolios each day to become aware of something that might require action. The best way to do this is to put all your portfolios into our system separately, like Mr. and Mrs. Jones Retirement Account, and so on. Our system will watch the portfolio or group of stocks for you like a cyber assistant. It will inform you by simply clicking on the activity button for each portfolio. This activity screen will outline any changes that require your attention with respect to the underlying portfolio. The process to do this is so simple. Just key in the symbols of each stock, mutual fund, bond, and so on that each client owns in their portfolios, into the DWA portfolio system or I prefer to simply place all the stocks all my clients own into one portfolio. The point I am getting at is this: the system will do the rest once it knows what to evaluate. Say you wanted to view each day anything that might require your attention in all your portfolios. You would simply go to your portfolio system and click on the "activity" button. In one second the system will separate all the stocks in all your portfolios and place them in groups like Double Bottom sell signals, RS change to negative, RS change to positive, Peer RS turned positive, and so on. In one click of the computer mouse you just evaluated every portfolio under your management in a matter of a few minutes. This activity would be done each morning before the market opening but since our charting system is updated the night before, you can get a jump on things by taking a minute to review the portfolio after the kids are in bed.

Each of you will find your own way of managing this information. We have clients who spend hours each night with the data and others that can easily manage their accounts with some easy 1, 2, 3 steps. As you work with Point and Figure analysis you will be amazed and delighted with your new found ability to take control of your and your client's investment endeavors.

Summary

When I was a broker back in the mid-1970s, I came to work unprepared every day. We simply didn't have a logical way of operating our business back then. We simply took firm research and passed it on to our clients hoping the stocks would rise so we could sell and replace them with other stocks that would then rise in price. It simply did not work, period. It wasn't until 1978 that I came across the Point and Figure method of analysis purely by accident. When I learned it, I realized I had found the Holy Grail of Investing. It was ECON 101, supply and demand. I knew then what I was put on this earth to do and that was to teach this method to my brothers and sisters in this business for the rest of my life. It is now 28 years later and I'm doing just that. This is not a book that is generally read once and then abandoned. I have read and reread this book and, even though I'm the author. Every time I read a chapter again, I am refreshed on something I have lost focus on. This book should be highlighted, underlined, dog-eared, scuffed up from use, and passed along to others. There is an old saying: "You can't keep it unless you give it away." You are one of my emissaries now and you should pass this on to others. Without you they may never have the opportunity to truly take control of their finances and, in the end, their retirement. Possibly between all of us passing the word we can help others attain a secure and comfortable retirement. This book will take an individual and his or her family much further in this endeavor than any government program can. Having read this book from cover to cover, you are now in the DWA family. Welcome.

ABOUT THE CD-ROM

This appendix provides you with information on the contents of the CD that accompanies this book. For the latest and greatest information, please refer to the ReadMe file located at the root of the CD.

System Requirements

- A computer with a processor running Pentium III or higher.
- At least 128 MB of total RAM installed on your computer; for best performance, we recommend at least 256 MB.
- A CD-ROM drive.
- Web Browser.

Using the CD with Windows

To install the items from the CD to your hard drive, follow these steps:

1. Insert the CD into your computer's CD-ROM drive.
2. The CD-ROM interface will appear. The interface provides a simple point-and-click way to explore the contents of the CD.

If the opening screen of the CD-ROM does not appear automatically, follow these steps to access the CD:

1. Click the Start button on the left end of the taskbar and then choose Run from the menu that pops up.
2. In the dialog box that appears, type *d*:\index.html. (If your CD-ROM drive is not drive d, fill in the appropriate letter in place of *d*.) This brings up the CD Interface described in the preceding set of steps.

What's on the CD

Learn the Point & Figure methodology from Dorsey, Wright & Associates in an interactive format with this educational CD. Designed to be used in conjunction with *Point & Figure Charting, 3rd Edition*, this CD will bring the concepts to life with additional examples and discussions as well as exercises and tests to refine your skills through a series of six lessons. The CD also includes a Glossary of Terms and additional writings from Tom Dorsey and guests.

Customer Care

If you have trouble with the CD-ROM, please call the Wiley Product Technical Support phone number at (800) 762-2974. Outside the United States, call 1 (317) 572-3994. You can also contact Wiley Product Technical Support at **http://support.wiley.com**. John Wiley & Sons will provide technical support only for installation and other general quality control items. For technical support on the applications themselves, consult the program's vendor or author.

To place additional orders or to request information about other Wiley products, please call (877) 762-2974.

INDEX

Accommodation, markets,
 309–310
Accumulation, 42, 65, 68, 330
Advance-Decline Line, 236–238
Alcoa (AA), 71, 132–133
Advanced Micro Devices (AMD),
 110
American Eagle Outfitters, 156
American Funds Growth
 (AGTHX), 165
American Funds New Economy
 (ANEFX), 318–319
American International Group
 (AIG), Dow Jones, 347, 349,
 353
American Stock Exchange
 (AMEX), 299
American Tobacco (BTI), 174
Apollo Group (APOL), 121
Apple Computer (AAPL), 26, 49,
 88, 124–125
Archer Daniels Midland (ADM),
 172–173
Ask Jeeves Inc. (ASKJ), 218
Asset class, 156–159, 350–356
AT&T (T), 7, 113–115, 146–147,
 153, 159
Auto parts (AUTO) sector, 170
Average Weekly Distribution,
 238–242

Back testing, 96, 279, 316
Ballistics (price objectives
 determination), 48–49, 51
Bank(s), 169

Bar charts (versus Point and
 Figure method), 11, 25, 42, 61
Barclays Global Fund Advisors,
 299, 353
Barron's Weekly, 253
Basketball analogy,
 profits/probabilities, 59
Bearish Catapult formation,
 73–79
Bearish Resistance Line, 41–42,
 46–47, 101, 330–331, 340
 examples, 126, 136, 307
 Exchange Traded Funds and,
  284–285
Bearish Signal, 69–70, 81
 Reversed, 58, 93–94
Bearish Support Line, 41, 45,
 47–48
Beazer Homes (BZH), 116
Belief/confidence, 5, 10
Bell curve, 190
 examples (Bullish Percent),
  263–274
 normal distribution, 239
 overbought (three standard
  deviations to right),
  239–240, 262–263, 266
 oversold (three standard
  deviations to left), 239–240,
  258, 262–264, 266–267
 regression to mean and,
  238–242
 Sector(s), 262–267
 standard deviations (six),
  239–240

Bernanke, Ben, 261
Biasiotto, Judd, 17–18
Big base breakout, 71, 341–342, 344
Biotech Sector (IBB), 307–308
Blumenthal, Earl, 90, 193
Bond(s), 102, 258, 279–291
Bottom fishing, 47, 87, 91
Box sizes, 342–344
   default/standard values, 25–27
   moving through a level, 38, 40–41, 50, 217, 244–245
Briggs & Stratton, 119
British Petroleum (BP), 154–155
Broadening Top formation, 92–93
Brokers:
   Point and Figure method, 15, 17, 18–19, 52, 61–62, 184
   relationship to investors, 5, 64–65, 253–254, 298, 365
Buffett, Warren, 62–63
Bull and Bear Club, 64
Bullish Catapult formation, 73–79
Bullish Percent (most important indicator), 73, 253
   All Fixed Income funds (BPMU99), 289, 291
   analogy to polling audience in *Millionaire* quiz show, 189–191
   bell curves using, 263–265
   bullish at the bottom and bearish at the top, 185–187
   Electric Utility, 256–262
   Exchange Traded Funds, 301–302
   first signal, 187–188
   history/development of, 185–188
   lessons from:
      1987 (The Crash), 183, 194–196, 236, 323
      1990 (Kuwait Invasion), 197–199

      1994 (Stealth Bear Market), 199–201
      1998 (Indices versus Stocks), 201–203
      2000 (The Two-Sided Market), 203–206
      2001 (9/11), 206–207
      2002 (No Place to Hide), 208–210
      2003 (Who Would Have Guessed), 210–212
      2006, 212–217
   market indexes (no correlation with), 186, 188, 226, 363
   measure of risk (not performance), 225
   mechanics of, 191–193
   mutual funds, 244–247
   Nasdaq Non-Financial (BPNDX), 225–227
   Nasdaq/OTC, 177, 203, 217–219, 363
   New York Stock Exchange (NYSE), 177–217, 363
   other equity indicators, 225–245, 247
   risk levels of, 193–194
   secondary market indicators, 223–247
      Optionable Stock Universe (BPOPTI), 225–227
      S&P 500, 225–231
   Sectors, 249–274
   use of, versus chart of an index, 189–191
Bullish Resistance Line, 41, 45–46
Bullish Shakeout formation, 85–87
Bullish Signal, 68–69, 81
   Reversed, 94–96
Bullish Support Line, 41–47, 75–76, 131, 134
   chart patterns, 80–81, 85, 101, 229, 281, 307

examples of, 126, 229, 231, 285, 330–331
Percent Positive Trend (trading above), 268–271
Burlington Industries (textiles), 64–65
Burlington Northern (railroad), 65
Burlington Resources (BR), 154
BusinessWeek, 280
Buy signal. *See* Signal(s)

Campbell's (CPB), 174
Capital Appreciation,
  opportunities for (Exchange Traded Funds), 353–356
Capitalization weighted, versus equal weighted, 107, 143, 150, 158, 163, 302–303
Cash Index Participation (CIP) unit, 297–299
Catapult formations (Bullish and Bearish), 73–79
Cavuto, Neil, 205, 265
Centex, 71
Channel, trading, 46
Chart patterns, 58, 63–65
  Bearish Catapult formation, 77–79
  Bearish Signal, 69–70
    Reversed formation, 93–94
  Broadening Top formation, 92–93
  Bullish Catapult formation, 73, 77
  Bullish Shakeout formation, 85–87
  Bullish Signal, 68–69
    Reversed formation, 94–97
  Catapult formation (Bullish/Bearish), 73–79
    trading tactics using, 73–77
  Diagonal Triple Top, 81–82, 92–93
  Double Bottom/Top, 65–68, 192, 194, 238, 269

High Pole Warning formation, 90–91
increasing success, 59–63
Law of Supply and Demand and, 55–57
Long Tail Down, 87–90
Low Pole Warning formation, 91–92
pattern recognition, 97–98
Quadruple Top, 72
Quintuple Top, 72
repetition in, 57–58
Spread Triple Top and Bottom, 82–85
Stop-Loss Points, 76, 87, 100–101, 335–336
Triangle formation, 79–81
Triple Bottom Sell Signal, 72–73, 81–82
Triple Top, 70–72, 81
Chartcraft, 217
Chartist, The, 235
Chase Manhattan (CMB), 145
Chevron Texaco (CVX), 154–155
Cialdini, Robert B., 220
Cisco Systems, 7, 8, 153, 189, 205
Citigroup, 101, 145, 303–304
CNBC, 56, 96
Coca-Cola (KO), 71, 109, 117, 118, 141, 156, 159, 167, 168, 172
Cocoa, 324, 326, 348
Coffee, 324, 348
Cohen, A.W., 14, 17, 77, 82, 186, 193–195
  and Stock Market Timing, 16
Cohen, Abbey, 184
Colgate-Palmolive (CL), 172
Collective solution hypothesis, 190–191
Columbine Capital, 140
Comcast (CMCSA), 118
Commodities, 117, 324–331
  as asset class, 350–356
    diversification, 350–352
    inflation, 352–353

Commodities *(continued)*
  beyond trading, 346–349
  compared to stocks (non-
      correlated comparison), 352
  Crash of 1987, 323–324
  evaluating opportunities in,
      323–356
  examples of, 323–325, 333–334
  Exchange Traded Funds
      (opportunity for capital
      appreciation), 353–356
  future contracts:
    chart patterns, 331–333
    risk management, 333–335
    spot charts, 328–329
    stop-loss points, 335–336
    trading, 327–328
    trend lines, 330–331
  Index Correlation Example, 349
  market index(es), 346–349, 355
    weightings of, 348
  Relative Strength (RS), 336–340
  support/resistance, 340–346
    big base breakout, 342
    changing box size, 342–344
    momentum, 344–346
    price objectives, 340–342
  trading, 325–326, 346–350
Commodity-Based Index Funds,
    355
Commodity Research Bureau
    (CRB) Futures Index,
    346–347
Comprehensive Capital, 190
Computer:
  performance of models versus
      people, 292
  power of, 15, 48, 63, 105, 316,
      320
  technological advances with,
      60–61, 254, 275
Confidence, 5, 6, 8
Consumer Reports, 105–106
Continuous Commodity Index
    (UV/Y), 338, 346–347
Contrarian view, 253, 284

Copper, 324, 329, 338
  versus Commodity Market, 339
Corning (GLW), 114, 148
Correction/crash, markets and,
    7–11, 22, 83, 118–121,
    147–148, 254–255, 317,
    321–322
Covered writing, 64, 300
Craftsman (world-class) status,
    20, 255
Crash of 1987, 183, 194–196, 236,
    323–324
Cummins Engine, 119

Dalbar study, 321–322
Danaher (DHR), 112
Dell Computer Corporation
    (DELL), 112
Delta, 78, 317
Depository Receipts
    (SPDRs/SPY), S&P, 226–227,
    299, 349
Diagonal Triple Top (Bullish
    Signal), 81–82, 92–93
Distribution corresponds to a top
    (resistance), 65
Diversification, 350–352
Dodge & Cox Stock (DODGX)
    fund, 165
Dominion Resources, 119
Dorsey, Wright, & Associates
    (DWA):
  background of, 177–182
  Dow Jones Secondary Oil Index,
      154–155
  Drug Index, 143–144
  Equal Dollar-Weighted Sector
      Indices, 169
  Food Sector Index (DWAFOOD),
      172
  information available from, 366
  International Matrix, 314–316
  Metals Non-Ferrous Index
      (DWAMETA), 132
  Money Management (*see*
      Money Management)

Oil Service Index (DWAOILS), 128–130, 155
  Relative Strength Chart Matrix, 169–171
  Retail Index, 143–144
  Secondary Oil Companies Index versus SPXEWI, 155
  Sector Index, 169, 171
  Software Index (DWASOFT), 271
  study on sector rotation, 251–253
  Telecom Sector Index, 146
Dot-com companies, 6, 71, 205
Double Bottom, 65–68, 192, 194, 238, 269
  with lower top, 69
Double Top, 65–68, 192, 194, 238, 269
  with rising bottom, 68
  with support, 68
Dow, Charles, 11–12, 16, 62, 65
Dow Jones, 7, 62, 212, 218, 297
  AIG Commodity Index (DJAIG), 347–349, 353
  bond index(es), 279–284
    20 Bond Average, 280
    Corporate Bond Index (DJCORP), 281–282
  index funds, 153–155, 159, 226, 313
  iShares, 150–153, 303–304, 310–313
  Nasdaq stocks in, 218
  Relative Strength, 107
  trading bands and, 49, 239
Drug sector, 303
Duke Energy (DUK), 123

Eastman Kodak, 7, 112
Economics in One Lesson, (Hazlett), 55
Economist, The 153, 160–161, 284
Edison, Charles, 34
Edison, Thomas, 34, 297

80/20 Rule (Pareto's Principle), 103–104
80-40-60 Rule, Percent of Stocks above Their Own 30-Week Moving Average, 236, 237
Electric Utility Bullish Percent, 256–262
Emerson Electric (EMR), 123
Emotional Intelligence, 356
Energy sector, 129, 153–156
Equal weighted, versus capitalization weighted, 107, 143, 150 ,158, 163, 302–303
Equities, versus Fixed Income, 290
E-Toys, 218
Euro FX, 343–345
Exchange Traded Funds (ETFs), 6, 216, 300–320
  broad market indices (no correlation), 226
  comparison of, 304–305
  evaluation of, 301–320
    trend charts, 306–308
  examples of, 307–308
  fixed income, 284–285
  future of, 320
  history of, 297–299
  international, 159–162, 304–305, 313–317
    Overseas versus United States: EFA versus SPX RS, 161
  iShares, 40, 315–316
  market indicators, 226–227
  mutual funds, 162–164, 317–320
  opportunity for capital appreciation (commodities), 353–356
  Point and Figure Method, charting, 40–41
  Relative Strength, 150–156, 310–313
    advanced concepts of, 313–320
  resources/web sites, 300–301

Exchange Traded Funds (ETFs)
    (continued)
    today's market, 299–301
    utilizing, 295–320
Exchange traded note (ETN), 347
Exxon Mobile (XOM), 154–155, 215
False courage ("buy-every-dip"
    mentality), 8

Fannie Mae (F), 118
Favored Sector Status, 265–267
    Percent Positive Trend Chart,
        268, 268–271
    Percent Relative Strength:
        on Buy Signals, 269–274
        in X's, 268–269, 271
    Sector Relative Strength,
        267–268
Fidelity Select Technology
    (FSPTX) fund, 165
Figuring (basis for Point and
    Figure method),12
Finding Religion among the
    Rapids, 10, 17
First signal, 187–188
First Trust Nasdaq 100 Equal
    Weighted Index Fund
    (QQEW), 303
Fixed income indicator(s):
    versus equities, 290
    example of (bonds), 279–289
    Exchange Traded Funds, 279,
        284–285, 286, 287
    versus interest rates, 285–286,
        287
    mutual funds, 291
FMC Corporation (FMC), 123
Food, Beverage, and Soap Stock to
    Stock RS Matrix, 173
Football analogy, 23, 84, 105, 181,
    184–187, 192, 195, 208, 212,
    217, 244
Forbes, 97
Ford (F), 117–118
Forest products and paper (FORE)
    sector, 170

Fortune, 153
FOX, 56, 265
Fund Score (Technical Ranking
    Method), and mutual funds,
    165–166, 301
Fundamental analysis, 13, 22,
    60–62, 84, 367
Futures contracts, 327–349
    Bearish Resistance Line
        (Downtrend Line), 330–331
    Bullish Support Line (Uptrend
        Line), 330–331
    examples of, 332–333
    risk management, 333–335
    spot charts, 328–329
    trading, 327–328

General Electric (GE), 62–63,
    156
General Motors (GM), 156
Gold Continuous Chart (GC),
    333–334
Goldman Sachs, 218, 351,
    354–355
    Commodity Index, 352
    Spot Return Commodity Index
        (GN/X), 347–349
Goleman, Daniel, 356–357
Golf analogy, 6
Good until Cancel (GTC) order,
    76, 101, 335–336
Google, 218
Granville, Joe, 99
Greenspan, Alan, 7, 261

Halliburton (HAL), 117, 128–130,
    134–137
Harvard University study, 220
Hazlett, Henry, 55
Hercules, 119
Herd mentality analogy, 250
Hershey's (HSY), 172
High Pole Warning formation,
    90–91, 238, 281
High-Low Index, 231, 233–236,
    243

HOLDRs, 299
Home Depot, 143
Horizontal count, 48, 51–52
Household goods (HOUS) sector,
170
Houston Industries, 119

IBM, 112, 188, 324, 330
ImClone (IMCL), 43–44
Index. *See* Market Index(es)
Individual Investor Institute, 17
Inflation, 352–353
Influence (Cialdini), 220
Integrated Devices (stock), 62
Intel (INTC), 107, 109–110, 156,
159
InterActiveCorp (IAC), 218
Interest rates, 214, 257, 261,
280–291
Dow Jones Corporate Bond
Index, 281–284
versus Fixed Income ETFs, 279,
286, 287
Interest Rate Sensitive chart,
285
Intermediate Term All Equity
Mutual Fund Bullish Percent,
245
International markets. *See*
Markets, international
Internet: 3–6, 8, 183, 223–224
availability of fundamental
information, 13, 21, 61
dot-companies, 6, 71, 205
Interstate Securities, 324
In-the-money, 78, 364
Intuit (INTU), 71
Inventory, creation of, 366
Investment News, 321
Investment process. *See* Portfolio
Investors Business Daily, 61
iShares, 40, 286
COMEX Gold Trust (IAU), 301,
353–354
Conservative Sector Manager
(2000 snapshot), 313

Dow Jones:
Energy Sector (IYE), 152
Financial Service Sector
(IYG), 303–304, 310–311
Healthcare Index (IYH), 150,
303
Internet Sector (IYV),
312–313
Real Estate Sector (IYR),
151–152
Technology Sector (IYW),
312–313
Telecom Sector (IYZ),
312–313
Total Market Index (IYY),
152, 310–312
Emerging Markets (EEM), 162
International ETF Matrix, 316
Latin America 40 Index (ILF),
314–315
Lehman:
Aggregate Bond Index (AGG),
288, 289, 349
20+ Year Treasury Bond
(TLT), 285, 287
Morgan Stanley Capital
International (MSCI):
Austria Index Fund (EWO),
304–306
Brazil Index Fund (EWZ), 162,
304–306
EAFE Index Fund (EFA),
160–162, 349
International Index Fund
(EWL), 304–306
Japan Index Fund (EWJ), 162,
314–315
Malaysia Index Fund (EWM),
304–306
NASDAQ Biotechnology Index
Fund, 308
Standard & Poor's:
S&P Europe 350 Index Fund
(IEV), 162
S&P 500 Growth Index Fund
(IVW), 318–319, 349

iShares *(continued)*
S&P 500 Small-Cap 600
Growth Index Fund (ITJ),
319
S&P Latin America 40 Fund
(ILF), 162
S&P Small Cap 600 Value
(IJS), 158

James River Talks, 57
Johnson & Johnson (JNJ), 303
Johnson, Norman, 190
Jones, Glen, 54

Kane, Steve, 16
KB Homes (KBH), 116, 119
Keep Peddling Zen Farmer, 17
King, Benjamin F., 181

Large capitalization, versus small
capitalization, 7, 156–159,
309
*Latent Statistical Structure of
Securities Price Changes,
The*, 181
Law of supply and demand. *See*
Supply/Demand, Law of
Lennar (LEN), 115, 148
Lockheed Martin (LMT),
123–124
London Gold (UKGOLD)/London
Gold Fixed PM, 301, 329
Long Tail Down, 87–90, 123–124
Long-Term Capital Management,
189
Long-term market
indicators/aspects, 247
Advance-Decline Line, 236–238
Average Weekly Distribution,
238–242
Percent of Stocks above Their
30-Week Moving Average
Index, 234–236
Low Pole Warning, 91–92, 238,
281–282
Lucent Technologies (LU), 5, 114

Magazine covers, power of, 153,
160–161, 195, 250–251, 284
Market, 142–149, 309–310
accommodation of, 309–310
correction of, 7–11, 22, 118,
254–255, 317, 321–322
divergence (positive and
negative), 118–121
evaluation of, 363
international, 159–162, 255,
316–317
Market index(es), 302
analogy to "phone a friend"
in *Millionaire* quiz show,
191
Bullish Percent (lack of
correlation with), 186, 188,
226, 363
commodities, 346–349
Correlation Example, 349
Nasdaq/OTC (*see*
Nasdaq/OTC)
Dow (*see* Dow Jones)
performance of versus
underlying stocks
(controlled by handful of
stocks), 188, 203, 205, 302
S&P 500 (*see* Standard & Poor's)
weightings, table of, 348
Market indicators, 224, 258,
364–365
Bullish Percents, 225–231
mutual funds, 244–247
other equity indicators,
225–245, 247
Advance-Decline Line,
236–238
Average Weekly Distribution,
238–242
High-Low Index, 233–234
Percent of Stocks above Their
Own 10-Week Average,
231–233
Percent of Stocks above Their
30-Week Average,
234–236

primary indicators, 73,
177–221, 253, 363
Nasdaq/OTC, 177, 203,
217–219, 363
New York Stock Exchange
(NYSE), 177–217, 363
secondary indicators, 223–247
Optionable Stock Universe
(BPOPTI), 225–227
S&P 500, 225–231
Sectors, 249–274
Summary Form, 242–244
Market Relative Strength. *See*
Relative Strength
Market timing:
versus sector timing, 252
Matrix, Relative Strength and:
DWA RS Chart Matrix,
169–171
stock to stock matrix,
171–174
Mauboussin, Michael, 119
Media (MEDI) sector, 170
Merck, 156
Meriwether, John, 189
Merrill Lynch HOLDRS, 299
Metals Nonferrous (META)
sector, 170
MFS New Discovery Fund
(MNDAX), 319
Microsoft (MSFT), 8, 156, 205,
258–259
Microstrategy (MSTR), 7
Momentum (periodic),
344–346
Money management, 52–54,
100–101, 139–140, 220–221,
254, 273–274, 292–293
Moody, Mike, 52–54
Morgan Stanley Capital
International Index(es),
160–162, 304–306, 314–315,
349
Morrison, Susan, 99
Moving Average Index(es), types
of, 231–236, 245

Mutual fund, 39, 244–247, 291
versus Exchange Traded Funds,
317–320
Fund Score, 165–166, 301
indicators, 244–247
Relative Strength, 162–165

Nasdaq/OTC:
Advance-Decline Lines,
236–238
Bullish Percent, 177, 203,
217–219, 364
Composite, 107
correction/crash, 8–10, 181,
265
Dow Jones (stocks in), 218
High-Low Index, 231, 233–234,
243
indicators, 243
iShares/Biotech Sector (IBB),
307–308
Non-Financial (BPNDX),
225–227
100 shares/QQQ, 226–227,
299
Percent of Stocks above Their
10-week average, 231
Percent of Stocks above Their
30-week average, 235
Nationwide Insurance Company,
53
Net asset value (NAV), 39,
244–245, 299
New York Stock Exchange
(NYSE), 7, 204, 363
Advance-Decline Lines,
237–238, 243
Bullish Percent, 177–217,
1974–1985 graph, 178
1986–2000 graph, 179
1987 chart, 196
1989–1990 chart, 198
1994 chart, 200
1998 chart, 202
2000 chart, 204
2000–2006 graph, 180

New York Stock Exchange (NYSE)
    (continued)
    2001 chart, 207
    2002 chart, 209
    2003 chart, 211
    2006 chart, 213
    High-Low Index, 233–234, 243
    Percent of Stocks above Their
        Own 10-Week Moving
        Average, 231–233
    Percent of Stocks above Their
        30-Week Moving Average,
        234–235
    80-40-60 Rule, 236, 237
New Yorker, 189, 292
Newspapers/magazines, as
    primary information source,
    31, 250–251
Newton, Isaac, 366
Noise, 23–24, 30–31, 37, 40
Nortel (NT), 114, 148
Nucor (NUE), 117
NYMEX crude oil (CRUDE),
    328–329

O'Neil, William, 100
O'Shaughnessy, Jim, 103
Occidental Petroleum (OXY), 154
Offense/defense, 109, 118, 177,
    184–185, 192, 195, 201,
    203–204, 225, 232, 245, 257,
    307, 364–365
Oil sector services, 117, 128–130,
    136–137, 152, 155, 170, 273
Operating system (organized
    method), 9–11, 182–185, 302
Option(s), 286, 323
    calls, 78, 216
    covered writing, 64
    Crash of 1987 and, 183, 194
    delta, 78
    Dorsey, Wright & Associates,
        14–17, 324
    Exchange Traded Funds, 40,
        149, 300, 307
    in-the-money, 78

premiums, 183
puts, 78, 183
trading, 78–79, 297, 320
Optionable Stock Universe
    (BPOPTI), Bullish Percent,
    225–227
Oracle Systems (ORCL), 71
OTC (over-the-counter). *See*
    Nasdaq/OTC
Other equity indicators, 225–245,
    247
    Advance-Decline Line,
        236–238
    Average Weekly Distribution,
        238–242
    High-Low Index, 233–234
    Percent of Stocks above Their
        Own 10-Week Average,
        231–233
    Percent of Stocks above Their
        30-Week Average, 234–236
Overleverage, 9, 182, 218

Pareto's Principle (80/20 Rule),
    103–104
Parker, Harold, 52–54
Pattern recognition, 97–98, 333
Peabody Energy (BTU), 117
Peer RS. *See* Relative Strength
Pepsi (PEP), 141, 167–168, 172
    NYSE chart, 232
Percent of Stocks above Their 10-
    Week Moving Average,
    231–233, 245
Percent of Stocks above Their
    Own 30-Week Moving
    Average Index, 234–236
Percent Positive Trend Chart,
    268–271
Percent Relative Strength in X's,
    268–269, 271
Percent Relative Strength on Buy
    Signals, 269–274
Pfizer (PEE), 303
Phelps Dodge (PD), 117,
    132–133

Philadelphia Stock Exchange
(PHLX), 297–299, 320
Gold and Silver Index, 297
Utility Index (UTY), 258–260
Phoenix Capital Growth
(PHGRX), 317–318
Planning/preparation, importance
of, 12, 59–60, 74
Point and Figure Method:
application of, 361–368
versus bar charts, 11, 25, 42, 61
charting:
art of, 3–8
basic tenets, 23–27
beginning of, 14–17
box sizes (standard/default),
25–27
buy and sell signals, 39
example, 24, 28–34, 39
Exchange Traded Funds,
40–41
flowchart, 28, 39
Internet, 21, 23–24, 26
mutual funds, 39–40
practice charts, 35–39
reversals, 30
S&P 500 Charts (2002 and
2005), 229–230
trend lines, 41–52
updating, 28–34
complete analysis tool, 277–292
fundamentals, 21–54
introduction, 3–20
market indicators (see Bullish
Percent and Market
Indicators)
origination of, 11–13
practice of, 35–39, 362–363
price objectives, 48–52,
340–342
relative strength, (see Relative
Strength)
risk management, 17–20,
321–322, 333–335
sector analysis/evaluation, (see
Sectors)

selecting group of
fundamentally sound
stocks from chosen sector,
22
stock selection guidelines, 85
supply and demand, 12–13,
21–22
tennis analogy, 13, 22–23
using ("putting all together"),
133–138, 165–166
why you should use, 11–14, 22
Point and Figure Method:
*Advance Theory and
Practice, The*, 48
Pologruto, David, 356–357
Portfolio, construction and
management of, 361
steps for, 363–369
evaluation checklist, 362
Portfolio Correlation Example,
351
Positive Technical Attributes
("putting it all together"),
133, 165–169, 174
criteria for, 134
High Positive Technical
Attribute Reading:
Halliburton, 134–137
Low Positive Technical
Attribute Reading: Wal-
Mart, 137–138
Positive Trend, 131, 136–137,
139, 267, 284, 331–332
Powershares, 300–301
Price(s), 183
bar charts versus Point and
Figure charts, and, 25, 42
box sizes, 25–27, 38, 40–41, 50,
217, 244–245
changes, supply and demand
leading to, 56, 93, 181
supply/demand, and, 49–50
objective, 48–52, 340–342
horizontal count, 51–52
vertical count, 49–50
Priceline.com, 7

Procter & Gamble, 6
Profits/probabilities, basketball
    analogy, 59
Pulte Homes (PHM), 116
Purdue University study, 97
Put options, 183, 216, 307, 324
Putnam study, 247–248

QQQ (Nasdaq 100 shares),
    226–227, 299
Quadruple Top, 72
Qualcomm (QCOM), 114
Quintuple Top, 72

Real Estate sector, 151–152
Regression to mean, 238–242
Relative Strength (RS), 221,
    166–174, 336–340
    advanced concepts of,
        141–175
    Bullish Percent concept and,
        194–217
    buy/sell signals, 86, 110–113,
        123–125, 127–128, 274
    chart matrix concept, 169–174
    divergence (positive and
        negative), 118–122
    Exchange Traded Funds (ETFs),
        6, 150–156, 216, 300–320
    foundations of, 103–140
    International exposure,
        159–162
    interpreting, 110–113
    Long Tails Up or Down,
        121–125
    Market (stock versus S&P 500
        Equal Weighted Index),
        106–107, 143–144,
        169–174, 258, 265–274
    calculating, 108–109
    versus Dow, 107, 150–151
    examples of, 113–118
    Matrix concept, 169–171
    mutual funds, 162–163
    examples of, 163–165
    fund score, 165–166

Pareto's Principle (80/20 rule),
    103–104
Peer (stock versus DWA Sector
    Index), 107–108, 150–151
    calculating, 109–110
    examples of changes for
        stocks, 126–133
Percent in X's, 112–113,
    121–125, 268–269
Percent on Buy Signals,
    269–274
Positive Technical Attributes
    ("putting it all together"),
    133–138
Sector(s), 142–143, 150–156,
    310–313
basic resources (2003), 117, 123
building sector (2000), 115–116,
    148–149
calculating, 143–144,
Exchange Traded Funds (ETFs),
    149–159, 169, 308–320
    asset class, applied to,
        156–159
    calculation and
        interpretation of,
        150–151
    examples of, 151–154,
        310–313
    subsector analysis,
        154–156
    healthcare sector (2000),
        115
    interpreting, 144–146
    telecom sector (2000),
        113–115, 146–148
    stock versus stock, 166–167,
        171–174
    example of, 167–169
    summary of, 139
    XM Satellite (XMSR),
        125–127
Resistance/support (defined),
    65–66
Restaurant (REST) sector, 266
Retail (RETA) sector, 266, 271

Reuters/Jeffries Commodity Research Bureau (CRB) Index (CR/Y), 347
Rickey, Branch B., III, 18
Risk(s), 18, 142, 227–228, 241, 256, 259
  definitions of (three), 333–334
  futures contracts, 333–335
  levels of, 193–194
  management of, 321–322
  market/sector accounting for 75 percent of stock's,
  measurement of, 193–194, 225
  reward and, 49, 52, 340–342, 346, 364–365
  taking (in investing/life), 17–20
Rizello, Joseph, 298, 320
Roethlisberger, Ben, 322
Rogers, Jim, 184
Roosevelt, Theodore, 19–20
Rotella, Robert J., 242
RSX (Relative Strength Percent in X's), 269–273
  RSXSOFT, 271
  RSXTELE, 269
Ryan Labs, 281
Rydex, 300–301, 320
Ryland Homes (RYL), 116, 148

Sample size/guessing, 191
Sara Lee (SLE), 172–174
Savings, investor, 247–248
Scana Corporation, 119
Secondary oil companies, 152–156, 159
Sector(s):
  analysis, 154–156, 231–233
  bell curves, 262–274
  Bullish Percents, 249–274
  Electric Utility Bullish Percent, 256–262
  evaluation of, 253–255, 365–366
  examples of, 170, 258–259

Favored Sector Status, 265–274
Index Funds, 169–170
Relative Strength, 169–174, 265–274
rotation method/tools, 249–275, 312, 314, 366
Select SPDRs, 299
summary of, 274–275
timing, 251–253
Sell signals. See Signal(s)
Semiconductor sector, 110
Shea, Cornelius Patrick, 8
Short selling, 68, 77–78, 298
Short-term indicators:
  High-Low Index, 233–234
  Percent of Stocks Trading above Their Own 10-Week Moving Average Index, 231–233
Signal(s):
  Bearish, 58, 69–70, 81
  Bearish Reversed, 93–94
  Bullish, 68–69, 81
  Bullish Reversed, 94–97
  buy/sell, and chart patterns, 39, 62, 85–87, 331–333 (see also Chart Patterns)
  Bearish Resistance Line and, 42–44, 47
  Bullish Support Line and, 42–44
  examples of, 49, 66–76, 91–97, 192, 195, 233, 238, 255
  Relative Strength and, 86, 110–113, 123–125, 274
  first, 187–188
  stop, versus trend stops, 335–337
Simon, Herbert, 97–98
Small capitalization stocks, versus large capitalization stocks, 7, 156–159, 309, 319–320
Smart Charts, 26, 306
Smith, Adam, 56
Snijders, Chris, 292

Software (SOFT) sector, 258, 266,
    270–274
  Favored Sector Status
    Evaluation for Software
    (October 2002), 272
Soulless barometer, 122, 185–186,
    216
Soybean, 326, 340, 341, 348
SPDRs. See Depository Receipts
Spot (defined), 328
Spread Triple Top and Bottom,
    82–85
Staby, Earnest, 185, 253
Standard & Poor's:
  iShares 158, 162, 318–319, 349
  Retail Index (RLX), 143
  S&P 100 (OEX), 323
  S&P 500, 9, 61, 156–160, 162,
      210, 212, 216, 286–287,
      297, 289, 302, 309, 316
    Bullish Percent, 225–231
    Capitalization-Weighted
        Index, 227–231, 309
    Depository Receipts SPDR
        (SPY), 226–227, 299, 349
    Equal Weighted Index
        (SPXEWI), 106–108, 129,
        143, 150–152, 154–155,
        162–165, 212, 266–277,
        273, 309, 338
    Growth (IVW), 158
    Point and Figure Chart
        (2002), 229
    Point and Figure Chart
        (2005), 230
  S&P 600 Small Cap Index
      (SML), 156–159, 309
  versus S&P 500 Large Cap, 157
  Small Capitalization Universe
      stocks, 7
State Street Global Advisors, 301
Statistical distribution. See Bell
    curve
Steel and iron (STEE) sector,
    170
Stock Market Timing (Cohen), 16

Stock(s):
  compared to commodities (non-
      correlated comparison), 352
  Positive Technical Attributes,
      133–138
  Ranking of, 106–107
  selection of, 42, 131–132
  versus Stock Relative Strength,
      166–169
Stock to stock matrix, 171–174
Stop loss point, 76, 87, 100–101,
    215–216, 331, 335–336
  Good Until Canceled (GTC)
      order, 336
  Trend Stops versus Signal
      Stops, 336–337
Strategic Asset Allocation, 60–61
Street Dot Com, The (TSCM), 7
Street TRACKS KBW Bank (KBE),
    303–304
Subsector analysis, example
    (Energy sector), 154–156
Sugar, 332, 342, 343, 348
Sullivan, Dan, 235
Sun Microsystems, 8, 205
Supply and Demand, law of, 4,
    7–8, 11–14, 21–22, 214, 224,
    244, 307, 363–367, 368–369
  example(s) of, 54, 62
  price changes, 56, 61, 75, 93,
      181, 221, 250, 262, 324, 327
  Point and Figure Method,
      24–26, 34, 44, 55–57,
      65–67, 73, 80, 101,
      284–285
  tennis match analogy, 13,
      22–23, 57, 69, 93, 96
Support Lines:
  Bearish, 41, 45, 47–48
  Bullish, 41–47, 75–76, 131, 134
  chart patterns, 80–81, 85,
      101, 229, 281, 307
  examples of, 126, 229, 231,
      285, 330–331
  Percent Positive Trend
      (trading above), 268

Support/resistance, 65–66,
340–346
big base breakout, 342
changing box size, 342–344
momentum, 344–346
price objectives, 340–342
Surowiecki, James, 189–190

Target, 143
Tax Deferred Annuities, 53
Technical analysis, 3–5, 13, 84,
366–367
commodities, 324–325
dot-companies, 6, 71, 205
Exchange Traded Funds,
312–313
mutual funds, 247
Technology sector, 8–10, 83,
147–148, 367
Technology, timing and, 297
Telecom (TELE) sector, 266
10 Year Yield Index (TNX), 285
1040 Bullish Percent (mutual
funds indicator), 245
Tennis match analogy, Law of
Supply and Demand, 13,
22–23, 57, 69, 93, 96
Tesoro (TSO), 154
Texas Utilities, 119
30 Year Index (TYX), 285–286
Three-box reversal, 25, 27,
299–30, 35, 50, 66, 75, 86,
88, 90, 191–192
Tidewater (TDW), 128–130
Timing, examples of, 252,
295–297
Tips, reasons for, 95–96
Toll Brothers (TOL), 115–116, 148
Toronto Index Participation
(TIPS) unit, 299
Toronto Stock Exchange, 299
Trading bands, 49, 239
Trading channel, 46
Transports nonair (TRAN) sector,
170
Treasury markets, 284

Trend lines, 41–52, 330–331
Bearish Resistance Line, 46
Bearish Support Line, 48
Bullish Resistance Line, 45
Bullish Support lines, 44
Trend charts, 119, 121, 317
Bullish Percent, 188, 199, 225
commodities, 342, 345
Exchange Traded Funds (ETFs),
306–308
market indices (bullish at
top/bearish at bottom),
186, 203, 253, 268
Percent Positive, 268–271
Positive Technical analysis
reading, 134
Triangle formation, 79–81
Triple Bottom Sell Signal, 72–73,
81–82
Triple Top, 70–72, 81

U.S. Dollar Index Weekly
Momentum, 345–346
U.S. Health Care Financing
Administration, 220
United Healthcare (UNH), 115
Utility, Exchange Traded Fund, 258

Valero Energy (VLO), 117, 154
Value investing, 186–187
Value Line (source of fundamental
information), 61, 107
Vanguard Financials (VFN),
299–301, 303–304
Vertical count, 49–51
Virginia Commonwealth
University, 17
Volatility, 19, 181, 218, 255,
316–317, 364–365
Bullish Percents, 205–206
Exchange Traded Funds, 163,
216
Point and Figure Method,
25–27, 33, 306

Wake-up call, 45, 100–101
Wall Street Journal, 247, 321
Wal-Mart (WMT), 117–118, 137, 143, 156, 158
Weather analogy, 227–228, 245
Weekly Distribution (WD) for All Stocks, 239, 241
West Texas Intermediate, 328
What Works on Wall Street, 103
Wheat First Securities, 324
Where's Waldo?, 159
Who Wants to Be a Millionaire? analogy, 189–191
Wieting, Steven, 101
Winder, Dave, 255
Winslow Green Growth Fund (WGGFX), 319

Wooley, Susan, 280
World-class (craftsman) status, 20, 98–100255
WorldCom (WCOM), 7, 113, 114, 146, 147, 153
Worth, 153
Wrigley's (WWY), 174
www.DIF.pt, 314

XM Satellite (XMSR), 125–126

Yahoo Finance, 31
Yahoo, 26
Yates, Jim, 59